D1599061

A Nation in Barracks

Oxford New York

A Nation in Barracks

Modern Germany, Military Conscription and Civil Society

Ute Frevert

Translated by
Andrew Boreham with Daniel Brückenhaus

Oxford • New York

First published in 2004 by
Berg
Editorial offices:
1st Floor, Angel Court, 81 St Clements Street, Oxford OX4 1AW, UK
175 Fifth Avenue, New York, NY 10010, USA

Berg is the imprint of Oxford International Publishers Ltd.

Library of Congress Cataloging-in-Publication Data
A catalog record for this book is available from the Library of Congress.

British Library Cataloguing-in-Publication Data
A catalogue record for this book is available from the British Library.

ISBN 1 85973 881 8 (Cloth)
1 85973 886 9 (Paper)

Typeset by JS Typesetting Ltd, Wellingborough, Northants.
Printed in the United Kingdom by Biddles Ltd, King's Lynn.

www.bergpublishers.com

Contents

Contents

Introduction: Military Conscription and Civil Society: Historical Trajectories

Aux armes, citoyens! The echo of that famous call to arms in revolutionary France has long since faded, though wars continue to be fought, even in Europe, as the history of the 1990s shows only too well. But such conflicts no longer demand vast conscripted citizens' armies clashing on the battlefields, as in the nineteenth and first half of the twentieth century. Instead, modern warfare focuses on deploying small, highly specialised and professional military combat units – a change opening a debate on universal conscription, whereby, in principle, every male citizen is summoned to arms. Now, after two hundred years, France, home of the modern conscript army, has abolished the draft, shortly after other continental countries like Belgium and the Netherlands, instituting a purely professional army instead. It is a path Germany, too, will most likely follow in the foreseeable future.

The American and British military model has triumphed, with a professional army comprising a stable group of long-term volunteers. Helped by geopolitical factors, neither country saw a need to establish a conscription system, merely introducing a short-term draft in times of war to cover recruiting and mobilisation needs.[1] In contrast, on mainland Europe, citizens were mustered and enlisted even in peacetime, and trained in military skills[2] – a policy dictated by military and strategic considerations, but in which differing political cultures, social and gender arguments also played a role.

Even today, supporters of conscription emphasise the institution's symbolic value and the benefit it brings in the political sphere, repeatedly claiming that the draft prevents social decay, acting as a reminder of civic virtues and the solidarity lying at the very heart of a democratic state. Advocates of conscription draw on a long tradition, going right back to the start of conscript armies in France and Prussia, appealing to the notion of the *soldat citoyen*, or citizen-soldier, as a figure bridging the structural gap between the armed forces and civil society and transforming the military into a societal institution.

In fact, military service is one of the very oldest institutions in the history of modern continental Europe, and generally older than the male franchise, a tradition tracing its roots to the late eighteenth century in France and the early nineteenth century in Prussia. Conscription has survived changing political systems and various constellations in security policy where the characteristics of democracy, fraternity and equality were not always immediately discernible, if at all. In Germany especially, the nation, donning uniforms and gathering under army banners, only rarely had institutionalised democratic structures. Certainly, Marx and Engels' comment in 1870 that Germany found 'unity in the Prussian barracks' still seems true today, but army quarters were hardly the place to practise models of civic order and values. On the contrary, as this book argues, the paradigm of a 'nation in barracks' is fundamentally opposed to the basic tenets and beliefs of civil society, and this itself is one main reason why support for conscription is dwindling at present.[3]

The terms themselves, whether *soldat citoyen*, citizen-soldier or the post-war 'citizen in uniform', all indicate how deeply conscription affected, and affects, civil life, and hence how much it needed, from the very start, convincing political, cultural and social justifications. In this way, the history of conscription, the struggle over alternatives, and the myriad acts of resistance against its introduction and implementation provide fascinating insights into how civil societies see themselves, a debate not only focusing on the relationship between civil societies and violence, and the state monopoly on violence, but equally questioning concepts of citizenship, social integration and gender policy.

In theory and historical practice, civil societies are distinguished by their efforts to organise their internal relations without recourse to violent means. Through rational insight, the citizen elects to forego violence, and it is this that makes him or her by definition a civilian. As a private individual, head of a family, or member of the middle-classes, they trust to the validity of a legal code to regulate their concerns; as *citoyen*, citizen, or *Staatsbürger*, they seek agreement in political agency, resolving whatever conflicts arise via debate and decision-making processes. These principles of liberal political theory can be found in nineteenth-century encyclopaedias, where '*bürgerlich*' and 'civil' were always considered synonymous and contrasted with the 'military estate', and civilian clothing regarded as 'civil dress, the uniform's antithesis'.[4]

'Military estate' and 'uniform' represent that institution legitimately housing the violence civil society *per se* cannot contain. The military, organised by the state and financed by the public coffers, is intended to guarantee the citizens' security, at home and abroad. The less it has to intervene in civilian life, the better, since its aims and governing principles stand so far removed from the nature of civil society that any contact ought to be avoided if at all possible. The military prepares its members to use physical violence, systematically practising its application as they learn how to overcome the culturally mediated barrier to killing. Soldiers are taught how to use lethal weapons, and how to obey commands given in combat ordering them to turn their weapons on the enemy. They also learn how to overcome their own fear of a violent death, using a mixture of group dynamics, ideological armament, and above all strict obedience, where cowardice before the enemy carries the death penalty.

On the one hand, adopting this sort of socialisation programme located the military outside the borders of civil society yet, on the other, it left the military providing civic society with a vital security service. In the early modern period, this ambiguity can be seen in the way continental European absolutist states maintained standing armies largely comprising mercenaries and volunteers, a segmentation abruptly halted by the modern invention of conscription. As the *Brockhaus* encyclopaedia noted in 1843, conscription removed 'the opposition between civil and military', since 'the soldier is never to cease being a citizen, and the citizen is never to sever himself from the cause of defending the fatherland'.[5] This was precisely the real revolutionary message in conscription: it blurred the borders between the military and civil spheres, carrying violence back into civilian life. From then on, citizens were forced not only to acknowledge the army as such, but actually to take an active role in it.

But the question of how and to what extent the armed forces and civil society actually converged remains unanswered, with the consequences similarly hard to define. It is relatively easy to describe the 'civilising' effect conscription had on the army, with, for instance, the military criminal code gradually mirroring civilian law, the troops enjoying better conditions and more humane treatment, and corporal punishment abolished. Nonetheless, the limits to such 'civilising' are obvious: the way the armed forces function, even today, resembles Erving Goffman's notion of 'total institutions', where members are not only subject to a unique socialisation and categorised into a specific subordination structure, but are also taught a set of skills that, in essence, are of little value outside that particular sphere.

The more difficult question, and the more interesting one, relates to the 'militarising' influences conscription had on civil society. This, however, is not meant to be understood as 'militarism', a common concern in older historical approaches, examining how the logic underlying military decision-making and agency dominated the political sphere.[6] Rather, the focus here is on whether societies with conscription prepare more intensively than others for a possible war scenario: does military service provide the impetus for bringing violence into society? Does it have the long-term and sustained effect of mobilising civil society for the collective use of violence? Providing a definite answer to such questions would require concentrating on societies at war, comparing those previously with and without conscription. This book, though, sets out along a different path, concentrating more on how peacetime military socialisation affects civil society structure and mentality than on the issues of how violence is unleashed in wartime, or possible preparation for it by military socialisation in peacetime.

Previous research has been unequivocal in condemning social 'militarism' as a key feature of Imperial Germany and paving the way for National Socialism, with Germany's '*Sonderweg*' and the deficit in civil society values largely traced to the influence of 'social' or 'civil militarisation'.[7] Such a reading of history seems less than convincing, given that it posits unbroken continuity. Yet didn't the Weimar Republic fundamentally alter the relationship between the military, politics and society transmitted by Wilhelmine Germany, presenting alternative, more civil society options for the future? Large parts of the population did not miss the military at all, or its pomp, lacklustre in a post-1918 world where male youths not only much preferred to join sports clubs than paramilitary organisations but did so in far greater numbers.

Elias Canetti maintained that contemporaries suffered most from the Versailles Treaty provision forbidding a conscription army, and hence this Allied stance planted the seed for the '*birth* of National Socialism', but such a claim is completely exaggerated, and has no adequate empirical evidence to support it.[8] Similarly, Canetti's claim that the conscription army is a characteristically German mass symbol of almost religious grandeur is extremely questionable. Was Imperial Germany really subject to a far greater degree of social militarisation than, for example, the French Third Republic or the British Empire? Recent comparative research finds no evidence to support such a hypothesis.[9] The question also arises of why only Wilhemine Germany is held responsible for the German population's military-friendly attitude – were Prussia and the other pre-1871 German states less 'militaristic'? Or were the middle classes, allegedly many of them helplessly mesmerised by the army after 1871, actually so much more civic-minded, un-martial, and opposed to violence before the German Empire was founded? As a rule, such questions remain unanswered by 'classic' militarism research, since this limits itself to Imperial Germany, disregarding the pre-1871 period.[10] But conscription is far older than Wilhelmine Germany, and its social, gender and cultural history opens up other perspectives and provides different insights.

In tracing how military service became a political icon and evolved into a social institution, offering a sphere of experience for millions of young men, this book examines three specific themes and theses that form a thread running through the chronological structure of the chapters.

● Conscription and Citizenship

From its initial introduction, conscription was regarded both as a duty imposed by citizenship and simultaneously as a citizen's right, excluding those who either were not citizens, or else had lost their honorary civic rights. In this constellation, there appeared to be a direct link between conscription and active citizenship, with one implying the other.[11] It was a construction with potential both for exclusion and inclusion, offering men from a range of social origins and faiths a chance to participate – however limitedly – in political and social affairs, while excluding women and foreigners. At the same time, or at least, that was the claim, it gave citizenship, both as an idea and in practice, a characteristic form which was oriented towards the state and coloured by the military. How marked this form was depended on those temporal, spatial and substantive constellations that changed markedly during the course of the nineteenth and twentieth centuries.

● Conscription and Nation-Building

From the outset, the conscript armies, as first created in France and Prussia, were dubbed 'schools of the nation', and occasionally even regarded as representing the nation as a whole. Political scientists and historians have also underlined the importance of the military in state- and nation-building processes.[12] This claim does not merely relate to the active role played by the army since the early modern period – up until the German 'wars of unification' in the 1860s – in expanding and consolidating a specific territory under a central government. The army affected nation-building too in a narrower sense by, firstly, supporting the formation of an association of all citizens as a nation (*Staatsbürgerverband*) and, secondly, trying to generate an awareness of national belonging. Making young men liable, in principle, to perform military service, irrespective of their regional, religious, or class affinity, ensured that they underwent a training in their formative years that attributed a key value to the nation or the 'fatherland'.[13] The bond to the nation prepared and practised during army service may not have entirely replaced other loyalties and identities, but it relativised and shifted previous rankings. It remains to be shown how far such aspirations were actually realised, and whether the shared, common experience of military service did indeed genuinely bridge social, religious and regional differences.

● Conscription and Gender Order

Furthermore, there are convincing reasons to assume that conscription and military training changed the relations between men and women.[14] Drafting tens of thousands, and later hundreds of thousands, of young men every year, and concentrating them in a space largely sealed off from the rest of society created a rift running between the genders, and this became ever more obvious as other social institutions abandoned the principle of gender separation. Churches and schools had only applied it partially, at any rate, and from the early twentieth century even the political system surrendered its male exclusivity and opened up the political arena to women, as both voters and politicians. Only the military remained as womanless as it had been since the early nineteenth century. But did it then really remain the exclusive 'school of masculinity' it had claimed to be before the First World War? Under which circumstances or in which social spaces could the military ideal of masculinity gain or maintain the upper hand, and what alternatives was it competing against? And how far might the notion of a woman unable to bear arms herself and hence in need of the protection proffered by the man rushing to her aid as the 'natural' arms-bearer actually have influenced social practices?

Writing a history of conscription stressing cultural, political, social and gender history perspectives means reading history not primarily as the history of war or the armed services but in terms of how society evolves. In other words, rather than concentrating on the army's concerns and recruitment needs, or military events where conscription 'proved' its worth, the decades of peace are taken as a focal point where the modern army had to present itself as a social event – and not least precisely because of the institution of conscription. Such an approach does not completely exclude war and the context of military technologies, but the permanent and intense influence exercised reciprocally by the military apparatus of violence and civil society are not revealed under the dramatically exaggerated conditions of war. Instead, they are best grasped through the unspectacular structures of peace.

In peacetime, the ground is prepared for war, and the after-effects of war are visible and discussed. Yet nonetheless, the function of military service is not simply covered by these two aspects, which is why this book primarily focuses on the more complex and sustained exchange processes conscription initiated and coined, examining a range of views and standpoints, from political decision-makers and military specialists to the common soldiers, from middle-class reserve officers to female spectators. The material presented draws on state files, parliamentary records, journals, newspapers and magazines, brochures and flyers, but equally traces the history of conscription through photographs, autobiographies, letters and songs. The texts used all come from Germany – or, more precisely, the various German territories united in 1871 under the German Empire – and from different periods, some from the eighteenth century, with the majority taken from across the long nineteenth century. This was the era when conscription was shaped and formed: it was planned and introduced in Prussia (Chapter 1); met with resistance in the political, economic and social arenas, but also opened up processes leading to conformity (Chapter 2), while the states comprising the Third Germany, above all the southern German states and Saxony, experimented with other, less socially inclusive recruitment models, with communal citizens' militias and civilian defence associations (Chapter 3); finally, Imperial Germany united the various models under the Prussian paradigm, increasing inclusion, and buttressing the political, social and cultural aura surrounding military service (Chapter 4). After the First World War, Allied pressure put an end to conscription, which was only reintroduced in 1935 as part of Hitler's long-term preparations for the Second

World War. After 1945, it took some years before either East or West Germany established a conscript army again, attempting the difficult task of mixing tradition with a total break with the past. This development is briefly sketched in the final part (Chapter 5), which concludes the book by arguing that the draft has not only served its term as a military strategy, but equally and above all, can be seen today, from political, cultural and social perspectives, as a model in the process of being phased out.

Notes

1. Chambers II, *To Raise*, and also *Draftees*; Strachan, *Politics*; Strachan, *Army*, pp. 3–48; Spiers, Army.
2. Foerster, *Wehrpflicht*, pp. 39 ff.; Moran/Waldron, *People*, pp. 8–188; Levi, *Consent*; Frevert, *Militär*.
3. *Marx-Engels-Werke*, vol. 17, Berlin, 1973, p. 269. On the concept of civil society as including the principle of non-violence, see Keane, *Civil Society*; Walzer, 'Concept'; Kocka, 'Zivilgesellschaft'.
4. *Universal-Lexikon oder vollständiges encyclopädisches Wörterbuch*, ed. H. A. Pierer, vol. 4, Altenburg, 1835, p. 487; *Meyers Konversations-Lexikon*, 5th edn, vol. 3, Leipzig, 1894, p. 708.
5. *Allgemeine deutsche Real-Encyklopädie für die gebildeten Stände*, 9th edn, vol. 3, Leipzig, 1843, p. 46.
6. Ritter, 'Problem', and also *Staatskunst*; Craig, *Politics*; Berghahn, *Militarismus*, and Berghahn, *Militarism*; Wette, *Militarismus*; Kühne/Ziemann, *Militärgeschichte*, pp. 23 ff.
7. Meinecke, *Katastrophe*, pp. 25–6; Ritter, *Staatskunst*, vol. 2, 1960, pp. 117 ff.; Wehler, *Gesellschaftsgeschichte*, vol. 3, pp. 880 ff. For a critical view, see Eley, 'Army'.
8. Canetti, *Crowds*, pp. 210 ff.
9. Vogel, *Nationen*; Ingenlath, *Aufrüstung*; Jahr, 'Prussianism'; Ziemann, 'Hauptmann', and also 'Sozialmilitarismus'.
10. Geyer, 'Geschichte'; Förster, *Militarismus*; Messerschmidt, 'Armee', and also 'Preußens Militär'; John, *Reserveoffizierkorps*; Rohkrämer, *Militarismus*.
11. Walzer, *Obligations*, pp. 77 ff.; Kerber, *Right*, pp. 238 ff.
12. Finer, 'Nation-Building'; Levi, *Consent*; Weber, *Peasants*, pp. 292–302; Treitschke, *Politik*, vol. 2, pp. 356, 405–6.

13. Although 'nation' and 'fatherland' are different in their historical meaning and origins, they were generally used as synonyms in the nineteenth century; even conservative officers talked of the 'nation', when they meant the monarchic and dynastic 'fatherland'. On the semantics and history of the terms see Langewiesche, *Nation*, pp. 14 ff., 190 ff.
14. Enloe, 'Canyon'; Isaksson, *Women*; Eifler/Seifert, *Konstruktionen*.

War, Nation, Gender Images: Core Concepts in Conscription in the Early Nineteenth Century

Universal military service for men is a modern project, engendered in the chaos of the French Revolution and the upheaval of France's subsequent wars. As early as 1789, addressing the Paris National Assembly, the military theorist and politician Edmond Dubois-Crancé advocated that every citizen ought to be a soldier and every soldier a citizen. Liberal resistance to this 'axiom' collapsed in 1793 when compulsory conscription seemed the only feasible way to generate the *levée en masse* France hoped would bring victory over invasion forces from England, Holland and Austria. In 1798, conscription was given a legal framework, providing the basis for Napoleon to recruit the army that spread war across the entire face of Europe, from Spain to Moscow.[1]

The notion that every male citizen ought to defend his own country can be traced back to the classical world, where the link between military service and citizenship was familiar to the Greek city states and the Roman Empire; yet the impetus this notion received in revolutionary France was new and far more radical, with the concept of *citoyen* coming to embrace a wider spectrum than the equivalent term in the Greco-Roman world. Furthermore, French contemporaries were not looking to Athens, Sparta, or Rome but taking the absolutist *Ancien Régime* and its professional army as their point of reference. The violent revolutionary act marking the end of the old system gave birth to a sovereign nation that envisaged a different military constitution embodying its own principles of *égalité* and *fraternité*. Initially, the hope was to preserve the third pillar of *liberté* by finding sufficient numbers of enthusiastic volunteers, but this had to be abandoned once the military challenges appeared to require enlisting all young men into a citizens' army.

If a move to universal military service provoked such fierce criticism in revolutionary France, how much greater might the resistance be in Prussia, whose political and social structures were still marked by absolutism and the precepts of a hierarchical social order based on traditional societal divisions? In fact, the introduction of military service in Prussia had to pass down a road strewn with many obstacles, and experienced repeated setbacks. With resistance coming from both civil and military figures, the aristocracy and middle classes, and men and women, it was by no means clear that military service would ever be finally accepted. Indeed, even the king was less than enthusiastic in his support, precisely because military service was so closely associated with revolution and middle-class emancipation – and it would take two wars, innumerable writings on reform, and endless meetings of various commissions before he changed his mind.

1. Criticism of Existing Prussian Army Structures

In 1806, when Napoleon's army of conscripts swept across Prussia, it not only brought the Prussian military to its knees but left the Prussian state, once so proud and powerful, shattered and broken. The 1807 Peace of Tilsit required Prussia to surrender half its population and lands and reduce its army from 235,000 to an initial 63,000 and later to only 42,000 men.[2] In this dramatic situation, high-ranking civil servants and officers developed reform programmes designed to help Prussia recover from defeat, release social and economic forces, and use them to expand the sphere of influence abroad. Put more precisely, the idea was to mimic the impressive success of the French Revolution in achieving a new spirit across society while avoiding the risk of violent political disruptions to the existing system.

The army itself was also the object of such changes. Its recruiting mechanisms and organisational structure had already been criticised in the late eighteenth century. Now, with Prussia ingloriously defeated at the hands of Napoleon, military reformers had no doubt that France provided a suitable model to emulate. In future, the Prussian army too should boast enthusiastic soldiers convinced of their vocation, and prepared to adopt more flexible and unconventional approaches to warfare. They saw the conscription method established under Frederick the Great as outdated, claiming mere drill and iron discipline enforced with draconian punishment was no longer sufficient to make soldiers ready and able to fight wars.[3] Such predictions were proved right, at the latest, on 14 October 1806: only two weeks after Jena/Auerstedt, Napoleon entered a Berlin hastily deserted by the king and government. The capital's inhabitants reacted with mixed feelings, as the diary entry for 26 October 1806 by the doctor Ernst Ludwig Heim attests. 'It is sad,' he wrote, 'that Prussia is being so humiliated. My one consolation is that the French are valiant warriors and we have been defeated by experienced soldiers and a mighty hero.' Four months later, after a dinner with Prussian officers being held as prisoners of war, Heim noted: 'Much as I pity these gentlemen, the military has, in general, deserved to be chastised and humiliated like this, since its overbearing manner and arrogant vanity knew no bounds before the war.'[4]

Similarly, the Prussian king, Friedrich Wilhelm III, found he could no longer ignore criticism directed at the military. In July 1807 in Memel, where he acknowledged Napoleon's conditions for peace, he drafted a series of measures that left nothing to be desired in terms of radical import. In his view, putting 'the army back on the old footing' seemed 'neither feasible nor advisable'. Instead, the 'sickly' officer corps was to be revitalised by 'completely altering' the recruiting system and 'admitting the non-aristocracy' into its ranks; enlisting foreigners was to cease altogether and fewer exemptions were to be granted. Such measures, he continued, assumed that military punishment would be 'just as strict but less defamatory'.[5]

The king's own thoughts on reform left his administration a free hand to introduce a programme of measures restructuring the army from the ground up – so much so that conservative officers immediately registered their opposition. Many found the notion of a national army and the prospect of opening up the officer ranks to middle-class men directly at odds with their traditional sense of a hierarchical social order. But younger officers, willing to reform, saw in these measures 'ideas suited to the new spirit and conditions'. Major-General Gerhard von Scharnhorst, entrusted by the king with heading a commission for reform, believed the coming 'inner regeneration of the military' should not only tackle the technical and tactical aspects, as his conservative colleagues suggested. In addition to the issues of formation, promotion, and exercises, he emphasised the need to 'strive particularly for morale'. 'The new army', he hoped, would 'approach its intended purpose in another spirit and enter into a closer and deeper alliance with the citizens.'[6]

What was to be understood by this 'other spirit'? Indeed, what was it supposed to, and what could it, convey to people in 1807? Positive definitions were hard to find; instead, the new was overwhelmingly defined as being different from the old, which itself was portrayed in the worse colours possible – with the Prussian army's traditional spirit pictured as a soulless machine, kept in trim by an unsophisticated, overweening officer caste. As direct servants of the crown, they enjoyed a number of privileges and felt themselves to be just as superior to all civilians as they were to the common soldier. The later war minister, Hermann von Boyen, reviewing the last third of the eighteenth century, claimed the 'warrior class' considered itself to be a 'self-contained part of the nation'.[7] Its feeling of self-esteem was not rooted in any 'alliance with the citizens' but lay in a personal relationship of loyalty to the monarch.

From the citizens' perspective too, the military appeared as an 'entrenched class', deliberately cultivating and maintaining social distance from 'the civilian class' and jealously guarding its privileges.[8] This distance found its most obvious expression in the code of corporative honour; in the eighteenth century, the idea that an officer's honour ranked far above a civilian's was reinforced and supported at the highest level.[9] But such precedence of honour was only enjoyed in the officer class – the common soldier was not treated respectfully, either by civilians or commanding officers. Officers and NCOs were none too fussy in their choice of the means to drum discipline into their subordinates. Ulrich Bräker, originally from Switzerland and serving in the Prussian army for a few months in 1756, still remembered the daily 'treatment' on the drill ground with horror many years later. This 'life of slavery' made him consider deserting more than once and he only gave up the idea on seeing how those caught again 'were made to run the gauntlet until they sank to the ground totally exhausted'.[10]

At that time, half of the Prussian army consisted of enlisted foreigners, like Bräker, and the other half of nationals recruited under a canton system first introduced in the 1730s. This system divided Prussia into cantons assigned to particular regiments and responsible for providing new recruits. Households were ascribed to cantons if their male members were 'enrolled', i.e. inscribed in the canton rolls, although whether they actually had to join up on their twentieth birthday or not depended both on their own personal situation and the regiment's needs; enlistment was waived in the case of a farm's direct heir or for only sons, and exemptions were also granted if men were not taller than 1.65 meters or could show impaired health. Regional research indicates that, at the end of the eighteenth century, only 7% of all those on the canton rolls actually joined the army. 'Cantonists' had to spend an initial two years with their regiment and afterwards were given leave of absence. The remaining years of service, usually ending at 40, assumed a presence and drill period of only two to three months annually; the recruits could spend the remaining time in their home areas. They were allowed to marry and, given a certain degree of luck and guile, they might find a farmer's widow or only daughter, take over the farm, and be discharged from the regiment.[11]

But the bulk of the cantonists from poorer rural families had no hope of such a release. Instead, their futures held long years of commuting between the regiment and their home, leading to increasing estrangement from the local population who believed, in line with popular sentiment, that soldiers in the army only learned 'idleness, drinking, and gambling'.[12] Parents were sorry to see their sons go because they feared the regiment's brutalising influence, unless the son had 'turned to the bad', when they hoped the martial discipline and order would do him good. The army might even enable him to step up the social ladder and, equipped with uniform and sword, return home more self-assured than before.[13]

The topoi of contemporary military discourse included the recurring image of soldiers taking certain liberties with civilians as a kind of retaliation for the draconian 'discipline' predominant in the regiments. This was the theme Friedrich Schiller immortalised in 1798 when he portrayed the soldier as a 'free man', taking no consideration of others, and enjoying his 'happy fate' in battle. Schiller, too, addressed the complex relationship between violence and 'wooing', when he wrote:

The rider upon his horse so fine,
He is an awesome guest,
The lamps in the wedding castle shine,
Uninvited he comes to the feast.
The time to woo he can scarce afford,
He takes by storm his love's reward.[14]

Court records in the eighteenth century eloquently testify to the kind of 'storm' soldiers employed in their brief period of courtship. Occasionally, however, women took rape by soldiers as a pretext to hide the real father, and the credence this met with in court indicates that such behaviour – though only an excuse in this instance – must have featured widely in other cases and corresponded to contemporary experience.[15]

The violence of soldiers met with general acclaim only when it occurred in war, in honourable and victorious combat. It was in a similar vein that the poet Anna Louisa Karsch (1722–91) wrote to her husband during the Seven Years War: 'And if the king should win the battle, and if the muse, my muse, should sing his triumph, my joy in victory would be twofold in knowing that one of my very own had played their part in it.' Despite the sympathy apparent in these lines, Karsch was first and foremost glad to have got rid of her husband, a tailor, more dedicated to alcohol than work who, as she put it, made her life hell. Since he squandered everything she managed to earn for herself and her children and never contributed anything to the family's upkeep, and, since she lived every minute of the day in fear of 'the unbridled rage of a husband devoid of reason', she drew him to the attention of the Prussian recruiting officer. In her biographical sketch written two years later, she pictured the scene on 21 January 1760, as her husband was collected, although she discreetly refrained from mentioning her own active role in the run-up to the event: 'Amidst my lamentations, they took him, who drew these from me, to follow the banners of war ... I was as someone awakening from benumbing dreams; I recovered myself and sang a song in praise of the king's birthday.'[16]

If this 'German Sappho' commended the army as a place to get rid of burdensome and unloved husbands, the 'more refined citizens' only sent their sons into the army if 'they didn't want to learn or conform with civic order',[17] while trying to spare those sons, brothers, or nephews from a soldier's fate if they had turned out better. The *Landrat* (district administrator) responsible for the levy of cantonists was flooded with protests from parents, who either offered to pay a ransom instead or encouraged the young men to go into hiding. The *Landrat* Ludwig von Vincke, in office from 1798 in Minden, Westphalia, described the period of dealing with appeals as the 'saddest days of my life' and went on: 'I had to appear heartless and cruel so often but truly I wasn't; I gave full consideration to choosing those that appeared most dispensable and yet still had to injure and distress some parents; I had to suffocate every human feeling, harden and steel myself against any impulse of sympathy.'[18]

Undoubtedly, the more prosperous sections of society had better chances of avoiding military service. In 1812, a disgruntled General von Bülow reported from Königsberg that 'every commercial clerk, copyist, tradesman, burgher or farmer's son that the entire commission found and recorded as indubitably suitable for conscription during the final appeal [generates] a more or less considerable exchange of letters before the authorities eventually get hold of him'.[19] While literate cantonists employed letters as their first line of defence, others simply voted with their feet; desertion was an everyday occurrence, especially in areas with a Polish population. According to the west Prussian *Landrat* von Schrötter in 1810, half of the recruits deserted before being enlisted. Along the borders particularly, many of those liable for conscription fled abroad and, even though a bounty was put on their heads, large numbers of deserters later returned to their hometowns and villages where they were able to continue their business unhindered.[20] The conscription authorities were powerless to do anything else but accept the situation; the threat of confiscating property as a punishment had no effect since generally the deserters had no possessions.

The population in those areas freed by royal decree from the canton system considered themselves very fortunate; this included not only large parts of Prussia's western provinces, but also towns and commercial regions – and they made a point of repeatedly having this status reconfirmed.[21] Consequently, the soldiers in compulsory military service came almost exclusively from the poor male rural population. The canton regulations that came into force in 1792 enlarged the group of people exempted from service even further. In 1811, the Silesian *Landrat* von Conradi noted that: 'From ten well-off subjects levied as cantonists, only two on average will definitely become soldiers and eight will avoid enlisting by buying plots of land. In other words, solely the young servant and son of the poor day-labourer are destined for military service.'[22] The latter must have considered serving under the flag discriminatory and a punishment; one could hardly expect them to be burning with desire to perform a duty apportioned so selectively, which most people attempted to discharge via the financial and social means at their disposal.

2. Conscription: Setbacks on the Road to a 'National Army'

As far as those advocating military reform were concerned, the situation required fundamental change, with exemptions abolished, or at least severely restricted, and all male subjects personally liable to perform military service. In this way, recruiting bottlenecks could be overcome and the 'morale' of the army improved. The French conscription army appeared to have proven that patriotism, eagerness, and readiness for combat only existed in a citizens' army that saw defending its country as an honour instead of a burden.

Lieutenant General von Blücher was utterly convinced of this idea and had already told his friend Scharnhorst at the beginning of August 1807 that he 'strongly recommended [Scharnhorst] organizing a national army'. Scharnhorst chaired the commission advising on new military guidelines and, here too, the position adopted was that 'All the state's citizens are its born defenders.' In July 1808, Scharnhorst described the 'introduction of universal conscription' as a 'national desire, debated in all manner of writings, which must be pleasing to all previous conscripts and welcome to all who love their country and hate the suppressor; the views of those few remaining weak and egoistical individuals do not need to be taken into consideration'.[23]

But Major-General Scharnhorst had taken his stance a little prematurely. Although military specialists may have believed implicitly in the need for and desirability of universal conscription, the politicians involved in financial and internal affairs took a rather different view, more akin to civil servant Barthold Georg Niebuhr's laconic remark of 'Adieu culture, adieu finances', made in 1808 on being told that Prussia was thinking of introducing conscription. As far as he was concerned, the idea appeared fundamentally 'pernicious'. He was certain it would not only ruin the state financially but, what was more, would lead 'to the degeneration of the entire nation, universal uncouthness, and the destruction of all culture and the educated classes'. In the army, future disciples of science or statesmanship would lose 'all respect for intellectual culture'. To place a person like that under the yoke of 'military slavery' like the 'rough farmer', where there was nothing to ruin anyway, was on a level with sheer Jacobinism and disgusted 'the true friend of liberty'.[24]

Just as Niebuhr, as an educated man, felt insulted by the principle of pre-scribed equality in conscription, the aristocracy was similarly scandalised by this 'revolutionary' axiom. In an 1808 petition to the Prussian king, the East Prussian *Standesherren* (mediatized princes) protested indignantly against the plan to make previously exempt nobles liable for military service: 'Including the nobility in a universal conscription that first saw the light of day in the birth of a revolution destroying all existing laws and constitutions in France, a conscription which by its very nature can only rest on the concept of universal equality, would lead, as we venture to suggest, to the complete destruction of the aristocracy.'[25] However, this was a threat that left the government unmoved. Freiherr vom Stein, a government minister, reminded fellow members of his class that their privileges were traditionally rooted in their readiness to 'sacrifice life and property for the state' and the order to regard them as equals with other citizens in future took account of the 'spirit of the nation', which needed to be 'united for our common purposes'.[26]

The Westphalian civil servant Freiherr von Vincke was also thinking of the 'spirit of the nation' when he approached Freiherr vom Stein at the end of September 1808. Sharing views similar to Niebuhr's, he considered conscription to be 'the grave of all culture, science and commerce, civic freedom, and every human joy'. It would 'inevitably lead [us] back to barbarianism', to a state where the army was not a means to an end but an end in itself. Vincke was only prepared to consider a universal duty for military service in the case of a *Landwehr* (enlisted army reserves), where these 'peacetime soldiers' would only be employed in military exercises for brief periods of time and without substantially 'removing them from, and limiting, civic trade'. The small standing army, on the other hand, was to consist solely of volunteers recruited primarily, if not entirely, from the lower social classes. Vincke was convinced that the trade apprentice or commercial trainee would be just as unenthusiastic about a military career as any student and would only take an active part in the defence of their country, if at all, as 'a peacetime soldier'. In his view, such an attitude deserved respect, not only in terms of a subject's 'personal freedom' but also in the interests of the state when properly understood, since a state could only truly flourish if the unfolding of military power rested on a solid economic and cultural basis; yet, as the critics of universal conscription unanimously agreed, integrating the middle classes into the military system would undermine this foundation and leave it permanently weakened.[27]

This line of reasoning is unmistakably located in the traditions of the early modern period and an order separating the civil and military spheres as far as possible – a model equally apparent in the eighteenth-century Prussian canton system, which may be regarded as an embryonic pre-form of compulsory military service. The older principle calling for citizens to take an active part in protecting and defending the common weal had fallen completely into oblivion, only continuing to exist pro forma in the free imperial cities which preserved their military sovereignty into the early nineteenth century. Even in the eighteenth century, municipal citizenship there was still only granted to those able to show they owned sufficient arms or who had permission to possess arms. But in reality, compulsory military service only existed on paper – anyone able to do so either bought himself free or paid for a substitute.

In fact, the city militias came to be purely symbolic bodies,[28] a fate that also overtook the *Schützengilden* (shooting clubs), which, after flourishing in the fifteenth and sixteenth centuries, had entered a period of gradual decline. Their loss of military significance went hand in hand with the cities' increased use of mercenaries for defence or their integration into the territorial state's defensive system. However, these clubs did survive in many places as sporting and leisure associations with clear church links even if, as the Prussian minister von Schroetter observed in 1808, 'general public participation in this institution has lessened over time, with a corresponding waning in respect and interest, until now the entire organisation has partially become degraded to offering nothing more than occasions for public carousal'.[29]

Most contemporaries seem to have regarded the strict division of labour between the army and civilians as relieving them from the burden of unpleasant duties. Even when, towards the end of the eighteenth century, the middle classes increasingly voiced criticism of the military's arrogance and privileges, this was never with any intention of removing such a division and opening the system up for all social classes. Instead, they were primarily concerned with reducing existing status differences and achieving equality between civilians and officers. The reformers' idea of 'an army drawn from the nation and returning to it' met with no enthusiasm in the 'nation' itself,[30] as can be clearly seen in the example of how a *Bürgergarde* (civilian militia) was established in Berlin. The French occupying forces ordered it to be set up in December 1806 to secure 'public peace and safety' throughout the city. A total of 2,185 male inhabitants of Berlin engaged in paying commercial activity and 'of good standing' were required to perform duties alternately on a 24-hour basis, with tasks ranging from guarding the gates, fire watchman duty, protecting public buildings, and accompanying post and goods wagons. They had to provide their own equipment (weapons and clothing) and the time spent on duty was unpaid.

From November 1807 on, Bijoutier Jordan, and the *Bürgergarde* commander, constantly bemoaned the large and apparently growing number of 'refractory citizens' unmoved by either threats or privileges in their refusal to enlist. The Silesian cities too were unable to 'awaken a lively enthusiasm for this matter'; within a few months the initial zealousness had 'cooled'. First of all, well-off citizens simply gave up their duties, employing 'paid watchmen, generally subjects in a wretched state', to take them on instead. The citizens themselves dismissed the *Bürgergarde* as a 'ridiculous *à la mode* sport' that 'no reasonable man can bother with unless he wants to become, quite justifiably, the material to amuse lazy *gourmands* at the dinner table'.[31]

The duties in the *Bürgergarde* were considered a sport because, in the final analysis, the tasks were policing functions and not military ones. Although they bore arms, in the official view they comprised a police troop rather than a militia. The reasons for this lay both in the general Napoleonic prohibition against militias and the Prussian king's interest in highlighting the essential distinction between a citizens' militia and the army. At the end of 1808, when he read that during public speeches and banquets 'the army is placed under the national guard', he did not mince words in ordering the city governor to curb the presumptuous citizens: 'The national guard, I repeat again, is *not an army* and should definitely not be considered as one and, what's more, neither should the army be slighted on its account.' The active patriotism demonstrated by the militia has 'certainly gained them the right to respect and recognition' since they 'have proved themselves worthy by keeping the peace *around the city of Berlin* as a police force would' but the regular army's merit is far greater. 'The troops have spilled their blood and put their bodies and lives at risk in *defending the fatherland*.'[32]

At the same time, the king showed himself quite willing to compensate for the decreasing appeal of the militia by offering symbolic badges of honour. In order to motivate the recalcitrant citizens to become officers in the militia and shooting clubs, 'I will be glad to maintain the allure of the uniform and consider the use of the existing Brandenburg ensign in red and silver suitable, and would even regard it an apt analogy to substitute the colour red for black in the crests'.[33] Not only does this generous provision give an insight into how obsessively the king occupied himself with the issue of uniforms, but it also indicates the importance he ascribed to a symbolic policy. Of course, he was assuming this would be welcomed by those affected, i.e. that educated, prosperous citizens were receptive to the 'allure of the uniform', regarding it as a suitable reward for paramilitary efforts that devoured both their time and their money. But just this was in doubt. After all, in 1817 the Berlin city council was still complaining about the 'burdensome militia guard duty' that required 50 citizens daily to be taken away from their business, and needed even 600 to 700 at parades. On the other hand, the burghers of Breslau, largely commercial traders and tradespeople, preferred to serve in the city's militia than in the newly organised *Landwehr* enlisted reserve army; apparently, they had more faith in the local militia than the new organisation, which might entail supra-regional deployment.[35] In any case, however, integrating civilians into the military was far from easy. The urban middle classes, from master craftsman to professor, revealed little inclination to succumb to the 'allure of the uniform', and the wealthier they were, the greater intransigence they showed in the face of various attempts to make them appreciate personal military service – not only at the level of police duties in the local citizens' militia but even more so when it came to universal conscription designed 'to preserve the fatherland'.

3. The Battle for the Middle Classes

The military reformers were well aware of how negatively military service was viewed, some even fearing that, in 1809, compulsory conscription might trigger 'unrest' among the 'more genteel classes'. For this reason, they recommended 'allowing a substitute (*remplacement*)', arguing that allowing such a measure preserved the love of the king as 'pure and unsullied' while gaining recruits who were capable, healthy, and able-bodied; in their view, young scholars and artists were useless for military purposes anyway since, as was common knowledge, 'their intellectual efforts left them unsuited to any sort of physical strain and, in most cases, a life of luxury or pampered upbringing from early childhood on had made them unfit for it'.[37]

However, this pragmatic logic found little support among the majority on the reform commission. Johann August Sack, councillor of state and ministry of the interior official responsible for the police, pleaded vociferously with 'state chancellor' Hardenberg to impose universal conscription and was equally vocal in his rejection of any kind of substitution, claiming it would otherwise degenerate 'into hired enlistment'. Friedrich von Raumer, a state councillor directly assisting Hardenberg, was only prepared to accept substitutes in extreme cases, with the king personally granting any exception necessary. In 1809, Freiherr vom Stein, while in exile in Brünn, spoke out against exemptions and substitutes. In his view, the whole point of conscription was to generate a 'martial spirit' across the 'entire nation', with the population acquiring the requisite skills. For this reason he insisted that 'every class in civil society' should have the duty to perform military service; it was the fundamental basis for shaping a 'noble, martial, national character' and engaging in a 'national war'. In particular, he believed universal conscription would curb the prevailing tendency in the 'commercial and academic classes' to an 'unwarlike and cowardly disposition', adding that this would 'counteract their drifting away from the state, encouraging the feeling throughout [all classes] of a duty to sacrifice one's own life to preserve it'.[38]

After 1807, this feeling of personal duty lay at the heart of all the debate in Prussia on the military. As far as Scharnhorst and his 'party' were concerned, military service formed both the basis for and proof of citizenship, an idea itself derived from the notion that 'rather than being a scholar, artist, etc., inhabitants of a state are first and foremost members of the state'; business people or artists needed civic order provided by the state before they could engage in their occupation, and they ought to be personally prepared to support and secure the state that guarantees it. Furthermore, this duty could not be delegated to others, since substitution would undermine the entire system, taking away its credibility.[39]

The reformers were constantly circling their key point – military service had to be universal to be effective. Where only 'the farmer and the poor citizen' are enlisted to defend the country, it must inevitably seem 'a burden and one far from honourable ... since one cannot buy oneself free from a question of honour'. In their view, a widespread feeling of duty and honour could only develop when wealthy and educated men shared the fate of the poorer and less well educated, and not until then would the 'battle for king and fatherland ... [be considered] something so holy and essential that everything else is subordinate to it'.[40]

Strictly speaking, the argument was circular: an appeal was being made to the subjects' patriotic sentiment – above all, in the 'upper classes' – while simultaneously assuming that this very same patriotism first needed military service to generate and shape it. This, however, reflected the contemporary perception of the 'more educated part of the population' as lacking positive 'sentiments' towards the Prussian state. As Hardenberg complained in 1808: 'Heartless cosmopolitanism is the order of the day' – a notion supported by Sack who, eleven months later, wrote of the 'upper classes' only being out for 'their own advantage' instead of desiring the 'common good'.

But how could 'warmth and enthusiasm' for the state be developed and transformed into support for conscription? One answer was to thrust it on the citizens 'by force'. If they failed to realise that their political interests were linked to conscription and wartime service, then more or less constant pressure had to be exerted in order to make them realise it. The 1810 draft bill on conscription in Prussia not only envisaged imprisonment as a punishment for men who failed to appear before the recruiting commission and avoided military service without any proven justification, but also allowed them to be deprived of their civil rights: they would be unable to purchase land, become burghers, have their own businesses, inherit, participate and vote in parish or municipal meetings, or take up any public or municipal office. These provisions were primarily directed at the professional urban middle classes, the self-employed in business and trade, and inn and hotelkeepers, whose sons were to forfeit all economic and political rights if they refused to perform military service. Hence, the failure to fulfil a citizen's duty directly cut oneself off from communal civil life – and, for all practical purposes, burghers and citizens had become identical.

A second way to make the upper and middle classes more receptive to this new military service might be to link conscription and political participation in the state more closely, with a constitution to reinforce such a connection. In March 1808, the reform commission indicated to the king that men would only be prepared to accept 'major sacrifices' for the army and the state if they were motivated by a 'love of their fatherland and its constitution', but such 'love' can only be expected if

> the government concludes a compact with the nation, creating a love for the constitution and trust in it, and making its independent status valuable. This spirit cannot be generated without a degree of freedom in the way to procure and produce the means to sustain independence. Whoever is unable to experience these feelings, cannot value them, and cannot sacrifice himself for them.[43]

In August 1808, Lieutenant-Colonel Neithardt von Gneisenau, a member of Scharnhorst's staff, put forward a similarly radical argument in a memorandum that advocated arming the general population, adding: 'However, if the people are to offer a spirited defence of their country, it is only appropriate and politic first to provide people with one'. It was essential, he continued, to have a 'free constitution' granting citizens a political franchise and making those in power answerable; a constitution and freedom created the basis on which men developed patriotic feelings and discharged their civic duties, including the defence of their country.[44] But neither the king nor his conservative entourage were prepared to go that far, merely deigning to organise the army in a slightly more 'civil' way, making it more palatable to the middle classes. In 1808, Friedrich Wilhelm III gave in to pressure from reformers to ban the humiliating punishments of cudgelling and running the gauntlet, promising further that every able soldier and non-commissioned officer 'irrespective of their birth' could become an officer, a clear indication that 'the conscription system would be extended to include the upper classes'.[45]

The question remained, though, of whether banning the whip and proffering potential officer status as a carrot would really be sufficient to awaken, as Gneisenau put it, 'the martial and civic spirit of the nation'. At all events, Scharnhorst was sceptical and was considering other possible bait: given that a 'free constitution' would not be granted, could certain privileges encourage the 'upper', 'educated', and 'cultivated classes' to join in this new system? Accordingly, the reform commission produced a first draft suggesting that men able to 'arm and clothe themselves, learning how to use these arms at their own cost' could form a 'reserve army' only required to exercise four weeks a year. In contrast, all others – including 'all citizens in farming and trade, and all hired day labourers' – were to be conscripted into a standing army to serve for several years and without a break.[46]

The suggestion, however, met with harsh criticism. Von Schön, clerk of the treasury, pointed out there was only one criterion for deciding who served in the standing army, and that was 'the ability to perform military service'; any other benchmark would 'more or less turn the soldier into a mercenary and the militias into the real defenders of their country'. Freiherr vom Stein too cautioned against demoting the standing army, warning of the consequences.[47] Some officers, though, were equally sceptical of the idea of militias – and it found no favour with the king. The reformers therefore pondered over what other means they could employ to gain 'upper class' support for the project of cross-societal universal conscription, concluding that even if these classes were to be incorporated into the standing army, they still needed to enjoy certain advantages, above all, a shorter term of service. On this issue, Scharnhorst felt that all recruits 'with a certain higher degree of intelligence and hence able to be trained as soldiers sooner than others' should only have to serve for four months in a three-year total period of service. Such an arrangement would leave the young men's careers and training undisturbed while providing them with the 'most basic military knowledge'.[48]

Interestingly enough, here the previous criterion of 'wealth' had simply been replaced by 'intelligence', with a shorter service period granted to all those studying at university or in the final year of an elite secondary school (*Gymnasium*). This emphasis on formal education might have originated in the tendency among officers and reformist state servants, themselves frequently not especially well off, to equate wealth with intractability and commercial egotism. In any case, the educated young men were nonetheless assumed to have certain financial resources since they were expected to pay for their own clothes, arms and subsistence if they wanted to enjoy a shorter period of service. However, including privileges for the educated seemed to avert the threatened ascendancy of Mammon feared by so many.

But whether 'educated' or 'wealthy' young men, independent militias or a standing army, symbolic or material advantages – in the final analysis all protagonists clearly understood that hardly any of the population were prepared to enlist for military service voluntarily. The prevailing division of labour between the military and civilian classes had only reinforced the civilian belief that defending their 'fatherland' was not their concern – a view so entrenched that not even wars had managed to change it. After all, the majority of the population thought wars had nothing to do with them and saw them as mere dynastic struggles and military skirmishes. Generally speaking, the vast mass of people considered the 'enemy of their country' as the 'enemy of their country's army' and had no aspirations to become personally involved. The Prussian reformers were certain that this attitude could only be altered by legal means and, where necessary, reinforced by police action; the only solution was a new conscription law able to 'provide the nation with the proper perspective on this matter'.[49]

4. Military Service, Wartime Service, and Manliness

Yet this law turned out to have a long period of gestation. It might have been publicly announced in 1808, but in the ensuing years it was written and revised several times and only finally enacted in 1813 – just as Prussia was preparing to pit its own military forces against the French national army. In this situation, the domestic and foreign policy considerations that previously kept the king and some of his ministers from succumbing to pressure for reform no longer played a role.[50] Now the most pressing concern was to establish a large, motivated army as quickly as possible to drive Napoleon's troops, in disarray after defeat in Russia, out of Prussia and the other German states. To this purpose, the groundwork was laid by a well-organised propaganda campaign accompanying the series of orders Friedrich Wilhelm III issued in rapid succession in spring 1813 calling his 'faithful subjects' to arms. After initially leaving all 'educated youths' free to 'show their good will by their deeds', a mere six days later the voluntary principle was revoked in a legal decree stating that 'all exceptions to the duty of military service' were null and void; two further decrees followed in March and April 1813 on organising the *Landwehr* (enlisted reserves) and the *Landsturm* (final reserves). This completed an 'arming of the nation' that foresaw every male citizen over 17 in one or other form of mobilisation.[51]

The general population's reaction to these measures was mixed. In some parts of the country, hundreds of men ran away to escape being drafted, going abroad or into hiding. In the regiments comprising the new *Landwehr*, desertion became increasingly frequent, causing the Westphalian civil governor Ludwig von Vincke to report to Berlin that, in many areas, unless he employed draconian methods, he would be unable to ensure 'men reporting for service who had previously failed to register'. Resistance was so great that it was only broken when the parents of runaways were arrested and their houses were threatened with being torched.[52]

The Breslau city delegates were 'surprised' to learn of a stipulation suspending all exemptions for cantonists for the duration of the war, including the one for their own city. Nine days after this decree appeared they asked the state chancellor to modify the enlisting age of urban youths, raising it from seventeen to twenty or even twenty-one, reasoning that urban young men enjoyed 'a more tender and genteel education ... than the countryman who is, from eight on, commonly used to personal service and the absence of ease and convenience'. Furthermore, the young people must be allowed to complete their training, whether in trade, business or academic life; interrupting their 'career' by 'forcing [them] into military service' would make them 'completely unfit to be citizens' and 'ruin' the commercial sector. In his reply, state chancellor Hardenberg left no doubts about his 'intense indignation' at what he termed the city fathers' egoistic policy of self-interest and 'lack of patriotism' when the issue at stake was the 'defence of the throne and the fatherland'. He was just as adamant in rejecting the request of a Breslau burgher who proffered a 'patriotic sacrifice' of 200 thalers in place of his youngest son's military service. As Hardenberg made unequivocally clear, 'money cannot discharge ... the sacred duty of serving the king and fatherland, body and soul'.[54]

Apparently, it must have soon become widely known that no exemption would be granted for military service to sons supporting their parents because many business and trades people, inn- and hotel-keepers, and landowners all presented doctors' certificates to prove their sons were sickly and weak and unfit for service. As early as the beginning of March 1813, the *Landrat* in Liegnitz reported that a number of wealthy merchants had used such medical evidence to support applications for their sons' 'dispensation', stating that although he did not wish to doubt 'the invalidity of the person concerned', he did not want the families 'to escape without receiving a considerable contribution from [them] for the benefit of the general good'. At his urging, the fathers donated a total of 2,100 thalers to pay for equipment and provisions for 'able-bodied or poor young soldiers'. The *Landrat* justified taking the money by arguing that: 'If this were in some sense a consideration for your able-bodied sons, I would have been wary of receiving it. But since the latter have been reliably determined to be unfit for military service, I do not regard it, in my humble opinion, as unbecoming to accept this offer.'[55] It was an approach that was widely imitated. Numerous burghers soon pronounced their readiness to supply, in place of their own incapacitated sons, uniforms and arms for other young men, 'penniless, but big and strong', and provide financial support for them during their period of service. This 'patriotic' offer was received 'with thanks'.[56]

Occasionally, close contacts in the right places and a suitably high donation could replace medical certificates. The Oranienburg *Landrat* managed to have his only son released from military service after the intercession of his son-in-law, president of the Liegnitz regional supreme court, and a public promise to donate 1,000 thalers to 'equip penniless volunteers'. As a large landowner, he had no inclination to lose his heir; moreover, his son was – of course – 'weak-chested and slenderly built, and brought up with such care and concern as has benefited his mind but left his physical constitution less positively affected. It is inconceivable that he could survive the hardships of a military campaign.' Hardenberg was not inclined to reject such an attractively gilded presentation of the evidence, reassuring the *Landrat* that: 'It is not the will of the state to appropriate the sole son and heir, imposing a loss on families that can also severely disadvantage them in respect of their material well-being.'[57]

The mass of documented cases like this one does convey the impression that the official line of Prussian subjects welcoming the war with keen enthusiasm was not reflected everywhere throughout the country. Precisely those classes previously spared the rigours of military service preferred to affirm their patriotic sentiment via pecuniary contributions rather than by sacrificing life and limb, as demanded by the state – an approach directly reflected in the social composition of the volunteers. Although the appeals and decrees of February 1813 were primarily directed at 'educated youths' with the necessary means at their disposal to pay for their own military equipment, the 1813–14 muster-rolls for volunteers only list 7 per cent as elite secondary school pupils and students, just under 6 per cent as government officials, and 11 per cent who were in business, commercial clerks or self-employed. In contrast, the majority came from trade (40 per cent) and agricultural milieus (20 per cent). In other words, these generally had neither education nor money and financed themselves by means of the 'collections and support' confirming the wealthy burghers' patriotic fervour.

In any case, the appeals for volunteers were not overly successful. Compared to some 120,000 men in the *Landwehr* and nearly the same number in the regular army, the 28,000 or so volunteers lost much of their lustre, and the figure suffers even further when one bears in mind the attractive promises given to entice the men to enlist; not only were they vouchsafed 'preferential' consideration 'in their previous civilian career', but given the prospect of forming their own artillery or rifle units, and rapid promotion as officers or NCOs. Conversely, those evading active service could reckon with neither job nor rank nor medals after the war.[58] What is more, this modest echo casts a different light on the vast propaganda efforts in 1813 designed to popularise the call to the colours. On Stein's orders, Ernst Moritz Arndt was the main figure to be entrusted with the task of mobilising the 'valiant Prussians' and 'German men' against Napoleon. In a pamphlet, printed twenty times with a total of nearly 100,000 copies, Arndt called for a holy 'national war'; the Prussian or German 'fatherland' could cast off its French shackles only if all the male '*Volk*' of the entire nation took to arms. Arndt invoked the 'ancient stories' bearing witness to manly valour and 'martial spirit', citing the Germanic myths and Nibelung saga as a guiding light for the 'farmers and burghers' to follow. Instead of seeing themselves as 'defenceless [men], unable to bear arms', they needed to rekindle 'traditional manliness', but this, he went on, required first and foremost being 'valiant' and capable of bearing arms. If 'Germany' wanted to free itself from the French, the 'German men' first needed to overcome their 'wretchedness and effeteness' and regain the virtues of their fathers.

Firmly located in the zeitgeist of the 'century of education', Arndt attributed the loss of these virtues to the wrong upbringing. In his view, men of his generation – he was born in 1769 – had been infected from their earliest days with 'puerile and womanish pleasures, laziness and cowardice'.[60] In this era, criticism against a supposedly unmanly, pampering approach to bringing up children was nothing new. In 1774, Johann Bernhard Basedow had already bemoaned the fact that 'my schools and mentors had not made me into a man'. In order to ensure 'future generations have men again', he taught the young charges in his Dessau Reform School 'practical and useful knowledge and skills' that 'women themselves don't possess' and which, consequently, greatly impressed them.[61] In the past, he continued, educating for gender differences had been criminally neglected and, as a result, the once sharp boundary between men and women among the nobles and educated classes particularly had become increasingly blurred. In 1786, the renowned professor of medicine, Johann Peter Frank, also censured the 'pampering education' common in those circles, claiming it had allowed Germany's 'heroic sons' to degenerate into 'dandified male puppets', debasing them into 'mollycoddled milksops' who displayed 'women's attributes' as much in their character as in their outward appearance. Frank's colleague from Halle, Johann Christian Reil, supported this view, writing in 1791 of how the sons of 'ancient, iron-hard Teutons' had become frenchified 'fops', 'thin as locusts, with no backs and calves' but instead with 'cramps, vapours and hysteria'.[62]

In the tradition of Rousseau, cold baths and vigorous exercise were recommended as the means to re-forge virile, tough men from what Frank called the emasculated 'grandsons of the iron-like Germans', to make them worthy of their ancestors and into men who kept women at a distance. Occasionally, the notion of 'military exercises' met with approval too, as something to be incorporated into male gymnastics for the benefit of a powerful physique and elegant posture. However, as Frank pointed out, this should not 'become the main concern' – after all, efforts directed at health education at the turn of the century were not aimed at having men trained as warriors. Instead, the idea was to shape a harmonious manly character, as exemplified, in 1793, by the reformist educator Johann Christoph Friedrich Gutsmuths, who dreamt of unifying the 'physical perfection of the natural man with the intellectual culture of the sophisticated earth-born mortal'.[63]

The numerous breviaries on manliness appearing around the end of the eighteenth century and in the early years of the nineteenth were also marked by a decidedly civilian emphasis. Yet although in his 1805 'character study' of the male sex, *Hofrat* Pockel may have asserted the 'superiority of power' and 'greater measure of courage, decisiveness, and firmness of sentiment' which, in contrast to women, allow a man to 'defend the freedom of his kin and his fatherland, devise [...] arts and sciences, introduce laws, establish societies, hold sway over countries and peoples, ruling them with enduring insight and might', he left no doubt that such truly male occupations were reserved for leading figures. The common man as little passed laws and ruled over other peoples as he defended his country. Instead, his destiny was to be 'the lord, *tutelary deity*, the *judge*, the *protector*, and *master* of his wife and children'.[64]

Similarly, one looks in vain in other writings at the turn of the century on the man *per se* for allusions to a possible model character of martial or military behaviour. Encyclopaedias may have qualified the term 'man' by adding strength, valour, or steadiness of manner – although it was actually more important to learn that one could only speak of a '*Mannsperson*' when he had completed his thirtieth year and attained a certain physical, mental and social maturity. However, nothing was said to indicate that this maturity was best obtained in military or wartime service.[65] Instead, if the army was mentioned at all, the tone was generally more critical. Johann Ludwig Ewald's 1804 two-volume book of advice entitled '*Der gute Jüngling, gute Gatte und Vater*' (The good youth, husband, and father), for example, describes the soldier's lot as one 'where unbridled freedom can be bought by strict obedience and meekly submitting to being a small part of a vast machine, and perhaps [a man] might gain honour and respect'. However, Ewald certainly did not believe that 'one could achieve true honour, or show manly strength and manly courage, solely in *this* station', anymore than did *Konsistorialrat* Friedrich Ehrenberg, a member of the Prussian protestant church administration, who in his lectures on the 'nature and disposition of the man' – already in its first reprinting in 1822 – wrote: 'In this way, the doctor who exposes himself to the risk of infection at the sickbed may show more courage than the soldier who, face to face with death, risks his life in battle.'[66]

The texts written in those days on the male self-image by middle-class men for an audience of fellow middle-class men did not attribute any particular merit to the army, let alone try to adopt it as a model of manliness. On the contrary, the soldier appeared as an antithesis to the middle-class man, as a social character not always in line with a civilian sense of values. The authors intensely distrusted the military milieu, and regarded universalising the prevailing conduct and norms in the military world as neither possible nor desirable. At the side of the ideal housewife, mother and spouse, they placed a man typified by the ambition to get on in his career, with a sense of family and communal values, but with none of the 'martial spirit' Ernst Moritz Arndt so praised in 1813 as the panacea to redress present ills and serve as a prospect to the future. In this sense, Arndt's call for 'educating citizens into soldiers' came close to a pedagogical revolution, directing the discourse of manliness onto a completely new track. However, he was not alone in his thinking. Many officers and civilians shared the views of this contentious writer and propagandist, similarly lamenting the unmartial nature of German citizens, disparagingly complaining that rather than having a 'military temperament', they showed every symptom of being infected by the 'commercial spirit'.[67] Similarly, high-ranking civil servants detailed to work on rebuilding and reforming Prussia after 1806–7 repeatedly called their fellow-men to task for being 'effete', and when, in 1810, Altenstein, a minister in the cabinet, sought to justify effeteness as an expression of greater 'intellectual capability' and 'ingenuity', he unleashed a storm of outrage. The high chancellor Beyme protested that separating culture and wartime service only led to misfortune and created the 'effete sex' presently populating the Prussian state, adding that: 'culture can very well be melded with wartime service, while culture without wartime service results in slackness of body and mind'.[68]

It was a view endorsed in 1811 by Sack and Raumer, two councillors of state. The former was principally concerned with the benefits to be gained for the army – the damaging caste spirit would be discarded and even the army's 'lower levels' would profit from 'more education and intelligence' – while the latter concentrated more on the anticipated benefits for the 'nation' from linking culture and wartime service'. He also insisted that 'art, science and public virtue' went 'hand in hand with heroic valour, the love of the fatherland, and the duty to defend it'. Raumer argued for an 'equable, early, and compulsory military service' to make the male populace aware of this duty, develop a 'national consciousness', and shed the 'effeteness and indolence stemming from the wrong upbringing'. As a further advantage, this would overcome the 'previous antagonism between the military and civilian classes' in two ways: firstly, by embourgeoisement of the officer corps and, secondly, by 'gradually spreading a military spirit and sense of order throughout the entire nation'. He envisaged an army reformed by integration into civic life and adopting a role as the nation's mentor, mediating key political and social values to male citizens (the former in the shape of 'national consciousness' and the latter as 'order, subordination and honour'). Since the army indiscriminately took in all young men, it also formed – in Scharnhorst's words from 1810 – a point of national unity 'linking' the male inhabitants within national territory one to another, overarching class divides and reinforcing society's 'inner harmony'.

For Raumer, too, it went without saying that the middle classes would not only be a part of this integrative task but would take on a vital, genuinely necessary role in preserving and supporting the state. He swept aside Altenstein's objection that their sons did not have the physical condition needed to serve in the army as a 'mere pretext', claiming they would rapidly improve with a proper training which did not simply stimulate 'intellectual pursuits' but actively encouraged 'physical exercises' – and he admonished middle class educationalists and parents to ensure that no one in future should be 'raised in such a way that, when still in the period of his greatest youthful vitality, he consider himself unfit to use war weapons or withstand the physical demands of military service'.[69]

The issue of physical education was not new in the political arena. As early as 1807, Freiherr vom Stein and other military reformers had advocated that 'gymnastic exercises ... such as fencing, swimming, horseback exercises, etc., related to war needs and designed to strengthen the physical constitution should be a part of school life' – and they were not thinking of military academies but wanted these skills included in the standard school curricula.[70] In 1811, Friedrich Ludwig Jahn spoke out in favour of founding gymnastics clubs to 'keep youths from listlessness and dissipation and make them suitably robust for future battles for the fatherland'.[71] Arndt, too, recommended holding competitions in weapons practice on Sundays during the summer for all 14- to 22-year-olds, with official competitions being held once or twice a year with 'married women and maidens' invited to a dance at the closing ceremony. Such 'physical exercises' would not only 'prepare [them] for the major business of war' but equally protect the young men 'in the years of pubescence' from their awakening sexuality, the 'sensual appetite' and the 'fevered dreams of their imagination'. As Arndt concluded, 'His heart must be directed towards a higher goal, his body must be trimmed and worn out with manly exercises. In this way, we'll produce a handsome, strong, and magnificent sex, protected from effeteness and lasciviousness by the ultimate appeal of manliness.'

While Raumer or Jahn viewed physical education for male children and youths as a pre-stage of military service, Arndt envisaged it as largely replacing service altogether, reckoning that an annual three weeks in the army would be sufficient to turn physically fit men between 16 and 45 into soldiers ready for battle. In this way, he continued, one could not only save two-thirds of military expenditure but benefit general cultural life too since 'in peacetime, standing armies are like stagnant pools breeding foulness and pestilence: the time spent on parade or loafing around, and living closely together in industrious inactivity inevitably leaves youths at the mercy of all kinds of desires and vices'.[72]

This description exactly tallies with Niebuhr's 1808 notion of 'stupid peacetime service'. Similarly to Arndt, he too initially wanted to limit 'arming' the population to critical cases of war – until wartime service became transfigured into a male initiatory experience. In his letters, he enthused: 'A period of real active service around the age of 20, when your heart and soul is fully in it, is a magnificent test; it steels the character, making you manly and complete as a human being.' Like others in his social class, Niebuhr had been exempted from military service and never enjoyed that steeling of the character he so praised, noting that it was 'a loss never to have passed through this school'. In 1813, the chance seemed to have come to make up for lost time: Niebuhr, Prussian state servant and scholar and then 36 years old, volunteered for active service.[73] Another volunteer at the time was the 16-year younger Westphalian merchant's son, Friedrich Harkort, who enlisted together with his 18-year-old brother. His letters to his mother showed how much he was enjoying the military campaign. On 13 February 1814, he wrote: 'Our soldier's life suits us rather well, despite the daily efforts and tasks ... As soon as I return via Paris, I'll have marvels to tell.' But the march back turned out to be anything but happy. He wrote to his betrothed: 'Every day my loathing for the military life becomes greater; for in my eyes the peacetime soldier is really an inconsequential figure.' The young Harkort had more or less enthusiastically joined up when it was a question of fighting, danger and gaining the laurels of victory, but the monotonous 'peacetime service' with the 'slavishly' practised drill exercises left him completely cold.

It is hard to say from this distance what motives the Harkort brothers had in enlisting voluntarily. There was certainly no overriding incentive for their future careers since both were firmly settled in business and had no intention of joining the Prussian civil service. They may, of course, have been attracted by the prospect of promotion to an officer's rank – for the middle classes, such advancement had hardly been possible previously, and indeed Friedrich Harkort took a lifelong pride in his achievement. A desire for adventure might have also played a role, especially when extremely young men 'are happiest and most ready to hurry to arms', as Ludwig von Vincke, the Westphalian civil governor, noted. They expected war to be a major, extraordinary experience, valued the mobility and comradeship, and felt the pull of power and danger. As Friedrich Harkort wrote, 'The greatest pleasure in a soldier's life is simply that you often sit down to eat in utter peace but before you're full, you're up and marching off again.' He enjoyed the rough and tumble of being with other young men too: 'One of us is shaved by the other – that's a great comfort on active service. And then we can all have a good laugh at the little accidents that happen. Me today, you tomorrow!' Finally, the uniform too seems to have contributed to his sense of well-being: 'Mama, I can assure you that I appear a very stately soldier.'[74]

The tendency to romanticise war, linking it with freedom and adventure, not only found expression in such letters but was also – literally – given voice in the numerous soldiers' songs of the time. In its first edition of 1799, the popular song anthology, the *Mildheimische Liederbuch*, only contained nine songs 'for the military profession'. In contrast, the revised edition in 1815 listed forty-one items under the same heading, designed for *'Soldiers and Reserves'*. The songs converted war into youthful male initiation or transformed it into a personal and political struggle for freedom, and ranged from Schiller's *Reiterlied* to rousing refrains written by the young Theodor Körner.[75]

The desire to experience war as a 'manly crusade', as Harkort dubbed it, not only entailed bidding farewell to the parental home and a sheltered but narrow life. For the Harkort brothers, volunteering meant, first and foremost, escape from an overbearing father and older brother. No member of their family had ever been a soldier before – in the Prussian era, they had been exempted, and under French occupation they had bought themselves free by providing a substitute. Furthermore, whether in Westphalia or the Brandenburg Marches, business circles had very little good to say of the army. It comes as little surprise, therefore, to find some relatives and friends commiserating with Harkort senior for losing his sons to the 'rough soldier's estate'. The deputy mayor in Lennep, Caspar Heinrich Stucke, wrote in a similar vein: 'I pity you for having to offer up two of your dear sons for the fatherland. It would be far better if they could dedicate their energies to the peaceful pursuit of business.' When news came of both brothers' names being put forward as officers in the *Landwehr*, Strucke commented: 'I am absolutely convinced that your noble sons will bring more honour to the officer class than that class brings to them. May Heaven protect them, as they will certainly protect the oppressed and peaceful citizens, so often the target of uncouth soldiery.'

Friedrich and Gustav Harkort shrugged off such concerns, though they sought to dispel the notion that they could become estranged from civilian life. As a lieutenant, Friedrich also showed an intense interest in his surroundings, sometimes even utilizing the military campaign as an educational journey, gathering information about the countries he passed through and reporting on them in his letters back home. But he was also aware of how war participation had enhanced his status. When they returned to the Altena barracks, he and his comrades were revered as 'their country's liberators' and showered with invitations, while balls and celebrations were held in their honour. The young war heroes lived 'as merrily as kings' surrounded, above all, by the 'patriotic female part of the population'.[76]

5. 'Female Patriotism'

Female patriotic ardour looked to a male heroism characterised by physical prowess and bravery, the readiness to take risks, and the certainty of final victory. Many women appear to have found men with battle experience attractive, especially if they had helped carry off the prize of victory. Could there be really any truth in Jahn's comments in 1810 on 'women's ... granting of favours', or his presumption that 'Whoever appears in uniform, bearing arms, will soon find himself loved; the soldier conquers her heart with greater ease'?[77]

Jahn's notions certainly did not reflect the complexity of the reality, nor was there any near anthropological reflex as he implied. Women did not inevitably experience an erotic attraction to weapons and uniforms, despite Jahn's claims, and those of many other later writers, to have observed it. In the early nineteenth century, the common soldier, even if adorned with 'uniform and weapons', enjoyed little respect, and though the officers were better off, it remains doubtful whether this was due to his military status and 'martial' character. Young women from the middle and upper classes may well have found officers interesting because of their aristocratic origins, proximity to royal power, self-assured appearance, and, not least, their proverbial skills on the dance floor.[78]

In fact, evidence from 1813–15 repeatedly shows that war actually had anything but an erotic effect on women. Very few mothers, wives and fiancées were delighted to learn that their sons, husbands or betrothed had decided to enlist. The 'lady from Berlin wanting a divorce on the grounds that her husband did not join the army' remained an absolute exception, striking a jarring note with many women and men alike. Peter Beuth, a senior financial officer and himself a volunteer, commented on this case with the words: 'I hold the patriotism of women in great esteem, but the home and the husband and the children must always be first and nearest and dearest.' This was no doubt why Beuth supported Eleonore von Vincke in her attempts to persuade her husband, Ludwig, to refrain from putting his 'foolhardy plans' into action and volunteering for the second campaign against Napoleon. Eleonore was opposed to her husband's plans, which stemmed partly from political disillusionment and partly from a feeling of being tired of his work. 'I can readily believe *you* would rather go than stay at home and torment yourself so much,' she wrote, 'but that is not my wish, my dearest, darling husband', adding, 'How can you believe that I am agreeable to your going as a rifleman volunteer; you know far better than that and that's why I am the only one you never asked ... don't think of such foolhardy plans a moment longer.' And her husband, so put to rights, confided in his diary: 'I received a dear letter from my Eleonore, although her aversion to my military plans grieved me sorely.'

Eleonore von Vincke did not see herself as acting unpatriotically in trying to keep her 40-year-old husband from setting out on his military adventures. 'You are assuredly of greater use in your present position', she wrote, 'than you ever will be as a single person, with no knowledge of military matters, in the vast mass of the army.'[79] Quite apart from the fact that his superiors and friends took a similar view, no one would have expected a wife to watch gaily as her husband departed for the war or even, as in the case of the Berlin woman cited above, put him under pressure to volunteer. On the contrary, there would have been general sympathy for the sighs uttered by Louise Henriette Funcke, a Westphalian industrialist's wife, when she learned, in 1813, that the French-occupied *Mark* was being reintegrated into Prussia. 'I fear, I fear our sons will be taken from us; they are the best goods God has given us. My heart is oppressed by this worry though otherwise I am glad to become Prussian and be the subject of that good king.' The feelings of her sister, Helena Teschemacher, married to a Wuppertal merchant, were less ambivalent. In a letter to her brother Johann Caspar Harkort, she made it quite clear she was not prepared to relinquish either stepsons or sons-in-law – and why not use Johann Casper's good connections, or even resort to bribery if needed, to free his sons from wartime service? Eighteen-year-old Auguste Mohl, daughter of a Barmen merchant and Friedrich Harkort's fiancée, had similar thoughts when she tried to convince Friedrich that it made no sense for him to volunteer.[80]

The different reactions women showed to the historically new experience of a patriotic 'people's' or 'national war' suggest different patterns of political and national identity. Their readiness to let their husband, son or fiancé enlist may have been reinforced or weakened by whether they felt themselves to be 'Prussian', like Louise Funcke, or belonging to the 'Grand Duchy of Berg', as did Helena Teschemacher and Auguste Mohl. But even among those born and bred in Prussia, there was a broad spectrum of reaction ranging from outright rejection to ardent devotion; it is noticeable, though, that there were no generally accepted, mandatory codes indicating how patriotic women should act. The experience of a war mobilising all citizens was too new and too abrupt: people's collective memory contained no similar experience to be recalled and taken as a guideline.

Those organising the war were well aware of this vacuum. Even in the run-up to the 'national levy', they had drawn on the help of men able to prepare suitable propaganda prior to and during the campaign against Napoleon. Consequently, there was a spate of martial and patriotic appeals to the public, pamphlets, and, above all, any number of poems and songs all aimed at legitimising the conflict as a 'national war' and trying to drum up male enthusiasm for it.[81] However, neither the Prussian king's official proclamations nor the semi-official calls to arms and patriotic songs were directed at women. In fact, women appeared only infrequently in the mass dissemination of nationalist writings and songs – either as a creature 'violated' by the French whose lost honour could be restored only by male combat, or else as a 'hero's mother' or 'warrior's wife', a homely adjunct to the martial male German.[82]

It was a new situation for women too. They were hard pressed to find models to follow, except in literature, where the principal figure of identification was provided by Goethe's Dorothea in his epic poem *Hermann and Dorothea*. Despite being the apotheosis of domesticity and modesty, Dorothea did not shy at defending a group of girls on a farm against 'a runaway plundering rabble'. Without male help, since all the men had enlisted, her 'mighty blows' made short shrift of five marauders, and then she locked the farmhouse and sat 'armed, until help came'. In two senses, Hermann was only transformed into a man by her love for him: firstly, as a husband, changed by marriage from a dependent youth into an independent citizen and father, and, secondly, in his transformation into a warrior. Although Hermann, the middle-class merchant's son, had sought exemption from military service for the final battle to run his father's business, Dorothea's example and love inspired him to the 'courage and strength' to 'confront our attackers'. Hermann's words 'if enemies threaten / Now or in future, then arm me yourself and hand me my weapons' are not only a pledge and admonishing of Dorothea, but equally distance him from his father who, in Goethe's poem, represents the peace-loving city burgher, concerned with 'order and cleanliness'. While his father trusts to the powers of nature, God and the 'valiant Germans' to protect his town from enemy occupation and destruction, Hermann wants, from now on, to be included among the 'fighters', saying: 'And if our countrymen all felt as I do, we'd all of us rise up: / Might against might would stand, and for all of us wars would be over'.[83]

Goethe's *'bürgerliche Idylle'*, first published in 1797, enjoyed a wide audience. It was as much an anthropological as an historical work, intending to identify 'the purely human aspect of life in a small German town', while 'reflecting in that small mirror the major movements and alterations on the world's stage'. Goethe's story, with a plot that 'did what the Germans wanted', was set in 1795, during the first coalition war, where the enemies were 'Franks' – in other words, the French – against whom the 'valiant Germans' were to fight either now or in the 'future'.[84] While male contemporaries were free to identify with Hermann's martial exhortation in the final verses, women could identify with the image of Dorothea. She was, after all, the main protagonist and, in many instances, showed herself to be Hermann's superior. The poem itself spoke of her 'magnificent stature' and the critic August Wilhelm Schlegel emphasised the 'heroic strength of her soul'. According to Schlegel, Dorothea united 'tender womanliness' with 'dauntlessness in facing any threat, either in general or to her own person', combined with a 'healthy physical strength which she uses to take the burdens of life on herself'. She served Goethe as a model of how the war could produce something good alongside the evil it generated: just as boys 'reveal' themselves as youths, and youths as men, so 'the weaker sex, as it is commonly called' shows itself to be 'brave and valiant and with presence of mind'. In an emergency, women like Dorothea could act like men – in other words, use weapons and defend themselves. But in the long run, the more important message was that they could also imbue men with 'courage and strength', arm them and hand them their weapons.[85]

Accordingly, the patriotism of women was principally expressed in proudly and gladly 'leading' their menfolk to enlist – sons, lovers and husbands – when 'honour calls', and not holding them back from their fatherland. Women could then look forward to being richly rewarded for this sacrifice by the masculinizing effects on soldiers returning home from 'war's storm and violence'. Jahn, at least, was firmly convinced that just as a man 'in the full sense of the word ... only [loves] the *womanly woman*', so a woman only desires the 'virile and manly man',[86] and to support the eternal truth of his statement, he quoted the appropriate verses from Klopstock's 1752 ode 'Hermann and Thusnelda': never, declares Thusnelda, did she so love Hermann as at the moment when, sweaty and dust-covered, he returned victorious from battle with the Romans.

> Come! I tremble with joy; give me the eagle,
> And thy sabre blood-reeking! Come! Breathe freely,
> Rest here in my embraces
> From the too terrible fight!

Klopstock's images and themes here are drawn from the classical world, principally using Homer's epic vision to give a literary setting for war – just as did other German poets and writers in the eighteenth and early nineteenth centuries. Dorothea, handing Hermann his weapons, could echo Thetis and Hecuba preparing their sons Achilles and Hector for battle. Thusnelda, trembling with joy and with the hero Hermann resting in her arms, might call to mind the fair Briseis, whose pleasures Achilles enjoyed during breaks in the fighting, or the faithful Penelope, who, after defying the feasting suitors, refreshed Odysseus with the 'sweet course of love' on the 'soft bedclothes' once he had returned from war and wanderings.[88] A further immediate source of such imagery came from Tacitus, whose portraits of German women encouraging their menfolk to fight and healing their wounds were known in every home interested in culture, and inspired the pictures hung on the walls. Many women did identify with their 'forebears'' fearlessness, and many poems praised the love of liberty these female Germanic ancestors embodied. The struggle to throw off the Roman yoke found its parallel in efforts to overcome 'France's hell' – and it went without saying that the 'German woman' had her part to play here 'not restricted to her homeliness but in the ancient ways of noble women, dedicated to her people heart and soul'.[89]

Returning to 'ancient ways', however, did not need to exclude Christian tradition. For example, the dramaturgy of church processions found a clear echo in scenes where young women, all dressed in white, lined the streets as the victorious soldiers marched past. The white clothing evoked the marriage rituals too: the women whose honour had been protected by the warriors' heroic deeds in fighting against the foreign 'violators' presented themselves as prospective wives to the victorious men. Hence, on a more abstract level, they symbolized the alliance of a nation, saved in its honour, with the men whose moral and physical strength had made the rescue possible.[90]

But between 1813 and 1815, women did not merely tend their peaceful hearths, waiting for their belaurelled warriors to return. In many towns, they formed associations to show 'their gratitude for the freeing of the fatherland from foreign suppression by expressing their active concern for the brave men and youths who have dedicated their blood and life to this higher purpose'. There is documentary evidence of around 600 of these associations, which received encouragement at the very highest levels of the government. Only a few days after the Prussian king had called on his 'people' to 'save their country' in March 1813, several princesses from the house of Hohenzollern appealed to the 'women in the Prussian state' to support the departure of their menfolk, calling for a mobilisation of women that embraced not only making donations but the 'sacrifice' of taking on other work.[91] This royal initiative was soon emulated elsewhere. In a proclamation in Hamm, for instance, women did not only want to be just 'idle spectators' or passive admirers of victorious manly deeds. Though their 'limited means' prevented them from directly participating in battle, they could nonetheless collect money and other donations (precious metals, linen, and wool), make bandages from rags, sew shirts or waistbands, and knit socks – for the good of those soldiers directly involved in combat, or lying injured in hospitals. This drew life at the front and at home close together. Women and men were fighting together for 'freedom and independence'. Involving women provided a moral armoury for men. 'Our men, sons, and brothers can encounter war's dangers with greater courage when they know that mothers, sisters, and relatives back home are busy on their behalf, already at work to relieve the pain that might result from illness or wounds.'[92]

The heartening effect of women's patriotism appeared to have been at least as important as exchanging gold wedding rings for iron ones. In any event, the charity shown by women called for a similar effort in return, placing a certain obligation on their beneficiaries. If women were prepared to sacrifice time, money and their emotions for the men in arms, they could hope and expect that men would show themselves worthy of such commitment. In this way, 'the active concern of patriotic women and maidens' was not merely one avenue used by women to establish a connection to the 'common good' or to express their 'gratitude' to their country's liberators. It also served by, as it were, a kind of osmosis to generate and strengthen patriotism in the 'male sex',[93] and for this reason it was also welcomed and supported by the government.

In Berlin, the royal princesses headed the Berlin Women's Association (*Berliner Frauen-Verein*), founded in 1813, while in the provinces this position was occupied by the wives of *Landrat*s or high-ranking civil servants. Their work received official recognition in 1814, when the Prussian king started awarding *Luisenorden* medals, named after his wife, Luise, who died in 1809 but was still widely revered for her indomitable courage. The provincial governors were obliged to gather information 'on the meritoriousness of the women and maidens distinguished by patriotism' and, in view of the 'not insignificant' number, 'strictly select' those most deserving. The lists sent in contained mostly married women involved in women's associations – single women were in a minority – and they read like a register of local and provincial notables: middle-class wives of privy councillors appear with the wives of aristocratic colonels and the widows of Jewish financiers. In contrast, the commercially active urban middle classes were hardly mentioned at all; aside from a few merchants' wives, one looks in vain for wives of chief wardens of guilds or landlords and innkeepers. It therefore seems questionable whether reality actually reflected the euphoric claims made by many mayors and *Landrat*s that 'the entire female population from every station and of every age' was involved in the women's associations, working for the good of the wounded or the 'defenders of our fatherland' on the battlefield. The initiative here was primarily being taken by women from 'the educated classes', above all, the wives and daughters of the state's civil service machinery.[94]

The other group of women especially active here came from the middle-class Jewish community,[95] since cooperating in local women's organisations and publicly working for the nation and *Volk* openly voiced their aspirations to integration and belonging. In this context, the writings of Rahel Levin are particularly impressive, as she reveals the frenzy of activity that gripped her in 1813. She had fled from Berlin to Prague and there, day in and day out, she looked after the soldiers, wounded or passing through. She collected money from friends and acquaintances, bought food and linen cloth, organised warm meals, and had shirts sewn. While before she had always felt poorly, she now enjoyed an 'iron constitution' and inexhaustible amounts of energy. She wrote to her fiancé Varnhagen, a captain serving with the Russian army: 'I am so happy to be able to *serve* the soldiers' – and, for her, such service held the dual aspects of both female and Jewish patriotism.

In a letter written to Varnhagen, she wrote: 'When I feel ashamed because you are all involved in the fighting, I console myself for my own comfort by the thought that I am also active in helping and healing.' But it was at least as important to take the chance to prove, as a Jewish woman, how seriously she took her national 'duty' and how much her help was needed. She suffered from her background all her life, complaining that she lived the life of a social pariah; in this context, she experienced 1813 as a real litmus test. She proudly identified herself with 'our Prussians', with '*our* people', who behaved in such a brave and courageous yet modest way. She thoroughly enjoyed being asked to help: 'My compatriots are seeking counsel, help, solace: Yes, and God has allowed me, small and worthless, lowly born and impoverished as I am, to give this to them.' Whereas she had previously often felt used and not truly acknowledged, she now experienced the joy of a 'broad outer and deep inner occupation'. 'Here, I am very effective and surrounded by people more than ever; not socially, but in a busy and charitable way.'[96] The Prussian government was glad to take note of this sort of patriotism and acknowledge her involvement publicly.

Indeed, from the first days of the war, a government order had ensured that all donors were honoured by having their names published in newspapers and official newssheets. However, this procedure did not always meet with approval – for example, the *Landrat* in Hagen thought it 'with all due respect, better and more to the purpose to honour in silence the virtues of the women and maidens engaged in this matter, precisely because in this way they can be honoured most'. In his view, 'Any marks of distinction, commendatory epistles, or named proclamations in official broadsheets' would 'bring future harm rather than benefit'.[97] Some contemporaries even viewed the public appearance of women and their collective organisation in associations as problematic and questionable. The higher purpose might not have been open to debate, but the uncustomary public behaviour of women as self-assured and independent was unnerving. Such concerns were always visible underneath the veneer applied by official reports pointedly praising the modest way associations engaged in good works, lauding their deeds as 'accomplished quite unpretentiously, without any public enumeration or fuss, simply and in silence'.[98]

The women involved in patriotic associations also seem to have been under the impression that they needed to justify their commitment. A Bremen women's association notice pointed out that 'in a normal age' it was indubitably 'the primary duty of the housewife to care for her own family and her own home'. However, 'in the present fateful times ... the great cause of the beloved ... Fatherland, as much as their own hearts, [must] call German women and maidens, first and foremost, to care for those whose great joy it is to protect us'.[99] Some women appear to have taken this 'primary duty' so earnestly that they did indeed put their own homes a clear second.[100] Moreover, for women, taking a public role and receiving public acknowledgment was by no means as odious as some male contemporaries would have liked to believe. In this context, it is revealing to consider an incident from 1815, when Anne von Wylich, superintendent of the Wesel women's association and wife of a privy councillor (*Geheimrat*), bitterly complained to Ludwig von Vincke about the high-handedness of Tendenberg, a reserves' commander. Her storm of indignation had been triggered by Tendenberg ordering the collection of linen for hospitals himself so that, as Anne von Wylich remarked, 'his name would appear in print'. She went on to ask Vincke to reprimand the commander and, in addition, to prevent his contribution being listed in the official bulletin. She regarded Tendberg's intervention as an inappropriate infringement of women's tasks. 'If men, and especially the reserves, become mixed up in this, we women will no longer be left anything to do with it.' And moreover, she added in injured tones, 'only gratitude and sympathy with our warriors, wounded *for us*, [can] sweeten the innumerable vexations we superintendents are exposed to'. But between the lines it was clear that public acknowledgement of their work was a further sweetener, greatly welcomed and jealously guarded, and one they had no desire to lose to male competition.[101]

While men remaining at home were not supposed to meddle in the patriotic affairs of women, the soldiers in the field were expected openly to express their gratitude and appreciation. Indeed, any number of entreaties and expressions of thanks reveal just how justified this expectation was. For example, a troop commander requested the military governor to ensure that the troop's thanks for the gifts 'is passed on to the requisite place; and I do not doubt that in future the brave Brandenburgers and East Friesians will preserve the honour of their compatriots and, in this way, seek to reward the glorious efforts of the women donors'.[102] An alliance between the sexes seemed to have been firmly forged –men fighting for women, women thanking and supporting them, the men then grateful for this support and so driven on to even greater heroic deeds. Yet this alliance could work only because, rather than the war being seen as a struggle between heads of state and governments, it was perceived as a battle between peoples and 'nations' – in essence, a matter that concerned everyone. The *Volkskrieg* or national war was an attempt to draw in all members of society across the social classes, generations, genders, religious faiths, and regions, even though this project was far from succeeding in all cases. Many women and men from different social backgrounds and denominations rejected the war directly or indirectly, for a variety of reasons. Nonetheless, the war made a whole range of new associations and experiences possible, significantly expanding the traditional perception of agency and accepted conceptual horizons.

There are three main points worth noting here: firstly, the experience of supra-local and supra-regional cooperation, which became accessible to a wider audience than just the drafted soldier meeting regiments in the field recruited from far distant territories. Through their work in associations, women too gained a wider perspective, developing an awareness of a 'national' solidarity beyond the sense of belonging experienced at a local, regional, or even state level. As an example, one might cite the instance of women from Schaumburg sending 800 bandages to Kassel in 1815 'with the express wish that, should they prove to be superfluous at the hospitals in Hesse, the bandages should immediately be delivered to a Prussian one'. In the same year, a Silesian women's association based in Breslau donated 4,000 guilders to the Münster provincial governor to help 'Prussian warriors' wounded in Belgium.[103]

Secondly, through the war, it was easier to overcome denominational barriers. Jewish women worked in the women's organisations in the same way that Jewish men, 'manly' volunteers, followed the colours, proving their desire to help 'save the fatherland' despite their special legal status.[104] For a social group previously able to shed its marginality only within the capital's tradition of literary and artistic salons, this represented a dramatic growth of integration and social recognition.

Thirdly, the borders previously drawn for women were transcended by the commitment of women – middle-class and aristocratic, Christian and Jewish – to the male 'warriors', organised locally yet effective on a supra-local and supra-regional level. This was a new form of social mobilisation marked by women coming together in their own associations, occupying specific fields of activity, and confidently guarding them from encroachment, and it had no existing model to draw on – despite the attempt to locate women's commitment within the Greco-Roman context. In general, their devotion to the *Volk* and 'nation' was accepted and valued for the duration of the war, although this changed once the fighting was over and peace descended across the 'fatherland' once again. In 1817, for example, one commentator wrote: 'The extraordinary state of affairs that inspired women as well to manly views and efforts is not permanent.'[105] After the war, although the majority disbanded, some women's associations remained active, dedicating themselves to combating local poverty.

What also remained was a remembrance of the 'extraordinary state of affairs' that turned women into patriots. The political wind of change sweeping through the years 1813–15 and women's part in it was repeatedly recalled, not only by the nineteenth-century women's movement but also in a journalism intended for a wider public. The collective memory did not simply preserve images of heroes' mothers and warriors' wives, hospital nurses and donation campaign collectors, but recalled the Amazons and 'heroic maidens' too – even though they were few in number. The women fighting in battle had moved furthest away from the female 'sexual character', as it had been coined since the late eighteenth century; instead of submitting to their 'destiny' and preparing themselves for a role as 'spouse, mother, and housewife', these young fighters had crossed into genuine male territory,[106] actually acting in a far more 'manly' way than many men refusing to perform military service. The fulsome praise lavished by veterans' organisations and the army on the memory of these women into the late nineteenth and early twentieth centuries, even to the extent of erecting monuments to their deeds, should not simply be read as approval of the extraordinary; instead, it should also be understood as admonishing male contemporaries. It is no coincidence that the verses of the young Friedrich Rückert were quoted in this context:

> I'd be ashamed to be called a man,
> If I couldn't use a sword,
> And wished on women the joy of using it themselves![107]

In 1814, when the poem was first published, Rückert was 26 years old – and what it meant 'to be called a man' was something his generation experienced during the Napoleonic wars, when male patriotism proved itself by following the flag and taking up arms to save the nation and the country. In an age already rich in innovations, this was one of the revolutionary 'principles' (or axioms, as Dubois-Crancé called them) that firmly imposed on every able-bodied man the duty to bear arms, irrespective of social affiliation, faith or region.

But only a few men eagerly embraced such new obligations. In those days, there was no common consensus that to be respected as a man, one not only had to be *capable* of using a sword but actually *had to want* to use it, as Rückert suggested. Moreover, the call for peacetime service met with even less enthusiasm than the duty of military service. The plans of Prussian reformers to give all young men a continual and thorough basic military training to be prepared for war unleashed a storm of outrage, with even those supporting the manly and masculinising military service, whether for political or personal motives, bitterly opposing any such universal service.

This rejection reflected the middle classes' deep-rooted mistrust of the army; as far as they were concerned, it was still trapped in the tradition of the *Ancien Régime* as a place of serfdom and bondage. Although the Prussian army sought to improve its reputation after 1806, by abolishing humiliating physical punishments for example, middle-class fathers still showed little inclination to have their sons enlist. In contrast, they warmed more to the idea of providing physical training for young men at athletics grounds, schools, or open-air exercise on Sundays, and teaching them to use weapons. This model of a substitute civil institution, however, was steadfastly resisted in army circles, which continued to press their claim to a monopoly on training and physical force and received broad support for it from the Prussian government.

Initially introduced for the war period only and afterwards hastily repealed, a law that permanently required 'the duty of military service' was finally decreed by the king in September 1814; in so doing, he was not only underlining the standing army's assertion to be the 'main training school for war for the entire nation' but was also giving way to the demands of reformers to send the *entire* nation through this school (of course, only the male part) and train them to 'defend the fatherland'.[108] In future, in Prussia too, every citizen would also be a soldier – though it remained to be seen whether every soldier would be just as much a citizen.

Notes

1. Vaisse, *Aux armes*, pp. 97–108, 118–30; Paret, 'Conscription', pp. 163–173; Krumeich, 'Entwicklung'; Smets, 'Dorfidylle'.
2. Jany, *Geschichte*, vol. 4, pp. 1, 20.
3. *Handbuch zur deutschen Militärgeschichte*, T. II, 1964, pp. 86–100; Kunisch, 'Puppenwerk'.

4. Heim, *Tagebücher*, pp. 140, 142; Münchow-Pohl, *Reform*, pp. 37 ff.; Gembruch, 'Publizistik'.
5. Vaupel, *Reorganisation*, pp. 8–10.
6. Vaupel, *Reorganisation*, p. 175.
7. Boyen, *Erinnerungen*, p. 121.
8. 'Besonderheiten'; Schwieger, 'Militär', see also pp. 191–2.
9. Frevert, *Men of Honour*, pp. 40–1.
10. Bräker, 'Lebensgeschichte', pp. 176–7.
11. Harnisch, 'Kantonsystem'; Kloosterhuis, 'Aufruhr'; and introduction to *Bauern*.
12. Frank, *Gesellschaft*, p. 14; Abbt, 'Vom Tode', p. 86; Harnisch, 'Kantonsystem', p. 163; Taylor, *Liberty*.
13. Pröve, *Heer*; Harnisch, 'Kantonsystem', p. 164; Kloosterhuis, 'Aufruhr', pp. 183–4.
14. Friedrich Schiller, *Wallensteins Lager*, in: *Schillers Werke*, vol. 4, Berlin, 1967, pp. 50–52; Translation: Friedrich Schiller, *Wallenstein and Mary Stuart*, ed. Walter Hinderer (New York: Continuum, 1991), p. 45. Schiller may have located his play in the mercenary milieu of the seventeenth century but his *Reiterlied* was swiftly incorporated into *Soldiers and Reserves* songbooks, indicating that contemporaries did not acknowledge the historical boundary he set.
15. Schnabel-Schüle, *Überwachen*, see also p. 291.
16. Wolf, *Karschin*, quotes pp. 275, 209, 188.
17. GStA Berlin-Dahlem, Rep. 74, O.O. Nr. 4, Volume I: Sack to Hardenberg from 26.1.1811.
18. Cited in Bodelschwingh, *Leben*, pp. 115–6, 215.
19. GStA Berlin-Dahlem, Rep. 74, O.O. Nr. 4, vol. I: v. Bülow to Staatsrat v. Hake from 9.5.1812.
20. Rep. 74, O.P. Nr. 3: v. Platen from 8.10.1812; Breslau government to v. Schuckmann dated 25.8.1812, etc.; *Historische Zeitschrift*, vol. 69, 1892, p. 449 (Schrötter); Sikora, *Desertion*; Sikora, *Disziplin*.
21. Cities recorded considerably less people enrolled and exempted than in rural areas. (Harnisch, 'Kantonsystem', p. 151).
22. GStA Berlin-Dahlem, Rep. 74, O.O. Nr. 4, vol. I: Denkschrift from 28.10.1811.
23. Vaupel, *Reorganisation*, pp. 27, 82, 500.
24. Gerhard/Norvin, *Briefe*, vol. 1, pp. 477, 495, 498, 501.
25. Vaupel, *Reorganisation*, pp. 748–9.
26. Freiherr vom Stein, *Briefe*, ed. Hubatsch, vol. II, p. 993.
27. Vaupel, *Reorganisation*, pp. 598–601; Scheel/Schmidt, *Reformministerium*, vol. III, pp. 704–717.

28. Gerteis, *Städte*, pp. 105–6; Kraus, *Militärwesen*, above all see pp. 74 ff.; Sander, 'Wehrhoheit'; Jung, 'Bürgermilitär'.
29. Scheel/Schmidt, *Reformministerium*, vol. III, pp. 1064–5; Pröve, *Republikanismus*, pp. 207–8, 438 ff.; Ewald, *Schützengesellschaften*; Michaelis, *Banner*, Chapter 1.
30. GStA Berlin-Dahlem, Rep. 74, O.O. Nr. 4 vol. I: v. Raumer dated 14.6.1811.
31. Vaupel, *Reorganisation*, pp. 40, 237, 720, 742, 765, 782; Scheel/Schmidt, *Reformministerium*, vol. I, pp. 63–65; GStA Berlin-Dahlem, Rep. 92 Nachlaß Vaupel, Nr. 42: Immediatbericht des Generalmajors v. Schuler, genannt von Senden dated 12.10.1809. Compare Pröve, *Republikanismus*, pp. 227 ff.
32. Kabinettsordre dated 17.12.1808, in: Vaupel, *Reorganisation*, p. 789.
33. GStA Berlin-Dahlem, Rep. 92 Nachlaß Vaupel, Nr. 43: Kabinettsordre dated 10.11.1809.
34. GStA Berlin-Dahlem, Rep. 74 O.P. Nr. 1: Schreiben dated 6.2.1817.
35. GStA Berlin-Dahlem, Rep. 74 O.Y. Nr. 11: Berichte dated 21, 23, 24, 27, 30.8.1817. On the Landwehr compare Chapter II 3.
36. GStA Berlin-Dahlem, Rep. 92 Nachlaß Vaupel, Nr. 42: Immediatbericht an den König dated 26.10.1809; Kabinettsordre dated 17.12.1808, in: Vaupel, *Reorganisation*, p. 789.
37. *Historische Zeitschrift*, vol. 61, 1889, pp. 104–109; ibid., vol. 69, 1892, pp. 437–440.
38. Ibid., pp. 432–461; Sack an Hardenberg dated 26.1.1811 and Raumer dated 14.8.1811 in: GStA Berlin-Dahlem, Rep. 74, O.O. Nr. 4, vol. I; Freiherr vom Stein, *Briefe*, edited by Hubatsch, vol. III, pp. 65–6.
39. GStA Berlin-Dahlem, Rep. 92 Nachlaß Vaupel, Nr. 39: Scharnhorst dated 10.7.1809.
40. *Historische Zeitschrift*, vol. 61, 1889, p. 103; ibid., vol. 69, 1892, p. 453.
41. Hardenberg an Altenstein dated 26.3.1808, in: Scheel/Schmidt, *Reformministerium*, vol. II, p. 468; Immediatschreiben Sacks dated 14.2.1809, in: Granier, *Berichte*, p. 358.
42. *Reorganisation*, vol. 2, Section 4, p. 108.
43. Vaupel, *Reorganisation*, pp. 321, 323.
44. Vaupel, *Reorganisation*, pp. 549–552.
45. *Reorganisation*, vol. 1, pp. 559, 580–81.
46. Vaupel, *Reorganisation*, pp. 82 ff.
47. Vaupel, *Reorganisation*, p. 201; Freiherr vom Stein, *Briefe*, ed. by Botzenhart/Ipsen, p. 200.
48. GStA Berlin-Dahlem, Rep. 92 Nachlaß Vaupel, Nr. 39: Scharnhorst dated 10.7.1809.
49. *Historische Zeitschrift*, vol. 61, 1889, pp. 99–100.
50. Craig, *Politics*, pp. 38–59.

51. Huber, *Dokumente*, vol. 1, pp. 48–53.
52. Bodelschwingh, *Leben*, pp. 551–59; Westphalen, *Tagebücher*, pp. 148–50.
53. GStA Berlin-Dahlem, Rep. 74 O.P. Nr. 3: Breslauer Stadtverordnete dated 18.2.1813.
54. GStA Berlin-Dahlem, Rep. 74 O.P. Nr. 3: Hardenberg dated 19.2.1813; A.J. Heinersdorf from 18.2.1813 and Hardenberg's answer dated 21.2.1813. Two hundred thalers was a large sum of money; the pro capita income in Prussia at the time was on average 66 thalers a year.
55. GStA Berlin-Dahlem, Rep. 74 O.P. Nr. 3: Landrat v. Vogten dated 2.3.1813; Liegnitzer Regierung from 26.2.1813.
56. GStA Berlin-Dahlem, Rep. 74 O.P. Nr. 3: Breslauer Kaufmann Lübbers dated 25.2.1813; Hardenberg dated 27.2.1813.
57. GStA Berlin-Dahlem, Rep. 74 O.P. Nr. 1: Dankelmann dated 26.3.1813; Hardenberg dated 26.3.1813.
58. Ibbeken, *Preußen*, pp. 393–4, 398, 405, 443–447.
59. Arndt, *Landsturm* (1813), pp. 2, 10, 11; Arndt, *An die Preußen*, in: Actenstücke, H. 1, p. 19; anon., An das Deutsche Volk, in: ibid., H. 3, p. 31.
60. Arndt, *Grundlinien*, pp. 23–4.
61. *J.B. Basedows Elementarwerk*, vol. 1, p. 37.
62. Frank, *System*, vol. 2, pp. 633–4, 693; Reil, *Hausarzt*, vol. 2, pp. 223–4; GutsMuths, *Gymnastik*, p. 17.
63. Frank, *System*, vol. 2, pp. 630, 642–3, 640; GutsMuths, *Gymnastik*, p. 152; Vieth, *Versuch*, p. 31.
64. Pockels, *Mann*, vol. 1, pp. 30, 29.
65. Frevert, „*Mann*", pp. 30–1.
66. Ewald, *Jüngling*, p. 46; Ehrenberg, *Charakter*, p. 240; Vieth, *Versuch*, p. 31.
67. Arndt, *Grundlinien*, pp. 12–13, 21–22; Vaupel, *Reorganisation*, pp. 333–4; Stein, *Briefe*, vol. III, pp. 65–66.
68. *Historische Zeitschrift*, vol. 69, 1892, pp. 438–9, 441.
69. GStA Berlin-Dahlem, Rep. 74 O.O. Nr. 4 vol. I: Sack dated 26.1.1811; Raumer dated 14.6.1811; *Historische Zeitschrift*, vol. 69, 1892, p. 460 (Scharnhorst).
70. Vaupel, *Reorganisation*, pp. 185–6; Scheel/Schmidt, *Reformministerium*, vol. I, p. 228; Neuendorff, *Geschichte*, vol. 1, pp. 445 ff.; Schodrok, *Jugend-Erziehung*, Chapter V and Appendix.
71. *Geschichte der geheimen Verbindungen der neuesten Zeit*, H. 1, Leipzig 1831, p. 200; Jahn, *Volkstum* (1810), pp. 188 ff.
72. Arndt, *Grundlinien*, pp. 21–2, 24–5, 28, 30–1, 40.
73. Gerhard/Norvin, *Briefe*, vol. 1, p. 498; vol. 2, pp. 376 ff., 384–5.
74. Soeding, *Harkorts*, vol. 2, pp. 519, 529–532; Berger, *Harkort*, p. 115.
75. Schneider, *Lieder*, pp. 319–23.
76. Soeding, *Harkorts*, vol. 2, p. 515; Berger, *Harkort*, p. 119; Hagemann, 'Mannlicher Muth', pp. 475 ff.

77. Jahn, *Volkstum*, pp. 188–9.
78. Just one example of many: At balls held in the Tübingen officers' mess during the early nineteenth century, officers were highly sought after as dancing partners and, as Robert von Mohl remembered later, their 'army uniforms' got the better of the students' 'black tail-coats' (*Lebens-Erinnerungen*, vol. 1, p. 104).
79. Westphalen, *Tagebücher*, pp. 540, 533–34, 156, 533.
80. Soeding, Harkorts, vol. 2, pp. 511, 514–15, 516–17.
81. Wilke, 'Aufbruch'; Weber, 'Lyrik'; Hagemann, '*Mannlicher Muth*', pp. 271 ff.
82. *An die Deutschen Fürsten. Und an die Deutschen vom Kriegs-Rath Gentz*, Leipzig 1813, pp. 12, 15; Arndt, *Zwei Worte*, p. 22, and also *Landsturm*, p. 10; *Actenstücke*, H. 1, pp. 18–9; H. 3, p. 31.
83. Johann Wolfgang Goethe: *Hermann und Dorothea, The Collected Works*, ed. Cyrus Hamlin and Frank Ryder, vol. 8 pp. 253–307 (Princeton: Princeton University Press: 1995).
84. Ibid., pp. 734–5, 737.
85. Ibid., pp. 741 (Schlegel), 482, 514.
86. Jahn, *Volkstum*, pp. 246–7.
87. Friedrich Gottlieb Klopstock, *Sämtliche Werke*, vol. 4, Leipzig 1856, p. 82; Schmidt, 'Apotheose'.
88. François Lissarrague, 'Figures of Women' in *A History of Women in the West*, vol. I: *From Ancient Goddesses to Christian Saints*, ed. Pauline Schmitt Pantel (Cambridge and London: Belknap Press, 1992), pp. 139–229, especially pp. 172–81; *Homer: The Odyssey*, trans. E.V. Rieu, Penguin Books, 1987.
89. Reder, *Frauenbewegung*, pp. 514–15, 159; Gleim, *Deutschland*, above all pp. 1 ff.; v. F., *Frauensteuer*, p. 57.
90. Berger, *Harkort*, p. 118; Hagemann, 'Manly Valor'.
91. Schmidt, *Charlotte Perthes*, p. 19; Reder, *Frauenbewegung*, pp. 489 ff., 52 ff., 43 ff.
92. Harkort, *Zeiten*, pp. 92–95.
93. StA Münster, OP Nr. 609: Aachener Plan zu einem allgemeinen Wohltätigkeitsverein achtbarer Frauen und Jungfrauen 1814 and Broschüre märkischer Frauen dated 12.5.1815; Gleim, *Deutschland*, pp. 8–10; Schmidt, *Charlotte Perthes*, p. 19; Weber, 'Emanzipation', p. 341.
94. GStA Berlin-Dahlem, Rep. 74 O.Y. Nr. 9: Bekanntmachung dated 31.3.1815; StA Münster, OP Nr. 610: Hofmarschall Groeben an Vincke dated 2.4.1816; Reder, *Frauenbewegung*, pp. 330 ff.
95. StA Münster, OP Nr. 610; Reder, *Frauenbewegung*, pp. 336–7.
96. *Das Volk braucht Licht*, pp. 481, 483–4, 486.
97. StA Münster, OP Nr. 610: Hagener Landrat dated 27.5.1816.

98. StA Münster, OP Nr. 610: Bericht über den Dortmunder Frauenverein, no date.
99. StA Münster, OP Nr. 610: Lübecker Frauenverein dated 12.7.1815.
100. StA Münster, OP Nr. 610: Hammer Bürgermeister dated 6.5.1816.
101. StA Münster, OP Nr. 609: v. Wylich an Vincke dated 27.6.1815.
102. StA Münster, OP Nr. 609: Schreiben dated 26.5.1815.
103. StA Münster, OP Nr. 609: Friedricke v. Meyer dated 15.10.1815; Öffentlicher Dank dated 17.7.1815 and 7.10.1815.
104. Reder, 'Aus reiner Liebe', p. 206.
105. Frevert, '*Mann*', p. 46; Hagemann, '*Mannlicher Muth*', pp. 383 ff.
106. Rückert's verse, published in 1814, formed the surround for a 'song in honour ... of Prochaska, a maiden from Potsdam' (*Rückerts Werke*, 1. T., Berlin 1910, p. 107). The lines were quoted in an article by Major Noel active in 1905 campaigning for suitable commemoration of the 'heroic maidens' of 1813–15 (*Die Schnur*, Nr. 35, 18.04.1905, p. 492), and soon afterwards called for a memorial to Johanna Stegen, a 'heroic maiden' from Lüneburg. The ceremony marking completion of the memorial was held on 26.04.1908 in the churchyard in Berlin's *Sophienkirche*, with a major turnout by military associations (*Die Schnur*, Nr. 48, 3.7.1908, pp. 699–702).
107. Huber, *Dokumente*, vol. 1, pp. 53–6.

–2–

'Both Citizen and Soldier'? Prussia in the *Vormärz* Period (1815–1848)

Prussia may now have had a law on conscription, but the resistance and reservations preventing its earlier enactment had neither weakened nor been resolved. Napoleon's defeat left Prussia at liberty to determine the shape and size of its army itself; but although freed from previous foreign policy concerns, domestic political issues remained very much on the agenda. In 1814, the king had succumbed to the pressure exerted by his war minister despite being vexed by universal conscription's expressly 'revolutionary' character. Even five years later, he was still criticising the new recruiting system as impractical, viewing it as 'a grave matter ... to turn everyone into a soldier'; no other state 'proceeded with a similar rigour'.[1] The Prussian subjects, for their part, were less than ecstatic to be called on to embrace the permanent duty of 'stupid peacetime service', as Niebuhr dubbed it, when it replaced the brief period of wartime service.

In this chapter, I intend to examine the form taken by opposition and protests to conscription, the interests involved, and the arguments and measures adopted by the government in countermoves. In addition, we will hear from the men required to perform military service on the basis of their year of birth, discover why they took the decisions they did, and learn about the experiences they had; we will see how they came to terms with a situation forced on them, using whatever legal loopholes they could find. Nonetheless, this strange duty imposed by the state did eventually become largely accepted, even to the extent that people even found it to have positive aspects, and advantages in social, political and gender-specific terms. Slowly but surely, in *Vormärz* Prussia, a rhetoric developed that had a sustained effect – a rhetoric praising military service not purely as a civic duty, but vindicating it as a means of social integration and cultural socialisation.

1. The Law on Wartime Service: Rules and Practices

In its final form, the conscription law was largely the work of the war minister, Hermann von Boyen, who borrowed both fundamentals and details from drafts produced, from 1807 on, by the reformers around Scharnhorst. These ideas revolved around two key notions: firstly, the attempt to use a strong, efficient army to help Prussia become a new force in international affairs and, secondly, the integration of the army into the steps deemed necessary to restructure the domestic and sociopolitical landscape. By 1814–15, Prussia had seen the majority of its foreign policy aims fulfilled and adopted a strong stance, both territorially and politically, with the anticipated reward of significant land gains at the Congress of Vienna; Prussia was also soon able to enjoy a key role in the German Confederation, successor to the Holy Roman Empire of the German Nation. On the domestic policy front, an ambitious legislature was initiating numerous economic and social reforms, while the royal promise to sanction a constitution and involve the entire population in government was still a part of current debate.

Against this background, Friedrich Wilhelm III proclaimed to his 'faithful people' that conscription would be retained. In doing so, he bowed to 'the alleged wishes of the entire nation' since 'a legislated system of arming the nation embodies the surest warranty of a lasting peace'. The law came into force, requiring from then on every man born in Prussia to perform military service. The normal case foresaw every 20-year-old serving for three years in the standing army before entering the army reserves for a further two years; finally, he was to serve in the *Landwehr*'s first reserves for the initial six years and afterwards in the second *Landwehr* reserves. In contrast to the army as the 'main training school for war for the entire nation', a task it was also to fulfil, especially in peacetime, the *Landwehr* was primarily active in times of war. Without any war to fight, it seemed sufficient to have brief refresher courses to maintain the level of military skills taught in the army.[2]

In this way, the Prussian military organisation was founded on two pillars that Boyen wanted to see existing independently of each other: service in the line army and in the *Landwehr*. The *Landwehr* had a largely autonomous organisational structure, with its own inspectors, commanders and an independent middle-class body of officers. However, in the early years especially, these two pillars suffered from considerable confusion over the division of tasks and responsibilities. Boyen, for example, assumed that the men in the *Landwehr* would receive their basic military training in the course of their three-year army service. The wording of the law, though, and the early organisational problems offered young men the chance of serving solely in the *Landwehr*. Since army funding restricted intake to no more than around 40,000 new recruits a year, the initial regular army turnover was too low to fill the *Landwehr* regiments. Consequently, until 1833, the *Landwehr* enlisted 'raw' recruits, hoping they would be turned into suitable fighting material by combining shorter periods of military exercises and the example set by soldiers serving in the standing army; in many places the majority of *Landwehr* troops consisted of men without any experience of serving in the line.[3]

In principle, all young men were liable for service in the line and the *Landwehr*, irrespective of their religion, social background or place of residence.[4] The only exception made was for those who had lost their 'civic honour'; criminals, who had 'besmirched' this honour, were considered 'unworthy to enter the ranks of those defending the fatherland'.[5] This stipulation reflected the intention of recasting military service as a civic duty both honourable in itself and a source of honour for those performing it. In other words, recruits should not consider military service as a punishment but as a reward for irreproachable moral conduct.

All previous regulations governing exemptions were revoked, whether for entire regions or groups of the population. In contrast to the eighteenth-century cantonal system based around households, the new, universal duty applied to the individual citizen and arose, as the ministry of the interior explained in 1819, 'as a result of the personal subject–state relations'. Consequently, the duty to perform military service was a personal duty, without the right to request performance by any substitute.[6] To ensure that there were no gaps in calling up those liable for military service, local districts and parishes compiled registers of young men born there or who moved there; the local worthies and officers who constituted the district recruiting commissions then used these lists as the basis for the annual levy. All 20-year-olds had to appear before these commissions and were examined to make sure they were fit for service, both physically and morally. If they met the army's strict health standards and could show no grounds why they should be 'objected to' or 'temporarily deferred until the following year', they 'remained' to be drafted. Since each army corps was assigned a recruiting district, it was then simply a question of mathematics to work out how many new soldiers were needed. Where the need for possible new recruits was less than the supply – and as a rule, from the 1820s it was – a selection had to be made; from 1825, this was done by drawing lots.

Complete exemption was, in principle, impossible, and legal provisions covered those cases where a recruit might have to be deferred. Army doctors were provided with detailed lists of inadequacies and given extensive instructions on the criteria for fitness. Recruits needed to be of a specified height (depending on the type of weapon to be used), while delicate and 'weakly' men were deferred until, after three years, they either appeared to have developed sufficient physical strength to cope with the hardships of military service or else were completely discharged. Appeals, too, were precisely regulated, and primarily dealt with men known to be the sole breadwinners in their original family, where enlistment would mean reducing their parents and siblings to beggary. But a farmer's or factory-owner's son could also be deferred if he could show he was indispensable and irreplaceable. Nonetheless, the recruiting commissions were instructed not to give the impression 'of favouring the rich over the poor and the higher over the lower', and measures such as publicly posting a list with the names of all those deferred were intended to ensure a high degree of transparency and control.[7]

Yet while the law on conscription and its regulations attempted to avoid any appearance of bias or inequality, it also contained provisions blatantly contradicting any principle of equality – above all, the controversial paragraph which provided that 'young people from the educated classes able to arm and clothe themselves' only needed to serve a one-year term in the army and foresaw them becoming *Landwehr* officers 'in accord with their abilities and circumstances'.[8] The justification for this privilege was threefold: firstly, the social and cultural respect owed to the educated and wealthy middle classes, traditionally far removed from all military matters – it being in the interests of the state, moreover, not to keep these future students from their university studies for too long; secondly, with these recruits predestined to be future *Landwehr* officers, the advantage of a one-year period of service was weighed against the duty of long-term supervisory tasks; and finally, the state saved the cost of equipment and provisions, since that was borne by these 'one-yearers'.

With the main cost-intensive army kept relatively small, the *Landwehr* tying up only a comparatively small proportion of funds, and the 'one-yearers' serving virtually at their own expense, the war minister could speak in glowing terms of the new army structure as nothing short of a bargain. Furthermore, despite clear guidelines, the new army appeared to offer sufficient flexibility to accommodate the demands of a 'martial training'[9] while respecting the needs of the economic and cultural sectors; it also fitted perfectly into the foreign policy landscape of the day, with the advantage of a small standing army (in 1826, numbering only 124,000 in a population of 11 million) hardly likely to awaken mistrust in those politicians preoccupied with the balance of power in Europe. The *Landwehr*, based on the model provided by the Swiss and English militias, was generally regarded as a purely defensive force; the first reserves in fact totalled nearly 180,000 men, but the lack of offensive potential blunted any threat to Prussia's neighbours.[10]

Nonetheless, the new laws gave rise to a wave of sharp criticism. As far as many middle-class men were concerned, the standing army continued to be too large and too expensive.[11] Manor estate owners raised their voices in chorus with the commercial sector, complaining of a 'situation almost indistinguishable from that of war itself'; they recognised, in principle, the duty of defending the fatherland but rejected any concept of peacetime military service. The list of those wanting exemptions was long, ranging from the Berlin *Schauspielhaus* theatre director for his staff, to the Paderborn prince-bishop and the Aachen capitular for their theology students, the copper mill owner in eastern Pomerania for his journeymen and apprentices, and the Königsberg merchant body for their members. Similarly, the Count of Stolberg-Wernigerode was just as much against any 'enforced military duty' affecting his sons, servants and foundry workers, as were the owners of a Neustadt mirror factory, the partners in a Barmen factory and the owners of the Siegen iron and steel works.[12] Such claims were nearly always based on eighteenth-century privileges and accompanied by the call for their continuation, while warning the government of dire economic consequences if they refused to give in – adding, of course, that economic ruin could hardly be in the interests of the state.

The failure of urban trade and commerce to push their interests through in the face of government opposition could certainly not be attributed to any want of trying: their applications and submissions filled file after file. In contrast, the rural population appeared to be resigned to their fate; after all, for them enlistment was, in a sense, nothing new. The cities did not lack influential advocates either, with, first and foremost, the state chancellor finding some of their suggestions interesting and their complaints well-founded, with the provincial governors rebuking the government for not taking the population's justified concerns seriously and allowing the 'seed of dissent' to grow.[13] Nonetheless, despite the enormous pressure neither the war ministry nor the ministry of the interior shifted its position; no ground was given on the principle that military service was not a 'burden' but an 'honour' in which 'every citizen should participate'.[14]

The Berlin government hoped that, given time, the populace would learn to value this 'honour' and place it above their specific individual interests. However, as is well documented in reports by district and provincial governors or municipal heads of the police, initial rejection and resistance was widespread, especially in the newly acquired territories. In the province of Posen, the requirement to perform military service met with stiff resistance from the Polish nobles there, while the other classes viewed it with 'discontent and hatred'. In the Rhineland, 'a large part of the inhabitants' viewed conscription as a 'misfortune and a hated burden'. The middle classes, particularly, longed for a return of French rule when they were able to escape army service by funding a *remplacement*.[15]

The situation was not eased by Berlin's rigid refusal to grant the new provinces any special dispensations. In urban areas, it was proving especially difficult to recruit the required numbers of soldiers with, for example, Aachen producing only two-thirds of the target number in 1817 even though the recruiting year comprised nearly 500 men. In the end, they could not even name one hundred as fit for duty; almost half (233) of the original muster were considered physically unfit, while nearly as many again were declared indispensable on the grounds of their 'family and trade situation'. After these deductions, only one-seventh of the total number of men liable for service could actually be drafted.[16]

It remains doubtful whether the other sixth-sevenths of this group were correctly discharged in all cases, and a certain scepticism about the decisions' objectivity seems appropriate, despite the efforts of the recruiting commission's members to point out the chronically poor standard of health among Aachen's youth and the financial plight many families were facing. Be that as it may, parents and employees were not alone in leaving nothing to chance to prove the young men were unfit or indispensable, and the youths due to be mustered were equally active – not shying at measures such as bribery or even self-mutilation. The police authorities repeatedly inquired into cases where doctors were paid to report that the young man in question was physically unfit. As early as 1818, the Koblenz provincial governor recommended entrusting only army doctors with the formal military examinations 'since the civilian doctors' work has frequently made them conversant with the conscripts to be examined or their relatives, resulting in a conflict between their interests and their duties'. But even army doctors were not immune to the temptation of accepting bribes to bolster their meagre salary.[17]

Civilian recruiting commission members too were not immune to any conflict between their 'interests' and 'duties'. They had the task of reviewing the young men liable to be drafted and selecting those considered fit to serve; they also received and dealt with objections, but how they applied the exemption criteria, whether strictly or loosely, was a matter for their own discretion. In this way, used positively, they could take local needs into account and minimize individual distress – but they frequently functioned *de facto* as a social filter. The commissions comprised the *Landrat* and four urban or rural landowners, and the notables with seats and votes tended to favour families they were acquainted with or knew well;[18] consequently, as the king noted in 1817 with 'considerable displeasure', 'the recruits are only being drawn from the lower classes'. In 1818, the Cologne government concluded that, as a rule, the men being deferred for a year due to family circumstances belonged 'to the classes of the rich'[19] – a group including those factory owners or their sons able to convince the commissioners that their enlistment would plunge numerous workers into unemployment, the merchants or their sons showing how a temporary interruption in their business would curtail their credit, or the well-to-do farmers or farmers' sons who knew how to make a case for being indispensable.

It is indicative of how unpopular the army was, even after the reforms and the spectacular victories over Napoleon, that it was precisely those already privileged by the legislature who were trying to avoid having to serve in the army at all. Instead of electing to serve for a year and subsequently cutting a good figure as an officer in the *Landwehr*, many men from educated and wealthy circles preferred to obtain complete release from military duty. In the Cologne administrative district in 1817–18, only forty-one men voluntarily reported for the one-year service – less than 1 per cent of the recruiting year, even though the group as a whole represented 3 per cent of the year.[20]

The 1814 law listed two criteria allowing for a reduction in service for men reporting voluntarily. Men of the 'educated classes' and those able to clothe and arm themselves were permitted to serve for one year: in 1816, outlay for equipment totalled between 40 and 214 thalers, depending on whether the volunteer intended to serve with the engineers or a cuirassier regiment (in comparison, the annual nominal income was then 94 thalers for non-self-employed persons in gainful work; Prussian elementary school teachers earned 107 thalers).[21] In the text of the decree, the emphasis was placed on education, though the tacit assumption was that the educated also have money at their disposal. At the same time, the term 'educated classes' was by no means defined precisely, as soon became apparent in practice. Journeyman locksmiths, for example, who had attended an elite secondary school (*Gymnasium*) for two-and-a-half years, considered themselves part of this group just as much as confectioners who knew how 'to give their cakes an individual form'.[22]

In 1816, the government defined the extent of education required for the one-year military service, recognising all those who had completed the '*Klein-Tertia*', the equivalent of middle school, i.e., those pupils entitled to enter the final years of elite secondary school. This move rapidly led, as the minister of the interior reported, to 'nearly all the sons of the middle classes, and even the sons of humbler artisans, attending the *Gymnasium* to attain the *Klein-Tertia* and the entitlement to serve for one year'. As the Cologne government lamented in 1818: 'Every commercial clerk considers himself a scholar, even if he has never learnt anything else besides copying out letters and invoices, and entertains no doubts of his right to serve for one year', while in Düsseldorf, Ruppenthal, a high-ranking civil servant, was even more direct:

> Since I was entrusted with military matters, I have been besieged with such attempted enlistments, with occasionally expressed objections of mine viewed as unlawfully arbitrary and biased, and I've had to put up with being told more than once that it is unseemly to place those who can write, read, dance, ride, fence and speak French alongside farmers' sons in the general rank and file.[23]

Undoubtedly, in the course of defending themselves against such a 'moneyed aristocracy', government officials like Ruppenthal may well have exposed a certain amount of academic ignorance, but their principal argument was a political one. If the borders for privileged people remained fluid and expanding, the regular contingent of conscripts would, in the end, have to be filled solely from the 'poorer working class', and the effect would be 'very disadvantageous', fuelling the discontent with this far from popular citizens' duty.[24] Such concerns led to commissions being founded in the 1820s precisely to objectify and standardise the procedures used to define privileged groups. All those unable to present a school certificate had to be tested, while third-party certificates, such as those from chambers of commerce, were no longer acceptable. In a further move, however, they successively expanded the number of educational institutions able to provide an acceptable certificate, including, from 1836, not only the *Gymnasium* but also secondary schools (*höhere Bürgerschulen* and *Realschulen*) as well, whose intermediate-level leaving certificates received the nickname of the 'one-yearer', reflecting its status of proving membership of the 'educated classes' and endowing the right to their privileges.[25]

Although growing numbers of young men were acquiring a certificate for admission to the one-year service, relatively few of them were actually serving. Between 1838 and 1848, there were only around 800 one-yearers serving annually beside the 40,000 drafted as 'normal' conscripts;[26] this imbalance was due to at least two reasons: the young men's lack of enthusiasm to serve and the officers' dislike of enlisting one-yearers. Many army officers found it less than pleasant to have to deal with the 'educated' short-term recruits, while the war ministry's reminders to treat them 'with forebearing' and not to 'expose them to all the common soldiers' hardships' merely generated spiteful ridicule among the regular aristocratic officers and lower-class NCOs. In their turn, the young students, business people and 'artists' did not overly value the chance of learning about army life from the inside and qualifying as a reserve officer – an aversion largely unaltered despite the state's attempts to make service agreeable, and hardly lessened even after army service was allowed to be combined with university enrolment. As was noted in an 1854 decree from the ministers for war and the interior, 'the majority of deception and deceit' during annual recruitment 'occurs in respect of the volunteers for one-year service'. But frequently they did not even need to bribe the recruiting staff or send an unhealthy look-alike to the muster since many army doctors tended to declare one-yearers 'unsuitable' anyway.[27]

In 1843, the ministers were complaining of a 'great increase' in cases where those 'conscripts eligible for one year of voluntary service wait to be drafted before they enter such service'. Yet from the young men's point of view such behaviour was perfectly rational, since the individual's chances of escaping military service altogether, legally and ingeniously, rose as the enlistment quota in real terms fell, reflecting the relationship between near-constant army numbers and expanding population growth – with 40,888 soldiers recruited from a general population of 11 million in 1820; 35,512 from 13 million in 1837; and 40,363 from 15.5 million in 1846. Even if a person was found to be essentially fit and available, the process of choosing recruits by lot could still produce the desired release from duty; if, contrary to the young man's hopes, the wrong number was drawn, there still seemed to be time enough to register voluntarily and exchange the two or three years of service for one. The government, though, had not originally foreseen conscripts adopting such a pragmatic approach and it subsequently forbade any late registration.[28]

In this particular instance, the Prussian state's general flexibility and readiness to compromise for its educated and wealthy citizens had apparently been taken beyond acceptable limits. In other cases, a greater degree of consideration was shown, as for example when both Catholic and Protestant theologians in the *Vormärz* period were 'spared' in recruitment procedures, without abandoning the principle of universal military service or succumbing to their wish to see, if possible, their exemption enshrined in law. In this way, the church 'enjoyed as a favour what it demanded as a right', and it was a favour that continued as long as there was a lack of priests and parsons to fill the existing livings.[29] Teachers, too, enjoyed initial temporary exemption 'in consideration of the need for public education' and, from 1827 on, those able to prove they had attended a training college were only required to serve for six weeks. This privilege originally applied both to elementary level and *Gymnasium* teachers, though the latter group lost this benefit in 1837 with the general ruling coming into force that allowed all candidates for higher teaching posts to register as one-year volunteers.[30] Armament factory workers enjoyed the same prerogative, providing they had distinguished themselves by 'industry and good behaviour' and had signed on with their employer for nine years.[31]

In the face of such numerous exemptions, the question arises of who actually served as a regular soldier for three years or, after the period of service was reduced in 1833, for two years. Who made up the tens of thousands serving every year? Who was being trained for the army, principally for the infantry, but also for the cavalry and artillery units? Unfortunately, exact figures on the recruits' social origins are not available, although it nonetheless seems reasonable to assume that the 'common' soldier came mainly from the lower classes – farmers' sons, farm workers, urban and rural day labourers, journeymen from various trades, and factory workers. Those volunteering for the full period of service, i.e., not as one-yearers, similarly came from this section of the population.[32] All young men could make use of this option before being called up, and some 2,000 to 3,000 did so annually. In this way, they obtained the right to enter military service before they were 20 years old – certainly attractive to some young men in view of their apprenticeships or work – and they were able to choose their own regiment, just as the one-yearers could. This latter privilege was extremely desirable since it meant they were sure of 'being allowed to remain near to their own kith and kin'.[33] In addition, quite a number of volunteers toyed with the idea of an army career as an NCO. Accustomed to hierarchies and subordination by their previous occupations or apprenticeships, they could reckon that, in the army, they would soon be allowed to give orders and not simply take them. Furthermore, the army offered, if not a life of luxury, at least a living wage and the future prospect, after active service, of obtaining entitlement to a government pension and, hence, a secure state benefit.[34]

In contrast, many of their contemporaries sought to use all the power at their disposal to evade military service: they pleaded illness, obtained certificates proving they were indispensable, bribed doctors and civil servants, emigrated or simply never appeared at any muster. On average throughout Prussia in the 1830s and 1840s, 4 to 6 per cent of the young men who were required to present themselves before the district recruiting commission, i.e., of all 20-year-olds, and those 21- to 24-year-olds who, at the previous muster, had been temporarily exempted or made to wait a year due to illness or for personal reasons, did not appear. Of those who did appear, between 66 and 76 per cent were not considered sufficiently large or strong enough for service and were declared 'permanently' or 'temporarily unfit'; 3 to 5 per cent were excused on social grounds. For the rest, there remained the hope of 'being excess to requirements'; after all, with the Prussian army's peacetime numbers in the *Vormärz* period remaining stable despite population growth, the need for recruits was generally lower than the number of those fit to serve and not seeking to excuse themselves on other grounds. As a case in point, in 1819 the Cologne government stated that, in its area, only 70 per cent of those recruited actually had to serve, and in 1831 this figure was slightly under 57 per cent. At that time, 62 per cent of all those 'remaining recruits' were enlisted in Prussia as a whole, and this was an exceptionally high quota. In 1830, the Paris July Revolution led to the army being partially mobilised, with a corresponding increase in the need for conscripts. In the end, the quota settled between 39 and 52 per cent, i.e., on average, less than half of those recruited and fit to serve actually went on to don the king's colours.[35]

2. The *Landwehr* as a Citizens' Militia?

The aversion many Prussian citizens felt towards fulfilling their 'most sacred citizen's duty' did not only apply to the standing army but equally to the *Landwehr*, where resistance was, in fact, even stronger initially. In 1818 nearly all the district administrators in Rhenish Prussia reported substantial resistance among the general population, while 1817 had seen the Prussian provincial governors complaining in unison that: 'An institution, which from its nature is designed to develop a universal feeling for courage and fervent patriotic sentiment and fix these as permanent character traits, is degenerating into a burden on the country.'[36]

At first glance, the widespread discontent seems hard to understand. After all, in contrast to serving in the regular army, service in the *Landwehr* was considerably easier, shorter and more convenient; instead of facing three years of unbroken service, *Landwehr* soldiers only had to don a uniform from time to time. The legal provisions may have prescribed regular exercises around the home area and an external review twice a year, but even if this were followed to the letter, the individual soldier suffered far less financially, physically and in terms of lost time than in the regular army. There was not even any loss in working days since the monthly drill exercises and shooting practices took place on Sundays. Accommodation too was in a familiar environment, with *Landwehr* soldiers lodging at home instead of in a barracks or unaccustomed private quarters. Attending a centralised military exercise was required, but only every two to three years and for four weeks at most, a time period easily planned and manageable in comparison to several years of regular army service.

Nevertheless, for a number of reasons, the *Landwehr* service came in for wide-spread criticism from everyone affected by it. The 1814 law on military service provided for all those who had already completed regular army service to serve in the *Landwehr* until they were 32 years old: one-yearers as NCOs and potential *Landwehr* officers, and the three-yearers as normal *Landwehr* troops. But until 1833, the *Landwehr* also included those passed fit at muster but not conscripted into the regular army; consequently, these men were without any military training. In 1832, more than 50 per cent of the *Landwehr* infantry came from this group[37] and they seem to have been precisely the ones protesting most vociferously against their new duties. Many men regarded the draft as a major intrusion into their 'civil circumstances', sometimes even regarding it as a blatant infringement of their civic rights.[38]

Organising the *Landwehr* took place far more at grass-roots level than in the regular army and, as a result, facilitated collective protests, for example, as in the case of Breslau in 1817. When a total of 396 recruits were to be publicly sworn to their colours, 110 of them were conspicuous only by their absence, and 222 of the remainder stated for the record that 'since they had already taken a civic oath, they were not willing to take any others'. Only eight burghers from the city were sworn in, drawing comments from the 'refractory' element that 'He won't be respected as a burgher of this town anymore, the scurvy dog! Let him just live off his dry army rations', and 'He must be a good-for-nothing and a blackguard since a real burgher wouldn't have sworn'. After these 'troublemakers' had been arrested – all of them tradesmen and businessmen – three to four hundred people stormed the town hall and government buildings, throwing files out of the window and sowing a trail of destruction through official residences and offices. The ensuing pitched battle between the garrison and the 'mob' left a 21-year-old tailor journeyman dead and seven other men, all apprentices, journeymen and master craftsmen, suffering from minor injuries, with thirty others arrested. In this way, the resistance was broken, and after the municipal authorities, town councillors, and government representatives had severely admonished them, the men liable for service in the *Landwehr* declared themselves prepared to swear the requisite oath. Only force of arms and the military occupation of the town had brought about their 'obedience' to an institution they apparently viewed as endangering their existence as citizens and city burghers, or at the very least, saw as contrary to that existence. In their eyes, rather than the *Landwehr* being a citizens' militia, it was but a useless appendage of the Prussian military machine and, without being made to, they had no intention of submitting to those strict laws enforcing military hierarchies that also reached into civilian life.[39]

The authorities reported a degree of discord, even where there was no collective resistance. The 'every soldier a citizen, and every citizen a soldier' axiom embodied in the *Landwehr* was visibly present everywhere, with every city gate adorned with the emblems of the city's *Landwehr* battalion,[40] yet the principle itself met with little support. The officers generally viewed it with suspicion, and even those few officers keen on the *Landwehr* continuing as an independent organisation pulled no punches when criticising it as untrained and undrilled. In their opinion, making men with only the most rudimentary military knowledge and no army experience into *Landwehr* soldiers violated the most basic Prussian army precepts and brought 'the entire edifice crashing to the ground'.[41] But what army staff found too little, the men themselves viewed as too much – and, in particular, found the longer, centrally arranged *Landwehr* exercises a burden. They not only received no pay for the weeks away from their job, but many employers shifted to taking on men over the *Landwehr* duty age. The problem was only exacerbated when the *Landwehr* soldiers were also the head of a household.[42] The vast majority of the 'innumerable objections' dealt with by the Arnsberg authorities in the summer of 1842 came from 'family fathers from the day-labourer and small farmer class'; during the father's period of *Landwehr* service, the government went on to explain, the wives and children needed 'poor relief'. But they were not granted it: not only was no compensation paid towards the wages lost, but neither the men themselves, nor their families, had 'any right to bread, soldier's pay, or other maintenance'.[43]

The lower social classes were not alone in submitting pleas for release from *Landwehr* service; manufacturers, merchants and lawyers similarly presented petitions, while doctors declared themselves to be essential workers, alleging a conflict of interests between the Hippocratic and military oaths as a justification for dispensation. In all of these cases, the recurring argument for exemption centred on the claim that, during peacetime, the *Landwehr* was, in reality, useless and superfluous. As one doctor put it in 1840, explaining his case for exemption due to his wife's first confinement: 'In an emergency, I would spurn using even the most sacred of family situations as any reason to prevent me offering those services required by the state: but in the present instance, the case is different.'[44] When the rapid spread of 'iniquitous objections' led some local authorities to attempt temporary suspension of *Landwehr* exercises, the king forbade it.[45] The tendency of many local and city authorities to grant their civil servants 'indispensable status' to support their petitions not to serve met with a similar reaction from the higher echelons. As Friedrich Wilhelm III informed the authorities in Silesian Oppeln in 1818: 'The brief *Landwehr* exercises cannot cause such grave disturbance to the official duties performed by a civil servant that, given due and appropriate provision, any untoward detriment need be feared.' He would be 'extremely displeased if authorities, who are the guardians of the law, set an evil example by withdrawing their staff from *Landwehr* service, and far rather expect them to demonstrate a positive spirit in strictly fulfilling the duties required, providing a model for the general populace to follow'.[46]

The authorities in Frankfurt an der Oder set a good example in 1817 when they ordered their civil servants not only to participate in the major reviews but also to take part in the voluntary exercises held on Sundays,[47] though it is hard to say how far their 'model' was imitated. Certainly, in contrast to the extensive accounts detailing resistance or reluctance to serve, there are reports noting '*Landwehr* reserves very willingly present' and praising the 'fine spirit' in the *Landwehr*. Such reports record how *Landwehr* soldiers from the Rhineland area, who had, for the most part, already 'taken part in campaigns', apparently used the Sunday exercises to relive their war experience in a ritualised form. There was, in any case, no lack of an audience – nearly all reports contain references to the presence of crowds come 'to watch their family and friends gathered in performing such an honourable profession'.[48] In some places, these exercises became thoroughly festive events, helped by the church taking the opportunity to hold services and bless the weapons. Such festivals unified not only the social classes, but also the generations and the sexes. 'The families, the old and young of both sexes, joined in the exercises heartily and enthusiastically, carrying the weapons to the reserves, encouraging them by their presence, regaling them in the breaks with draughts of refreshing drinks, and complimenting them as the future defenders and protectors of their goods, their possessions, and their homelands.'[49]

Occasionally, districts with major exercises arranged festivals where 'the reserves are feasted extremely well, even to excess'. Private people donated food and drink too, for example, the 'estimable burgher of Groß-Strehlitz' in Upper Silesia who 'voluntarily' donated several barrels of brandy to the reserves to mark 'the anniversary of the battle of *La belle Alliance*'.[50] Communities demonstrated 'patriotic zeal', too, if they funded 'outward ornamentation' for their reserves, e.g., providing additional equipment to embellish their uniforms. The group of private sponsors included not only high-ranking crown civil servants, who were officially urged to donate, but local landowners, businessmen and merchants too; for example, in 1819, the Minden merchant body presented their local 2nd *Landwehr* Battalion with 'decorative braid aiguillettes for the cavalry jackets', while other well-to-do citizens dipped into their own pockets to provide 'what was lacking' in the shape of jackets, hats or sashes.[51]

Such donations suggest that the middle classes, at least, were gradually coming to terms with the new organisation: now the *Landwehr* was a fact, they tried to make the best of it. It was no surprise, then, that the uniforms were precisely the aspect inspiring a desire to support the reserves – after all, the uniform was the primary and key outward symbol of a military person.[52] Moreover, it was well known how highly the regular army valued uniforms, and how crucial and telling the smallest differences were in cut, material and equipment. With the cheaper and simpler *Landwehr* uniforms, what could be more obvious than 'decorating' and 'embellishing' them as much as possible? This did not merely raise each individual reserve's feeling of worth and self-esteem, but simultaneously underlined the right of the *Landwehr* to be an equal part of the 'armed force', as stated in the 1814 law on military service.

However, although such initiatives say nothing of how lower-class men coped with the imposed *Landwehr* service, there are indications that this new military status steadily became more attractive for them as well – and here too, the uniform played a significant role. For many men with a low income, they were not only receiving a piece of clothing of better quality and harder-wearing than their normal clothes, it also came free of charge. The uniform's importance might be easier to understand if one bears in mind that, when drafted, many young people were unable to produce even the pair of long trousers, jacket, shoes and two shirts required, and the local community had to provide them.[53] Viewed in this light, it is less surprising that many reserves not only tended to wear their uniforms during periods of service but continued to do so in everyday civilian life as well. While the 1815 *Landwehr* regulations only permitted reserves on furlough to put on uniforms for festive occasions, the Upper Silesian authorities reported in 1816 that 'the men on leave were constantly in uniform', whereas, in 1818, the district administrator from Simmern in the Rhineland recorded that the reserves 'would consider themselves more honoured' by the privilege of wearing their uniforms in Sunday exercises 'than by being given sabres'.[54]

Such reports make clear how far the uniform was regarded as something more than just a piece of clothing providing warmth or offering personal embellishment. Instead, it also symbolised honour – the honour of belonging to a class especially close to the Prussian throne. But there was a price to pay for such an honour: as von Hake, the war minister, emphasised in 1825, the reserve on furlough 'voluntarily' presents himself 'as a soldier', and hence has to behave as a soldier and respect military orders. The concrete concern was to ensure that all reservists in uniform 'treated their officers with the honour due to them' and could be punished if they did not or, even worse, were 'refractory'.[55] In fact, *Landwehr* reserves on furlough were subject to civilian criminal jurisdiction and did not fall under military law; nonetheless, if wearing the uniform made them recognisable military personnel, they had to accept the laws valid in and for the army. In other areas too, they were not totally free from the 'watchful care' of battalion commanders and officers, who were to keep an eye on them and intervene, for example, in cases of conflict with their 'masters'. As a result, military superiors reinforced the power relations existing in civilian life, making the 'reserves' aware 'that they can only become worthy of their profession and partake of my mercy by exemplary fulfilment of the duties incumbent on them'.[56]

In the context of the relationship between military and civilian authorities, it is interesting to note the king's warning that military supervision over *Landwehr* reserves on leave should never 'devolve into a procedure which might diminish the respect due to the authorities or the reserve's master'. In other words, the concern seems to have been that the reserves in their military 'status' could place themselves above public service officials or employers, and be supported by their military superiors – and a *Landwehr* reserve's complaint to his divisional commander in 1841 shows that such worries were not entirely unfounded. The local district *Landrat* had had the reserve whipped; the man then complained that this treatment was both dishonourable and unbecoming to his military status. Reserves took their status, too, as a reason to apply directly to the king, asking for 'redress of presumed abuse occurring in civil life'. In these cases, their 'position as members of the military' was used to lend 'greater importance to their gatherings and a greater weight to their decisions, with the public and the authorities' and ought to help them push through their own civic interests.[57]

Such incidents go to show that serving in the *Landwehr* was not merely irksome or burdensome; it actually opened up possibilities. Lower-class men, in particular, could employ their status as honourable defenders of the fatherland to demand to be treated with honour and respect in their civilian lives, and, possibly, even with courtesy. It was also conceivable that social dependencies were reversed within the military environment: a plough boy who practised diligently and was a good marksman may have become an NCO over his less-talented master, while a day-labourer may have given orders to a factory owner. In this way, the *Landwehr* system introduced 'a genuine revolution across all civic relations'.[58] Once they had donned the king's colours, some of the reserves had learnt 'pride' and this new self-assurance had an effect beyond the confines of the parade ground.

But, vice versa, civilian relations also affected the army. The king had made it clear that he required all the inspectors and staff-officers 'carefully to bear in mind' the 'special position' of reserves and shun 'any unnecessary prolongation of tasks, roughness, and severity'.[59] This was not always easy, especially for officers directly detailed from the regular army, and they needed repeated reminders to show more moderation. The new army structure, reaching deep into civil life, made it imperative to consider the soldiers' 'personal situation, customs and character'. For this reason, before implementing harsh punishments, the *Landwehr* commander ought 'to confer beforehand with the responsible civil authorities on the official standing of the person to be punished'. Above all, such 'attentiveness' was absolutely essential for the recruits from 'the educated classes' if one did not want to confirm those 'wrong notions' on 'treatment by Prussian soldiers' that were prevalent principally in the Rhenish provinces.[60]

Although corporal punishment had been abolished in the army in 1808 (except in the punishment brigade), compared to civil law, military criminal law continued to be marked by far greater rigidity and severity. The contrast was especially noticeable in the Rhineland, still using the liberal French civil law; the discrepancy was so striking in the *Landwehr* that it repeatedly culminated in conflicts and protests. The harshness of military punishments stood out even more prominently in the context of rapid and repeated shifts between civilian and military life, and this, of course, did little to make such service more appealing. Furthermore, the situation was exacerbated by military court judgments extending into civil and civilian life. In the view of the Berlin minister of public safety (*Polizeiminister*) anyone 'expelled from the army for a serious felony' should not be allowed to take up public office or be granted municipal citizenship; the 'felonies' demanding such measures included stealing, which was the most frequent offence soldiers were accused of. However, neither the Cologne government nor the municipal authorities wanted to bow to such an interpretation, and, in 1838, their protest against the unconditional transfer of military values and categories onto civil affairs was finally successful. The military back-pedalled on the issue of granting municipal civic rights and land ownership, allowing the cities to determine which definition of 'a blemished character' they wanted to follow in future, in accordance with their own laws. The war ministry, though, showed no inclination to compromise where sovereign rights or symbols were at stake. A man dishonourably discharged from the army could never take public office, wear the national cockade or display any military honours on his chest.[61]

The assertion of a military hegemony was especially apparent in cases of conflict between civilians and army personnel, and attacks were common. Even *Landwehr* officers suffered from the overbearing behaviour of their fellow officers from the regular army, who did not take them seriously and treated them 'with disdain and scorn'.[62] Although this may have been understandable in the early phases of the *Landwehr* when many officers had been appointed without any military qualifications, the status difference showed no signs of eroding later either, when the officers were recruited from 'one-yearers' with regular army training. The attitude was further fostered and reinforced by the Prussian army policy of filling vacant *Landwehr* commander posts with regular officers in order to bring the *Landwehr* 'in line';[63] this, however, awoke the distrust and anger of the *Landwehr* officers from the civilian population, who felt ignored and slighted.

In 1845, an open conflict broke out in Bielefeld over just this issue. When a regular officer, initially invalided out of the army and then reactivated, was to be pushed into the post of *Landwehr* captain, most *Landwehr* officers gave voice to their resistance, preventing the appointment. Interestingly enough, the opponents largely came from the men who, in civilian life, were 'independent', primarily from the commercial or manufacturing sectors, while those in favour tended to be 'in official positions', apparently believing they had to take into account the clearly expressed views of their military superiors – and this, of course, was precisely the objection of those *Landwehr* officers insisting on the institution's independence. Hermann Consbruch, a Bielefeld merchant and *Landwehr* officer since 1835, wrote of it serving 'one and the same purpose' together with the regular army, but not in a role inferior to it, hoping for relations built on 'concord and mutual trust' and not made to suffer under the regular army's assertion of a military hegemony.

Middle-class *Landwehr* officers did not only object when such assertions affected military service matters; they were also sensitive to what they saw as regular army interference in their civilian lives. In 1845–6, for example, a conflict erupted between the garrison's officer corps and the local Bielefeld Gentlemen's Club (*Ressource-Gesellschaft*). After a new club statute was voted in prohibiting the wearing of arms, the commander prosecuted those members of the club directorate who were also *Landwehr* officers in a court of honour for their alleged anti-military stance. The latter group protested vehemently, putting forward two reasons in support of their case: firstly, their votes in favour of the new statute were not intended as a 'demonstration' against the regular army, and, secondly, in their view, the commander had no grounds to interfere in their civilian lives at all. As citizens they had the right to exercise their 'personal convictions' without 'having to answer as officers'.[64]

Such disagreements bear witness to the fluid borders between civil society and the army, and the ambivalence in the behaviour and attitudes of middle-class men. The old established Bielefeld bourgeoisie were certainly interested in mixing with the local garrison officers, who were not only allowed to become club members but, until 1845, were even excluded from the balloting procedure that normally regulated membership in this exclusive institution. Moreover, many men felt themselves to be personally connected to the army: the eighteen club members deciding on the new statutes in 1846 included some veterans from the 1813–15 campaign, while many of the remainder were *Landwehr* officers or NCOs 'heart and soul'. Yet, on the other hand, they were always at the ready to defend their civilian status, and were very self-assured in their approach to doing so. They regarded regular officers' attempts to tie *Landwehr* officers to the 'rules governing an officer's honour' when they were not serving as arrogance, claiming they were first and foremost civilians and only liable to military regulations when in active service. If the army chose to overrule such 'manly views, [...] in the end there would be few civilians willing to become *Landwehr* officers'.[65]

In fact, the majority of young middle-class men in the 1815–48 period demonstrated a marked lack of enthusiasm in applying for a *Landwehr* officer position, with only 40 per cent of the one-yearers acquiring the required qualification.[66] Moreover, simply because a man was entitled to become a *Landwehr* officer did not mean he was actually intending to pursue such a career. Military and civil authorities were constantly complaining of one-yearers turning down the chance of being appointed as a *Landwehr* officer, which, as the provincial governor Ludwig von Vincke pointed out, 'incurs His Majesty's most serious displeasure'. In future, every refusal to serve was to be reported to the king, who expected that 'in such instances, efforts would be undertaken to awaken a greater inclination for it'.[67] It is now hardly possible to know whether the lack of such a 'greater inclination' was primarily due to the distrust created by the anti-civilian airs of regular officers and *Landwehr* commanders or stemmed from other, less political, motives. Nonetheless, we can say that many men apparently saw little benefit in wearing a *Landwehr* officer's uniform, leading regular drill and shooting practice, and being drafted for annual four-week training exercises.

The volunteers and reserve officers who served in the 1813–15 war retained a certain loyalty and affection for the army, starting veterans' organisations, arranging local commemorative events, and celebrating jubilees in the *Vormärz* period.[68] The 'young commercial traders, merchant's clerks and businessmen', however, were more restrained when it came to filling vacant officer positions – an odd contrast with the liberal public's attitude of unilateral support for the *Landwehr* and their praise for its virtues, especially when compared with the standing army. David Hansemann, like other figures in commercial and banking life, extolled the *Landwehr*'s 'civil manners' and non-violence, while encyclopaedias emphasised its 'democratic' character and 'moral spirit'.[69] In 1839, Carl Welcker, a member of the Baden parliament and co-publisher of the influential state encyclopaedia, praised the Prussian *Landwehr* system as 'the most glorious and blessed institution of this state', allowing the 'army and the people' to enter into an 'organic *union* and *reciprocal relation*', claiming that, while the army gains in 'moral strength' and military efficiency, the people feel themselves 'uplifted', strengthened in their manliness and their 'sense of fatherland'.

Despite Welcker never actually experiencing the drill ground himself, nor serving in a barracks, he drew on his time as a professor in Bonn, where he 'had been able to observe the daily military exercises taking place directly in front of my windows' and, additionally, had personally known 'a number of privates and officers'. His observations – and even more, his political convictions – led him to view the *Landwehr* as the perfect alternative to the standing army system, and regard it as the school of 'civic sense, courage and patriotism'.[70] But the Prussian citizens' sons who had to go through this schooling were of a different opinion; instead of revering the *Landwehr* as a drill ground for a civic character and 'manly' virtues, they first and foremost saw it as doing nothing more than upsetting their social, family and business relations, and protested against it as vociferously as possible. As the years passed, though, the protests stilled, or emerged in another form. While, for example, in 1817 the new recruits in Breslau had refused to participate in the swearing-in ceremony, or collective pleas were entered petitioning a release from duties, later strategies to avoid the burden of *Landwehr* service were more individual. In any case, it was certainly not possible to talk of an eagerness to serve, or even an enthusiasm for it, despite examples of men reconciled to their situation and, in some instances, managing to turn it to their own advantage: a becoming uniform, a status commanding respect, and, for *Landwehr* officers and NCOs, an authority reinforcing their own influence.

3. Citizenship and Masculinity: The Jewish Population Demands Participation

Men from the Jewish population seem to have had few objections to the new Prussian army structure. The military authorities bear witness to their constant 'good will and attentive completion of duties', giving special mention to the fact that 'they presented themselves punctually for the *Landwehr* exercises' and 'distinguished themselves by great obedience and a quiet manner'.[71] In this way, Jewish men presented themselves as the ideal model soldiers, above all, because, in contrast to the Breslau *Landwehr* reserves, they saw military service as offering entry into Prussian civic society – as the cornerstone of political and social emancipation, and complementary to it.

As early as 1783, Christian Wilhelm Dohm, a Prussian civil servant in the war ministry and committed advocate of Jewish emancipation, had already given his opinion on military service as a key condition for 'improving [their] civic condition', and commented that 'the Jews cannot claim equal rights with the remaining branches of society, if they have not first proved themselves to be just as willing to perform military service as they are capable of doing so'. He staunchly held to his views against all the critical voices citing religious, physical and moral obstacles to the Jewish population's readiness to fight; instead, he believed the Jews would be 'just as loyal and capable' of dying for their country 'as everyone else [...] once they are given a country'. It was a stance supported by Moses Mendelssohn, a well-respected figure in the Berlin Jewish community and regarded as their spokesperson on political and religious issues.[72]

Interestingly enough, this line of reasoning figured prominently in the ongoing debate on 'improving the situation of the Jews' during the 1780s. At a time when non-Jewish citizens were celebrating exemption from military service and fiercely defending the privileges allowing it, the national and Jewish emancipation discourses were already setting different, universal accents. Here, the Jewish subjects appear as the prototype of modern citizens – long before the non-Jewish population adopted this definition as their own. In the period of reforms under Stein and Hardenberg, this interlinked package of military duty and civic rights came under closer scrutiny. In 1808, justice minister Carl Wilhelm von Schroetter asked the king to answer the question of whether he 'considered the Jews to be worthy of conscription'; Schroetter himself did, pointing out that without the draft 'no extension of rights and privileges could be granted to the Jews'.[73] Stein's 1807 October Edict had reflected this latter view, excluding those inhabitants 'whose religious notions prevent them from fulfilling the entire range of civic duties' from participating in the unrestricted freedom of goods traffic. The ruling was severely criticised in 1808 by Mendel Oettinger from Breslau, who argued that those civic duties implied 'nothing less than the duty of military service', even though the authorities obviously believed this could not be harmonised with laws governing Jewish ritual. But Oettinger disagreed; as far as he was concerned, the vast majority of educated Jews openly acknowledged the 'sensible idea' that 'the duty of constantly contributing, if possible, to the welfare of his monarch and fatherland' is of greater value than respecting the Sabbath, and added that he was personally 'prepared to submit to the burden of military service just as the Christians do'. However, in return, he expected to be granted 'all civic rights, and especially the permission to possess goods'. While Mendel Oettinger only spoke for himself, in 1810 the Berlin community made a joint declaration on behalf of all their 'fellows', accepting all civic duties and asking in turn to be allowed to enjoy all civic rights.[74]

But this was indeed the crux – and precisely the point that made the government uneasy. The 1812 Edict on Emancipation skirted around the issue of laying down clear and generally binding provisions on military service and admission to public office. In 1813, this lack of clarity left recruiting authorities hesitating over whether the royal decrees on lifting all rights to exemptions in the course of establishing the *Landwehr* affected Jewish men or not. While the government in Mark Brandenburg tended to enlist Jewish men, since 'supplying the fresh levies of reserves becomes more difficult every day', in the eastern military government, in part, a different approach was adopted, allowing Jewish men to buy themselves out of the *Landwehr*. In contrast, in 1814, the military governors of the lands between the Rivers Elbe and Oder considered that 'treating the Jews differently from all other citizens in this matter is just as unnecessary as it is damaging'. After all, they continued, the experience of war has shown 'how resolutely many of this nation's members behaved, and how many volunteers among them have truly distinguished themselves'.[75]

Indeed, several hundred Jewish men had volunteered to serve in the war, and some Jewish communities had even equipped their poor Jewish volunteers as a proof of their 'noble patriotism'.[76] However, this show of support did nothing to gain them recognition as equal citizens. The king may have promised, in 1813, that all educated men who volunteer for service and distinguish themselves by their 'bravery, zeal, and patriotism' would be 'given preference in their future civil service career', but once the war was over, such talk ceased as far as the Jews were concerned. As justice minister von Kircheisen put it in 1815, 'transitory valour' cannot weaken the 'presumption of *less morality*' – and von Schuckmann, minister of the interior, agreed. In the latter's view, courage was not, in the final analysis, 'the only virtue required as a public servant'. Other qualities were equally essential, such as social honour and unquestioned loyalty to the political system; with Jews, however, one could never know whether they would place their 'national', i.e., Jewish, identity above any service in the interests of the general good. Although in 1817, the ministry of the interior let it be known that Jewish men were certainly required to perform military service 'just like all other citizens', they added that this would not affect 'any other personal rights and obligations, including those concerning the civic sphere'. The permission to take up university and teaching posts granted in the 1812 Edict was rescinded in 1822 and a year later all the Jewish public legal officials in the newly acquired Rhenish provinces received notice of dismissal.[77] Performing military service may have been a necessary condition for being granted civil rights, but it was certainly not a sufficient one.

While reformers such as Gneisenau and Scharnhorst had still gravitated towards military service as a logical outcome of citizenship (first political emancipation, then military service) and the advocates of Jewish 'improvement' read the link in reverse (first military service, then civic emancipation), Prussia in the *Vormärz* period denied any direct connection between the two at all. Prussian policy thought it enough for the state to provide its citizens with 'protection under law'. Nothing further was required – this alone was sufficient to expect due gratitude from the beneficiaries. In 1845, the minister of the interior, von Bodelschwingh, pointed out, more or less in justification of this stance, that these views were shared equally by the Jewish population too, citing as evidence the most recent petitions filed and applications submitted.[78]

In fact, in 1842, two years after Friedrich Wilhelm IV came to the throne, Jewish citizens had initiated an unparalleled joint action, protesting in unison against his plans to exempt all Jewish men from the draft and merely grant them optional entry into the army, which Jewish intellectuals, elders and rabbis regarded as an attempt to bar Jews from the fatherland's 'evolution' and prevent their civic emancipation. In Prussia, the argument ran, 'where the army and the people are identical', 'every proscriptive approach to the army presupposes a proscriptive approach to the people and the fatherland. We would cease to be completely Prussian, we would once again be the excluded, the separated, only belonging to our country conditionally.'[79] Contrary to the support indicated by Bodelschwingh, those signing this petition did not believe military service was merely paying off a debt of gratitude for the personal and property rights granted by the state. The dream of complete equality still survived intact, even though, given the contemporary political developments and the revitalisation of the concept of the Christian state under Friedrich Wilhelm IV, realising it seemed less likely than ever. In this situation, the aim was to secure the rights they already had and ensure continued access to military service.

Another line of argument was put forward by Ludwig Philippson, a rabbi and liberal Magdeburg newspaper editor, who had formulated the petition signed by more than eighty Jewish congregations: for the 'still inferior Jewish masses' the army offered a crucially important 'means of education', teaching them 'orderliness, punctuality and respect for the law' as well as imparting 'a correct and superior understanding of social life'. Moreover, disputing the Jews' right to this means of emancipation was tantamount to consciously undermining the 'civic improvement of the Jews' achieved since 1781.[80] The idea of the army as the 'main school for educating the entire nation' harked back to the wording in the 1814 law on conscription, whose author, the war minister Hermann von Boyen, gave a more precise definition of what this phrase really meant two years later. He wrote to the Westphalian provincial governor Ludwig von Vincke in 1816 that: 'If our standing army is to fulfil the task entrusted to it, it must not only be regarded and treated as a training school for war for the entire nation, but also as a school teaching all those virtues every citizen needs.' Rather than the army merely providing the professional skills needed for shooting, marching and drilling, it was to teach the soldier 'what he absolutely must know to become a good citizen'.[81]

Such a broadly formulated educational programme, applicable to all recruits across the board, was first actively called for when military service for Jewish men became an issue. In 1817, for example, the Bromberg government emphasised the 'salutary effect training the Jews in the army must have on their lowly level of culture'. Ten years later, von Vincke expressed himself even more candidly when he spoke out for 'compelling [the Jews] especially to serve' in the army, since in this way they would not only be 'removed from higgling and haggling for three years, given a certain body of knowledge, become accustomed to physical exertion, and freed from certain caste prejudices' but also and 'particularly' prepared for conversion to the Christian faith, since 'in the same way as the school assimilates the child, the army makes the Jewish young man similar to the Christian young man'.[82]

Over subsequent years, these reasons, though slightly modified, developed into a set point of reference in the landscape of political debate. For example, they appeared in the Prussian state ministry appeal in 1832 to conscript the Jews in the former Polish territories as well, while the commission reporting on affairs in the eastern province of Posen similarly recommended military service as 'the most important means of education for Jews', not only for the Jewish soldier while serving but 'for the salutary effect [this will] exercise on his return to civilian life on his surroundings and, in future, principally on his children'. It was a view reflected by the interior ministers in the 1840s too, with von Rochow commenting in 1842 in an official vote on 'Regulating Jewish Matters' (*Regulierung des Judenwesens*) that 'experience has shown' that nothing contributes to the 'education and improvement of the Jews' as much as military service, and for this reason it is both in the interests of the state and the 'moral interest of the Jews'. This firm stand by Rochow, similarly adopted by his successor von Bodelschwingh, clearly opposed the king's intention of applying the special provisions governing the Posen Jews throughout the entire kingdom, since 'the Rhenish Jews and those living under the 1812 Edict' would inevitably perceive this as 'a political degradation, and a national disgrace'; after all, they were 'not unjustified in regarding their call to the colours as a major *political right* which they share with Christian subjects'.[83]

In these debates, alongside the political, social, and moral arguments, gender issues played a key role. Jewish men were repeatedly accused of cowardice, an allegation denying them the core male characteristics of bravery and valour. The 'nation's view' that Jews are fearful by nature was never shaken even by experiences during the campaigns against Napoleon, and when the Berlin Jews in 1842 put forward arguments that their example in the 1813–15 war had dispelled all prejudices about Jews being 'cowardly' and 'unfit for service', these were rejected out of hand. To the extent that military service was institutionalised after 1814 and seen as a general agency of socialisation, it appeared essential for Jews specifically to partake of this 'flower of honour' and have themselves trained as 'real' men. Anyone not passing through this school soon became suspected of effeminacy and cowardice – accusations quick to be levied against Jews. In the 1830s, the young Jewish writer and journalist Gabriel Riesser considered this the 'most defamatory of all slurs', and neither the spoken word nor written form would suffice in response – the only adequate reply for a 'man of honour' was a challenge to a duel.[84]

Similarly, Riesser viewed the demeaning treatment awaiting Jews in the army as equally humiliating and disrespectful. They were practically excluded from any promotion beyond the rank of sergeant major and, until 1847, the guards did not accept any Jewish recruits at all, on principle. In 1827, Ludwig von Vincke also complained of the 'army's marked aversion to Jewish recruits'. According to the figures in his research, only 189 soldiers of the Jewish faith were serving in the standing army and the army reserves, where they comprised nearly 0.1 per cent of the total amount, with, at the time, the Jewish population representing slightly more than 1 per cent of the entire populace; the *Landwehr* showed somewhat less incongruity, with, in 1827, 908 Jewish men serving in a total force of around 175,000 reserves.[85]

Undoubtedly, these figures give a distorted picture since they do not allow for the large proportion of Prussian Jews, especially in the province of Posen, who were not even subject to conscription until 1845. They also do not consider the fact that the majority of the Jewish population was urban, and, generally speaking, townsmen were not drafted as often as their compatriots in rural areas. Yet even given these constraints, the impression remains that the military and civilian members on recruiting commissions regarded Jewish recruits as less valuable than Christian ones and wanted to deny them the education promised in the army.

4. The Army as the 'Training School' for War and Peace

If men without army experience found they were increasingly regarded as unreliable, weakly, immature and incomplete, this could partially be attributed to a number of parallel measures that upgraded military service into a basic requirement for access to a range of civil rights on the level of both community and state. Although the first war minister's plans to tie local voting rights to completed military service were never implemented, the king did instruct local authorities to grant municipal civic rights only after the applicant had submitted proof of appearing before a recruiting commission.[86] A similar thrust can clearly be seen in the provision requiring all those applying for a position in the civil service first to show that they had complied with the draft requirements.[87]

Young men should preferably only marry after they had finished their time in the army, too. In the eighteenth century, many soldiers had been married but, in contrast, the nineteenth-century recruit ought to be young, single and not yet a parent – but to ensure no-one imagined marriage might offer a reason not to be drafted, provincial governments' official gazettes regularly pointed out that married men remained just as liable to be enlisted. Moreover, all priests and, later, registrars were instructed to remind all men subject to conscription of this fact when they initially submitted written confirmation of their intention to get married. The army reforms also cut totally the financial allowances previously made to wives and children.[88] The desire for celibate soldiery was justified, on the one hand, by the need to avoid paying welfare, since neither the state nor the local authorities wanted to take on benefit payments for families of enlisted soldiers left without sufficient means of support; on the other hand, recruits without family ties were thought to be more willing to accept the draft and see army service as less of a burden.

Indeed, the message that regular army soldiers had to be single was repeatedly driven home, but this norm simultaneously expressed a new idea: the notion of military service as a transition between youth and adulthood. Contemporary popular opinion saw marriage and independence as largely synonymous. At least, among the rural farming population, but also in the urban middle and lower-middle classes, acquiring the material basis for an independent life came before marriage, and a celibate soldiery reinforced this pattern of behaviour. The soldier was regarded as marriageable only once he had been released from his duties in the standing army – and it was only then that his real life as a man began, marked by starting a family and providing the economic security needed for them.

In this way, the years of military service formed a block between youth, where the future recruit finished secondary school, learnt a trade, or worked as a farm or day labourer or in a factory, and adult life, where he had to shoulder greater responsibility in both the public and private spheres. Once an adult, he not only became a husband and father, but also a local burgher and subject of the Prussian king – and this entailed political duties which he was expected to discharge in a conscientious and responsible manner. The army harboured no doubts about its role as defender of the monarchist model, clearly rejecting any movement towards constitutional, liberal or, even worse, democratic principles. From the army perspective, fulfilment of duty was quite simply identical with conservative and royalist beliefs. For this reason, for example, in the *Vormärz* period, a special 'watch' was kept on students completing their one year of service who were deemed to hold 'dubious opinions'. Such a policy had two aims: firstly, to prevent opposition political notions from spreading among the soldiers and, secondly, to try and reclaim such 'subjects' in the army, converting them to 'pure and lawful sentiments'. In 1816, the king decreed that, in addition, every soldier was to be given 'an overview of the country's constitution', so that he will 'leave his service with sufficient knowledge of his duties as a loyal subject'.[89]

The core of these duties can be summarised briefly in a few sentences. The key point is contained at the very top of the list of a soldier's duties read out at the swearing-in ceremony: 'The soldier's primary duty is to serve his royal majesty and the fatherland loyally.' Furthermore, it was expected that every soldier demonstrate 'military skill, valour in all calls of duty, and courage in the face of battle, obedience towards superiors, honourable conduct in service, and, in addition, is honest and upright in his dealings with his fellow soldiers'.[90] The significance attributed to this code of duties can be clearly deduced from the way it was directly embedded in the swearing-in ritual and its complex initiation ceremonies. Prior to the swearing-in ceremony itself, the recruits were divided by religious confession, with initial preparation from the different clergy. Afterwards, they met again at the place chosen for the ceremony, usually a barrack yard or other large square. Here, officers first explained to them the 'symbolic significance' of the oath, then read them the soldier's duties, and finally swore the recruits in. In garrison towns, the oath was taken 'on the colours or canon', but otherwise it was sworn on 'the officer's sabre or sword'. In this way, the colours, canons, or side-arms were included in the swearing-in ceremony and, as it were, consecrated. Where 'circumstances' proved suitable, a 'special religious ceremony' might follow the swearing-in.[91]

Only once the swearing-in was completed with 'solemnity and dignity' was the recruit considered 'enlisted' and 'admitted' into his regiment. He then underwent another medical examination, since the army wanted to be absolutely sure their soldiers were carrying no contagious diseases and would be able to cope with the physical demands made on them. Standards were high, and the list of 'physical defects' long. The requirements varied, depending on the type of troops: the infantry was thought to make the greatest demands physically, and a soldier here had to be 'a strong, healthy fellow', with a 'strong neck and broad shoulders, a good broad chest, supple arms and hands, and healthy feet', while cavalry recruits could be somewhat less robust and well-built. The highest standards were reserved for the guards: their soldiers not only had to be especially tall, but also to have 'an appealing outward appearance'. However, in all other cases, the criteria was 'ability', not 'good looks'.[92]

These criteria, which the recruiting commissions and military doctors were urged to follow stringently, excluded a large number of the young men who had to attend the mustering from following the king's colours. The quota of those declared unfit was not fixed but depended on the year and region, and seems to have been slightly higher in the cities than in the countryside; on average, in the Prussia of the 1830s and 1840s, more than two-thirds of those mustering were rejected.[93] Accordingly, the army only comprised the strongest and most physically powerful men for any given year of birth, while the weaker ones had to or were allowed to stay at home. There is no evidence to believe they viewed this as a personal blemish – quite the contrary, the records of self-mutilation (which became 'rampant', as was reported in 1825), simulated illnesses, and ostensive accentuation of physical defaults suggest many young men preferred to be considered sickly and ill and escape the draft in this way.[94]

On the other hand, for those recruits enlisted because of their stamina and fitness, the army endeavoured to awaken a kind of pride in their physical prowess; because they were strong and well built, they were qualified to perform an honourable duty – and could thus rightly feel they were superior to their unfit friends. Yet in the same breath they were told their bodies were anything but perfect. At best, they were superficially flawless, but in reality marred by any number of faults, cumbersome, unwieldy and ungainly. The army's task was to 'apply particular rules to marshal the limbs that have been left to the course of nature since youth' and prevent the man from becoming degraded to the 'slave of a mawkish, effete body', and they set about it using a precisely ordered sequence of incessant exercises in drill and gymnastics, and marching and shooting. They not only practised the famous, notorious march past where the Prussian soldiers were presented to their supreme commander, but they practised ordinary march pasts every day until the procedure became a part of the soldiers' flesh and blood. And that was exactly the point: drilling, marching, presenting arms, loading, aiming and shooting had to be performed with a steady movement, mechanically, without thinking, let alone doubting; a command had to trigger an immediate reaction, without exception, in all soldiers, in the same rhythm and at the same pace. The frequency of marching steps per minute was prescribed, as were their length and the height of the leg when turning, or the angle between the upper and lower arm when shouldering a rifle. It all went to create the classic military 'posture' that still characterised the soldier 'long after he has hung up his uniform, and suggests we are looking at a man who knows no fear, nor simply bows to his fate'.[95]

This 'posture' was not only the product of a solid and continuous 'physical dressage' over years – and one did talk, in no way critically, of 'harnessing' and 'drilling' recruits – but consciously broke with all habits the new soldiers brought with them from their civilian lives. For most of them, it took considerable effort to adapt to this new regime and, consequently, the officer in charge (generally a young lieutenant or captain, though frequently an NCO) found sufficient opportunity to reprimand the recruits for their mistakes, usually in the gruffest and harshest style. Although the recruits' officers were repeatedly lectured by their superiors to treat the young soldiers kind-heartedly, gaining their 'affection', their 'trust', and even their 'love',[96] the frequency of such admonishments suggests certain things were going seriously amiss. Many officers found the role of drill sergeant trying. Military literature in the first half of the century contained numerous indications that, even in the army itself, the new military structure was subject to criticism. Instead of constantly having to drill squads of changing recruits, army officers would have preferred to see previous structures reinstated. Indeed, their recurring cry was that there is no 'standing army' and 'warrior caste' any longer – merely a 'transition', 'a school' with new students joining and old ones leaving.[97] From the professional point of view, a conscription army undoubtedly had certain disadvantages.

Many officers, too, were unable to – or unwilling to – understand the general educational tasks the army was to master in future. To their way of thinking, the army was the long arm of the king, enhancing the Prussian monarch's prestige abroad and guaranteeing public security at home – and it was quite beyond them why it suddenly had to be transmogrified into a 'means of education for the general population'. They felt misused and over-challenged in their new role as the 'people's teacher'. And why indeed should they have hankered after teaching thrift, orderliness, 'abstinence and cleanliness' to 'uneducated creatures'? How did it help battle skills and military efficiency if the soldier was engaged in refining his 'moral and intellectual abilities' and learning to recognise 'his own value as a citizen of the state'? Officers reacted sceptically to the idea of the 'military dispositions passing entirely into the character of the people' and this 'effecting a recasting of their being' across 'all of the nation'.[98] After all, a reverse movement was equally conceivable, and instead of 'militarising' the people, the army might become the object of possible attempts to 'civilise' it, and, in order to reinforce its unity and efficiency in implementing its core tasks, many military specialists would far rather have sealed the military caste off altogether against every civilian influence.

Indeed, such reverse influences were already visible in the *Vormärz* period. It was not enough that regiments and battalions had to check the recruits' school education and ensure that, for example, poor penmanship or weak German skills would be remedied before they were discharged;[99] in addition, in the 1840s, temperance societies tried to enforce teetotalism on the army, with, from 1845 on, soldiers permitted to have the tot of rum officially provided during manoeuvres to be paid out in money instead. Appeals to commanders to wean their troops from the consumption of alcohol eulogized the 'infinite advantages' of such measures: 'After all, 45,000 strong men are returning to civilian life from the school of the army every year, taking with them the impressions, the teachings, and the habits they have acquired while in military service.' But a counterargument was easily found: even if each instance of 'immoderate partaking of rum' was evil, there could be no question of doing without it during wartime or on manoeuvres as a 'means of relief' and a 'restorative'. The army's fighting power would suffer under the soldiers' forced abstinence.[100]

Using the army as a school for civil life and a training institution of the nation awoke the sceptics' distrust, not least because they suspected that misusing and overstraining the army would weaken its military functions; this was one reason why many superior officers tended to approach the required hours of instruction in a dilatory fashion. The training plan may have demanded that recruits were informed daily on 'The why of their actions' and given background political knowledge, but the vast majority of officers seemed neither willing nor able to fulfil such tasks. Moreover, they did not have sufficient teaching materials. There was, of course, the *Soldatenfreund* (Soldier's Friend), the brainchild of the military journalist and court actor Louis Schneider, which originally appeared in the early 1830s as an almanac and was later transformed into a weekly journal. This publication received Prussian war ministry support and could be found in officers' messes, or was passed on to sergeant-majors and NCOs and read to soldiers during the instruction periods. Yet measured against the mass of tracts, compendiums and journals appearing after the 1850s, the *Soldatenfreund* at that time was no more than a lonely voice crying in the wilderness. Apparently, in the first half of the nineteenth century, its message largely fell on deaf ears, though this was to change after the 1848 revolution.[101]

However, the army could draw on other, less explicit and less obvious means to provide their soldiers with an enduring education – for example, via the entire 'internal service' and, first and foremost, the provisions governing rooms, clothing and personal hygiene. During their military service, recruits were supposed to learn how to fire a gun, use a bayonet, and march in rank and file, yet they also learned to wash daily, to change their underclothes regularly and make use of medical services. Furthermore, they had to repair and clean their uniforms, look after their leathers, tidy their kits and sweep their rooms. Such activities were not normally a part of a young man's education: washing, sewing on buttons or cleaning was a woman's work. Men were not bothered with such tasks, neither in the urban tradesmen's or day labourers' households, nor in the rural homes of farmers and labourers. In the army, though, delegating these tasks to women meant having to pay for them. A soldier could indeed have his washing done by an NCO's wife, but only if he was willing to sacrifice some of his paltry wage. Interestingly enough, however, expecting soldiers to perform 'female' work does not appear to have been viewed as an imposition. In any case, there are no records of protests, and even if some were able to buy themselves out of having to do such jobs, as a rule there were other, less well-off men ready to take them on.[102]

It is indicative of the army's character as a 'total institution' that this juxtaposition of 'masculine' active service outside and 'female' service in the barracks was not seen as contradictory.[103] The army not only tried to seal itself off and maintain its autonomy, it also read itself as a social microcosm, incorporating all the essential functions needed to survive and realising them without external help. Since this microcosm was only accessible to men, and should remain so, it follows that the men had to be involved in all those activities incumbent on women in the world outside. In a certain sense, they even became more masculine, asserting their independence and autonomy free from female assistance, pursuing a policy of 'Be a man and do it yourself'.[104]

It seemed so self-evident that the army was exclusively a male space, it was hardly ever questioned. In 1831, when the Bavarian officer Albert von Pappenheim published his 'military fantasies' suggesting that women should be drafted, he immediately qualified his proposal by saying they should be liable for a cash tax, not personal military service. Yet even in this watered-down form, the idea was totally ridiculed. The military journal *Allgemeine Militär-Zeitung* considered the notion 'unworkable' and pointed out that it endangered 'the benefits of the law for women'. More importantly, highlighting the damaging consequences for the army, it pointed out: 'Apart from any question of morals, more likely than not, the password would no longer be a secret.' It was not only women who had to be protected from the army; the army also, and above all, had to be protected from women.[105]

There was no support forthcoming either for Pappenheim's plea for 'the female sex' to be granted 'the same civic rights as the male'. The logic of the argument was clear, and had already played a key role in the debate on Jewish emancipation: if women are to fulfil every duty of a subject, they ought to be allowed to enjoy every subject's rights too. In 1838, Carl Welcker put forward a similar line of reasoning, although he came to a different conclusion. Welcker considered it completely inconceivable for women to be granted the same political rights as men, since, on principle, they were unable to perform military duties. The right to vote and take decisions in the civic community, he continued, presupposed that one was prepared to defend this community 'to the death', but women had always been prohibited from doing just this, their 'natural disposition' forbidding any sort of martial undertaking. After all, 'the physical nature of the stronger, braver, freer man' marked him 'as the active founder, master, bread-winner, and protector of the family, drives him into the external life to act outwardly and work, drives him into the fight for justice and the clash of arms'. In contrast, the 'weaker, more dependent and timid woman' was predestined 'to be the man's protégée' and had her place in 'the quieter hearth and home'.[106]

However, by no stretch of the imagination did this normative portrayal of gender relations find its parallel in reality. All contemporaries were well aware that courageous and spirited women existed who felt themselves to be anything but too weak and tender for 'male' battles and conflicts. The series of such 'Amazons' and 'heroic maidens' from the 1813–15 Wars of Liberation were still well known, their memory preserved during the *Vormärz* period (and beyond), although, simultaneously, care was taken to present them as exceptions and not as role models. The majority of people remained convinced that wars had to be fought by men; only when male protectors were lacking, or in an absolute emergency, were women allowed to take up arms themselves as, for example, Goethe's Dorothea did in days of old.[107]

But not all men were actually capable of playing the role of protector and defender of the fatherland. Welcker proved to be overly hasty in taking the basis of physical differences between the sexes to deduce a natural law prescribing differences in moral cognisance and attitudes to life. The 'male destiny' did not offer every man a foundation for 'greater boldness, manly courage and both physical and active valour'.[108] Military experts, especially, knew only too well that bravery in the face of the enemy was rare and, in most cases, had to be artificially stimulated. Decorations, like the Iron Cross for instance, were designed to reward and encourage imitation, while draconian punishments, fixed in martial law and familiar to every member of the ranks, were intended to intimidate and the rigid discipline and 'harnessing' to suffocate potential disputes.

The question of how men could learn courage was a constant theme running through military publications in the nineteenth century. A revealing answer, in more ways than one, was given by the author of an article published in 1829 'on courage, its causes and the means to instil it in soldiers'. The writer postulates passion as the principal cause of courage, distinguishing between four types: religious fanaticism; ambition; love of one's country; or passion for a woman one hopes to impress by bravery. The task of military training, therefore, is to 'set ablaze' just such passions in the troops. However, he continues, with religion now 'a matter of indifference' for the vast majority of people, religious fanaticism has run its course as the 'cheapest means' at any government's disposal, and since passion for a woman is solely effective with individuals, the only prime causes remaining are patriotism and ambition. However, he continues, the city republics in the ancient world and in Switzerland have shown patriotism to be linked to freedom and pride in citizenship; in monarchies, in contrast, the principal motive is the 'noble passion' of honour. Consequently, the goal must be to inflame such feelings in the ordinary soldier too, to allow this sentiment to act like the 'strongest spring', powering their courage and leading them on 'to victory'.[109] Irrespective of such passionate and passion-inducing causes, courage, for soldiers, was related equally to awareness of physical strength and the proper use of weapons – one reason why weapon use was practised especially intensively in the initial training phase.[110] Simultaneously, though, recruits learned that rather than the sabre, rifle and bayonet merely being the 'tools of the trade', they had a 'great patriotic significance', and should therefore be treated with 'a certain respect', while the soldiers 'ought to be proud of being allowed to use them'.[111]

In peacetime too, the military formed an 'armed' caste, with officers and soldiers always appearing armed in public – and even if civilians were scandalised, or landlords occasionally demanded that soldiers remove their swords, the army unwaveringly asserted the right to carry arms, arguing that 'public house brawls' took place without swords too, and under certain circumstances, table legs or stools could even be more dangerous. Wanting to deny the soldiers' right to their sabre was put on a par with emasculation, since 'bearing arms' was conducive to 'stimulating and maintaining the sensation of manly vigour'. 'The manly feeling of carrying a splendid weapon' belonged to a soldier's 'manliness'. In 1828, an officer expressed his extreme regret that the times no longer tolerated this sort of masculinity and instead intended to turn soldiers into 'refined civilians'. The next war, he believed, would demand something more from soldiers 'than those quiet civic virtues', though it was to be feared the 'nation's martial spirit would then be merely a historical memory, and the abandoned swords destroyed by rust'.[112]

For the soldier, then, the sword was intended as a constant reminder of his vocation to fight and win wars. It was, moreover, supposed to, literally as well as figuratively, keep in check any civilians criticising the military. The sabre marked its bearer as military personnel, a guarantor of security for the unarmed and hence defenceless civilian. But it equally reminded the citizens to show a suitable degree of respect to their protectors, and to treat them with suitable deference – acknowledging their social standing and granting them precedence. If such respect were found wanting, the soldier could use his sword to demand it. And indeed, conflicts with civilians were commonplace, generally for everyday reasons, but the use of the sabre gave them a special quality. Such disagreements were frequently due to women – hardly surprising in view of the ages of the men involved. There was nothing unusual about young, single men competing for women's favours at village or small town dances, or for such competition to end in scuffles. However, the presence of soldiers changed this traditional picture. Firstly, the soldiers appeared as a group and were immediately recognisable as such; consequently, from the very start, the fights always took the form of group conflicts. Behind every individual soldier making advances to a woman stood a group of his fellow-soldiers, and any civilian lover not wanting to have his dearest stolen by a soldier in uniform was sure to have his group of young lads behind him too. Secondly, youth culture in the *Vormärz* period was relatively closed, and the soldiers comprised a disturbing and disquieting element: in the towns, they were strangers who stayed only briefly, while their visits to the villages where they were quartered for the annual exercises were even shorter. Everywhere they entered into the fixed 'territory' that young men in the area were trying to divide and control among themselves. At that time, soldiers were exceptionally mobile, only comparable, if at all, with urban journeymen, and this allowed them to live out their erotic and sexual needs more freely, and with fewer attachments, than was normally the case. As was commonly observed, soldiers frequently followed the precept of 'another town, another girl'.[113]

Even in their songs, they portrayed themselves as libertines, to the 'delight' of some superiors, and the indignation of others concerned about 'military discipline' and the army's public image. In 1818, only a few soldier's songs were found to be 'heroic and poetic'; most contained 'immoral, indecent ideas, inciting debauchery and describing such scenes'.[114] Not every soldier took the maxims to heart that such songs praised, yet, nonetheless, their unfamiliar surroundings offered numerous inducements to what critics termed 'moral turpitude'. Older, more experienced fellow-soldiers had a significant influence, while relationships with women were certainly facilitated by the custom of quartering soldiers in private houses, due to the lack of available barracks.[115] The list of soldiers' duties implicitly dealt with such dangers, urging recruits to practise 'orderly' moral conduct and warning against 'dissoluteness' and 'profligacy'. First and foremost, this was understood to be the 'unbridled satiation of natural drives', an 'immoral impulse' that had a negative effect on the 'soldier's health' and filled the military hospitals – a veiled reference to sexually transmitted diseases, which, however, were only taken seriously, in both medical and military police terms, from the second half of the nineteenth century on.[116]

The unfamiliarity of the culture in the garrison experienced by most new recruits and the perils awaiting them in their new surroundings underlined the need to bind the young men firmly within the body of soldiers – another point where the modern conscription army differed from its predecessors. While soldiers in the eighteenth century, recruited under the canton system, generally spent only a few weeks a year with their regiment, the soldiers after 1814 were together for three or, later, two years of military service, excluding short periods of furlough. During this time, the aim, at least, was for the soldier to come to view the army as his new home, and see 'his superiors as his parents, and his fellow-soldiers as his brothers',[117] and the further away a soldier was from his hometown, the more important this seemed. Recruits were largely drawn from rural areas, and for them the garrison towns were like a foreign world. They were not conversant with the social manners in the towns where they were quartered, and even if they knew the dialect, there was much they did not understand.

This unfamiliarity was heightened if the regiment drew its recruits from a number of recruiting areas – as was the case in particular for those troops stationed in East Prussia, Upper Silesia and the province of Posen. These troops included men speaking Polish or Lithuanian and, what was more, mixed them with soldiers from within the 'old' Prussian borders. In other provinces, regiments were relocated from time to time, to counteract any tendency to become 'settled' and to ensure they were ready for military deployment. If Boyen, the first war minister, had had his way, all units would have been thoroughly mixed, with men from the Rhineland in Silesia, Silesians in Posen, and Polish soldiers in the Rhineland.[118] But Boyen was unable to push his ideas through against the king and his advisers who favoured keeping the custom, popular with everyone, of assigning particular recruiting areas to regiments. Such links were fixed for a longer period creating cross-generational long-term bonds, with the son serving in the same regiment as his father or grandfather, and had the added advantage of leaving recruits relatively close to their hometown, making it easier to fall back on family resources – an advantage not to be disdained given the recruits' paltry pay. Similarly, regional homogeneity appeared to encourage the troops' feelings of solidarity and their political reliability.

Boyen's plan to mix all recruits had one particular aim in mind: transforming the army into a 'national' organisation, where in place of local and regional identities, soldiers would take the entire state as the dominant point of reference. A soldier from the Königsberg area, for example, was to exercise alongside a fellow-soldier from Cologne or Westphalia, and discover they were all Prussians, despite worshipping in a different church, speaking a different dialect, or preferring dumplings to potatoes. On the one hand, the army ought to reflect the Prussian state in all its regional, religious, cultural and social diversity, yet, on the other hand, it should also overarch and minimise such diversity, recasting its 'students' into a uniform and uniformed mass.

Such 'recasting' was most systematic in the guards regiments, stationed in Berlin and Potsdam. They drew their recruits – around 12 per cent of all those enlisted – from all the Prussian provinces, providing they were large enough and with suitably 'appealing' looks. Mixing provinces entailed mixing the religious confessions, though, as Jewish men were not accepted into the guards until 1847, this initially affected only Catholics and Protestants. Under the 1832 Military Church Regulations (*Militärkirchenordnung*), the Catholics, though a clear minority, could only be required to attend a Catholic service. However, Friedrich Wilhelm III ordered the soldiers of both confessions to attend the Sunday worship in the Potsdam *Garnisonkirche* that preceded the regular 'Church Parade' where he personally reviewed the troops. He instructed the pastor 'to give a short sermon, and not to preach on controversies' and use an 'inoffensive litany', arguing that, ultimately, before battle every soldier prayed together for success and the sooner one could convince the Catholics that Protestants were also Christians, the better.[119]

His intervention indicates the central importance religion and the church had for the army. They not only paid for a (Protestant) chaplain-general and employed military pastors to provide spiritual guidance for the troops, but also ordered the men on guard to say a prayer at reveille and tattoo, and urged all soldiers to attend Sunday service at least once a month. In a similar vein, constant emphasis was placed on religion and piety as the 'fixed pillars of military training', which had to be 'maintained by discipline and made publicly visible'.[120] Conversely, the military exercised a substantial influence on the church and religion. The pervasive presence of religious references and practices in military routine could help counteract the erosion of links to the church which, it was claimed, had already been observed among the general population in the 1820s. However, rather than promoting all denominations equally, the army favoured the established church in Prussia. Despite an official policy allowing freedom of worship, there were repeated instances of commanders forbidding their soldiers to attend the services of free-thinkers. Also, Friedrich Wilhelm III's order that Catholic recruits attend a moderate Protestant service follows the same pattern, not only annoying Catholic representatives but simultaneously entrusting the army with yet another educational task that had implications in the social sphere: Catholics, under the inflammatory influence of their 'clerics', should come to recognise the validity of the New Testament for both Christian denominations and acknowledge that Protestants also believe in God. This experience would then resolve the accursed antagonism or, in stronger terms, the battle between the faiths, and promote unity, not just among the troops, but throughout the nation.[121]

Rather than just vouchsafing unity and harmony in religious matters, the modern Prussian conscription army was supposed to do the same across society too: men from a range of social backgrounds serving side by side should turn 'military service into a school of equality, awakening and nourishing a public spirit'.[122] In fact, it was only the Prussian army that did have recruits from well-to-do, middle-class families; in other German and European states, military service remained the province of the poor. Even if the number of volunteers in *Vormärz* Prussia remained far below the figures the authorities had hoped for, each company counted a few sons of merchants and civil servants among their troops, especially in university town garrisons. However, the conditions for middle-class and lower-class recruits in the army were far from equal. To begin with, because the one-yearer volunteer had to provide his own uniform, it was frequently better made and of better material; it also bore a distinctive feature – an epaulette – clearly identifying the wearer as a one-yearer. Such recruits tended neither to look after their clothes themselves, more often than not, paying a longer-serving soldier to take on the task, nor did they eat with the other troops, since they had to pay for their meals themselves; moreover, even when barracks were available, they lived in private quarters. Finally, as potential future *Landwehr* officers they received less drilling and, if they proved suitable, were soon entrusted with leadership tasks.

On the other hand, superior ranks did not always show such lenience in dealing with their middle-class subordinates, nor did they always treat them preferentially, and frequently they even drilled them especially mercilessly. From his own experience, Theodor Fontane reported how, in the 1840s, one-yearers were still ascribed a low 'military esteem' and frequently perceived as a 'burden', above all by NCOs.[123] In his memoirs, Rudolph Delbrück, too, recalled how, in 1841, he had to bribe his sergeant with alcohol to win him over. But, in turn, being able to buy relief increased the distance between the one-yearers and 'normal' recruits, and together with the much greater free time the former enjoyed, could lead to envy and antipathy.[124]

In short, despite equality and thorough mixing of recruits in principle, visible differences remained on the social, religious and regional fronts. Equality only really existed before the martial law that subjected all troops, no matter what their origin, to a strict order of discipline, prescribing ways of behaviour applicable across the board, and stipulating the requisite punishments for breaches of regulations. In addition to the terms specifically governing military matters – desertion, betrayal of military information, or cowardice in the face of the enemy – provisions also covered more general areas, requiring the soldier to lead 'an orderly life', to incur no debts or play games of chance, and refrain from 'drunkenness or other forms of dissoluteness'. Conscripts could not marry as they liked, but first had to obtain their commander's permission. The worst 'common', i.e., non-military, offence was considered theft and in case of reoccurrence the offender was punished by being 'drummed out of the regiment'.

The duty to unconditional obedience and comradeship lay at the heart of the code of behaviour defined under martial law. A superior's orders were to be obeyed 'promptly' and without protest. Relations with other soldiers, in turn, were to be marked by good comradeship, which meant above all, a soldier 'living in harmony with his fellow-soldiers', doing 'everything in his power to help them' and 'staying together in battle, need and danger'.[125] Admittedly, the notion of comradeship did not extend beyond borders of social class and rank: neither NCOs nor officers viewed the 'common' soldier as their comrade in arms. The response to libellous or defamatory behaviour, the 'point of honour' so crucial to the army, was differentiated along group-specific lines too. If a rank-and-file soldier felt insulted by another, he was not allowed to challenge him to a duel, since this was a privilege exclusively reserved for officers; but no officer would challenge an ordinary soldier who had insulted him to a duel any more than the soldier who felt his honour had been besmirched would send his second around to a captain to demand satisfaction. The officer corps may have regarded itself as a society of equals internally, so that a lieutenant could demand satisfaction from a general, and the troops felt themselves, despite all the apparent differences, to be 'comrades' all together, but between the groups there lay distinct, insurmountable barriers.[126]

5. Soldiers and Civilians – Soldiers as Citizens?

Accordingly, the army also formed a stratified society, only appearing unified and homogeneous when it presented itself to the outer, civilian world, when troops, NCOs and officers were united in their 'superior profession', in their noble, selfless, self-sacrificing service for king and country – which immediately distinguished them from civilian citizens, who merely indulged in their own 'private advantage'. The military man's commitment to the 'greater good of the state' may not have brought him riches, but it did assure him of his king's thanks and acknowledgement:[127] it brought him honour – a benefit not to be compensated for in monetary terms and that the 'common' soldier could rarely transform into cash, but which implied a preferential social ranking, placing all army personnel above civilians. Among officers, this status was expressed in the way every lieutenant, in principle, could be received at court while civilian public servants needed a far higher grade, but it was less obvious for the lower rank-and-file, as common soldiers frequently had to struggle hard to have it recognised, as is witnessed by the numerous brawls and violent attacks on record.

In many places, unruliness began with the mustering. Ordinary citizens continually complained about the young men's behaviour as they marched to the mustering location, accusing them of 'all manner of nonsense' and damaging of other people's property: they destroyed garden fences, knocked fruit from the trees, uprooted cabbages, broke beanpoles in half, turned over washing baskets, and set up 'a great cry'. In addition, soldiers billeted on civilians frequently behaved in a 'beastly' way towards their hosts, taking freedoms underlining their claim to a special status. They insisted on their right to be called to account only by their military superiors and resisted, by force of arms, any attempts by the local police to discipline them.[128] An incident in Westphalia in 1849 showed how strong the soldiers' sense of power was and the function it could have: a farmer was ordered to take the luggage of twenty-four *Landwehr* reserves from Paderborn to Rietberg, but when he refused to allow the men on his horse-cart as well, they set about abusing him, verbally and physically.

This case indicates how quickly civilians turned into soldiers, adopting both a military viewpoint and army manners. The called-up reserves had also been civilians prior to receiving the call-up orders although they may not have been exactly glad to be mustered since, in the troubled times around 1848, there was no telling where they would be deployed and when they would be discharged again. But they took it out on the wagoner, who had not been enlisted. This might have reflected class tensions: the 'gentleman farmer' with his horse-cart belonged to the agricultural middle or upper class, while the reserves were primarily farmhands or tied cottagers, and hence members of the rural lower class. Military status, though, provided the reserves with an effective means of evading the hierarchies of civilian life and even overturning them completely. The farmer's protests and the public sequel to the conflict also proved, however, that civilians were not prepared to tolerate such high-handedness. When the regional newspaper, the *Westfälische Zeitung*, published a 'public rebuke', provoking an official inquiry into the incident, it set clear limits on the military's claim to superiority.[129] While a growing number of citizens proved increasingly willing to live at peace with the standing army, they were not prepared to accept any behaviour from military personnel – and the fact that, as the Rhenish banker Beckerath phrased it in 1848, 'our sons, our brothers' were serving in the army allowed them to take a critical view of this 'thoroughly popular institution'.[130]

But this institution was allergic to criticism. Whether the issue at stake was the extent of military funding, or civilian reservations about military law, the Prussian army was not to be moved. From the army perspective, its actions were entirely legitimate, merely putting into practise the key idea behind an *esprit de corps*: unconditional loyalty and internal solidarity, founded on radical encapsulation from civilian society. Nor did it matter that such complaints were less common and milder in Prussia than in the constitutional states in southern Germany. The military, as was repeatedly stated, followed its own laws and regulations; these had to be accepted 'outside' and could never be revised by reference to the civic model.

This claim to autonomy, though, severely hampered every attempt actually to transform the army into a 'popular institution'. For the officer corps, autonomy was vital: it secured their power base and the operational availability of the troops, who, they believed, required iron discipline and the deterrent of harsh punishments. 'Military discipline' was particularly crucial in a conscript army: after all, every year the army was equipping tens of thousands of young men with instruments of violence and teaching them how to use them properly. Soldiers dealt with sabres, bayonets and rifles on an everyday basis – and they even wore their sabres when not on duty. As both officers and civilians knew, this represented an accumulation of potential violence that needed to be firmly checked and kept within defined boundaries; the latter group, too, clearly saw the inherent political dangers deriving from men's widespread skills in the use of weapons. In 1840, for example, David Hansemann warned that the Prussian army statutes were gradually kindling an awareness 'of their power' among 'the lower classes' and, consequently, they were a prime 'democratic force'.[131] In southern Germany, where troops were only recruited from the 'scum of society', contemporary observers feared the unpropertied classes, who could use weapons, would rise against the rich, who could not. The only remedy lay in the 'power of discipline' and an *esprit de corps*, specific to the army, insulating it from the civilian population and their ambitions.[132]

Innumerable instances where the Prussian regular army was deployed internally during the *Vormärz* period testify to their success in producing and sustaining this spirit.[133] The soldiers did not hesitate to combat political or social unrest; any hint of class solidarity evaporated under the systematically practised following of orders, even though the soldiers frequently came from the same social strata as the people on the other side of the fixed bayonets. Not surprisingly, the liberal democrat perspective saw the soldiers as supporting the 'absolutist system'. In 1848, Leue, the Cologne representative in the Frankfurt National Assembly, harvested ready 'approval from the middle and the left' when he observed that the people 'have learnt over the last 33 years that the army, instead of protecting them against external enemies, has frequently been deployed to suppress civic freedoms and been employed against the citizens themselves'.[134]

As far as the army was concerned, the education based on harsh discipline and military encapsulation had borne fruit – and proved to be stable even under the conditions prevailing in 1848–9. Some revolutionaries hoped the soldiers would see themselves as citizens and turn their weapons away from their fellow citizens, but such hopes remained unfulfilled, whether in Berlin, Mainz or Rastatt, and this despite a mass of broadsheets and newspaper articles, primarily by democrats, setting out to solicit the soldiers' good will, proffering the 'hand of brotherhood'. Soldiers and NCOs garrisoned in Berlin publicly denounced a brotherhood 'demanding a price as high as perjury and treason'; the military oath, especially, pledged them to allegiance to the king personally and obliged them to stay away from any opposition movements critical of the monarchy. Officers and the war ministry civil servants did their utmost to support the rank-and-file, starting a major ideological and political offensive attacking efforts to fraternise. The extremely successful propaganda campaign bolstering discipline, buttressing the loyalty of the troops, and mobilising them against the alleged enemies of the king ran under the slogan 'Only soldiers help against democrats'.[135]

Simply because soldiers were active in maintaining the prevailing order, though, did not mean they were uninterested in reforms. The democrats' broadsheets or speakers were best able to gain influence over the troops when they examined the soldiers' concrete concerns and promised to follow a 'legal path' to change. Indeed, in 1848, the voices calling for better food, more pay, increased furlough, and easier service became steadily more vociferous. Although soldiers were not allowed to present petitions or attend political gatherings, they found other ways and means to make their discontent and wishes known.[136] The complaints emerging in the public sphere in 1848 made a mockery of all official accounts of soldiers being well off in their regiment, with nourishing food, a suitable wage, and a physically beneficial rhythm of exercise, though simultaneously it became obvious that, despite the grievances, the army was unified and did function. There were no successful attempts to trigger mutinies or initiate mass desertions among regular soldiers. The *esprit de corps*, the force of discipline and the ideological lines that officers sharply accentuated, guaranteed deployment of troops wherever needed. The normal friction with civilians, mutual insults and scorn raised the soldiers' levels of aggression when occupying territory, storming the barricades or securing the public peace.[137] However, it was just in 1848–9 when the expectation of being treated with special respect and preference in public was being taken less seriously than usual that many soldiers adopted a hard confrontational course.

The troops remained totally untouched by the changes in military policy called for during the 1848 period. Nowhere among the list of complaints compiled by the Prussian regular army rank-and-file in 1848 was there any mention of swearing allegiance to the constitution instead of the king, voting in officers, or dissolving military academies, as the Frankfurt and Berlin National Assemblies demanded; hardly any of the soldiers could understand why they should swear obedience and loyalty to a piece of paper instead of the flesh and blood of their sovereign monarch. As far as those immediately affected were concerned, liberal and democrat interests in fundamentally altering the standing of the military in society and state remained an external concern, and this too, as Friedrich Wilhelm IV gratefully noted in 1849, also proved the success of a military training in inculcating 'total loyalty' and 'total obedience'.[138] In 1852, the head of the Königsberg police confirmed that 'the military's condition' provides 'a universal basis for patriotism and loyalty to the crown'; the soldiers were markedly less likely to have democratic tendencies than the part of the population which were far removed from the military sphere.[139] Moreover, the fear of universal conscription posing a danger to the monarchical system proved to be unfounded during the period of the 1848 revolutions. Despite the close links between the army and civil society and the relatively short period of service, the young recruits had apparently been successfully shaped into obedient soldiers and shielded against political influences from society.

But even if the 1848–9 revolution provides a wealth of material documenting how efficiently obedience and education functioned in the Prussian regular army, this says nothing about the long-term effects of such a socialisation. At best, one can find evidence of this among the army reserves and *Landwehr* reserves, who generally had spent several years serving in the regular army before returning to civil life and being recalled in 1848. However, their behaviour does not form a single, unified picture. In 1848, large cities such as, for example, Berlin and Breslau, saw the formation of both democratic and conservative *Landwehr* associations. While the former were calling for 'free elections of officers' and abandoning familiar forms of address to soldiers, which they found demeaning, the latter wanted 'to effect the maintenance of law and reason under the *Landwehr*'.[140] Many of the mobilised and active *Landwehr* battalions in the provinces of Posen, Saxony, Brandenburg, Pomerania, and Silesia in 1848 functioned perfectly, and the Prussian king personally thanked all of those 'brave *Landwehr* men', 'happily' leaving 'house and home, wife and child' behind, to re-establish law and order in the fatherland.[141] On the other hand, during mobilisation in November 1848 and spring 1849, there were instances of unrest and political opposition, especially in the Rhineland and Westphalia. In May 1849, for example, in Elberfeld, regular army troops were deployed to bring to reason the *Landwehr* reserves who were refusing 'to use their arms against their relatives and struggles for freedom'.[142]

In the same period, Kayser, a Prussian major and commander of a Westphalian *Landwehr* battalion, had to use brute force to get his troops into uniform, put them through their paces and set them marching off to the south, where he intended them to fight those insurgents and soldiers in Baden and the Palatinate endeavouring to defend their new republican governments against the Prussian and imperial troops called upon by the princes as they fled. Despite 'democratic agitators' and 'false heroes of freedom' inciting Kayser's *Landwehr* men to 'excesses' and desertion, they proved, after initial difficulties, to be disciplined and loyal in skirmishes, showing no solidarity at all with the republican troops. This was less a result of political differences, and more due to the feeling of foreignness. As Kayser knew, 'the most effective measure against loose discipline' was

> removal from the home district; nothing works better to stop dangerous fraternising between soldiers and civilians than taking the troop to an area with a different religion than the majority of them follow; and if there are a few instances of insignificant brawls [with civilians] which give no cause for excessive countermeasures, you can then be absolutely certain of the troop's reliability.[143]

The events of 1848–9 underlined the validity of Kayser's experience. The *Landwehr* men in their home area, surrounded by a range of political influences and interests, were frequently reluctant to obey the call to arms. Few were thrilled by the prospect of being separated from their families and work for an undefined period and being detailed to garrison a distant province, or even foreign states. After years on furlough under the conditions in the army reserves or *Landwehr*, the grip of the army they had known during their regular service had loosened. Only troop relocation could neutralise the gravitational pull of their civilian lives and reassert military discipline, and only then did the troops perceive themselves as soldiers again, obeying their superior officer's orders and avoiding fraternisation with civilians.[144]

In other words, army training did not always turn recruits into vassals loyal to the king and the higher authorities for the rest of their lives, and even if a recruit's interest was awoken in military concerns and ways of thinking, this did not automatically and inevitably entail adopting the corresponding political attitudes, as the example of Friedrich Engels demonstrates so well. Son of a Wuppertal factory owner, Engels served as a one-year volunteer in a Berlin Artillery Guards regiment in 1841-2, an experience that made a deep impression on him. For example, in June 1842, while still serving, he was engaged in an exchange of letters with the writer Arnold Ruge, who mistakenly addressed Engels as 'Herr Doctor' and was corrected in no uncertain terms: 'By the way, I am not a doctor and can never become one. I am a businessman and a Royal Prussian Artillerist.' In later life, in both politics and his writings, Engels kept this dual identity; he wrote easily and knowledgeably on military topics and, in so doing, felt himself 'still so much a soldier' that he often gave greater weight to military achievements than to political considerations, as is evident in his commentaries on the Crimean War and the Prussian constitutional conflict. Yet, at the same time, his service in a Prussian guards regiment hardly turned him into a conservative monarchist. Whether in his role as adjutant in a Palatinate volunteer regiment in 1849 or as a socialist politician, he remained a citizen actively participating in 'progress' and the 'century's advancement'.[145]

Friedrich Engels belongs to the very few men from the first half of the nineteenth century who have left us direct evidence of their military experience. Undoubtedly, other soldiers similarly wrote letters home, but, in most cases, they have been lost or destroyed. Contemporary memoirs mentioning military service are rare too and, if they exist at all, come exclusively from middle-class writers. For that reason, it is impossible to say what impressions army service left on men from the lower classes, or what their experiences, observations and opinions were. Nonetheless, one can safely assume these were richer and more varied than the ones army critics and apologists have attributed to them, and their views would neither have emerged as paeans of praise to the military and their own 'magnificent profession', nor have merely painted military service as a burden to be tolerated, where it was just a question of 'sitting out one's time'. Even if soldiers did keep a calendar crossing off 'another day down' on the way to their discharge, this does not mean that they simply wiped two or three years out of their lives.[146] It is hardly conceivable that they found the army solely a time of *ennui*, and that the experience left no mark at all; for that, it was too long a time, too different and too intensive. Furthermore, former soldiers were given sufficient opportunities afterwards actively to recall military service – whether through the cycle of *Landwehr* exercises, celebrations and jubilees, or at regular Sunday meetings in the local tavern.

Engels's entertaining letters to his sister Marie give a ready insight into his experience and feelings. He does not seem to have suffered at all during his year's service in a respected Berlin Guards regiment. Instead, he appears to have enjoyed it as a welcome break in his commercial training and work. In comparison with the 'common' soldier, he certainly lived a life of luxury, with his own valet, who cleaned and catered for him, elegant private rooms, and meals of his favourite 'regional specialities' taken at a Rhenish restaurant. He does not seem to have been over-taxed, either, by his daily tasks, although he did find exercises irksome and unnecessary. However, they took so little time in total that he saw no further need to comment on them.

Engels spent his generous portions of leisure time investigating life in Berlin. He habitually wore his uniform while visiting theatres, concerts, and reading-rooms, or attending lectures at Berlin University, and felt very well in it; in fact, when he described it in a letter to his sister, he became quite enthused: 'By the way, my uniform is very attractive, blue with a black collar, with two wide yellow stripes on it, and with black, yellow-striped lapels and red-lined coat-tails. Then come the red shoulder epaulettes with white edges, and, believe me, the effect is magnificent.' And he tried out the effect straight away on civilians, describing, half-seriously, half-impishly, how he had driven a lecturer 'distraught' with his uniform: 'While he was lecturing, I was sitting directly in front of him and the poor chap couldn't take his eyes off my shiny buttons and completely lost the thread of what he wanted to say.' But Engels too seems to have succumbed to the effects of external symbols as well: in a letter to Marie, he proudly recounted how he had been promoted to an NCO, with the rank clearly worn on the uniform. 'By the way, I've been a corporal for four weeks, and am wearing the stripes and braiding and the blue collar with red trimmings.' His new rank did not merely provide new decorations, but gave him a different standing of honour and right to command. As he wrote, being a corporal 'allows me to order around all the common soldiers in the entire Prussian army, and all of the common soldiers have to salute me'. Evidently, Engels enjoyed this prominent status that distanced him from the bulk of the troops and edged him closer to the officer corps. He encountered his superior officers with a mixture of outward respect and inward equanimity. However, he has nothing to say about the rest of the regiment's recruits, not even in a humorous anecdote.

In contrast, in his autobiographical sketches written fifty years later, Theodor Fontane at least remembers the other one-yearers serving at the same time as him, in 1844–5, in the three battalions of the Berlin *Kaiser-Franz-Regiment*, referring to the 'comrades' he shared guard duty with, while the rest of the regiment was out on manoeuvres. Later, as an NCO starting to give orders, he became aware of the 'rank-and-file', describing the 'chaps' as 'easy to handle', and, in the guardroom, letting them 'tell all kinds of stories from their hometowns'. The difference in military rank here, though, only went to underline the social gap between Fontane, the apothecary and budding writer, and the ordinary ranks, preventing any relationship of real comradeship, let alone friendship. Fontane preferred to spend his time with young officers, who took him to a literary club, and inspired him to write 'patriotic' poems about Prussian war heroes.[147]

Rudolph Delbrück similarly does not appear to have sought contact with the 'common' soldier. Prior to his military service, he had spent his time exclusively with students, higher civil servants and officers. Moreover, at 24, he was older than the majority of soldiers. He had already finished his studies in law, taken his second set of law exams and spent two years working as an articled clerk for the Merseburg authorities. In other words, he came from a world far beyond the horizon of experience shared by his 'fellow soldiers'. His age and education also separated him from the youthful and boyish Friedrich Engels, whose one year of service was in the same regiment at the same time. But rather than strolling down Berlin's Unter den Linden boulevard and showing off his uniform, Delbrück used his year in the army to prepare for his exam as a junior judge, which he passed brilliantly in June 1842. Military service, in his case, was far from being a welcome break, or offering a period to defer key decisions on the direction of his life. Instead, it forced itself unwanted into the precisely prescribed sequence of steps in Delbrück's education on the road to the higher civil service.

Originally, Delbrück planned to become a professional officer, even as a child, though later, when he wrote his memoirs, he could no longer remember the reasons why: 'It might have been the pull of military fame that Berlin and Potsdam exercised, or perhaps the splendid uniform that dazzled my eyes as a boy, or possibly it was the thought of protecting the crown prince' – whose teacher, in the early years of the nineteenth century, had been Delbrück's father himself. Even after Delbrück had finished his secondary school education, he still intended to pursue his plans for the army, but an uncle persuaded him 'that completing a university degree first would be beneficial for a military career'. It was only when he reached the end of his studies that he finally gave up the idea and settled on public administration as his future vocation.

To put his 'military circumstances' in order first, in 1841 Delbrück entered the 12th Berlin Artillery Guards regiment, choosing the artillery because 'service with this weapon was considered less time-consuming than the infantry'. His limited funds would not allow him to join the cavalry, and, in any case, the barracks were 'conveniently situated'. Delbrück's father was a friend of the commander, 'and so I was assured of all consideration possible, especially because I immediately explained when asked that I had no intention of taking the officer's exam, which at that time was not yet obligatory'. In so doing, Delbrück broke completely with his childhood dream; even if the exam would not have helped him to become a regular army officer, it would at least have assisted him in becoming a *Landwehr* officer, and allowed him to wear the uniform that had so dazzled him as a boy. Since he decided against it, he obviously did not believe it would benefit his career; at that time, a higher-ranking civil servant did not yet need to have a rank as a *Landwehr* officer.

Delbrück completed his service as a one-year volunteer correctly, but without enthusiasm or enjoyment. He must have performed his duties adequately, since, like Engels, he was also promoted to corporal. Nevertheless, he did not find military service easy – since he already knew 'what time is worth', the hours spent in the barrack yard or exercise yard, or at the shooting range in the north of Berlin, seemed to be 'a total loss for my life'. He would have considered it infinitely more sensible if he could have bought himself out, as was possible in the southern German states. He acknowledged the 'justification' of the Prussian military system 'solely in the abstract principle of equality before the law', which would not allow for substitution by monetary payment or provision of another recruit.[148]

Delbrück's reasoning combines the experience and attitudes of his time and society. Even in the 1840s, thirty years after the new 'revolutionary' army structure had been introduced in Prussia, many citizens still believed that they – or their sons – were actually out of place in the army. The further the glorified, mythical 1813–15 campaigns slid into the past, the more the awareness of being truly useful in defending the fatherland became dulled. The long period of peace was trying not only for officers: among civilians, it awoke and reinforced doubts about funding the upkeep of an expensive army, and about the need for personal military service, which seemed a sheer waste of resources.

This defensive position was hardly dented by the alternative views that the military disseminated. Since many officers were sceptical about political and educational notions of upgrading the army into the 'nation's training school', the question of how far it was the military service's mission to benefit the whole of society remained unresolved. Other attempts by some military reformers, such as Boyen, to turn military service into the basis for citizenship had also come to nothing. As far as commonly held beliefs were concerned, the duty of army service was demanded from subjects, not from citizens. Jewish men alone considered military service a national duty and a proof of active citizenship, and protested vigorously against any attempt to exclude them from it.

In contrast, in non-Jewish circles, after massive initial protests and public shows of resistance, a more pragmatic approach set in to the new 'body tax'. Once it became clear that the authorities refused to give way and insisted on this tax being paid, people applied the strategy of dealing with the conditions on a case-by-case basis, fully utilizing whatever leeway existed; here, urban inhabitants showed greater flexibility and inventiveness than the rural population. There were ever fewer cases of total and collective refusal based, for example, on old rights to exemption or the claim to being essential for the state; and as the draft became less rigorously imposed in practice, such tactics appeared increasingly superfluous. In the 1830s and 1840s, the chances of any young Prussian man actually performing military service were less than one in ten.

If individuals welcomed a more relaxed policy on enlistment as a means of pursuing their own interests, such practices also violated the abstract principle of equality embodied in the statutes governing the Prussian army, and indeed, the fact that a small proportion of the male population bore the burden of military service, while the majority effectively went free, was a constant bone of contention. As early as 1817–18, Prussian provincial governors had pointed to this asymmetry as the cause of massive discontent with the new recruiting system. In 1843, with notoriously low recruiting figures, the Prussian and Westphalian provincial estates petitioned the king again to ensure more equality in conscription, since the low draft quota made it difficult to anchor 'the sentiment of a moral obligation to military service' in the general population.[149] Apparently, the conscription law's rhetoric of equality had firmly taken root, with many seeming to believe that only maximum inclusion could redress the gradual erosion in legitimacy and lift military service to the unquestioned duty of every male citizen of honour – the very status it had been asserting since its introduction.

Notes

1. *Historische Zeitschrift*, vol. 67, 1891, p. 55; vol. 70, 1893, p. 284.
2. Dittmar, *Heeres-Ergänzung*, pp. 1 ff.; *Preußische Landwehr*, pp. 21 ff. The period of service was later altered (apart from the Guards); from 1820 to 2½ years for infantry and from 1833 to 2 years; in a parallel move, the period for service in the reserves was increased from 2 to 2½ or 3 years. Soldiers in the cavalry had to serve for 4 years. In proportional terms, the numbers serving in the infantry, cavalry and artillery were 76:14:10. Twelve per cent of all soldiers joined Guards Regiments. (Dieterici, *Mittheilungen*, pp. 325–64, primarily p. 363).
3. *Preußische Landwehr*, p. 61; Jany, *Geschichte*, vol. 4, p. 154; *Historische Zeitschrift*, vol. 67, 1891, p. 75.
4. The only exceptions were princes of the royal house and sons of the mediatized princes, who were exempt from military duties in all states in the German Confederation. In addition, the Mennonites primarily settled in East and West Prussia continued to be exempt in line with the canton exemption originally granted to them in the eighteenth century; however, they had to pay a form of military tax. The few Mennonites living in other Prussian provinces were

similarly able to attain an exemption but were required to pay an annual tax, In addition, they were prohibited from acquiring any further land and were not accepted into the state civil service. (Dittmar, *Heeres-Ergänzung*, pp. 1–2).

5. Dittmar, *Heeres-Ergänzung*, p. 245.
6. Verfügung dated 30.09.1819, in Dittmar, *Heeres-Ergänzung*, p. 19.
7. Dittmar, *Heeres-Ergänzung*, pp. 84 ff.
8. Dittmar, *Heeres-Ergänzung*, p. 6.
9. Meinecke, *Leben*, vol. 1, p. 418.
10. *Allgemeine Militär-Zeitung*, Year 1, 1826, Columns 196, 203. The second reserves were planned specifically for men from the *Landwehr* between 33 and 40. This service, though, actually existed only on paper, since the military exercises they were supposed to take part in had not taken place since 1820 due to lack of funds. The same applied to the *Landsturm* (last reserves), originally intended for the men between 40 and 50, but this plan was similarly never implemented.
11. Hansen, *Briefe*, vol. 1, p.73–4 (Hansemann); Mürmann, *Meinung*; Pinkow, *Kampf*.
12. See the numerous petitions and correspondence from 1815–19 in GStA Berlin-Dahlem, Rep. 74 H IX Stände 3, vol. II; O.O. Nr. 4, vol. I; O.P. Nr. 8; Rep. 77 Tit. 332 t, Nr. 16, 40, 47; Tit. 332 l, Nr. 6, vol. II.
13. GStA Berlin-Dahlem, Rep. 74 H II, Generalia Nr. 14: Denkschrift der Oberpräsidenten dated 30.6.1817 and subsequent individual reports 1818; Lüdtke, "Wehrhafte Nation", primarily pp. 14 ff.
14. GStA Berlin-Dahlem, Rep. 74 O.P. Nr. 8: Kriegs- und Innenminister dated 23.6.1818; Hardenberg dated 24.3.1818.
15. GStA Berlin-Dahlem, O.O. Nr. 4, vol. I: Posener Regierung dated 25.10.1816; O.Y. Nr. 10: Aachener Militärgouverneur v. Dobschütz dated 7.6 and 29.8.1815.
16. GStA Berlin-Dahlem, O.O. Nr. 4, vol. II: v. Schuckmann dated 8.8.1822; O.P. Nr. 8: Aachener Bericht dated 15.12.1817.
17. GStA Berlin-Dahlem, O.P. Nr. 8: Ingersleben dated 22.4.1818; HStA Düsseldorf, Reg. Köln Nr. 1691: Wipperfürther Landrat dated 14.5.1819; Dittmar, *Heeres-Ergänzung*, pp. 77–8. On the quite frequent attempts at bribery and misrepresentation see also StA Detmold, M1 IC Nr. 20; HStA Düsseldorf, Reg. Köln Nr. 1718 and 1719.
18. From 1839 on, the town councillors, who voted in the civilian members, were also allowed to elect burghers without property – a measure facilitating the election of state civil servants onto urban recruiting commissions. Previously, the industrial middle classes were the prime group represented there (Dittmar, *Heeres-Ergänzung*, p. 66). In addition to the *Landrat* and four civilian members, the local recruiting commissions included three officers and an army doctor.

19. GStA Berlin-Dahlem, Rep. 74 O.O. Nr. 4, vol. I: Friedrich Wilhelm III. dated 19.4.1817; H II, Nr. 8 Niederrhein: Pestel/Ruppenthal dated 18.1.1818; O.P. Nr. 8: Kölner Regierung dated 1.4.1818.
20. HStA Düsseldorf, Reg. Köln Nr. 1691: Kölner Regierung dated 22.6.1819.
21. StA Detmold, M1 IC Nr. 57: Instruction dated 19.5.1816.
22. GStA Berlin-Dahlem, Rep. 74 O.O. Nr. 4, vol. II: Kabinettsordre dated 14.3.1819; Berliner Magistrat dated 17.7.1822; Rep. 74 H II, Nr. 8 Niederrhein: Pestel/Ruppenthal dated 10.1.1818.
23. GStA Berlin-Dahlem, Rep. 74 O.O. Nr. 4, vol. II: v. Schuckmann dated 8.8.1822; O.P. Nr. 8: Kölner Regierung dated 1.4.1818; Rep. 74 H II, Nr. 8 Niederrhein: Pestel/Ruppenthal dated 10.1.1818.
24. Ibid; StA Detmold, M1 IC Nr. 17: Minden government dated 16.11.1818; HStA Düsseldorf, Reg. Köln Nr. 1724: Aachen government dated 8.8.1819.
25. Dittmar, *Heeres-Ergänzung*, pp. 387 ff.
26. C.v.W., *Denkschrift*, pp. 12, 36. It is not possible to say what statistical relationship existed between those entitled to one year of service and the one-yearers actually serving in the *Vormärz* period; the figures for this comparison are only available from the 1860s. In 1862, the percentage was 12.4% (Engel, 'Institut', p. 249).
27. Dittmar, *Heeres-Ergänzung*, pp. 594–5, 345, 349, 353; StA Detmold, M1 IC Nr. 30: Decree dated 22.5.1854.
28. Dittmar, *Heeres-Ergänzung*, pp. 395–6; Dieterici, *Mittheilungen*, pp. 327–8; Stenographische Berichte, vol. 3, 1863, p. 632; Zunkel, *Unternehmer*, p. 114.
29. GStA Berlin-Dahlem, Rep. 77 Tit. 332 t, Nr. 26, vol. I: Koblenz and Köln provincial governors dated 21/30.8.1818; Altenstein dated 20.8.1818; Dittmar, *Heeres-Ergänzung*, pp. 95 ff.
30. Dittmar, *Heeres-Ergänzung*, pp. 96–7, 102–3, 106, 418 ff.
31. GStA Berlin-Dahlem, Rep. 77 Tit. 332 t, Nr. 65: Kabinettsordre dated 24.10.1834. In 1862, the requirement of enlisting for a nine-year period of service was lifted.
32. HStA Düsseldorf, Reg. Aachen Nr. 1426 and 1428: Lists of voluntary three-yearers from 1860, 1861, 1865, 1866. We can assume the social profile was similar in the *Vormärz* period.
33. StA Detmold, M1 IC Nr. 57: Minden government dated 15.12.1829.
34. In 1820, a royal command was issued obliging all urban administrative authorities to fill all the lower civil service posts with men enjoying such entitlements – which led to increasingly vociferous protests from the cities, but no change in policy (*Sammlung sämmtlicher Drucksachen*, vol. 1, 1860, Nr. 27, pp. 1 ff.). Compare Helmert, *Militärsystem*, pp. 75–6; Messerschmidt, 'Militär', pp. 57 ff.

35. Dieterici, *Mittheilungen*, pp. 327–8, 342 ff.; HStA Düsseldorf, Reg. Köln Nr. 1691: Köln government dated 22.6.1819.
36. HStA Düsseldorf, Reg. Köln Nr. 1691: Wipperfürther Landrat dated 14.5.1819; GStA Berlin-Dahlem, Rep. 74, H II, Generalia Nr. 14: Denkschrift der Oberpräsidenten dated 30.6.1817.
37. Jany, *Geschichte*, vol. 4, p. 154; only 46 per cent of *Landwehr* infantry had previously served in the line army. Lüdtke, "Wehrhafte Nation", pp. 13, 23 ff.
38. GStA Berlin-Dahlem, Rep. 74 O.P. Nr. 8: Cleve government dated 3.6.1818.
39. GStA Berlin-Dahlem, O.Y. Nr. 11: Breslauer Regierung dated 21, 24 and 30.8.1817; Generalleutnant v. Hünerbein dated 23.8.1817; regional governor dated 27.8.1817.
40. *Allgemeine Militär-Zeitung*, Year 8, 1833, Column 784. In villages, such plaques were attached to the outermost village houses.
41. At least, that was the opinion of General von Müffling in 1821, who simultaneously 'professed his faith' in the *Landwehr* (*Historische Zeitschrift*, vol. 70, 1893, p. 285). On the criticism coming from conservative officers see Schmidt, *Landwehr*, pp. 117, 124 ff.
42. HStA Düsseldorf, Reg. Köln Nr. 1691: Bonn *Landrat* dated 8.8.1818. At the end of the 1850s, on average, every second *Landwehr* reserve was married; in the first year age-group it was 30%, in the fifth 46% and in the seventh 63% (*Stenographische Berichte*, vol. 5, 1860, p. 1226; *Stenographische Berichte*, vol. 3, 1863, p. 635).
43. GStA Berlin-Dahlem, Rep. 77 Tit. 332 p, Nr. 10: Journal article by the Arnsberg government dated July 1842; Schmidt, *Landwehr*, pp. 220–1.
44. GStA Berlin-Dahlem, Rep. 77 Tit. 332 p, Nr. 10: Dr Lievin dated 25.7.1840. His argument proved unsuccessful.
45. GStA Berlin-Dahlem, Rep. 77 Tit. 332 l, Nr. 10, 2.2.1. Nr. 32110: Extract from the 7th Westphalian *Landtag* adjournment dated 30.12.1843; *Preußische Landwehr*, pp. 48 ff.
46. GStA Berlin-Dahlem, Rep. 74 O.Y. Nr. 10: Kabinettsordre dated 12.12.1818 and 18.10.1817.
47. *Militair-Wochenblatt*, Nr. 73, 1817, p. 364.
48. *Militair-Wochenblatt*, Nr. 39, 1817, pp. 91–2; Nr. 63, 1817, pp. 284–5; Nr. 105, 1818, pp. 620–1.
49. *Militair-Wochenblatt*, Nr. 80, 1818, pp. 422–3.
50. *Militair-Wochenblatt*, Nr. 110, 1818, p. 663; Nr. 80, 1818, p. 420.
51. *Militair-Wochenblatt*, Nr. 110, 1818, p. 663; Nr. 154, 1819, p. 1013. Similar reports appeared continuously from 1819 on. *The Allgemeine Militär-Zeitung* interpreted these cosmetic touches as a sign that 'the nation has taken the insitution of the *Landwehr* to its heart' (Nr. 10, 1829, Column 76).

52. Brändli, "Offizieren".
53. Dittmar, *Heeres-Ergänzung*, pp. 153–5.
54. GStA Berlin-Dahlem, Rep. 77 Tit. 332 1, Nr. 10: Oppeln government dated 24.7.1816; Koblenz government dated 13.1.1818.
55. GStA Berlin-Dahlem, Rep. 77 Tit. 332 1, Nr. 10: Kriegsminister v. Hake dated 30.4.1825.
56. GStA Berlin-Dahlem, Rep. 77 Tit. 332 1, Nr. 10, 2.2.1. Nr. 32108: Instruction by Friedrich Wilhelm III dated 10.12.1816 (and the following quote).
57. StA Detmold, M1 IC Nr. 75: Kriegsminister dated 16.7.1857; Eifert, *Paternalismus*, pp. 167–8.
58. *Allgemeine Militär-Zeitung*, Nr. 83, 1831, Column 661.
59. GStA Berlin-Dahlem, 2.2.1. Nr. 32108: Instruktion 1816.
60. HStA Düsseldorf, Reg. Köln Nr. 1692: Daily order by von Hake dated 4.8.1818.
61. HStA Düsseldorf, Reg. Köln, Nr. 1722: Correspondence between Sayn-Wittgenstein, the minister for public safety, and the Cologne government 1816, Kabinettsordre dated 31.5.1838. The fierce debates in the first united *Landtag* in 1847 showed that the military-civil conflict over criteria for felonies had not yet been resolved (Frevert, *Men of Honour*, pp. 37 ff.).
62. GStA Berlin-Dahlem, Rep. 74 O.Y. Nr. 10: Thile dated 21.1.1816.
63. *Preußische Landwehr*, pp. 96–7.
64. Johanning, *Vorgänge*, pp. 100 ff., 63, 55, 57–8, 52.
65. Johanning, *Vorgänge*, pp. 63, 110–11.
66. *Stenographische Berichte*, vol. 3, 1863, p. 634.
67. StA Detmold, M1 IC Nr. 73: Vincke dated 12.6.1837.
68. Harkort, *Zeiten*; Trox, *Konservativismus*, pp. 43 ff., and also 'Kriegerfeste'.
69. Hansen, *Briefe*, vol. 1, p. 73 (Hansemann 1830); *Allgemeine deutsche Real-Encyclopädie für die gebildeten Stände*, 6. Aufl., vol. 9, Leipzig 1824, pp. 221–223.
70. Welcker, *Anhang*, pp. 592–3, 597–8; *Verhandlungen der Stände-Versammlung*, 4. Beilagenheft, 1831, p. 38. See Chapter 3.3 as a comparison.
71. GStA Berlin-Dahlem, Rep. 77 Tit. 332 t, Nr. 4, vol. II: Denkschrift v. Bodelschwingh dated 15.9.1845.
72. Dohm, *Verbesserung*, T. 2, pp. 223, 237; Mendelssohn, ibid., pp. 72–77.
73. Freund, *Emanzipation*, vol. 2, p. 210.
74. Scheel/Schmidt, *Reformministerium*, vol. I, pp. 328–32 (Oettinger); Freund, *Emanzipation*, vol. 2, pp. 413 ff. (Berliner Judenschaft).
75. GStA Berlin-Dahlem, Rep. 74 O.O. Nr. 4, vol. I: Militärgouvernement dated 15.1.1814.
76. GStA Berlin-Dahlem, Rep. 77 Tit. 332 t, Nr. 4, vol. I: Immediateingabe Bromberg dated 4.1.1831; Fischer, *Judentum*, pp. 47 ff.; Lindner, *Patriotismus*, pp. 61 ff.

77. Freund, *Emanzipation*, vol. 2, pp. 466–7; Fischer, *Judentum*, pp. 60–1;GStA Berlin-Dahlem, Rep. 77 Tit. 332 t, Nr. 4, vol. I: Innenminister dated 3.1. and 8.4.1817.
78. GStA Berlin-Dahlem, Rep. 77 Tit. 332 t, Nr. 4, vol. I: Innenminister dated 8.7.1817; Denkschrift v. Bodelschwingh dated 15.9.1845.
79. *Allgemeine Zeitung des Judenthums*, Year VI, Nr. 14, 2.4.1842, p. 200. Already in 1831, the elders of the Jewish community in Bromberg had petitioned the Prussian king to ask for Jews living in the Posen province to be allowed to enter military service – from 'patriotic feelings' and because, as the interior minister Schuckmann commented they saw the release from military service as 'disgracing them' (GStA Berlin-Dahlem, Rep. 77 Tit. 332 t, Nr. 4, vol. I: Bromberger Gemeindevorsteher dated 4.1.1831; Schuckmann dated 26.1.1831). Riesser, *Schriften*, vol. 3, p. 469.
80. *Allgemeine Zeitung des Judenthums*, Year VI, Nr. 14, 2.4.1842, p. 200.
81. Westphalen, *Tagebücher*, p. 562.
82. GStA Berlin-Dahlem, Rep. 77 Tit. 332 t, Nr. 4, vol. I: Bromberger Regierung dated 12.3.1817; Vincke dated 15.4.1827.
83. GStA Berlin-Dahlem, Rep. 77 Tit. 332 t, Nr. 4, vol. I: Staatsministerium dated 12.11.1832; v. Rochow dated 12.4.1842; Bodelschwingh dated 15.9.1845; Fischer, *Judentum*, pp. 212–13.
84. Freund, *Emanzipation*, vol. 2, p. 210; Fischer, *Judentum*, p. 216; Riesser, *Schriften*, vol. 3, pp. 60–1; vol. 2, pp. 152–3.
85. GStA Berlin, Rep. 77 Tit. 332 t, Nr. 4, vol. I: Berliner Regierung dated 5.11.1818 with notes by Schuckmann dated 29.11.1818; Vincke dated 15.4.1827; Übersicht der bei der Linie und Landwehr I. Aufgebots Anfang 1827 dienenden Juden; Votum v. Schuckmanns from 4.6.1827. The king first permitted Jewish one-yearers and three-year volunteers to serve in the Guards in 1847 and 1848 respectively (ibid, vol. II: Schreiben dated 30.3.1848).
86. Meinecke, *Leben*, vol. 2, p. 125; Kabinettsordre dated 28.6.1827, in: Dittmar, *Heeres-Ergänzung*, pp. 218 ff.
87. See the extensive correspondence generated by cases where this provision has been infringed, in: GStA Berlin-Dahlem, Rep. 77 Tit. 332 t, Nr. 12.
88. GStA Berlin-Dahlem, Rep. 92 Nachlaß Vaupel, Nr. 43: Kabinettsordre dated 28.11.1809; StA Detmold, M1 IC Nr. 27; HStA Düsseldorf, Regierung Aachen Nr. 1426: Amtsblatt dated 4.1.1866.
89. Dittmar, *Heeres-Ergänzung*, pp. 377–8. (Kabinettsordre dated 24.2.1824); *Militär-Wochenblatt*, Nr. 13, 21.9.1816: Kgl. Verordnung dated 11.1.1816.
90. *Militär-Wochenblatt*, Nr. 32–34, 1844: Articles of War (*Kriegsartikel*) from 1844.
91. From 1847 on, the Prussian army was sworn in using this unified procedure; previously, there had been local 'differences'; in some places the swearing-in

was led by a priest, occasionally even by an NCO (Dittmar, *Heeres-Ergänzung*, pp. 166–9).

92. Dittmar, *Heeres-Ergänzung*, pp. 591–3, 132–3.
93. Figures based on Dieterici, *Mittheilungen*, pp. 327–8. The variation in regional figures does not confirm the commonly held opinion that cities or industrial regions generally had a much higher percentage of those unfit than rural areas. For example, in the heavily industrialised government district of Düsseldorf, the figure for those mustered and found unfit were 64% in 1831 and 63% in 1854; in Berlin these figures were 64% and 70% respectively. In the rural district of Köslin the figures were 70% and 75%, and in the eastern Prussian area of Gumbinnen, similarly rural, the corresponding figures were 58% and 86 % (pp. 347 ff.).
94. Dittmar, *Heeres-Ergänzung*, pp. 240 ff.
95. *Militair-Wochenblatt*, Nr. 38, 1817; Nr. 44, 1817, p. 141; Nr. 12, 1843, p. 96; Nr. 2, 1846, p. 8; *Allgemeine Militär-Zeitung*, Year 6, 1831, Column 86, 375; Year 8, 1833, Column 790.
96. One case of the many examples can be found in the *Militair-Wochenblatt*, Nr. 232, 1820, pp. 1642 ff.
97. *Militair-Wochenblatt*, Nr. 15, 1845, p. 64; *Allgemeine Militär-Zeitung*, Year 6, 1831, Column 470, 582.
98. Quotes from articles in the *Militair-Wochenblatt*, Nr. 142, 1819, pp. 917–18; Nr. 2, 1846, p. 7. Also see the *Allgemeine Militär-Zeitung*, Year 2, 1827, Column 203; Year 6, 1831, Column 86. On the officers' scepticism compare *Allgemeine Militär-Zeitung*, Year 3, 1828, Column 217; on their professional ethos see, Craig, *Politics*, pp. 79–80.
99. Kgl. Verordnung dated 11.1.1816, in *Militair-Wochenblatt*, Nr. 13, 1816; Verfügung des Kriegsministeriums dated 3.8.1832, in Dittmar, *Heeres-Ergänzung*, p. 57. Soldiers who did not speak German were generally either of Polish or Lithuanian extraction. See, Helmert, *Militärsystem*, p. 68.
100. *Militair-Wochenblatt*, Nr. 41, 1845, pp. 172–5; Nr. 46, 1845, pp. 196–7 (counter argument); Nr. 48, 1845, pp. 204–6; Nr. 49, 1845, pp. 209–10.
101. *Militair-Wochenblatt*, Nr. 142, 1819, p. 917; Nr. 2, 1846, pp. 7–8. On the Soldatenfreund see Trox, *Konservativismus*, pp. 86 ff.
102. How unquestioningly accepted it was for soldiers to carry out 'female' work can also be seen in the suggestion published in 1817 by a retired aristocratic lieutenant and holder of the Iron Cross in the Militair-Wochenblatt, where he proposed overcoming the shortage of good NCOs by giving 'soldier boys' a good military training including sewing and cooking (Nr. 42, 1817, pp. 116–20). In the Prussian military school, Militär-Knaben-Erziehungs-Institut zu Annaburg, even into the 1870s the young boys there learnt how to 'sew a good seam and knit and darn a sock' (ibid., Nr. 5, 1874, p. 37).

The daughter of the Ludwigsburg governor, von BaurBreitenfeld, recalled soldiers and NCOs in the 1850s who preferred to use their waiting time for needlework and busily stitched the most colourful slippers, braces, and such like ... Even in the streets opposite the barracks you could see soldiers sewing in their free time and no-one ever came even close to imagining this was not military or proper' (Schumacher, *Kind*, pp. 181–2).

103. Goffman, *Asylums*, pp. xiii, 6.

104. When Georg Meyer was a soldier, his captain used the remark 'Be a man and do it yourself' (Selbst ist der Mann!) in pointing out a seam on Meyer's uniform that needed repairing (*Lebenstragödie*, pp. 48–9). The enduring effect of this lesson can be judged by the example of Albert, a bricklayer, who entered the army as a volunteer in 1869, and later taught his little sons how to darn their own socks. When his wife protested 'that's girls' work', Albert insisted he 'had had to darn his socks himself during his army time and we [the sons] also have to be able to do the same' (Albert, *Jugenderinnerungen*, p. 14). See also Rychner/Däniker, 'Unter "Männern"'.

105. Pappenheim, Fantasieen, p. 31; *Allgemeine Militär-Zeitung*, 1832, Columns 727–8.

106. Welcker, Geschlechtsverhältnisse; Frevert, "Mann", pp. 21 ff. Female writers too wrote of war and the army being 'unnatural' for women and 'completely at odds with the women's natural profession of motherhood' (Woltmann, *Natur*, pp. 183–4).

107. This was even conceded by Woltmann, *Natur*, pp. 186–7. Compare the anthology Die edelsten vaterländischen Frauen der vergangenen Zeit; für Deutschlands edle Frauen und Töchter, Magdeburg 1831, primarily the text on "Adelheid von Thurn, ein Beispiel ehelicher Treue und weiblichen Heldenmuths": Adelheid, who initially acknowledges her female 'frailty', sees herself forced, in the absence of any male protectors, to defend her honour by force of arms, and she defeats the person who insulted her in a duel – making her into a 'role model and paragon for German women' (pp. 206–17).

108. Welcker, 'Geschlechtsverhältnisse'.

109. *Allgemeine Militär-Zeitung*, Year 3, 1829, Column 349–52, 357–60, 364–7, 372–4, 379–82, 389–92.

110. On the intensive and complex discussion on military training compare *Allgemeine Militär-Zeitung*, Year 3, 1829, Column 351; Year 6, 1831, Columns 630, 643; Year 7, 1832, Columns 109–12, 122–6; Year 8, 1833, Column 173; *Militair-Wochenblatt*, Nr. 232, 1820, pp. 1640–4; Nr. 38, 1845, pp. 159–62.

111. *Allgemeine Militär-Zeitung*, Year 3, 1829, Column 788.

112. *Allgemeine Militär-Zeitung*, Year 2, 1828, Columns 775–6; similarly Year 11, 1836, Columns 739–44.

113. *Allgemeine Militär-Zeitung*, Year 3, 1829, Column 382.
114. *Militair-Wochenblatt*, 14.11.1818, pp. 782–3.
115. In 1819 only around 50% of the soldiers were in barracks. The remainder were quartered with civilians (Lüdtke, "Wehrhafte Nation", pp. 27, 52). Even in the 1850s, only two-thirds of the Prussian troops were actually in barracks (Stenographische Berichte, vol. 3, 1865, p. 2015).
116. *Militair-Wochenblatt*, 14.11.1818, p. 783; Nr. 34, 1844, pp. 141, 143 (Article of War [Kriegsartikel] 46); Nr. 232, 1820, p. 1642.
117. *Allgemeine Militär-Zeitung*, Nr. 51, 1833, Column 407.
118. Meinecke, *Leben*, vol. 2, pp. 119 ff.; Lüdtke, "Gemeinwohl", pp. 298 ff., 329; *Historische Zeitschrift*, vol. 67, 1891, pp. 65–6.
119. *Militär-Wochenblatt*, Nr. 100, 1888, Column 2065.
120. *Militär-Wochenblatt*, Nr. 104, 1818, p. 615; *Allgemeine Militär-Zeitung*, Nr. 44, 1829, Column 360.
121. Compare the protests by free-thinking religious groups against a decree by a Magdeburg general dated 15.3.1859 (Sammlung sämmtlicher Drucksachen, vol. 5, 1865, Nr. 257, pp. 4–7). On the Catholic representatives' annoyance see Schubert, *Provinziallandtag*, vol. 5, pp. 137–143.
122. *Allgemeine Militär-Zeitung*, Year 8, 1833, Column 791; *Militair-Wochenblatt*, Nr. 142, 1819, pp. 917–8.
123. Fontane, *Zwanzig*, pp. 152–3; Spielhagen, *Finder*, vol. 2, pp. 6–7.
124. Delbrück, *Lebenserinnerungen*; Hasenclever, *Erlebtes*, p. 14.
125. Articles of War (Kriegsartikel) from 1844 in *Militair-Wochenblatt*, Nr. 32–34, 1844.
126. *Allgemeine Militär-Zeitung*, Year 1, 1826, Column 54; Year 5, 1830, Column 516; Frevert, *Men of Honour*, pp. 36 ff.; Dieners, *Duell*, primarily pp. 174 ff.
127. *Militair-Wochenblatt*, Nr. 32, 1844, p. 134; Nr. 86, 1818, p. 469.
128. StA Detmold, M 1 IC Nr. 298: Amt Schwalenberg dated 20.9.1841, and numerous other complaints; GStA Berlin-Dahlem, Rep. 77 Tit. 329, Nr. 4: Ahrweil Landrat dated 23.7.1831.
129. StA Detmold, M1 IC Nr. 298: Beilage zu Nr. 73 der Westfälischen Zeitung dated 27.3.1849.
130. Wigard, *Bericht*, vol. 2, p. 804.
131. Hansen, *Briefe*, vol. 2, pp. 221–2.
132. *Allgemeine Militär-Zeitung*, Nr. 10, 1.2.1834, Column 79; also see Chapter 3.
133. Lüdtke, "Gemeinwohl", pp. 283 ff., 291 ff.
134. Wigard, *Bericht*, vol. 2, p. 952.
135. *Vossische Zeitung*, 4.6.1848; Hettling, 'Bürger'; Trox, *Konservativismus*, pp. 114 ff., 159 ff.

136. Müller, *Soldaten* (1999), primarily pp. 196, 198, 251 ff.
137. Müller, *Soldaten* (1999), pp. 247 ff.
138. *Militair-Wochenblatt*, Nr. 106, 1879, pp. 1866–67. (New Year's message from 1.1.1849); Nr. 30, 1848, p. 135.
139. GStA Berlin-Dahlem, Rep. 77 Tit. 332 t, Nr. 4, vol. II: Wochenbericht dated 30.1.1852.
140. Trox, *Konservativismus*, pp. 118–19, 162.
141. *Militär-Wochenblatt*, Nr. 106, 1879, p. 1867; *Preußische Landwehr*, pp. 103–4.
142. Goebel/Wichelhaus, *Aufstand*; Trox, *Konservativismus*, pp. 162 ff.; Müller, *Soldaten* (1999), pp. 294 ff.
143. Schütte, 'Landwehrbataillon'.
144. *Preußische Landwehr*, p. 106.
145. *Marx-Engels-Werke*, Ergänzungsband, 2. T., Berlin 1973, pp. 490–501.
146. *Militair-Wochenblatt*, Nr. 104, 1818, p. 615; Willich, *Heere*, p. vii.
147. Fontane, *Zwanzig*, pp. 150–7, 172–7, 192–3; Spielhagen, *Erinnerungen*, pp. 237, 253.
148. Delbrück, *Lebenserinnerungen*, pp. 39, 51, 63, 121–2.
149. Landtagsabschied für die zum achten Provinzial-Landtage versammelt gewesenen Preußischen Provinzial-Stände dated 30.12.1843, Königsberg 1844, pp. 34–5; GStA Berlin-Dahlem, 2.2.1, Nr. 32110: Extract from 30.12.1843 from the 796th Westfalian Landtagsabschied.

Military Systems in the 'Third Germany'

But were there any viable alternatives to the Prussian model of universal male conscription across all social classes? The question was, in fact, not new. From the early years of the nineteenth century on, it had inspired many heated debates on the pros and cons of various military models, whether in cabinets and parliaments, in associations and newspapers, or at a range of meetings. The fierce and profound disagreements it engendered were only finally resolved in the late 1860s; in the end, the view that emerged victorious was the one favoured by such disparate figures as the Prussian war minister Albrecht von Roon and the socialist activist Friedrich Engels. The latter had lauded universal conscription in 1865 as Prussia's 'only democratic institution', commending it as an 'enormous advance', far superior to recruiting and drafting.[1]

Engels's stance was upsetting to many of those who shared his other views but were critical of Prussia's military service system, advocating a militia model closer to 'armed civilians' (*Bürgerbewaffnung*) or 'citizens' militia forces' (*Volkswehren*) found, for example, in Switzerland. The Prussian system came under attack from 'bourgeois' circles too, where it was criticised for its extreme inflexibility and condemned for the 'unbending single-mindedness' with which it 'blindly intervened in civil life'.[2] It was, in fact, the strictest conscription system in Europe at the time. Britain, for example, adhered to the volunteer army principle even during the Napoleonic Wars, retaining this model until the First World War.[3] On the continent, the largest standing armies were found in France and Russia and under the Habsburg monarchy, yet the latter still employed an extremely selective recruiting system until 1868, not only excluding civil servants, clerics, farmers and students, but all those able to pay for a substitute. And in France, whose *levée en masse* provided the original inspiration for the Prussian system, conscription might have survived all the changes in government throughout the nineteenth century, but only at the cost of substantial restrictions; under the lottery system, if any man was due for military service, he could buy himself out and provide a *remplaçant*.[4]

This French model found imitators in many German territories too, especially in the states of Baden, Württemberg, Bavaria and Saxony, which all had previously been part of the former Rhenish Confederation except for Saxony. As a result, Germany had various systems in force simultaneously – providing an incentive for contemporaries to observe and compare different models. They not only intensely scrutinized aspects such as funding, technical details or the problems of military efficiency, but tackled concerns of wider import too, in particular, the social, political and cultural conditions governing the range of recruiting practices and the consequences these had. In the years of peace following 1815, when the era of wars in the late eighteenth and early nineteenth century finally ended, the public sphere's main concern was not so much the army's ability to wage war, but its ability to wage peace. The central questions revolved around three key issues: how could an army be integrated into civil society with as few points of potential friction and conflict as possible? How large should the army be, what basic model should it follow, and what were its tasks? And finally, how permeable should the borders be between the military and civil spheres – which transfer effects and intersections were desirable, and which should be prevented? There were a myriad of answers to these questions, reflected in the diversity of military practices in the states comprising the 'Third Germany'. Yet despite numerous internal differences, they were unified by one overreaching concern: rejecting the Prussian model and insisting on their own system of conscription and substitutions. And even though some military experts took a contrary stance, they had to wait until 1866 before they could push their views through on the back of, first, the military defeat against Prussia and, later, the shared victory over France. It was this victory that lent sufficient authority and legitimacy to the principle of universal military conscription and powered the political will needed to apply it in Baden, Württemberg, Bavaria and Saxony, despite its widespread unpopularity.

1. The Move from Exemption to Substitution

In the beginning was Napoleon – and nowhere does this commonplace historical phrase apply more than in the founding of the Rhenish Confederation's military structures. In the early years of the nineteenth century, the states looking radically to modernise their military systems tended to be those benefiting most from French assistance in substantially enlarging their territory. The drive to reform was not solely engendered by pressures accompanying territorial expansion, but was equally a product of integration into the Napoleonic alliance system, which inexorably necessitated a fundamental enlargement and restructuring of each individual state's army.

Bavaria, for example, had previously relied primarily on recruiting soldiers at home and abroad, and, to an extent, forcefully drafting destitute subjects, but in 1804 it issued a decree establishing the universal duty of military service. Although, like Prussia in the previous century, it granted a wide range of exemptions, these were cancelled five years later. They then adopted a substitute regulation, following the

French model, 'to make the present ruling more popular'.[5] The 1812 Conscription Law confirmed these provisions and, in a further step, made the granting of personal and civic rights dependent on fulfilling military service: only those men fit for service who had served for six years, or paid for a substitute, were allowed to settle, marry or enter public office.[6] Developments in Baden and Württemberg were similar, with an 1806 Conscription Law offering generous provisions for exceptions and substitutions. Yet despite such allowances, these laws did achieve their aim of enlistment, generating large numbers of troops for the French 'protector's' campaigns.

The local population, though, more or less overwhelmingly rejected such foreign and unfamiliar practices, while among the populace in territories acquired after 1803–6 during these medium-sized states' consolidation processes, resistance to such measures was especially stubborn. Many men simply disobeyed orders to appear for mustering, and desertion was held to be a legitimate means of avoiding the new sovereign's outrageous demands. There were repeated cases of recruits being openly 'insubordinate', or provoking collective 'excesses' and engaging in 'seditious conspiracies', frequently invoking the old regime, which they wanted to see reinstated, not least because of its 'lenience'.[7]

Conscription was far from being a force for integration, least of all under the extreme strains of wartime – and, without any national war, the southern German and Saxon sovereigns could not draw on its potentially integrative force. Ultimately, they were behaving just as the *Ancien Régime* had: dispatching newly enlisted troops to serve in a war fought for 'alien' interests to promote a foreign power. Consequently, in contrast to Prussia, the Rhenish Confederation's motivation to introduce military service was not rooted in national policy concerns, nor enhanced by national feelings and interests. Instead, it came like a thief in the night – an administrative act imposed from above without any promise of participatory measures. Nonetheless, despite the unpopularity of conscription, the southern German states retained it even after the Napoleonic alliance collapsed and the Rhenish Confederation was dissolved in 1813.

Since the Congress of Vienna did not reverse their territorial gains, the southern German states maintained their status as medium-sized powers, located geographically between Austria and Prussia. As sovereign and independent states, they appear to have seen a need for a substantial army, and even in the German Confederation, the 'Third Germany' ensured it was represented by a suitable military force: Bavaria, for example, provided one of eight army corps, while Baden and Württemberg jointly shared another with Hesse-Darmstadt, and the division from Saxony was mixed with the Hessian–Thuringian troops. Yet the importance and prestige that the ruling princes attributed to a strong army found no echo in their subjects' feelings. The assembly of estates in the southern German states, considerably enlarging their sphere of influence after the introduction of constitutional systems in 1818, viewed the military ambitions of their respective sovereigns with concern. As the Württemberg representatives critically noted in 1815, 'Conscription and the large standing army are largely responsible for the state becoming like a huge prison, with widespread destitution and immorality',[8] while the vast majority supported the view that only extensive provisions on exemptions or the possibility of substitutions could save the country from penury.

In these circles, the radical Prussian practice of disallowing either exemption or substitution was regarded as a specific, non-exportable characteristic of that 'extremely military state'[9] and unanimously rejected. In contrast, they claimed, one was proud of the more civil traditions cultivated in southern Germany. In parliamentary exchanges on the military statutes and budgets, assembly members in Baden, Württemberg or Bavaria bluntly described military service as an 'evil', an 'illness' or a 'burden'. They certainly acknowledged the duty of all male citizens to defend their country in a time of war, as von Liebenstein, a Baden assembly member, emphasised in 1820, drawing a parallel with the constitutionally enshrined principle of equality before the law: 'When the hour of danger sounds, *everyone* must fight for a fatherland that grants all of its children equal rights and protection.' But in times of peace, the standing army should be kept small and the burden on each citizen, both financial and personal, eased as far as possible.[10]

Initially, though, there was no general agreement on how this should be done. In Baden, the parliament found itself at odds with the government's preferred policy of leaving untouched those traditionally established privileges in the religious, economic and social spheres, seeing no reason why, *per se*, Mennonites, armaments workers or new settlers in Konstanz should be exempted from the 'primary civic duty'. Under a constitution guaranteeing equal rights and demanding equal duties, any majority agreement over exemptions on principle was impossible – even if individual assembly members repeatedly took a stand against the precept of equality, which they saw as a revolutionary axiom that was drenched in blood.[11]

But *one* exception to the rule of no exceptions did find widespread approval: one son from each family should be exempted from military service if this was deemed necessary 'to preserve the family's well-being and civic standing'. This provision primarily targeted families in rural areas, but equally encompassed urban trades, where the family functioned as an economic unit, dependent on their growing children's labour; if all the male children were drafted, such a unit would disintegrate. The argument ran that since a son's duty to support his parents had primacy over all other civic duties, and it would be presumptuous of the state to set other priorities without risking its own annihilation, one son, at least, was to remain at home to secure 'domestic happiness' and, with it, the 'basis for public well-being'.[12]

It was not only at points like these that one notices how the vast majority of assembly members argued for 'civil' interests, oblivious to the level of state concerns. Rather than arguing over principles, they were attempting to find pragmatic solutions to the issue of how to combine civil life with the 'sacred duty' of defending one's country. Baden, in the early constitutional phase, did not invoke the political rhetoric found in Prussia under Hardenberg and Stein, closely linking military service and active citizenship. Apparently, the civic rights guaranteed under the Baden constitution were regarded as so well secured that it seemed superfluous to take military service as a basis for their legitimisation. This, at least, is suggested by the reverse case, where the regional assembly (*Landtag*) overtly criticised the government's proposal to grant civic and municipal rights to foreigners who voluntarily served in the army. For the assembly delegates, since foreigners serving in the army did so 'in their own interests', they did not need to receive civic rights automatically as a reward - although they could, of course, apply just like anyone else who met the 'requirements necessary'.[13]

The matter-of-fact way that all assembly members demanded unrestricted substitution similarly indicates that they saw no inevitable link between citizenship and military service. According to Liebenstein, substitution was the only measure that could make 'the universality of a duty to military service bearable' and, he added, anyone should be allowed to buy himself free without having to reveal his motives for doing so. Rather than the state having any right to play the role of guardian and to fetter 'the free will of its citizens', he continued, all those liable for military service should be at liberty to find and pay for a 'substitute'. It went without saying that this was only viable for those with sufficient means at their disposal, and only one subordinate clause mentioned that 'admittedly' 'very poor citizens' would be excluded from enjoying the blessings of a substitute.[14] Such statements reflect the assembly members' ties to their social class: in addition to the traditional middle-class 'worthies', it included the new ambitious men of 'property and education', and a broad swathe of the independent middle classes. When citing 'popular opinion' and balancing civic freedom against legal equality, they spoke for their equals; the lower classes, unable to afford such a freedom, did not figure in their equation and had to make the best of equality.

Given that civic spirit and not patriotism was the key slogan of early liberalism in Baden, as organised in the second chamber, the delegates also considered it unnecessary to justify military duties by recourse to patriotic feelings. And, first and foremost, civic spirit was demonstrated at local community level rather than in a state body politic dominated by civil servants.[15] When one chamber delegate lauded 'love of the fatherland' as the driving force motivating future soldiers, calling on schools and the press to awaken such an emotion more intensively in the general public, no fellow delegates supported him.[16] After all, equating patriotism and military service would label as egotistic and unpatriotic all those submitting a substitute rather than performing military duties themselves. If at all possible, such a hasty conclusion was to be avoided, since civic spirit could also, first and foremost, be put into practice in other contexts and at other places than, of all things, in the army.

Traditionally, middle-class society in the southern German states had been removed from the military, and this distance formed a distinct civic point of reference permeating their views. Under the *Ancien Régime*, in the social division of labour, the 'respectable urban classes' had only pursued civilian occupations and, consequently, their knowledge of the army came solely from second-hand accounts, where it was painted as a downright horrifying institution, with members forming a closed caste subject to their own rules. This, of course, had been no different in Prussia. There, though, in the eighteenth century, political motives had endowed the army with a status of honour, largely lacking in southern Germany. For this reason, the movement taking place at the start of the nineteenth century to reshape the military caste as a civic institution could not feed on the same political capital as had been accumulated in Prussia previously. Neither could the southern German armies draw on the approval enjoyed by the Prussian army, the *Landwehr* and volunteer civilian militias in the political arena, which stemmed from involvement in the Wars of Liberation. As far as the subsequent generation was concerned, the Rhenish Confederation armies had been fighting on the wrong side, and were late changing over. The propaganda *über*-myth of burgeoning German patriotism across all social classes culminating in common war efforts in 1813 largely found no resonance here – despite each government's best efforts to reconstitute it for its own state. For example, in 1833 Ludwig I, king of Bavaria, directed an obelisk to be built in memory of the 30,000 Bavarian soldiers who lost their lives fighting for Napoleon during the 1812 Russian campaign. The obelisk was located centrally in Munich's inner city with an inscription around the base, personally composed by the king himself, reading: 'They also died to free their country'. At the ceremony unveiling the memorial, in an attempt to repair political damage, Ludwig offered a crucial link between Napoleon's invasion of Russia and later defeat on the Leipzig battlefield by saying: 'The Bavarian army has always been loyal to the king, is so now and will continue to be so in future.'[17] But he was unable to conjure up the heroic and patriotic aura surrounding the Prussian army in general and the *Landwehr* in particular after 1815, and which they maintained so adroitly. The Bavarian army could not claim the prerogative of being instrumental in realising 'national' interests and emotions, nor being a means of expressing them, nor could it claim to embody the mythical birth of a popular civil national movement.

Against such a background, the middle classes in Baden, Württemberg, Bavaria, or Saxony saw no reason to relinquish their traditional distance from military affairs. When 19-year-old Heinrich Brockhaus, a publisher's son from Leipzig, went to be mustered in 1823, he presented certificates from his regular doctor that led to his release from military duties 'without any further inconvenience'.

However, his concern over being 'made a soldier' did not stem from health or financial worries, but was rooted in his dread of the ensuing social and cultural tedium. As he confided to his diary, 'It would have been the death of me to be garrisoned in some small town', casually adding that, of course, he recognised the 'duty of every citizen to defend his country in times of need'.[18] Apparently, in 1823 such times seemed to be long past; Brockhaus could fall back on his doctor's help with a clear conscience. The state, similarly, left his conscience to sleep in peace since, in contrast to Prussia, neither Saxony nor any of the southern German states employed the rhetoric of an ethical or political discourse. Instead, they all presumed their citizens were unwilling to perform military service and, working on this basis, devised ways and means to make the 'great sacrifice', the 'burdensome circumstances' and the 'onerous discomforts' more bearable.[19] The citizens, for their part, gratefully accepted such solace without ever having to feel they were behaving egotistically.

After all, they were only applying the right enshrined in law to appeal against the mustering of one son and to have him released from the duty of military service. In Baden in 1827, 1,190 appeals of this nature were officially granted, allowing more than a quarter of all able-bodied youths liable for service to stay home.[20] In Württemberg, where there was no general release on the grounds of 'family circumstances' but only provisional exemption for a year (which in fact came to the same thing), the 1850s and 1860s saw every seventh 'able-bodied' recruit released from his duties.[21] The second legal means to escape this unloved state service consisted in finding a substitute. As in Prussia after 1825, the southern German states had introduced a draw to select the recruits actually needed. If, despite applying all the standard folk rituals to ward off misfortune, someone drew the 'wrong' number, he was still able to provide a substitute.[22] He concluded a contract with this 'guarantor', which then had to be officially certified. The guarantor declared his willingness to join up in place of the named recruit and remain in the army for the entire period of service, generally six years; in return, the guarantor received a freely negotiable sum of money, deposited with the military, to be released in a single lump sum when he was discharged. During his period of service, the guarantor was already able to access the interest and an extra 'bounty' payment that varied according to the economic situation, but could even be as high again as the original guarantor sum.

The only factor governing such payments was the going market rate, with, for example, payment needing to be higher if guarantors were in short supply, or if a war appeared imminent. In the mid-1830s, financing a substitute in the Baden infantry regiment cost around 450 guilders, with substitutes for the cavalry regiments asking at least 500 guilders – approximately the equivalent of a day-labourer's annual income. Since at the same time senior mid-range civil service clerks received around 1,200 guilders a year and free lodging,[23] it would have been feasible for a thrifty civil servant to save the money needed to buy his son free from military service, while this would have proved practically impossible for the day-labourer. As a rule, the latter's son was more likely to have been taking the payment as guarantor, providing he had drawn a 'lucky' number and was not enlisted himself.

Trading money against personal services in this way was principally attractive for young men from lower social strata, and many of them concluded one guarantor contract after another, providing them with sufficient money at the end of their army service to facilitate their start in civilian life. But the money parents invested in this exchange was similarly beneficial for those men released from service, buying time for better vocational training, leading to better remuneration in the long term – which was why everyone sought to find the means needed to pay a guarantor if they possibly could. For the Mannheim merchant Friedrich Ludwig Bassermann, himself a lieutenant colonel in the local militia, there was never any question of doing anything else but buying his sons out of the army in the 1830s and 1840s, while, in 1831, the Heidelberg professor Carl Welcker announced to the Baden regional assembly: 'I myself, a father of sons, frankly admit I would, just as all other fathers in my situation, give the last penny I had squirrelled away to buy my son free from the sacred duty of defending his country, if he were not himself interested in a career within the officer class.'[24] And neither the urban lower-middle classes, nor the well-to-do rural and agricultural populace, would have disagreed.[25] In many communities, families even got together to form clubs, contributing a regular membership fee as insurance against the risk of their sons being enlisted. If a member's son was 'unlucky' in the draw and had to join up, a certain amount was paid out, which could then either be kept or used to pay for a substitute. It seems that such clubs attracted primarily 'less well-off' parents who did not have the full means to pay for a substitute themselves.[26]

Since the total funds for guarantors deposited with the army were administered centrally, these figures provide an insight into how often substitutes were used. In Baden during the 1840s, the total amount held on account varied between 183,000 and 238,000 guilders annually; assuming each substitute cost an average of 450 guilders, there would have been around 400–500 guarantors annually (for the 2,000–3,000 enlisted recruits each year). More than 1,000 guarantor contracts were concluded in 1848 alone, with the acute threat of war pushing up the sum agreed to a higher rate than usual; in other words, that year every third enlisted man opted to buy himself out and let another serve in his place.[27]

There is hardly any record of protests against the substitution system. The guarantors benefited just as much as the local authorities, since the agreed capital sum paid out to the soldier or NCO on discharge was a buffer against impoverishment and dependency on poor relief. As far as the civil sphere was concerned, the substitute system was 'one of the most beneficial institutions for citizens', to quote the Baden liberal Itzstein in 1822; the state, for its part, valued the equalisation of burdens it entailed. In this way, the army could acquire a sufficiently large body of NCOs at no extra cost, with, for example, all of the colour sergeants and most of the sergeants in the 1840s originally having entered the army as guarantors. It was only when post-mid-century industrial expansion led to more jobs and higher wages that Baden took control of the guarantor system itself, reserving the right to reward NCOs with higher bonus payments as a way of combating the considerable attractions of employment in the industrial sector.[28]

In Württemberg too, the state played an intermediary role between the recruit and the substitute. The war ministry kept a list of men willing to act as substitutes, or who had already done so; anyone wanting to find a substitute then paid the government a set fee of 400 guilders and a person was chosen from this list. The system functioned totally anonymously, with neither the recruit nor the substitute knowing the other, and in this way prevented any personal dependencies or individual bartering over the guarantor's lump sum payment. In Württemberg between 1817 and 1849, around 15,000 men paid for substitutes, with an average of 450 men per recruitment year taking a substitute during the 1840s, i.e., roughly 16 per cent, with the figure rising to 22 per cent in the 1850s.[29]

2. Army Service: The View from Inside

Substitutes were not simply a source of cheap future NCOs. The army also appreciated their coming from lower social strata, since the lower the common soldiers' status, the less officers, primarily from upper- and middle-class families, needed to show restraint in the way they treated them. It was quite standard for the lower ranks to be addressed either in the third person or the familiar second person singular *Du* form – a contempt similarly reflected in the degrading punishments meted out. Corporal punishment - officially banned in schools - was extensively used, and occasionally even administered publicly.[30] Such practices underlined the hierarchical divide between officers and the troops and gave an added social slant to the military structure of subordination.

Nonetheless, from the soldiers' perspective inside the barracks' walls, the reality rarely matched the picture middle-class fathers painted of the army as a place of dread and horror. For a start, enlisted soldiers actually only spent around seventeen to eighteen months in barracks – a small proportion of their standard term of military service which, in Baden, Bavaria and Württemberg, totalled six years for the infantry.[31] To be sure, even during the long phases of furlough, their mobility was limited and they remained under military law, as a rule, unable either to marry, start a business as a master craftsman, or benefit from communal land or facilities. However, they were then only loosely connected with the army and were busy earning their living and participating in normal civilian life. Secondly – and despite the very obvious disadvantages – even the time in barracks brought certain benefits. The wage may have been meagre but it was guaranteed and regular, partially paid in money and partly in kind (bread).[32] Especially in the first decades of the nineteenth century before industrial and commercial development got into its stride, with work outside the agricultural sector hard to find, the army's basic economic provision was not to be sniffed at, encompassing as it did clothing and regular meals.[33] Undoubtedly, the soldiers' quarters in barracks and private homes were less than ideal, although middle-class contemporaries' indignation over the standard 'two-soldier' bed conveniently forgot that, for the majority of civilians in those days, a single bed was an unattainable luxury. Finally, even the physical demands placed on soldiers were, in comparison, not as bad as sometimes claimed. Quite the contrary – contemporary observers were constantly highlighting how favourably military service affected young men's physical development. Admittedly, as officers confessed, many of the exercises were tantamount to 'a kind of torture', yet they led recruits, even in their first year, to adopt a 'better posture'; as a result, one could immediately tell ex-army men from others, even in later life. According to a Baden assembly delegate in 1841: 'Just watch a village congregation leaving their church, and when you see the young lad with delightful posture and an easy countenance, his entire appearance will tell you at once: he was a soldier.'[34]

One might object, though, that such a perception was merely a projection and would not necessarily stand up to any empirical test; furthermore, by declaring the vast majority of those mustered as 'unfit', the army had already pre-selected the 'best-looking young men'. In Baden during the 1820s, two out of three men liable for the draft were declared unfit, and in Saxony in the 1840s, this figure was as high as three out of four, while in Württemberg in the 1850s the relation between those medically examined and found fit was two to one: 40 per cent were considered totally unfit for service, and 16 per cent were temporarily exempted until the following year's mustering.[35] In other words, just as Prussia did, the armies in the medium-sized German states also only recruited healthy, tall and sturdy men: neither the tailor's emaciated apprentice, reflecting the popular image of the day, nor the shoemaker's lad with the bent back, nor the flat-footed farmer's boy would ever even have had the chance of improving their posture under the army's strict regime of exercises. Yet in comparison to working on the land or in the urban trades, military service was hardly more damaging to the recruits' health, or placed greater physical demands on them – if anything, the opposite was the case, as exemplified in the Württemberg soldiers' song from the 1850s: 'Should I be a farmer's slave, earn my bread by my sweat each day? No, my friend, that's not my way. I'd rather live where the canons cry, under canvas and the open sky, where we talk of guns all day, No, I won't be a farmer's slave.'[36]

However, the soldier's life had other elements than just the romance of the campfire or the popular shooting exercises, and there were few soldiers who enjoyed hours of exercise and drill. In 1859, an anonymous Bavarian soldier criticised the 'mass of commands from above' that suffocated any pleasure or independence, adding that the drill ground resembled a 'slaughtering block'.[37] Although soldiers formally had the right to complain to a higher instance about their immediate superior officers' behaviour, they rarely did so, more often than not from the fear of being really put through it afterwards.[38] As a result, any public denunciation of abuse in the army frequently came from outside military circles, as in 1833 when civilians in Dippoldiswalde, Saxony, protested against a guard being whipped after they had been alerted by unusually loud screams. At that time, corporal punishment was a part of everyday military life and, moreover, was officially allowed under Saxony's military criminal law. When, from the 1830s on, concern for public opinion played a major role in the war ministry's insistence on a close reading of the law to restrict corporal punishment as far as possible, the move was strongly resisted from within the army, which still often had offenders whipped even where the lock-up was prescribed under military law. The Dippoldiswalde cavalryman who fell asleep on guard duty should 'only' have received four to six weeks locked up with fatigue duties, instead of which the commander added 'fifty strokes on the backside' as 'a punishment to act as a deterrent', meted out by a major in the presence of numerous officers, NCOs and common soldiers.[39]

If, in that case, the punishment was thought to fit the crime, any officers exceeding their authority got away all but scot-free; for example, a Dresden lieutenant who severely injured a guard on duty was sentenced to be confined to quarters for forty-eight hours.[40] But such crass inequality awoke almost no echo in the public sphere: while parliaments missed no opportunity to attack the military budget, which they saw as too high, and urged the army to keep enlistment figures as low as possible, they had no desire to become embroiled in the army's internal affairs, and turned a deaf ear to the plight of the troops. Under such circumstances, the soldiers were largely left to their own devices, and some, confronted with the army's rigid punishment system, saw suicide as the only way out. There are constantly recurring reports of soldiers hanging themselves while in detention or being so terrified by the thought of their punishment that they shot themselves with their service gun.[41] Others, though, gave vent to their anger and frustration in anonymous letters. In Munich's English Garden park in 1835, a threatening letter was found, contrasting the officers' 'life of luxury' with the troops' vexed and harassed existence, and warning that if this did not change, the soldiers would soon lose patience, start a 'revolution' and 'give the fine officers a thrashing'.[42]

Revolution in the army was every government's nightmare – and times of political unrest in particular gave it renewed sustenance. The idea of troops rising against their officers was bad enough, but worse still was the thought of soldiers joining forces with rebellious civilians and turning their weapons on the authorities, the state and the government. The authorities imagined such an attack potentially lurking behind every 'drunken brawl' and when, for example, in 1846, soldiers in Dillingen, Bavaria, protested against the exorbitant price of beer, the Munich interior ministry read it as an attempt to 'create a state of unbridled anarchy and chaos'. The greatest danger, they commented, lay in the 'age's pernicious doctrines' gaining acceptance even in the army, transforming it into a base for 'tumultuous acts of violence'.[43]

From the army's perspective, this danger was best banished by submitting soldiers and officers to strict disciplinary control. Just as in Prussia, though, limited funds for building new barracks left many soldiers still living in private quarters, making it extremely difficult to construct any effective social barrier to the civilian 'enemies of law and order'. But even when soldiers were in barracks, their time off-duty could be spent in mixing with civilians, primarily in pubs and inns, where they could read newspapers and become involved in political discussions. Undoubtedly, such contacts occasionally led to fully fledged fights, but they also established personal relationships, and even sometimes friendships between soldiers and the urban population, encouraging a flow of ideas that were not to the military authorities' taste.[44]

In 1846, a Bavarian divisional commander suggested regularly exchanging garrisons as the only way to stop this transfer and avoid the 'troops fraternising with rioters' and 'assimilation into the civilian populace'. The Munich war ministry, though, rejected the idea as impracticable. However much the political context might give one cause to frown upon any 'civil assimilation of the military', the disadvantages of exchanging garrisons would be too great. 'The regard due to be paid to the conscripts' home circumstances in every possible instance, as His Majesty the King has ordered, would have to cease totally; the unpopularity of military service would grow, giving rise to increased instances of desertion, and seemingly turning the duty of conscription into an odious burden.'[45]

In fact, in the Third Germany too, it was common to enrol soldiers in regiments based near their hometowns, and, given the extensive periods of furlough, this seemed only reasonable.[46] Yet, especially in politically volatile times, this practice represented a further constant source of danger for the army, as was shown, at the latest, by events in 1848–9.[47] In the southern German states, far more than in Prussia, soldiers seized the moment to approach their superiors and make their wishes known. These lists of 'justified demands' were far from revolutionary, focusing primarily on being treated with greater respect under improved material conditions.[48] While some commanders did try to ensure soldiers received better victualling and increased payments for food, others resorted to intimidation and scare tactics. But in 1848, as a first step, the military in Bavaria and Saxony abolished corporal punishment – forty years after Prussia. They also reminded soldiers of the oath they had sworn on the regimental colours, and painted the revolutionary movement for greater civil rights in the blackest terms as simply a group of traitors and law-breakers. The three strands of this immunisation process – the carrot, the whip (or lack of it) and propaganda – apparently bore fruit. The majority of troops functioned as expected, even when used against civilians and in pitched battles on the barricades.

In fact, soldiers rarely changed sides. In May 1849, numerous Bavarian and Baden soldiers guarding fortifications at Landau in the Palatinate deserted and joined the republican volunteer corps, after being 'worked on' and 'corrupted' by civilians. Reports from Kempten mentioned local citizens sparing neither 'words nor drinks nor money' in their efforts to entice the soldiers to take up 'the people's cause', while a commander in Lindau bemoaned how 'discipline, military obedience, and the loyal and dutiful spirit of soldiery have all substantially declined. Repeated instances of excesses are reported, recurrent cases of insubordination, and continual complaints of disrespectful conduct towards officers.'[49] Yet by 1850 the Bavarian troops too were as 'reliable' as ever, with, just as in the past, soldiers mainly taking civilians as the butt of any 'excesses', rather than their military superiors.[50] Desertion, similarly, had all but ceased; any remaining instances can at most be attributed to individual cases of protest. If men really had no intention of serving after being mustered and drawing the 'wrong' lot, they were usually long gone before the swearing-in ceremony took place. Such cases in Württemberg accounted for 3 to 4 per cent of recruits in the late 1850s and the early years of the 1860s, while during and shortly after the 1848 period of unrest, this figure had been over 6 per cent.[51]

3. Civilian Counterparts: An Armed Citizenry and a Man's Right to Bear Arms

As we saw above, middle-class men had no need to take such radical steps – they could simply buy themselves out. Nonetheless, this did not necessarily imply a principled stand against every kind of armed duty: despite successfully escaping military service, and harshly condemning a standing army as a place of misery and squalor, back-breaking drudgery and inhumane, degrading treatment, they were equally at pains to point out the great political significance of bearing arms and to state unequivocally their own basic willingness to do so. This discourse was found particularly in early liberalism and, partially intentionally and partly unwittingly, resembled and borrowed from the ongoing debate over military reform in Prussia.

The initial impetus in developing this discourse came from the Freiburg history professor Carl von Rotteck in 1816. Against the background of the recent wars with and against Napoleon and in the context of the new conscription system, he posed the pivotal question: 'Do we want to make the nation itself into an army, or turn soldiers into citizens?' His own answer was unambiguously clear. In his view, society needed citizen-soldiers, but with the emphasis more on citizen than soldier. Too pragmatic to have any illusions about the utopian ideal of permanent peace, Rotteck acknowledged and accepted the 'national war' as a symptom of the modern, post-revolutionary era. In this new sort of war, all citizens might be needed since conflicts of this type were fought 'at the nation's behest' and 'for the true benefit of the state'. Men were to be kept fit to fight and ready for combat in the '*Landwehr*' – in Rotteck's terms, a troop unit meeting periodically, organised on the local level with freely elected officers. In addition to this 'national militia' (*Nationalmiliz*), there would be a standing national defence force (*Nationalwehr*) with soldiers 'recruited on a voluntary basis'. While recognising that an effective professional army was essential, Rotteck vehemently opposed universal conscription, arguing that no citizen should be obliged to serve in it.[52]

His position did more than simply reflect civil criticism of the standing armies in the *Ancien Régime*. It also betrayed a deep and profound mistrust of military forms as such. It seemed as though an army inevitably involved rigid hierarchies, blind obedience and mindless drilling, and, moreover, such structures were essential for it to function effectively; yet they stood in fundamental opposition to the basic tenets of a civil society, which, in an ideal form, was founded on actively involved adult (male) citizens voluntarily taking up responsibility for themselves. Not surprisingly then, for Rotteck, transferring military principles of organisation to civil society, seemingly inevitable under any conscription system, was to be avoided at all costs. Nevertheless, he still envisaged all citizens being trained as 'national fighters' – but in a substitute civil institution rather than in the army.

But why did Rotteck, a liberal intellectual and politician, believe any such training was needed at all? And, given that he thought it was, why was the necessary evil of a regular army not sufficient in itself to the task? Rotteck's reasoning may well have rested on two basic premises. Firstly, it seemed most likely that, even after Napoleon, modern national wars would be mass affairs, hardly capable of being won by professional armies restricted by budgetary constraints. Yet a major national defence force was absolutely vital, as had been shown by Great Britain needing to activate its militia during the Napoleonic wars to keep the French conscription army in check – and although this force was only needed in times of war, it needed to be ready to be deployed in an emergency. Training was essential, since a well-drilled conscription army had to be met with more powerful weapons than mere enthusiasm and patriotic fervour.

But in viewing all male citizens as potential 'national fighters', Rotteck was not simply following the dictates of military logic. Instead, the idea drew on a political notion that he dated back to the classical world, with active participatory citizenship accompanying the readiness to defend one's country in times of need – and in taking this approach, he was reiterating Gneisenau's belief, expressed in 1808, that constitutionalism and military service were linked. In contrast to the enslaved vassal, the free citizen was a fervent patriot, equating his own personal freedom with the liberty of the civic community and their shared 'fatherland', and ready not only to defend this liberty with words, but with deeds too; furthermore, because he also acknowledged this task as implying a 'universal social duty', he was not willing to leave it to a professional 'military caste'. And in Rotteck's view, it was precisely this stance that characterised the free citizen as mature and self-assured, with an awareness of the responsibility he bore.

In 1823, a similar line was taken by Friedrich Wilhelm von Ellrodt, a Frankfurt colonel, commander of the local urban militia, and a member of the permanent citizens' assembly (*Bürgerrepräsentation*). He too argued for a self-sufficient 'citizens' army' comprising all male members of the populace, irrespective of wealth or origins, where substitution was not permitted. As far as Ellrodt was concerned, bearing arms went hand in hand with personal independence: 'The principal distinguishing feature of the free man is being able to use weapons and knowing how to defend and protect his liberty and independence himself. Anyone not constantly prepared to do so, or anyone not having learnt how to do so, betrays a slave mentality.'[53] The image of Germans being 'slaves ... since the citizen no longer bears arms' recurred in a rousing speech to 'fellow German citizens' given by Becker, 'citizen and fervent lover of liberty', at the *Hambacher Fest* meeting of around 30,000 democrats and liberals in May 1832. In a reference to the conscription army, which he viewed as a tool of the prevailing authorities, he maintained weapons had previously adorned every free man, but now were 'only carried by slaves', bayonets instantly at the ready to suppress any protest by a 'defenceless and weaponless citizenry'. The only recourse was the 'universal arming of all citizens' – only in this way, Becker thought, could free constitutions be guaranteed and a limit put on the governments' 'whims and arbitrariness'.[54]

In 1839, the liberal politician Carl Welcker indicated the implications for domestic policy if all citizens were capable of bearing arms. Constitutional liberty requires a 'martial spirit', epitomising both the readiness and ability to defend and protect this liberty at home and abroad. Since, in Welcker's view, liberty and this martial spirit were intrinsically linked, involving the male populace in a 'citizens' army' along the lines of the Prussian *Landwehr* was creating both the political and moral foundation for a 'constitutional citizenry' *and* its crowning glory. This citizens' army functioned like a 'school', teaching 'the proudest of all feelings – a self-reliant sense of civil rights and liberty'; a man graduating from this school was well prepared to rebuff 'in a manly manner' any 'misconduct' in the personal or political sphere. In this way, he guarded the constitutional state's integrity in both war and peace, and protected it from any attempts to restore an absolutist monarchy without a constitution.

Welcker's positive reading of military service deviates radically from the unfavourable attitude dominant in the southern German states, prevalent in their assemblies and widespread in public opinion there during the *Vormärz* period. Instead of depreciating military service as an irksome burden, he upgrades it into a decisive element in modern citizenship, transforming it into a right that represents an integral part of political freedom. Moreover, he ranked 'martial training' as a crucial factor in the programme of male education, taking a stand against a trend that he regarded with a certain ambiguity. In his view, the older, rougher forms of masculine manners were being edged aside everywhere by 'tamer and more sophisticated customs and laws', and while this was to be welcomed as an indication of civilisation advancing, it was, at the same time, a worrying sign of society losing vitality and stamina. A concerned Welcker asked: 'Where will spinelessness, triviality, weakness and cowardice meet their master?' – finding the ready answer in a 'national armed service' (*vaterländischer Waffendienst*), a useful corrective for civil servants, the scholarly or the well-off: all men whose lifestyles had suffered most from the new customs.[55]

Such reasoning was vociferously developed in the liberal military discourse of the 1830s, and packaged to create maximum public debate. But it did not merely reflect the fault lines running through the political landscape. It offered a new, more militant notion of citizenship and masculinity. The citizen, as imagined by the Hambach festival speaker or leading figures in southern German liberal thought, was no longer to be primarily a family father, worker, or local burgher, but first and foremost a citizen of the state, guarding his rights and actively exercising them. In this view, acquiring and defending rights needed more than just a populace endowed with education, economic independence and a civic spirit; instead, it was essential for citizens to demonstrate their 'civil courage and civil commitment' as well, and take up arms to defend 'honour and liberty'. As Welcker put it in 1838, 'Men and nations have to defend their honour themselves, or else they lose it.'[56]

In this sense, it was only logical to place the concept of individual valour at the heart of liberal thought, and turn to the classical world for historical justification or, nearer to home, evoke the traditional city states in the medieval and early modern period. Under the *Ancien Régime*, the principle of urban citizens' militias had been steadily abandoned as it came under attack from two sides: firstly, the burghers, even in the Free Imperial Cities (*Freie Reichsstädte*), steadily opted to pass time-consuming parade and guard duties onto substitutes, and, secondly, the state authorities were increasingly keen on assuming the military functions themselves and delegating them to the standing army. Nonetheless, right up to the early years of the nineteenth century, it was quite common in many places for men to own arms, even when they were not needed for defence purposes. In Württemberg, for example, state law required that any man marrying or acquiring municipal civic rights had to prove ownership of a musket and breastplate, and when the king rescinded the law in 1809, decreeing general disarmament, he triggered massive unrest among the general population. All urban and rural inhabitants, with the exception of nobles, landowners and royal civil servants, were ordered to sell their weapons or surrender them at the town hall; however, the population at large was reluctant to obey. The rural populace especially offered a significant degree of resistance, yet it was in the countryside particularly that officials had been instructed to implement the law stringently to put a stop to poaching or violations of manorial hunting rights.

In 1815, there was yet another example of how strongly the citizens felt about the issue of owning weapons. In this case, members of the Württemberg assembly of estates protested indignantly during advisory discussions on the new constitution against any 'meddling in property and natural freedoms', demanding that the 'good old right' of owning weapons was reinstated. In 1817, the new king relaxed the strict provisions his father had introduced, allowing those citizens to carry a musket who claimed they felt a greater need for security. In the end, the state's constitution left this point of dispute unresolved, indicating that it would be regulated in a law later. However, later never came – even though both public functionaries and city delegates pushed to have the issue finally settled. In 1843, the local governments too took a decisive stand on freely owning weapons as the 'honorary privilege of every Württemberg citizen', simultaneously pointing out that a people 'familiar with weapons' could be employed to defend the state if it were threatened by external forces.[57]

The right of all male citizens to bear arms reappeared on the political agenda during the revolutionary period of 1848–9. A petition presented by the Freiburg patriots' association (*Vaterlandsverein*), with its nearly 800 members, to the war ministry in Saxony declaimed 'bearing arms is the supreme right of the free man'.[58] According to the Mannheim lawyer Friedrich Hecker, outspoken in March 1848 in the Karlsruhe parliament in favour of an armed citizenry and civilian militias (and himself a colonel in the Mannheim militia), the musket should be 'dear' to each citizen, and 'sound like the bugles' blast' in their ears. In Hecker's view, every male member of the population should have his own musket, paid for himself and passed on to his son, as in 'the wilds of Kurdistan'. Bearing arms was not only a sign of patriotism, but reflected a justified feeling of distrust against the authorities – since, if they provided the weapons, they could collect them in again. This though, according to Hecker, was exactly what the citizen should never allow: after all, the 'armed nation' is the 'certain protector of its liberty and rights'.[59]

Hecker, a democrat and later leader of a band of volunteers, was not alone in his views; his emotive speech resembled that given in August 1848 by Ernst Moritz Arndt as the Bonn delegate to the Frankfurt National Assembly. Arndt, well advanced in years, also wanted to ensure that 'every German man' would be granted the 'manly and honourable right' of bearing arms, although he saw this right as being limited to service in a 'citizens' militia' (*Volkswehr*), subject to the 'orders of authority'.[60] In other words, just as Welcker had done seventeen years before, both Hecker and Arndt placed the individual's right to bear arms within a political and military context, where it appeared bound to the issue of protecting rights to political freedom and coupled with ideas around collectively organising the men bearing arms.

Nonetheless, the debates in 1848 were particularly revealing in showing how, in the view of many contemporaries, the individual's right to bear arms was not exhausted by political and military functions. Welcker, for example, had previously announced on several occasions that he regarded the use of arms as perfectly legitimate in other, private affairs – in this particular instance, for defending personal honour.[61] In the process of debating basic constitutional rights, the 1848 Frankfurt Parliament had to spend time considering a minority opinion maintaining that the 'right of every German to carry arms' should be expressly guaranteed in the Imperial constitution (*Reichsverfassung*). The democratic delegate, Professor Franz Wigard from Dresden, underlined that this right was 'a primal, genuine German right', which 'should never ever be forfeited again'. And this right, as the majority of National Assembly members were quick to point out, was not exhausted by a general duty to serve in either the army or civilian militia (*Bürgerwehr*). Instead, this right should be enjoyed equally by those whose 'physical constitution prevented them serving in the militia' or who were over service age.[62]

Interestingly enough, Wigard saw no need to justify this democratic proposal further, or provide any other endorsement of it. Indeed, it is now difficult to reconstruct clearly what notions of personal freedom and self-affirmation these advocates of an individual's right to bear arms had, since they appear to have been content with references to rights enshrined in ancient customs and tradition. Nonetheless, it is noticeable that they extended the right to bear arms to 'every German'. In this way, though, they placed themselves beyond that 'primal' instance they were invoking. Neither the Greek city-states in antiquity nor the Roman republic knew of any universal right to bear arms undifferentiated along social lines – and such an idea was even less likely to have emerged from any medieval or early modern cities. On the other hand, if the desire for democratisation expressed in 1848 aimed at transcending such social differences, it still clearly remained within set gender borders – and despite the Frankfurt *Paulskirche* witnessing any number of lengthy debates, this issue was never touched on in the course of the speeches there. Apparently, all delegates, irrespective of their political leanings, felt it went without saying that this right extended to men alone. Similarly, the idea of requiring women to perform military service was never incorporated into debates on creating new military structures that would be valid throughout the empire. And when one delegate spiced up his exceptionally confused argument by remarking that, at times of greatest peril, not only men but women too would 'delight in using arms', he was met with a storm of riotous 'laughter' and 'uproar'.[63]

In fact, in 1838 Welcker had taken the opportunity in the state encyclopaedia (*Staats-Lexikon*), the bible of early liberal thought, to underline the fact that both the right to bear arms and the corresponding duty to fight to defend the fatherland were exclusively male prerogatives. In addition, he highlighted the key political significance inherent in the rights and duties incumbent on weapons owners, maintaining that, from the dawn of time, every free people had linked 'the right to vote directly and participate in political decision-making in the civic community with the duties of defending it to the death: anyone with the right to decide on war must be in a position to fight it'. And the implication was so obvious it hardly needed to be spelled out: since women were allowed neither to bear arms nor to take part in campaigns, they could make no case to enjoy any of the associated political rights.[64]

The logic of the argument, though, was less than convincing. There were simply no cases of any direct link between political rights and bearing arms, neither in Prussia nor in the southern German constitutional states. Furthermore, it was not the case that every man with access to political rights had been trained in the army to defend his country and, conversely, not every soldier of the appropriate age was entitled to take up political office or vote for delegates in the corporative assemblies of estates. In fact, a perfect congruence between political rights and military duties in the *Vormärz* period never existed, despite liberal theory steadily closing the gap between them and certain practices suggesting that such a link really had been forged. For example, men in Prussia and Bavaria were obliged to clarify their military status prior to marrying, settling or emigrating. Serving personally was not an essential prerequisite to obtain these rights, but the men needed to prove they had attended a mustering before the recruiting authorities and, in this way, had, in principle, recognized their calling to defend their king and country.

Liberal politicians drew on these practices, but went far beyond them in upgrading military service to an exercise in civic education and masculinity. In doing so, their views contradicted those of all fellow-citizens who, over the years, had reconciled themselves to the principle of conscription while seeing it as neither applicable personally nor valid for their sons, whom they chose to buy out. In so doing, these pragmatic fathers were actually employing the same notion Welcker himself favoured under prevailing conditions – but Welcker, in contrast, was hoping for a different style of army in future, an inclusive military structure leading to a genuine citizens' army. He regarded this as essential, not least to ward off the threat of a 'mobocracy'; especially 'at a time when the poor might, given the right circumstances, start a war against the rich', it was counterproductive to pursue a military organisation teaching the poor how to use weapons and leaving the rich 'unmartial'. In contrast to Rotteck in 1816, such considerations led Welcker to support the idea of compulsory military service across the social spectrum, following the Prussian model. This would not only put an end to the 'cowardice' found in the middle and upper classes; it would also reconcile and resolve social differences, since, he believed, if the 'higher' and the 'lower' were brought together as equals, they would learn to respect each other as 'fellow-citizens'. In this way, common military service for the fatherland would create new bonds across society and, in the long run, prevent a civil war between the poor and the better off.[65]

When Welcker first introduced these ideas into the Baden parliament in 1831, they received initial support; in the end, though, he was unable to gain a majority. The main point of dispute centred on his call to abolish substitution, which he placed on a par with a modern form of the 'traffic in human flesh'. In 1832, the newspaper for army affairs, the *Allgemeine Militär-Zeitung*, maintained that only a 'constitutive assembly of estates comprising confirmed old bachelors' would accept a conscription law that excluded substitution.[66] It was, in fact, not until 1848, when the wave of popular revolutionary rhetoric on equality met the equally widespread middle-class fear of a 'mobocracy', that family fathers appear to have accepted the need, whether they liked it or not, to surrender the right to buy their sons out of military service.

Nonetheless, most delegates continued to have trouble digesting the concept of universal conscription, as the history of paragraph 137 of the March 1849 Imperial constitution goes to show. This section of the basic law succinctly states that 'Conscription applies to everyone; no substitutions are possible.' But the first draft did not contain the second clause. This led to a minority in the constitution committee tabling an amendment excluding the use of substitutes and justifying it in plenary session by arguing that the practice of buying oneself out of military service was contrary to equality before the law, encouraged social unrest, and hindered 'the uniform organisation of armed forces' throughout all territories. No delegate dared publicly to vote against the motion. Even the majority on the committee thought it wise to keep their own counsel after the chairman of the military committee had condemned substitution as an offence 'against a principle of higher morality'. But such determined resistance was first needed before a prohibition on substitutions was included in the articles of Imperial constitutional law.[67]

In 1848, another of Welcker's concerns was on the agenda of the Frankfurt Parliament. In 1831, he had introduced the idea in the Karlsruhe assembly of combining the military and citizens into a 'citizens' army' (*Bürgerheer*) which would then form the principal core of the armed forces. At the time, however, although his vision did not receive majority support in the constituent assembly of estates, it awoke far greater interest and support outside. Throughout the 1830s local authorities in Baden continued to petition for 'the introduction of a general armed citizenry', seeing it as a means of overcoming the problem of 'military institutions that are too costly'. In September 1847, the Baden democrats incorporated this idea in the political programme embodied in the Offenburg manifesto, and in February 1848, 2,500 citizens from Mannheim called for the Baden parliament to use their influence to have an 'armed citizenry (*Volksbewaffnung*) with freely elected officers'.[68]

In 1848, citizens in other German states, including Prussia, were calling for some form of arming civilians, or armed citizenry, and a 'popular military organisation'.[69] Everywhere, resentment over the existing armies had grown to substantial proportions. Funding was not the only issue at stake; anger was widespread over the armies' political stance and their 'morale'. In the 1848 Frankfurt Parliament, the existing armies were condemned as 'reactionary' tools, suppressing any social movement that incurred the authorities' displeasure. The answer, they claimed, was to tie the army to the constitution: such attacks would be stopped if, instead of swearing their oath of loyalty to the king, soldiers swore by the state's constitution. Moreover, as Tübingen's Professor Vischer argued, it would be more suited to the spirit of the new age if the armed forces 'were fused organically with the nation'; the populace would never agree to it being employed against their own. Instead, they would use it to defend constitutional and civic liberties. Such arguments moved many of the delegates gathered in Frankfurt's *Paulskirche* to support the introduction of an 'armed citizenry' (*Volksbewaffnung*) as soon as possible.[70]

Despite the enthusiasm for this 'most popular idea of the day', notions on how to implement it practically remained 'utterly confused'.[71] Moderate liberals argued for keeping the standing army to defend the state from any external threat, while a *Landwehr* took over tasks to ensure internal peace and security; democratic delegates replied by supporting the concept of a 'citizens' militia force' (*Volkswehr*), which would erase the 'unholy distinction between the armed and unarmed citizen'. Inside this military structure, 'democratisation' would be guaranteed by having 'freely elected superiors'. Furthermore, since the soldiers would be sworn in on the constitution, they would be obliged to protect civic liberties in the political sphere.[72] Opinion in the Frankfurt Parliament was equally diffuse and divergent on the relationship between an 'armed citizenry' and 'civilian militias'. Although one could easily have gained the impression that both terms referred to the same thing, some delegates insisted that the civilian militias were only a part of the 'citizens' militia force' and distinct from the 'standing army'. The assembly's military committee, entrusted with the task of establishing a new empire-wide military organisation, wanted to see 'civilian militias' set up in all municipalities but, to avoid interfering too much in their 'civilian and commercial life', left the individual states and communal authorities to decide how they should be organised and used. In this way, it merely consolidated the status quo that had already existed since spring 1848, leaving a situation many delegates felt was urgently in need of a general and binding ruling.[73]

4. Civilian Militias during the *Vormärz* Period and in 1848–1849

By 1848, civilian militias were nothing genuinely new; they could be recalled as a relic from the early modern principle of urban civilian defence forces. During that period, the original military functions had become transformed into a symbolic show – a mere 'game' with colourful uniforms and festive parades.[74] In 1809, the Württemberg king put an end to this by abruptly deciding that all citizens' militias and old traditional shooting clubs (*Schützengesellschaften*) were to be disbanded. He only permitted a civilian guard force (*Bürgerwache*) in Stuttgart to do duty at the palace and city gates when the army was absent. The other medium-sized German states saw a similar development too.

After the Paris July Revolution in 1830, a wave of new militias was founded. The local populations in many towns came together to form civilian guard forces (*Bürgergarden*) and defence organisations 'to secure public peace and protect property'. Above all, the group of property-owning civilians was active in seizing the initiative and forming local militias, generally supplying the officers and commanders for them. Such civilian self-empowerment was at its most pronounced in Saxony, which in 1830 saw local militias established throughout the state as an element in the process of introducing constitutional structures. The government took a positive attitude towards such groups providing they concentrated on policing tasks within the local district, but tried to prevent them taking on any areas of military competence.[75] From the civilian perspective, though, crossing that demarcation line seemed to have its attractions, as the dispute over the local militias' uniforms and weapons clearly illustrates. Militias in Saxony stubbornly persisted in trying to model uniforms and insignia on military designs, despite the war ministry's equally persistent attempts to prevent them. No matter how much the militiamen, who came from the lower and middle classes, sought to erase the external differences between them, the army showed itself equally determined to stop them. There were protracted struggles over every detail of the uniforms, with the local militia commander-in-chief having to intervene time and again to call local units to order after disobeying the ban on 'military insignia'.[76]

This argument over military signs and symbols reflected fundamental differences over the sense and purpose of the local militias (*Kommunalgarden*) within the entire military context. The 1830 decree authorizing a local militia defined it as 'an association of well-disposed residents from all social classes, to secure general security and public order', adding that it was also seen as 'a means to promote civic spirit'. Consequently, although government authorities tended to interpret this provision rather restrictively, the local militia were at pains to improve their standing within the political and military landscape in Saxony – and for that they needed, not least, to be properly armed. An unarmed militia was totally inconceivable – even the idea itself was simply laughable. Local commanders, generally members of the propertied and educated classes, regularly applied to the war ministry requesting muskets, ammunition and sabres, but the authorities were less than forthcoming. By the time the local militias were fully organised in 1832, they had received a mere 5,000 muskets – approximately one for every fifth militiaman. With the exception of the Dresden militia, whose 6,000 men were completely equipped from armoury supplies, other local militias largely had to pay for their uniforms, weapons and ammunition themselves. The authorities in Leipzig, for instance, only provided 500 bayonets, while 1,408 were paid for and purchased privately; in Pirna, the figures were 20 supplied to 209 purchased. In this way, since the local authorities rarely offered to buy the missing weapons from public funds, the individual militiaman was faced with a significant personal investment.[77]

The underlying conflict between the central authorities and local citizens was present too in the battles of will over weapons. While the militiamen, in their role as an organisation maintaining public order, wanted to bear all the insignia symbolising military worth, the war ministry was taking a firm stand on the army monopoly of military functions, jealously guarding against all devolution of tasks. From the war ministry perspective, 'arming a citizen' was 'always a dangerous method', and made him 'more refractory'. The ministry of the interior regarded the ambitions of the local militias more favourably, citing experience to support the claim that they could protect public order better than the army, whose deployment tended to inflame the situation as citizens often saw it as inappropriate.[78] The dramatic sudden unrest in Leipzig in August 1845 provided a prime example of what they meant.

The events there escalated after the local population had given vent to its frustration with Prince Johann, who was held accountable for the rigid attitude taken towards free-thinking religious movements. But when the local garrison was called out to control the mob and fired on them, killing seven demonstrators, a major wave of 'turmoil' broke over the city. To calm the situation, the commander passed police and guard duties over to the local militia. They presented themselves in a dual role: firstly, they underlined their position as a part of the Leipzig citizenry protesting against the army attacks by being prominently involved in the demonstrators' funeral cortege. 'At the head of the procession rode a part of the mounted local militia force, followed by the coffins in intervals, each accompanied by their mourners, and escorted by local militiamen and students.' Secondly, the local militia functioned as a civilian police force, monitoring the procession and endeavouring to control any disturbances.

In any case, as became clear when the government both praised and censured the militia for its behaviour, the latter saw itself as an independent municipal body and not as under the government's command. As far as the militiamen were concerned, 'praise or censure from the state government is all one, since they believe in the power in themselves.' It was a self-confidence that found similar expression in the song of the Leipzig militia guards: 'Militiamen won't rest until we get the best, not the mob possessed, nor tyrants that oppress. The best is in between. Our suffering was extreme. Our rights are what we claim. A citizen's no slave.'[79]

While the conflict in Leipzig in 1845 took place in the context of a political struggle between the government and the people, with the militia principally on the side of the civilian population, their deployment during social tensions in the local area was more equivocal. In such instances, they embodied the interest of the urban middle classes in stability and order – which is no surprise since only resident and self-employed men were entitled to enlist in the militia. As a result, their ranks were full of tradesmen, businessmen, innkeepers, doctors and, in some cases, civil servants, all appearing admirably suited to protect middle-class property rights and keep in check the danger posed by the growing industrial proletariat.[80] And when such dangers loomed and political or social conflicts erupted, the propertied citizens were very ready to become involved in a civilian militia.

In 1830, for example, in Leipzig, the 26-year-old publisher Heinrich Brockhaus, whose older brother Fritz was already a local *Kommunalgarde* officer, joined the militia too. After the unrest in September, he reported that it was 'quite wonderful to see the citizens with muskets and sabres standing on guard' and 'keeping the mob in order'.[81] In the spring of 1848, many communities organised their own security forces, as did the town of Schwäbisch-Hall, reasoning that they needed to protect themselves against 'the violent acts of the unruly riff-raff'. The Stuttgart and Dresden governments were flooded with constant requests for the weapons needed if the local civilian militias were to secure middle-class property. Apparently, not only was 'civic order' under threat from 'reactionary' forces but also from 'anarchy and insurrection'. At the end of March 1848, Wilhelm von Kügelgen, court painter in the Duchy of Anhalt, noted that trouble 'is brewing in the lowest classes', and by November 1848, he 'seriously' feared 'the mob launching an attack on my house'.[82] Even in the small town of Ballenstedt where he lived, the situation called for a local civilian guard force – and Kügelgen was promptly chosen as its commander. As far as he was concerned, the call for 'arming civilians' contained primarily a social import. He remained a stranger to the political hopes liberals and democrats associated with it, although it was precisely such hopes that gained in force and conviction in the months of revolution. The immense public pressure led the grand duke of Baden and the king of Württemberg to introduce laws on 1 April 1848, providing for civilian militias in all districts. Eleven days later, Saxony followed by issuing a decree on strengthening the local civilian militias, aimed at 'preparing a universal arming of the people to protect the fatherland internally and, if need be, externally'.

These laws contained numerous innovations, altering the status of civilian militias even where they already existed. Firstly, they made it clear that civilian militias were not purely local institutions, but played their part within a general, state-wide system of armed citizenry (*Volksbewaffnung*), and, secondly, in so doing, they explicitly ranked militias as military units and not as a police force. Finally, the mode of social inclusion and exclusion underwent a change: whereas to begin with, in the spirit of the *Vormärz* period, social borders had been clearly drawn, with militias exclusively recruiting men who were 'independent, with their own income', able to afford their own equipment, such provisions later fell into abeyance. From June 1848, Württemberg local districts were permitted to arm men at their own expense if the men were unable to pay for their own weapons. In contrast, the civilian militia law in Baden did not contain regulations excluding a part of the society, and when the Mannheim local authorities passed a resolution in 1848 only admitting urban burghers to the civilian militia, they provoked a storm of outrage; even moderate liberals like Welcker declared the move inadmissible and succeeded in introducing measures to have non-burghers admitted.[83] In Saxony, democratic associations registered their protests against day labourers and destitute people being excluded from the militias in a petition where they stated: 'Not providing for the universal arming of citizens testifies to a mistrust that cannot be justified by any danger. We still do not have a general armed citizenry, which, moreover, we have been promised. We demand it as a sacred right. The worker is just as worthy to carry a weapon as the civil servant, or the wealthy member of the middle class.'[84] The Saxon government could not ignore such pressing demands coupling the claim to citizenship with the desire for weapons and civilian militia membership, and from November 1848 day labourers, journeymen and factory workers were also obliged to enlist in the local militia.

In this way, the character and function of local militias shifted significantly. Instead of being a local burghers' defence troop acting as a shield against violent acts by the 'mob' as in the past, their future role was centred around cultivating the citizens' ability to fight, protecting the constitution and guaranteeing public order. Some militiamen went even further, dubbing the militias and defence forces as 'a place where the population receives an intellectual and moral education', while yet others praised their social function. For example, a petition signed by 324 men from the Saxon district of Neu-Ebersbach in 1850 applauded universal service in the local militia as removing 'the barriers between gentleman and commoner, the high and the low, the scholar and the unschooled; in other words, everyone here is what they have to be and should be – a human being and a citizen!'[85]

It is hard to say whether this reflected the reality of local militias, or was simply a tactical move – after all, the petition was submitted in support of keeping their defence force. In fact, the information documenting local militias presents a very diffuse picture, and it varies from state to state, region to region, city to city, town district to town district, and even from month to month. Above all in the early revolutionary phase, many men enthusiastically welcomed the call to arms and provision of weapons, taking a stand on defending 'the rights and liberties embodied in the laws from both inner and outer enemies', with even those who had bought themselves out of regular military service active in the civilian militias.[86] To begin with, since memories of the Napoleonic war had left a legacy of belief in aggressive French expansionism, attention primarily concentrated on the 'outer enemy' in the shape of France, but soon the 'inner enemy' took over as the focus of concern. Some civilian militias became totally absorbed in defensive measures against assumed or real actions undertaken by the 'mob', while others considered their basic remit was to protect the constitution or, after spring 1849, the Imperial constitution. In summer 1849, numerous Württemberg civilian militias mobilized to support the Baden revolutionaries (which included many civilian militiamen) in their struggle against Prussian troops.[87]

The more civilian militias took a stance on political issues, identifying the 'inner enemy' not in the guise of the revolutionaries but as embodied in the traditional authorities, the closer they were subjected to government monitoring. In twenty-four cases, regular troops were deployed in Württemberg villages and towns to disarm the local civilian militias. In Saxony too, once the May uprising in Dresden had been suppressed, numerous local militias were disbanded and those remaining placed under strict supervision.[88] The year 1850 found the war ministry bemoaning that 'nowhere' had the militias deployed in 1848–9 justified 'the government's trust even to a moderate degree', but instead they had, sadly, fulfilled 'the hopes of the revolution'.[89] Undoubtedly, such an assessment was strongly related to their own perspective, since there is no general picture of militias in Saxony choosing 'rebellion' and actively fighting against the military authorities, despite there being numerous accounts of militias actually doing just that. However, many villages and towns never even founded a militia force, and Pietist communities objected to them on religious grounds. Rural communities too demonstrated considerable reserve in starting militias, voicing the opinion that the very idea was a thoroughly urban contrivance and the countryside had no need for it. In 1848–9, records show slightly less than a third of all rural districts in Saxony with a local militia force, and many of those were only a reality on paper, with no intention of ever arming themselves and practising military drills.[90]

The majority of civilian militias, and the best organised, were found in major cities. In 1848–9 in Leipzig, for example, 12,000 men were in militias, and Hanover reported 3,000 militiamen from a population of 30,000; in October 1848, Heilbronn recorded a civilian militia of over 1,200 men, while in spring 1848 the militia in Stuttgart was numbered at several thousand. In addition, Stuttgart boasted a youth corps, a *Jugendbanner*, with around 250 men under 25, largely comprising *Gymnasium* pupils, commercial clerks, members of athletics associations, and students from the technical university. They also invoked civic duties as the reason for their involvement and cited the 'urge to learn how to fight that drives every young man'. When they described the purpose of their organisation, echoes of the liberal *Vormärz* rhetoric could clearly be heard, intensified by the euphoria of experiencing, and even helping to shape, a historical period of transition: it was not only designed to promote a 'genuine public spirit', but also to 'call to the ranks the kind of men needed for the future of this country'.[91] But a more martial tenor was equally present, exemplified in the reports sent by the 45-year-old Wilhelm von Kügelgen to his brother Gerhard in distant Petersburg. In spring 1848, Kügelgen was writing enthusiastically about the daily drills and exercises, adding, 'Basically, there's nothing I'd rather do than pack my musket on my back and take part in a campaign. And not only me, lots of the others would too, as bit by bit a growing flood of martial spirit is sweeping across the entire population.'[92] Even men who had been exclusively involved in civilian occupations suddenly found the military 'movements' totally fascinating – aided, no doubt, by the interest in them shown by the female half of the population. After all, most drills and exercises were performed publicly and attracted a large audience of both sexes.

Women and men met on other occasions too, though in different roles. Women sewed and embroidered civilian militia flags and banners and were given pride of place at the presentation of the colours, which was not only conducted with great pomp and circumstance but also in public. In April 1848, women in Constance near the Swiss border, insisted on attending the local council meeting that was debating how to help organise the *Heckerzug*, an armed march led by the southern German democrats Friedrich Hecker and Gustav von Struve. The women did not want to join in, although one or two actually did so, but felt directly affected as mothers and wives. Moreover, they were adamant about their moral influence: 'Inside and outside the house, the women's spirit is a decisive factor in whether some men take up arms and gladly march off for their country, or whether they are indifferent, unwilling or cowardly and avoid joining in the general fray.'[93]

Here, women were asserting their shared responsibility in the political sphere, staking out their own key role in the armed war fought by men. They perceived war as a joint concern even if they never, or rarely, took up arms themselves – and even if exceptions generally received a sharp public rebuke and were ridiculed as Amazons, viragos, and 'drunken maenads'.[94] In a way reminiscent of the wars against Napoleon in the early nineteenth century, 1848–9 saw women taking on a whole range of tasks and functions, ranging from moral encouragement to symbols of manly valour (the banners), from secondary skilled jobs (preparing cartridges, making linen surgical dressings, and looking after the wounded) to collecting money for weapons and naval equipment, and providing social support for families of soldiers or militiamen. All of these tasks defined them as part of a political gendered community where responsibilities and competences were clearly separated but mutually interdependent.

For men, this was simultaneously both a confirmation and a challenge. Undoubtedly, the active participation of women put them under pressure not to fall short of the anticipated measure of martial patriotism – and this duty was underlined when women handed over banners and weapons to the men: 'When the weapon to defend the fatherland is handed to him by a woman, who would be cowardly enough not to fight with it to the death?'[95] And if men shirked this duty, women could add physical weight to what had merely been symbolic pressure, as in Freudenstadt in June 1849 when the wives and daughters of civilian militiamen who had mobilized behind the Baden revolutionaries came out 'carrying sticks' to punish the militiamen accused of cowardice for staying behind. Women from northern Germany and Württemberg were active too when support was needed to implement the Imperial constitution resolved on by the Frankfurt Parliament. They published appeals to 'our German warriors' in broadsheets, posters and newspaper advertisements warning their menfolk not to be misused as the bailiffs of a 'tyrannical duchy hostile to the people', and threatened to withdraw marital rights and suspend relations with their sweethearts if their pleas fell on deaf ears.[96]

It is impossible now to say how widespread or serious such threats were, or judge how they affected the men, but at least it is known that men were also using the women's topos of the mocked, contemptuous and despised coward. For example, in May 1849, when the local Gmünd club (*Volksverein*) called for a volunteer corps to be formed to fight in the struggle over the Imperial constitution, it did so expressing the hope that 'no-one will need to be told by our young women: leave us alone, you coward, we want men who have the courage to defend our highest good, our honour, our liberty, our life and our home.'[97] The 1848 public debates on 'arming the people' were pervaded by the image of the 'manly' man, characterised by his martial valour, coupled, as it were, with the complementary image of the (virginal) woman needing and deserving protection.

The flags women embroidered for the militiamen – unrivalled in symbolism as a pledge of masculine unity, vigour and determination – expressed the women's concern with the issue of their men's valour. Holding the colour presentation ceremony in the women's presence indicated that men were conscious of the women's expectations and demands, and accepted them. This interlacing of duties was succinctly summarised in a poem, quoted by a teacher and civilian militia officer in 1848 at a presentation of the colours in Stuttgart: 'The German tribe delights in rushing / to follow the women's call to arms / The women's glory to bestow this honour / And your glory too, to belong to free men'.[98]

In evoking the Germanic past, this part-time poet drew on memories of when every man was presumed armed and responsible for defending his own home. This trinity of masculine liberty, valour and fitness to marry met with great resonance in 1848–9, with some Württemberg districts even suggesting that men should only be allowed to marry if they could provide their own uniform and arms – an idea that both the ministry of the interior and the chamber of deputies viewed favourably. In 1849, according to Wolfgang Menzel, a writer and parliamentary delegate, 'Anyone unable to manage to furnish themselves with a musket and arms shouldn't get married', a notion echoed by Tafel, a fellow deputy, who proclaimed: 'In future, a weapon has to be the essential equipment for every young man.' Such views did not merely cite traditional customs in Württemberg as their authority but invoked contemporarily valid law in Bavaria too, which required every member of the *Landwehr* to appear before the altar in his complete military regalia.[99]

Forming a link between fitness to marry, valour and suitability as a citizen falls under the heading of what one might term 'inventing a tradition'. The era being quoted lay so far back in history that memories of it were only located within a mythical surround. In addition, it was conveniently forgotten that only a small part of the male population benefited from the *Heerbann*, or the right to bear arms; moreover, the way previous generations of civilians, purportedly so crazy about using weapons, had shirked military service, evincing a distinct lack of enthusiasm over it, or even openly resisting, was similarly consigned to oblivion. Hence, the adamant affirmation of tradition and 'good old customs' cast more light from the present onto the future than it did on the past. And as the broad debate on 'arming the people' made only too clear, the future was reserved for men who, in association with other men and supported and honoured by women, were able and ready at any time to take up arms and fight for the state, the constitution and the civic order. Such views, moreover, seemed to receive initial confirmation in practice. Civilian militiamen gloried in their roles as freedom fighters and guardians of the law, 'true to the ruler but never a slave', and drew political self-confidence from their new military functions.[100] But precisely this attitude frequently culminated in conflicts with their duties under military discipline and the army's hierarchical system, which the militiamen regarded as constrictive and alien; and the longer civilian militia service went on, the harder it became to motivate them to accept these practices. Furthermore, the superiors responsible for maintaining discipline often had little real authority since the 'lower ranks' mostly knew them from civilian life, where they considered themselves equals.

In the long run, guard and parade duties seemed as superfluous as a ridiculous 'masquerade', to quote Brockhaus, and, despite the abundance of heroic rhetoric, the prospect of military action also failed to generate enthusiasm across the board. When the conflict over adopting the Imperial constitution came to a dramatic head in Dresden in early May 1849, and the strategy of petitions and addresses appeared to have been exhausted, many in the militia backed away from the use of arms. In his diary, the actor and local militiaman Eduard Devrient cursed 'It's all dull, indecisive, and insipid', condemning the readiness of his comrades 'to go home and let their weapons be taken off them. Those male mollies! They loved playing at soldiers, but they aren't even capable of making a decision when needed.' But Devrient also found himself vacillating on the question of using his weapons against the Saxon and Prussian military, despite his embarrassment over his 'cowardice' moving him 'to tears'. It was also radically at odds with the 'pluck' of the Chemnitz militia, mobilising to lend active support to the provisional government and welcomed by Dresden women waving shawls and kerchiefs. Only the 'hale and hearty young men, robust and courageous' mobilised in the Dresden civilian militia, while family fathers felt themselves bound by their private duties – just like Devrient, at the time 47 years old and the head of a large household. As early as the turbulent March days in 1848, he had noted: 'If there were not so many lives dependent on me, I know what use I'd make of mine.' This inner discord drove Devrient into such a rage that he took refuge in radical pronouncements: 'Why do wives and children have to enslave us so! My own lived experience has brought me to the point the democrats are making when they want to abolish the family to set men free.'[101]

Behind such a view lay the notion that, although civilian militiamen were no longer 'the ruler's slaves', they had proved to be 'under their wives' thumbs', placing family duties above any 'political civic spirit'.[102] The symbolic alliance between men and women had given no indication of the complexity and complications in the relationship between civilian militias and gender order, where men and women were confronted by a divisive experience and concrete conflicts of interests. Initially, male readiness to accept a political and military responsibility transcending the private sphere meant distancing themselves from their house and home, with even standard exercises in the local area promoting links between the men rather than to their families. Indeed, many documents contain complaints over the 'disturbance to family life': 'The military exercises provide an opportunity to visit inns and lead to diverse expenditure; neighbouring civilian militias pay visits to each other; you don't want to own a musket simply to take on exercises; you go hunting and take part in target practice.' And all of this was not done alone, but in the company of other men – in the meantime, the women and children 'starve' and 'discord grows between man and wife'.[103]

All of this meant that civilian militia service brought the men noticeably more together in male groups, drawing them away from the family context, and such an observation gains force if one recalls the militiamen's age and family status. The men liable for civilian militia service were all middle-aged, with an average age of over 30, and mostly married.[104] While young, single men were expected to spend their free time with their peers, family fathers were supposed to adopt a different sort of behaviour, closely integrated into their family situation. Civilian militia service negated this notion, encouraging a displacement from family structures. But, as Devrient's comment on his experience in Dresden indicates, such a displacement stopped once the situation became 'serious', when 'playing at soldiers' was over and real military action against armed troops was imminent. Then, many husbands and fathers tended to regard themselves, first and foremost, as heads of the household, and only secondarily as brave citizen-soldiers. Women, too, only sustained the political gender alliance until the economic and social position of the family appeared endangered, and where the man's absence threatened to result in acute need, they recanted on any pledges of solidarity.[105]

Admittedly, such conflicts were predominantly played out within the private sphere; in the public arena – above all, in the parliamentary and district-level debates on civilian militias – they played no role whatsoever. Here, the idea of the armed citizen as the foundation stone of political liberty was, in general, very positively received. A man serving in the local civilian militia was not merely defending his home and private property but was, as the Baden Law on Civilian Militias specifically stated, defending his country and its constitution. In doing so, the citizen had advanced into a novel and notably political role, where state citizenship was ranked higher than municipal citizenship. But this was not all – the experience of politics as having something to do with a struggle was similarly new, with conflicts of interest not only expressed in words, but equally with muskets and pikes, and, moreover, with every citizen expected to take an active and personal stand on the issues.

In this way, however, the political message accompanying these experiences cast the enormous problems and difficulties inherent in the militia experiment into shadow, and even survived the demise of the militias themselves. The early enthusiasm over the new military status rapidly evaporated in the face of everyday demands. There was a vast gap between the politically and culturally motivated demands to bear arms and the readiness 'to take on the discomfort and burden it involves'. Instead of drilling, standing guard or fighting the regular army, many militiamen quickly discovered that they would rather dedicate their time to pursuing their civilian occupations. Involvement in militias tended to be low, except when political movements peaked. Only the major towns had a constant force of militiamen – the others were deterred not least by the high costs for weapons and clothing, partially to be paid for by the individual militiamen and partly by the local authorities. By 1850 less than 8 per cent of all local districts in Württemberg had established a militia force, a situation reflected in the terse remark by a Stuttgart parliamentary commission in 1851 that: 'There is no longer any response anywhere to the call for a civilian militia.' Even Baden rescinded its 1848 Law on Civilian Militias two years after it appeared on the statute books, providing instead for each local district to decide autonomously on whether to form a militia or not – primarily to 'suppress the mobs' violent acts against members of particular classes or estates'. In this instance, just as in Saxony, civilian militias were reduced to a purely public order function and their link to a universally armed citizenry, as had been planned in 1848, was no longer an element in political discourse.[106]

5. The 'Martial Spirit' in Military Associations or Dreams of a Democratic Army

Consequently, when the post-Revolution governments filed away the idea of an armed citizenry, they could do so claiming that the citizens' theoretical recourse to their ability at arms had aroused little lasting or practical interest. The debate on substitutes in military service too raised doubts over 'the' people's readiness to take up arms, that notion evoked so persistently and with such pathos. Apart from Prussia, all the states permitting substitution prior to 1848 retained it in the 1850s and 1860s, after a brief revolutionary intermezzo. Everywhere saw a rush to rescind the abolition of the substitute system, introduced in the Frankfurt Parliament, usually justified by citing 'the many esteemed opinions presented by the people' and the experience in 1848–9. According to the Württemberg war minister, 'Requiring men to bear arms to this extent' did not reflect the views 'of the vast majority of our people'. For the middle classes represented in parliament, such a statement was balm to their ears, since they remained just as keen on buying themselves out of military service after the Revolution as before, and saw no further need to justify their views.[107]

Yet, nonetheless, a defensive tone gradually started to creep into their arguments. Apparently, the consensus on an equal universal military service for all, anchored in the 1848 Frankfurt Imperial constitution, could not be completely ignored. It was repeatedly invoked by speakers in parliamentary debates, who then banished it again with either the triumphant or sorrowful cry that it had proved impossible to implement in practice. They then went on to warn that abolishing substitution would be ill advised before military service was established for all fit young men throughout the country. Among other reasons, the delegates vindicated their unwillingness to – as they saw it – put the cart before the horse by pointing to the serious consequences this step would have in terms of both legislation and funding. Many of those advocating substitution under the given conditions were, at the same time, actually engaged in vigorously praising the virtues of a citizens' militia force. Above all, from the 1850s on, southern Germany saw a steady increase in the volume of support for the Swiss militia model, regarded both as cheap and democratic. In contrast, those speakers taking up Welcker's position on a Prussian *Landwehr* system were open to the criticism that it was too costly and, furthermore, too dependent on a standing army system. In 1865, a Württemberg parliament delegate summarised the majority's reservations in his comparison of the Prussian army and the Swiss militia: in Prussia, he said, a young man spends more time in military service – this lends him a 'certain military character'; in addition, he becomes accustomed to a 'subordination he then transfers to his civilian life'. In Switzerland, though, this relationship is reversed, since there they transfer 'the liberty and equality found in the civic sphere wholesale into military life'. In other words, in Prussia, the civic sphere is militarised, while in Switzerland, the military sphere is civilised.[108]

It was obvious that even militias needed to observe military principles, such as discipline and obedience, if they wanted to achieve a minimum of unity and tactical efficiency, but the lack of professionals, and the short periods of practice and drill, ensured that the prevailing civilian atmosphere there continued unchanged. In Switzerland, too, any purely military dominance was hampered by the way civilian and military spheres were interwoven, far more than in Prussia, with a constant exchange of roles between the citizen and soldier: a Swiss militiaman always bore in mind that he was equally a local citizen and, for example, family father and artisan or farmer or doctor, and sought to ensure a suitable balance between his roles. In contrast, over the two or three years of active service, a Prussian soldier was trained to forget civilian customs and concentrate, heart and soul, on life in the military. But, for a majority of middle-class citizens across the southern German states, this was precisely the crux – and the very idea was both alarming and repellent. Even though the formal active service period in southern German armies was far shorter than in Prussia, there was still a general concern that men could become infected with the garrisons' 'military spirit'. Instead, as a positive counterpart, fighters should become bearers of the 'martial spirit', to be 'cultivated from youth on' and 'refined and intensified by a martial training'. And that, as the Württemberg parliamentary delegate Fetzer emphasised in 1865, was only viable in a 'national army' (*Volksheer*), which ought to replace the standing 'garrison army' as quickly as possible.[109]

This differentiation between a 'military' and 'martial' spirit (*militärischer und kriegerischer Geist*) could draw on a long tradition, going back to Ernst Moritz Arndt and Carl von Rotteck, and had played a part in the calls for an armed citizenry in the years around 1848. Yet, even in the 1850s and 1860s, the model of a people's army organised along militia lines lost none of its political allure, while military events throughout those years did nothing to dim its continuing topicality. The decades between the Congress of Vienna and the wave of revolutions across Europe in 1848 formed a relatively peaceful period, but the years afterwards were marked by numerous military confrontations, spawning the idea in contemporaries that political conflicts could best be resolved via military means. Whether the tensions between Prussia and Austria at the end of the 1840s, the 1859 uprising in northern Italy against the Habsburgs, or the Crimean War – they all led to greater public awareness of war as a means to achieve political ends. But despite the belligerent mood gripping, in particular, large parts of the liberal middle classes in the late 1850s, they were not blind to the deficits in the national military system.[110] Quite the contrary – this attitude actually resulted in increased readiness both to consider reforms and implement them. In this context, the most vocal group calling for defence associations (*Wehrvereine*) to be established was the *Deutscher Nationalverein*, founded in 1859 as a mix of liberals and democrats in a party-like structure with members throughout all the German states. They envisaged voluntary defence associations in all districts, teaching 'weapons skills' to single men between 18 and 35 without any previous military experience and, according to Wilhelm Rüstow, former Prussian lieutenant and writer on military affairs, this would only require a concentrated drill period of eleven days at most.[111]

In his Zurich exile, Rüstow dreamed of using such defence associations to develop a revolutionary army, though this was an idea that met with no support among the *Deutscher Nationalverein*'s members. They were largely constitutionalists, envisaging the defence associations as a 'cement between people and army', a troop of volunteers reinforcing regular army forces in the case of war. Furthermore, these associations were to keep alive the notion in the general population of alternatives to a standing army and underline the idea that citizens could also show a readiness to fight in other ways than by enlisting in the regular armed forces. Certainly, the military training in defence associations was meant to be 'earnest' and followed the Prussian drill regulations, but left out 'presenting of arms, march pasts and similar nonsense'. In this way, the defence associations represented a prototype of a future 'people's army' or 'militia army', embodying the liberal-democratic movement's perspective on military policy.[112]

However, despite their energetic start, the *Deutscher Nationalverein*'s ambitious defence programme rapidly fizzled out. Most Prussian members were against any campaign to found a dense network of defence associations across every single German state, claiming they would be neither practical nor realisable in Prussia itself, especially since, as Hermann Schulze-Delitzsch objected on the basis of his own personal regular army and *Landwehr* service, Prussia already had 'a legal obligation to universal military service'. In their view, defence associations could only be usefully called into life where universal military service did not yet exist. But even in such cases the *Deutscher Nationalverein*'s initiative met with little resonance.[113] Above all, the men's gymnastic clubs and associations, originally chosen as a potential breeding ground for the defence association movement, kept a reserved distance. In Coburg, at the first German athletic sports festival in 1860, the convening body of gymnasts may have recommended 'weapons practice, namely target practice with firearms', but the majority of its members rejected making this into an obligation, similarly dismissing the concept of gymnastic clubs as the 'core of a general armed citizenry' and the idea of them establishing any centralised organisational structure. In 1862, of 134,000 gymnasts in total and 80,000 active gymnasts, only around 18,300 took part in fencing, shooting and drill exercises – and even the 1861 Coburg 'Model Company' comprising members of the local gymnasts' club and equipped with bayonet rifles, uniforms and various accessories did not survive for long, despite a prestigious start.[114]

The *Deutscher Nationalverein* hoped to have better luck with the shooting clubs. In the uncertain *Vormärz* period, these had already been entrusted with paramilitary and police duties, and 1848 had seen many of the urban shooting clubs voluntarily joining the local militia groups. However, simply a glance at the statutes would have made clear that their primary interest lay in pomp and pageantry. Their uniforms, deprecatingly dubbed 'clown's coats' in the *Deutscher Nationalverein*'s broadsheet, comprised as brilliant and variegated a range of colours, materials and styles as had ever been seen, with (lower) middle-class whimsy in questions of ornamental and distinguishing features allowed a completely free rein. Despite arranging processions that resembled military parades, the shooting clubs traditionally were at great pains to stress their distance from the army and underline the differences between them – and indeed the central focus of club life was not any military-style exercise, but 'convivial gatherings', especially the annual rifle-match fête held every summer.[115]

In contrast, the members of the Frankfurt Shooting Club pursued a totally different line on what their association wanted to achieve. Founded in 1860 at the behest of radical democrats, its declared aim was to promote the 'nation's training in how to use firearms' in order to build a bridge between the 'people and the army'. There is no clear indication of how far this club was able to transfer its ideas to other riflemen's associations, although it did provide the impetus for the first national rifle-match festival in 1861, held in Gotha, with a core concern expressed as 'Manliness is Valour at Arms' (*Mannhaftigkeit gleich Wehrhaftigkeit*) – an image constantly evoked in many rhetorical appeals and speeches. The idea even underlay the notion prevalent in the German Marksmen's League (*Deutscher Schützenbund*), founded in the same year, of being 'placed at the side of the army, like a reserve of honour'. However, northern German delegates, who firmly rejected any idea of linking the army and the shooting clubs too closely, stalled moves among southern German marksmen eager to immediately debate 'armed citizenry and military-style organisations'. Consequently, at the 1862 Frankfurt national rifle-match festival, held jointly with gymnast and choir clubs, a more measured approach was adopted, with, for example, Hermann Schulze-Delitzsch, guest speaker and Prussian member of parliament, praising the 'promising' initiative of the gymnastic and shooting clubs to arm the 'nation' and create a free and constitutional 'people's army'. Yet simultaneously, there were repeated indications that many shooting clubs had little interest in the idea of that 'united nation in arms' so enthused over by Georgii, an Esslingen lawyer and member of the *Nationalverein*.[116]

In this way, then, the *Deutscher Nationalverein*'s efforts to convert gymnasts' and marksmen's clubs into defence associations with a military value largely came to nothing, despite the gymnastic associations – under the influence of its key founding figure, '*Turnvater*' Jahn – and the traditional shooting clubs both being convinced that their activities had military worth. But apparently they were opposed to turning this military currency into their principal *raison d'être*. In the same way that the army wanted to ensure that the border to civilian life was sharply drawn, civic associations wanted to preserve their civilian character, and all groups took issue with any blurring of differences between the military and civilian spheres of operation, as proposed under the defence association concept.

Nonetheless, this experience did not prevent democratic politicians from continuing to enthuse over militia armies, armed citizenry and youth defence groups as counter-models to existing army structures. Even in 1865, visions of a fundamental militarisation gearing the 'complete national education' towards infusing men with 'a martial spirit' and 'love for weapons' still exercised 'a certain allure'. More than anywhere else, in southern and central Germany terms like a people's army or universal military service were deemed to have 'a ring about them that can be quite seductive', a view supported by the numerous petitions in 1865 from local communities all calling for 'the introduction of universal military service'.[117] But as the subsequent years went to show, this by no means implied directly copying the Prussian system. Indeed, the greater the acknowledgement Prussia received as a model German state – especially for a military system so dominantly successful in 1866 – the louder were the calls from those politically motivated opponents clinging to the notion of militias and a people's army. After the Stuttgart chamber of deputies passed a new military service act closely mirroring the Prussian system in early 1868, opposing democrats collected 150,000 signatures in protest against it.[118]

Wilhelm Liebknecht too issued a forceful call to southern German delegates meeting in 1868 in Nuremberg at the fifth conference of the German workers' associations to tear off 'the noose of the military agreements Prussia has thrown around your necks', openly admitting his preference for the Swiss system of a 'universally armed nation' as the only truly 'democratic' model. In contrast, he continued, the standing armies in Prussia and other European states are 'absolutist' and 'dynastic'. Liebknecht's fiery speech contained all the arguments and criticisms already voiced in 1848, and even his list of demands had nothing original to offer: the slogan of 'every citizen a soldier, and every soldier a citizen' had accompanied the birth of the French *levée en masse*, initiated the Prussian *Landwehr* system, spurred on the civilian militias in the 1848 Revolution and inspired the defence associations in the early 1860s. Yet he did not let the failures distract him from his argument, pointing to the USA and Switzerland, where 'the nation itself' takes on the task 'of defending the fatherland'. The Nuremberg delegates, representing a total of 14,000 members, took what he said to heart and declared it was 'the worker's duty, explicitly and unceasingly, to work with all means possible towards removing the standing armies and introducing a universally armed citizenry'.[119]

At the same time, the arguments did contain two new nuances. Apparently, some delegates wanted to go further than Liebknecht, arguing for 'universal disarmament'. However, he dismissed this by claiming the time had not yet come for such measures; first of all, the 'enemies of the people' needed to be brought to task, starting with French and Prussian 'Caesarism' before moving on to Russian 'despotism' – and that, he said, would 'take a long time'. In the meantime, 'peoples' needed to remain armed; here, he carefully underlined that he meant the peoples and not the 'standing armies'. The second change from the 1848 period concerned the role of the *Landwehr*. Whereas many liberals, even in the 1830s and 1840s, had regarded it as a model of 'universally armed citizenry', after the 'reorganisation', at the latest, it had been knocked off its democratic pedestal, with the general approval it had formerly enjoyed simply evaporating. Now, in Nuremberg, the Prussian *Landwehr* was firmly located within the topos of standing armies, and as far as Liebknecht was concerned, it no longer deserved the name of a 'citizens' militia force'.[120]

Liebknecht's argument, which the delegates unanimously supported, clearly shows that the position developed in 1865 by Friedrich Engels, a guiding light in socialist thought, found no echo either in the democratic movement or in the emerging socialist workers' grouping. Engels regarded militia organisation as a sheer 'fantasy' for countries like Prussia; in principle he endorsed a similar reinforcement to the line structure as implemented in Prussia in the early 1860s. In his view, 'Germany's working classes' should be keen on receiving 'intense' military training in the army: 'The more workers who are trained in the use of weapons, the better.' Universal conscription, in a form as inclusive and intensive as possible, represented 'the necessary and natural corollary of universal suffrage; it puts the voters in the position of being able to enforce their decisions gun in hand against any attempt at a *coup d'état*'. Here, Engels may have been thinking of his own experience as a Prussian one-yearer, and how his army experience left him far from being a conservative and monarchist. Given the choice, he would have opted for a solid military training over the democratic spirit in a militia army with, 'as it were, no term of service at all'. In contrast to Rüstow, a tremendously influential figure in liberal and democratic circles, with his eleven days of training, or August Bebel, who in 1867 advocated a three-month training period, Engels stood by a two-year period 'following the flag' as essential to maintaining a viable, combat-ready army. Furthermore, he was convinced that precisely because the Prussian army consisted of conscripts, it could 'neither wage an unpopular war nor carry out a *coup d'état* which has any prospect of permanence'.[121]

It was not a view widely shared by other socialists. In 1862, Ferdinand Lassalle had dubbed the Prussian army a 'prince's army', the king's disciplined 'instrument of power', and the 'most decisive and important of any organised power instruments'. For Lassalle, reducing service to six months was an essential step in transforming the army into a 'people's army' that was not fighting 'against the nation'. Ferdinand Lassalle played a key role in organising the General German Workers' Association (ADAV), effectively the first labour party, founded in Leipzig in 1863, which similarly spoke out for a purely defensively structured 'citizens' militia force'; this was a stance finding support equally at the German workers' associations' annual meetings and in the Social Democratic Workers' Party, established in 1869. On the question of military policy, the gulf separating different wings in the labour movement on other issues suddenly vanished (although, in general, it actually awoke little interest, except in Engels's case). Moreover, they were completely at one on a policy of searing criticism against Prussia, with Liebknecht's voice only part of the chorus accusing it of 'high treason against the German nation'.[122]

However, in the 1860s, such anti-Prussian sentiment was not limited to socialist or democratic circles; it was similarly prevalent in looser groupings in the Third Germany that were not bound to such a strict core ideology. Despite there being, as Bebel observed, 'no institution within the Prussian state exploited as much as the law on the so-called universal conscription to arouse the German population's sympathies for Prussia', this promotional acclaim was not successful everywhere,[123] as can be seen in the acrimonious controversy raging in Bavaria, both inside and outside parliament, after the war between Austria and Prussia in 1866. The question of introducing the Prussian military constitution may have found unanimous support among the army authorities, but it was heavily criticised in parliamentary debate, with the opinion leaders only voting for the law in the end after the ministries had invested considerable time and effort in persuading them to change their minds.[124]

In the general population, though, the issue was far from resolved. In spring 1868, when the reorganised Bavarian *Landwehr* was first called together, the entire country experienced an unrest marked by 'excesses' and 'tumults'. In Trostberg, for instance, there was 'a veritable insurrection' against the commanding officer who had ordered the men to appear for a swearing-in ceremony and instead was subjected to 'complete ridicule'. When the captain wanted to start the ceremony, 'there was a scream from some of them, which most of the others picked up "what, we're not going to swear Prussian, besides we've already sworn for our king, we want to stay Bavarian", and "chuck him out, he's just a Prussian in disguise" – whereupon they raised their sticks and pushed the captain back'. A second attempt to instigate a swearing-in ceremony with support from the regular army often failed too, since in many districts, the *Landwehr* men simply did not attend – in Passau and Traunstein, for example, only half of those liable for *Landwehr* service were actually present. In other places, such events attracted an audience of people who were not liable to serve themselves, but fuelled an atmosphere of protest.[125]

Initially, such protests were directed against the new *Landwehr* organisation and the additional burdens this entailed. Bavaria had, in fact, had a *Landwehr* from the early nineteenth century, although it was similar to the Prussian one in name alone. The Bavarian form was a locally organised civilian militia, comprising all local men from the towns, up to the age of 60. *Landwehr* members had to equip themselves and their tasks fell largely into the sphere of local public order duties, although they increasingly took on a show role for local prestige. Their combat-readiness was extremely limited, as events in 1868 demonstrated: when the 'old' *Landwehr* was ordered to turn out to put an end to the unrest among the 'new' *Landwehr*, they simply did not appear – many *Landwehr* members, often tradesmen, were not in the town, others did not hear the signal, and 'many were held back from doing their duty by their wives, out of worry and fear, or by others, out of spite and *Schadenfreude*'.[126]

In comparison to the old *Landwehr*, the new one was not only more socially inclusive, it was also more 'military', with members regularly called up for exercises, taught theory and practice, how to drill and fight with bayonets, military law, and all about their 'new social position'. In this process, they learnt the 'notions of military discipline and order' – a step viewed by Bavarian citizens as 'Prussianisation'. The fallout from the fierce political debate over army reform even reached the rural population, either via the local broadsheets or as a part of the local priest's Sunday sermon, and the majority took sides 'against Prussia' – and there was no lack of wild rumours to fuel the flames. Farmers in upper Bavaria, for instance, had heard that 'now the *Landwehr* has to swear to the king of Prussia, and drill all year round and, before you know it, everything's got to be Lutheran'.[127] But an aversion to Prussia was not restricted to the traditional heartlands of Catholic Bavaria, where people cited a 'hereditary feeling of loyalty and devotion to its king and the royal house'. It was similarly evident in Baden and Württemberg, and even apparent in politicians who had no objections, in principle, to introducing the new military structures. When Moritz Mohl, a Württemberg liberal, warned in 1868 of a 'further Prussianisation of the morale in our army', he was primarily thinking of the arrogance the Prussian military showed towards civilians, which they used to buttress their claim to superior status.[128]

In contrast, it was less than surprising that the Württemberg officers were unanimous in supporting this new spirit, even though, rather than officially putting their case on the issue of prestige, they concentrated on efficiency. When asked in 1866 which form of universal conscription they would prefer to see introduced, they all spoke out in favour of the Prussian system. After all, they noted, it 'was not solely the needle gun' that 'secured Prussian victory, but the excellent military training, the compact structure, imbued with the spirit of duty, earnestness and self-sacrifice, and the intelligence pervading all ranks of the army', adding that including 'the sons of educated and well-to-do families' was especially 'advantageous' for the 'army's moral and intellectual state'. In this way, they upgraded 'the entire material' and the army could enjoy 'a far more independent and reliable element, capable of being used far more confidently for many purposes', with, moreover, a sense of duty that did not 'require constant supervision'.[129] But it was just this promise of 'versatility' that made opponents of the Prussian system sit up and take notice. Impressed by the Prussian victories in 1864 and 1866, they still could not help but remember the appearance of the Prussian army in 1848–9, when it was revealed as an efficient instrument for the reactionary forces. For many southern German officers, though, those were the years when they found their own troops to be 'unreliable' and unwilling to protect the prevailing order adequately. In officer circles, militias met with little enthusiasm too: they were considered as a means employed by 'artful democrats' to weaken military institutions and have them labelled as 'a system of general worthlessness'.[130]

Yet underneath these differences lay one notion bridging both groups – the idea of an 'armed nation', whose males were taught from an early age to bear and use arms. Their disagreements took place on the level of the concept's purpose and political ends: democrats wanted to protect basic civil rights against social restrictions and political incursions, while army officers and official authorities saw preserving given power relations as the primary goal. The two groups also favoured integrating the armed citizens into different organisational forms: the democratic movement envisaged a loose association of civic soldiers, donning their uniforms for only brief periods, electing their own officers and disciplined via inner conviction rather than obsessive drill; officers took the regular army as their point of reference, imagining the *Landwehr* or reserve troops grouped around that focal point, which was, just as in Prussia, a 'school' attended by all men for several years before they transferred into other formations, with fewer demands made on them.

It took the Franco-Prussian war in 1870–1 to finally put an end to this incessant wrangling in the southern German states over their internal policies on the form and purpose of their military organisations. In 1870, they acceded to military conventions with Prussia and adopted Prussian military structures, finally putting the seal on the dream of the citizen-soldier – a dream that had been born in the early years of the nineteenth century, nourished in the *Vormärz* claims to the right to have an armed citizenry, sustained in the militia experiments in the 1848 Revolution, and which had lingered on in the private defence associations of the 1860s. But a military institution scrupulously avoided by the middle classes and exclusively reserved for lower-class men similarly no longer reflected the zeitgeist. With the substitution system abolished, the educated and propertied members of the middle classes would also see their male offspring having to serve personally in the army; they too would have to pass through that same 'training school for the entire nation' that their Prussian peers had been attending since 1814.

Notes

1. Engels, *Die preußische Militärfrage und die deutsche Arbeiterpartei*, in Karl Marx and Friedrich Engels, *Werke*, vol. 16, Berlin 1976, pp. 44–5, 54. (English quotes from: *The Prussian Military Question and the German Workers' Party*, Trans. Barrie Selman, International Workingman's Association).
2. Rosenberg, *Publizistik*, vol. 2, p. 502; Zunkel, *Unternehmer*, p. 209; on the Swiss militia see Jaun, 'Bürger-Militär'.
3. Colley, *Britons*, pp. 287 ff.; Best, *War*, pp. 122 ff., 231 ff.; Spiers, *Army*.
4. Wandruszka/Urbanitsch, *Habsburgermonarchie*, vol. V, pp. 240 ff., 485 ff.; Helmert, *Militärsystem*, pp. 40 ff. Hungary and the *Siebenbürgen* settlement of ethnic Germans were excluded from conscription until 1849. On Russia, Hagen, 'Levée'; on France, Ingenlath, *Aufrüstung*, pp. 34 ff.
5. HStA München, Abt. IV, A II 1 b Nr. 26: Konskriptionsgesetz from 1804; Nr. 27: Note des auswärtigen Ministeriums dated 6.4.1809.
6. Gruner, *Heer*, pp. 42–3.
7. Wirtz, '*Widersetzlichkeiten*', pp. 54 ff.; Sauer, *Revolution*, p. 27.
8. Sauer, *Heer*, p. 13.
9. *Verhandlungen der Zweiten Kammer Baden*, 1822, Protokollheft 8, p. 538.
10 *Verhandlungen der Zweiten Kammer Baden*, 1822, Protokollheft 7, p. 165.
11. *Verhandlungen der Zweiten Kammer Baden*, 1822, Protokollheft 7, pp. 355, 358–9, 379, 525 ff. In 1818, the Baden constitution foresaw all citizens having to contribute 'without exception, to all burdens on the public purse' but in return enjoying all the same civic rights too. It noted expressly that 'differences in birth and religion' do not provide a reason for 'exemptions to military duties'. (*Die Landständische Verfassungs-Urkunde für das Großherzogthum Baden, Karlsruhe 1819*, p. 4, Paragraphs 8, 10). Mediatised noble families (*standesherrliche Familien*) declared exempt in the Vienna Act on the German Confederation (*Wiener Bundesakte*) were the sole exception.
12. *Verhandlungen der Zweiten Kammer Baden*, 1822, Protokollheft 2, pp. 154–155; Protokollheft 8, pp. 388 ff.
13. *Verhandlungen der Zweiten Kammer Baden*, 1822, Protokollheft 9, p. 140; Protokollheft 2, Beilage 79, § 47; Kommissionsbericht p. LXXIX.
14. *Verhandlungen der Zweiten Kammer Baden*, 1822, Protokollheft 7, p. 165, LXXXIII.

15. Nolte, *Gemeindebürgertum*, primarily pp. 211 ff.
16. *Verhandlungen der Zweiten Kammer Baden*, 1822, Protokollheft 8, p. 371.
17. *Allgemeine Militär-Zeitung*, Nr. 89, 1833, Columns 705–708.
18. Brockhaus, *Tagebücher*, vol. 1, p. 66.
19. *Verhandlungen der Zweiten Kammer Baden*, 1822, Protokollheft 2, p. 151.
20. *Verhandlungen der Zweiten Kammer Baden*, 1828, Beilagenheft 5, Nr. 8, p. 2. According to the 1825 Baden Conscription Law every family was permitted to have one son released from military service; after 1828, recruitment shortfall meant that only 'indispensable' sons would be freed from service.
21. The figures are based on the 1866 records of the Württemberg *Oberrekrutierungsrat* (senior recruiting council) contained in: HStA Stuttgart, E 271 c Nr. 1495.
22. For more details on the widespread superstitious practices designed to help produce a favourable draw, see Wuttke, *Volksaberglaube*, pp. 454–5; Meyer, *Volksleben*, pp. 238 ff.; *Bavaria*, pp. 365–6.
23. *Verhandlungen der Zweiten Kammer Baden*, 1835, Protokollheft 2, p. 155; Nolte, *Gemeindebürgertum*, pp. 134–5.
24. Gall, *Bürgertum*, p. 241; *Verhandlungen der Stände-Versammlung des Großherzogthums Baden im Jahre 1831*, Beilagenheft 4, Karlsruhe 1831, p. 37. Even when, in 1843, the Württemberg government adopted the Prussian model allowing sons of middle-class citizens only to serve one year, they still preferred to pay for a substitute (Sauer, *Heer*, p. 94).
25. One example representative of many: in 1837 the Bavarian carpenter Jacob Scheffel paid for a substitute for his son Wilhelm, a trained joiner, because otherwise he 'would be forced to give up his trade as a joiner, which brings me a real benefit from practising both professions together, added to which I would be unable to nourish my family adequately from my carpentry trade alone' (HStA München, Abt. IV, A II 1 b Nr. 74: Scheffel dated. 31.7.1837).
26. *Verhandlungen der Zweiten Kammer Baden*, 1822, Protokollheft 8, pp. 477, 480–1; Lutz, *Offizierskorps*, p. 25; *Verhandlungen Württemberg*, 1851/53, I. Beilagenband, 1. Abt., pp. 96, 194.
27. *Verhandlungen der Zweiten Kammer Baden*, 1847–9, Protokollheft 1, p. 138; 1st Beilagenheft, p. 64; Protokollheft 8, p. 222. In 1848, 3,200 men were enlisted, around a quarter of those of the same age (Lutz, *Offizierskorps*, Tab. p. 25).
28. *Verhandlungen der Zweiten Kammer Baden*, 1822, Protokollheft 7, p. LXXXI (Itzstein); 1847–49, 1st Beilagenheft, pp. 62–3.; Protokollheft 8, p. 222; 1850–51, Beilagenheft 7, p. 436; 1865–66, 4th Beilagenheft, p. 36; Helmert, *Militärsystem*, pp. 71–2.
29. *Verhandlungen Württemberg*, 1851/53, I. Beilagenband, p. 195 (1817–49); IV. Protokollband, p. 3768 (1840s).; 1854/55, I. Beilagenband, p. 435 (1851–54);

1855/61, I. Beilagenband, 1st Abt., p. 132 (1854–56) and 3rd Abt., p. 1602 (1857–59).

30. *Verhandlungen der Zweiten Kammer Baden*, 1833, Protokollheft 10, pp. 3–4.
31. *Verhandlungen der Zweiten Kammer Baden*, 1822, Protokollheft 8, pp. 79–80.
32. Bruder, *Nürnberg*, pp. 427 ff.; Jäger, *Militärwesen*, pp. 49–56.
33. Blessing, 'Disziplinierung', p. 471.
34. *Verhandlungen der Zweiten Kammer Baden*, 1825, Protokollheft 10, p. 366; 1833, 1st Beilagenheft, p. 51; 1841, 4th Beilagenheft, p. 162.
35. *Verhandlungen der Ersten Kammer Baden*, 1828, Protokollheft 1, pp. 156, 160; HStA Dresden, Kriegsarchiv, Nr. 6408 (Statistics 1847); HStA Stuttgart, E 271 c Nr. 1496: Results of medical examinations 1850–57.
36. Pfister, *Zwietracht; Militair-Wochenblatt*, Nr. 48, 1845, p. 205. [*Sollt ich's einem Bauern dienen / Und mein Geld im Schweiß verdienen? / Bruder, nein, das tu'ich nicht. / Lieber will ich bei Kanonen / Im Gezelt und Lager wohnen, / Wo man von den Waffen spricht; – / Einem Bauern dien'ich's nicht.*]
37. HStA München, Abt. IV, M Kr Nr. 2821: Schreiben v. 1.7.1859.
38. Petition Leipziger Soldaten in *Deutsche Volks-Zeitung u. Leipziger General-Anzeiger* dated 20.4.1848.
39. HStA Dresden, Kriegsarchiv, Nr. 659: v. Below dated 2.7.1833.
40. HStA Dresden, Kriegsarchiv, Nr. 659: Dresdener Kommandeur dated 3.7.1833.
41. HStA Dresden, Kriegsarchiv, Nr. 695:1057–1075.
42. HStA München, Abt. IV, A IV 2 Nr. 113: the undated letter was found on July 8,1835.
43. HStA München, Abt. IV, A IV 2 Nr. 113: Innenministerium an Kriegs-ministerium dated 6.5.1846.
44. Schmidt, *Stadt*, see particularly pp. 275 ff.; Bruder, *Nürnberg*, pp. 464 ff.
45. HStA München, Abt. IV, A IV 2 Nr. 113: Divisionskommandeur dated 4.5.1846; Kriegsministerium dated 5.5.1846 with commentaries.
46. Schmidt, *Stadt*, pp. 50–1; Bruder, *Nürnberg*, pp. 44–5.
47. HStA München, Abt. IV, A IV 1 Nr. 58: Report dated 3.9.1849.
48. HStA Dresden, Kriegsarchiv, Nr. 1435: Deutscher Vaterlandsverein Leipzig dated 2.5.1848; Steinhilber, *Bürgerwehren*, p. 37; Calließ, *Militär*; Müller, *Soldaten* (1999), pp. 185 ff.
49. HStA München, Abt. IV, A IV 1 Nr. 57: Rittmeister v. Rechberg (Kempten) dated 3.5.1849; Nr. 58: Kommandeur Lindau dated 3.9.1849; Nr. 59: Festungskommando Landau dated 21.5. and 25.6.1849; Müller, *Soldaten*, pp. 45–46, 50.
50. HStA München, Abt. IV, A IV 1 Nr. 57: War minister from 15.4.1850. On attacks on civilians, primarily after mustering, HStA Stuttgart, E 271 l, Nr.

166: Reports by the Oberämter Backnang, Stuttgart, Weinsberg, Leonberg 1832/33; Verhandlungen der badischen Abgeordnetenkammer, 1857, 6th Beilagenheft, p. 2.

51. Verhandlungen Württemberg, 1851/53, I. Beilagenband, 1. Abt., pp. 406–7 (1848–1850); 1854/55, I. Beilagenband, p. 435 (1851–1853); 1855/61, I. Beilagenband, 1. Abt., p. 132; I. Beilagenband, 3. Abt., pp. 1602–3 (1857–59); 1862/65, I. Beilagenband, 1. Abt., pp. 246–7 (1860–1862).

52. Rotteck, *Heere*, pp. 54, 58, 86–7, 106, 115, 130–6.

53. Ellrodt, *Zweck*, pp. 65, 67–8, 69.

54. Wirth, *Nationalfest*, H. 2, pp. 85–8.

55. Welcker, *Anhang*, pp. 589–607.

56. Welcker, *Geschlechtsverhältnisse*; Welcker, *Bürgertugend*; Rotteck, 'Gemeingeist', pp. 518–19.

57. Sauer, *Revolution*, pp. 26 ff., 36–37, 52 ff.

58. HStA Dresden, Kriegsarchiv, Nr. 1435: letter from 15.6.1848.

59. *Verhandlungen Baden 1848*, Protokollheft 3, pp. 330–31, 340.

59. Wigard, *Bericht*, vol. 2, p. 1337.

60. Wigard, *Bericht*, vol. 2, p. 1337.

61. On Welcker's favourable views on duelling see, Frevert, *Men of Honour*, p. 138.

62. Wigard, *Bericht*, vol. 2, p. 1328.

63. Wigard, *Bericht*, vol. 2, p. 801.

64. Welcker, *Geschlechtsverhältnisse*; Lloyd, 'Selfhood'; also see Chapter 2.4.

65. Welcker, *Anhang*, pp. 592–3, 596–8. This article is almost identical with the '*Motion auf eine constitutionellere, weniger kostspielige und mehr sichernde Wehrverfassung*', Welcker proposed in the Baden assembly of estates (*Ständeversammlung*) in 1831 (Verhandlungen, 1831, 4. Beilagenheft, pp. 27–67).

66. *Verhandlungen*, 1831, 7. Protokollheft, pp. 7 ff.; 13. Beilagenheft, pp. 90 ff.; *Allgemeine Militär-Zeitung*, year 6, 1832, Column 728.

67. Wigard, *Bericht*, vol. 2, pp. 1327–31; Huber, *Dokumente*, vol. 1, p. 318.

68. *Verhandlungen der Zweiten Kammer Baden*, 1833, 23. Protokollheft, p. 26; Obermann, *Flugblätter*, pp. 48, 54.

69. Obermann, *Flugblätter*, pp. 60 ff.; Pröve, *Republikanismus*, pp. 165 ff.

70. Wigard, *Bericht*, vol. 1, pp. 206 ff.; vol. 2, pp. 796 ff., 926 ff. (Zitat Vischer p. 931). On the calls for the army swearing an oath on the constitution, which appears in all the petitions and lists of demands during the 1848 Revolution (and already had a long tradition in the southern German states from the *Vormärz* period), Höhn, *Verfassungskampf*, pp. 81 ff.

71. *Verhandlungen der Ersten Kammer Baden*, 1848, 1. Protokollheft, p. 62.

72. Wigard, *Bericht*, vol. 2, pp. 802–6; 926–9; vol. 4, p. 2746.

73. Wigard, *Bericht*, vol. 1, pp. 207, 684; vol. 2, p. 930; vol. 6, p. 4400.

74. *Verhandlungen der Zweiten Kammer Baden*, 1841, 4. Beilagenheft, p. 162; Schmidt, *Stadt*, p. 23; Jung, 'Bürgermilitär'.

75. Ruhland, *Untersuchungen*, 2 vols; Ruhland/Zeise, 'Entstehung'; Hammer, *Volksbewegung*, pp. 389 ff. On developments in the electorate of Hesse and Prussia, see Pröve, *Republikanismus*, pp. 159 ff., 294 ff., 372.

76. HStA Dresden, Kriegsarchiv, Nr. 886; Nostitz Drzewiecki, *Communalgarden*.

77. HStA Dresden, Ministerium des Innern, Nr. 993a: In 1832, the local militia had 4,966 muskets from the main royal arsenal, 5,112 were owned by the militia members and only 740 were provided by the local authorities. This allowed every second militia member to be armed (there were a total of 32 militias with 23,145 members).

78. Ruhland, *Untersuchungen*, vol. 1, pp. 91–2; Hammer, *Volksbewegung*, pp. 395–6; Sauer, *Revolution*, p. 43, for Württemberg.

79. HStA Dresden, Kriegsarchiv, Nr. 1003: Oberst v. Buttlar dated 13.8., 15.8. and 16.10.1845; Leipziger Zeitung, Nr. 239, 6.10.1845; Ruhland, *Untersuchungen*, vol. 1, p. 81 (Lied: *Es will die Bürgerwache, allein die gute Sache, nicht Pöbels Raserei, doch auch nicht Tyrannei. Das Gute liegt inmitten. Wir haben viel gelitten. Wir fördern unser Recht. Der Bürger ist kein Knecht*); Hammer, *Volksbewegung*, p. 393.

80. Beutel, *Bürgersoldaten*, p. 52; Sauer, *Revolution*, pp. 58–61.

81. Brockhaus, *Tagebücher*, vol. 1, pp. 165, 170–1, 173, 433; vol. 2, p. 41, 77. Nostitz Drzewiecki, *Communalgarden*, pp. 21–2.

82. Sauer, *Revolution*, pp. 75 ff.; HStA Dresden, Kriegsarchiv, Nr. 2083, 2084; Pröve, 'Bürgerwehren'; Kügelgen, *Bürgerleben*, pp. 346, 361.

83. Sauer, *Revolution*, p. 85; Gall, *Bürgertum*, pp. 297–8. The Baden Law on Civilian Militias was largely formulated by Friedrich Hecker, then colonel of the Mannheim militia, and was approved by parliament in summary proceedings (Verhandlungen Baden 1848, 3. Protokollheft, pp. 329–47, 354–61).

84. HStA Dresden, Kriegsarchiv, Nr. 1435: Petition by the Leipzig democratic association (with 540 signatures) dated 17.6.1848; Ministerium des Innern, Nr. 994: Decree dated 11.4.1848; Kommunalgardengesetz from 22.11.1848.

85. HStA Dresden, Kriegsarchiv, Nr. 993a: Petition dated 1.9.1850; Brauns, *Bürgerwehren*, pp. 36–7.

86. Badisches Bürgerwehrgesetz, in *Großherzoglich Badisches Regierungsblatt*, Nr. 20, 3.4.1848, p. 73. In late summer 1848, in Bavaria's Lower Franconia 11% of adult men and 27% of married men belonged to a local civilian militia (Harris, 'Arms', pp. 142, 149). Julius Bassermann, who had bought himself out of military service in 1839, was active in 1848/9 in the Mannheim civilian militia (Gall, *Bürgertum*, pp. 241, 350).

87. Steinhilber, *Bürgerwehren*, pp. 55 ff.
88. *Verhandlungen der zweiten verfassungsberathenden Versammlung des Königreichs Württemberg*, Stuttgart 1850, p. 341; Ruhland, *Untersuchungen*, vol. 1, pp. 179 ff.
89. HStA Dresden, Kriegsarchiv, Nr. 886: Kriegsministerium from 3.3.1850.
90. HStA Dresden, Ministerium des Innern, Nr. 1078b: Generalkommando der Kommunalgarden from 13.8.1849.
91. Sauer, *Revolution*, pp. 101–2. (Stuttgart); Goldammer, *1848*, pp. 617, 636 (Leipzig); Brauns, *Bürgerwehren*, p. 19 (Hannover); Steinhilber, *Bürgerwehren*, p. 22 (Heilbronn).
92. Kügelgen, *Bürgerleben*, pp. 346–7.
93. Hummel-Haasis, *Schwestern*, pp. 25–6, 90–1; Sauer, *Revolution*, pp. 104–5; Pröve, 'Mann', pp. 110 ff.; Koppmann, 'Exercitien', p. 94; Lipp, *Weiber*, p. 344.
94. Hummel-Haasis, *Schwestern*, pp. 105 ff., 185 ff.
95. This, at least, was Kathinka Zitz's rhetorical question when she founded a women's association in Mainz in 1849 and called for members to donate their jewellery for weapons, which were then presented to the democratic associations with the name of the donor engraved on them (Hummel-Haasis, *Schwestern*, p. 265).
96. Lipp, *Weiber*, pp. 124–5; Hummel-Haasis, *Schwestern*, pp. 27, 22–3, 24–5.
97. Lipp, *Weiber*, p. 368.
98. Lipp, *Weiber*, p. 348 *(Es eilt so gern der liebende Germane / Zum Waffendienste auf der Frauen Ruf; / 's ist Eu'r Ruhm, die Männer so zu ehren, / Und Ruhm ist's, freien Männern zu gehören.)*
99. Sauer, *Revolution*, pp. 181, 190, 196.
100. Brauns, *Bürgerwehren*, pp. 40 ff.
101. Devrient, *Tagebücher*, pp. 478–9, 481–2, 425.
102. Welcker, 'Bürgertugend', p. 769.
103. Verhandlungen der zweiten verfassungberathenden Versammlung des Königreichs Württemberg, Stuttgart 1850, pp. 340–1; 'Erinnerungen eines alten Bürgerwehrmannes', Schwäbischer Merkur, Nr. 443, 22.9.1900.
104. Harris, 'Arms', pp. 145 ff. In Baden, age of entry was 21 and members could be up to a maximum of 55; in the majority of other states, men were between 25 and 50.
105. Lipp, *Weiber*, pp. 152–3.
106. Verhandlungen Württemberg, 1851/53, I. Beilagenband, 1. Abt., pp. 254–9; Verhandlungen der Zweiten Kammer Baden, 1850/1, 7. Beilagenheft, pp. 75–84; HStA Dresden, Ministerium des Innern, Nr. 993b: Report from 30.11.1869; Ruhland, Untersuchungen, vol. 1, p. 184.

107. Verhandlungen der dritten verfassungsberathenden Versammlung des Königreichs Württemberg, Stuttgart 1850, p. 100; Verhandlungen Württemberg, 1851/53, I. Beilagenband, 1. Abt., pp. 95–6, 194–6.
108. Verhandlungen Württemberg, 1862–65, IV. Protokollband, p. 3089. On the Swiss military system see Jaun, 'Bürger-Militär'.
109. Verhandlungen Württemberg, 1862–65, I. Beilagenband, 3. Abt., p. 2116.
110. Biefang, *Bürgertum*, pp. 122–4.
111. Biefang, *Nationalverein*, pp. 107–109.
112. Biefang, *Nationalverein*, pp. 107, 109; *Bürgertum*, p. 182.
113. Thorwart, *Schriften*, vol. 3, p. 183; Biefang, *Nationalverein*, pp. 102, 171; *Bürgertum*, pp. 174 ff., 185.
114. Biefang, *Bürgertum*, pp. 160 ff., 177; *Nationalverein*, pp. 96, 362.
115. Ewald, *Schützengesellschaften*, pp. 18, 66 ff., 210 ff.; Pröve, *Republikanismus*, pp. 443 ff.; Biefang, *Bürgertum*, pp. 164–5.
116. Weismann, *Schützenfest*, pp. 7, 12, 17, 96, 108; Biefang, *Bürgertum*, pp. 169 ff.; Michaelis, *Banner*, Chapters 3–5.
117. Verhandlungen Württemberg, 1862–5, IV. Protokollband, pp. 3073 ff.
118. Sauer, *Heer*, p. 219.
119. Dowe, *Berichte*, pp. 174–80.
120. Dowe, *Berichte*, pp. 177–8, 180; on reorganisation cf. Chapter 4.1.
121. Engels, 'Militärfrage', pp. 51, 54, 63, 66, 78; Dowe, *Berichte*, p. 179; Stenographische Berichte, vol. 1, 1867, pp. 453–4 (Bebel).
122. Jenaczek, *Lassalle*, pp. 73, 81–3, 86 (At that time, just like his friend Rüstow, Lassalle toyed with the national association's goals of setting up defence associations – cf. Biefang, *Bürgertum*, pp. 182–5); Dowe, *Protokolle*, pp. 176–7 (1870), 493–4 (1874); Fricke, *Handbuch*, vol. 1, pp. 105–6 (1873); Protokoll 1869, pp. 32–3; Bebel, *Heer*, pp. 43 ff.; Dowe, *Berichte*, p. 176.
123. Stenographische Berichte, vol. 1, 1867, p. 453.
124. Leyh, 'Heeresreform', pp. 28 ff.; HStA München, Abt. IV, A II 1 b Nr. 76: Denkschrift from October 1866; Außen- und Kriegsminister dated 17.1.1868.
125. HStA München, Abt. IV, A II 1 b, Nr. 80: Major Raith from 27.5.1868; Freiherr von der Tann from 16.4.1868.
126. HStA München, Abt. IV, A II 1 b Nr. 80: Landwehrbataillonskommando Traunstein from 1.4.1868.
127. HStA München, Abt. IV, A II 1 b Nr. 80: Augsburger Generalkommando from 8.5.1868; Kriegsministerium dated 9.4.1868; Markt- und Gemeindeverwaltungen from the Trostberg district end of April 1868; Hauptmann Haack aus Cham dated 6.4.1868.
128. Verhandlungen Württemberg, 77. Sitzung, 14.2.1868, p. 1835.

129. HStA Stuttgart, E 286 Nr. 33: Commanders' statements dated 14.9.1866; E 271 c, Nr. 1453: Reports from 18.9.1866, 1.10.1866, 28.10.1866.
130. HStA Stuttgart, E 271 c Nr. 497: Oberstleutnant v. Suckow, Betrachtungen über württembergische Militärverhältnisse (ca. 1867); Nr. 1454: First draft by the Württemberg war minister v. Hardegg (undated, end of 1866); Nr. 1453: Stuttgarter Infantry Regiment from 28.10.1866; Nr. 1456: Report by Hauptmann E. v. Arand, Nov. 1866; Nr. 1459: Report by the Oberrekrutierungsrat (senior recruiting council) from 17.1 and 2.2.1867.

–4–

War and Peace: Imperial Germany in the Prussian Barracks

In Prussia too, the wars of the 1860s represented a tectonic shift in domestic and military policy. They effectively quelled criticism of the army, so particularly vocal in 1848 and still widespread in the 1850s, set a firmer course towards a civic *Realpolitik*, and acted as a brake on the quest for alternative policy models – that *leitmotif* of early nineteenth-century German military history. The constitutional struggles of the early 1860s may have seen the Prussian chamber of deputies utilising the issue of the restructuring of the conscript army to stonewall government policy completely but, at the latest by 1866–7, after the army left the battlefields of Schleswig-Holstein and Königgrätz victorious with Prussia's aspirations to power within Germany realised, delegates made their peace with that very same institution.

Yet Prussia's rise to hegemony over Germany, supported by its army and culminating in the founding of Imperial Germany in 1871, did not merely hail the victory of the Prussian conscription model over the other German states' recruiting systems. It also heralded higher recruiting quotas and greater 'military equitability' (*Wehrgerechtigkeit*), leading to a far higher proportion of young men performing military service. Even if the army never became a 'training school for the *entire* nation', and numerous young men were never drafted (not to mention all the young women), the army steadily evolved into an extremely influential and valued instance of socialisation. In contrast to the *Vormärz* period, the army now actively sought to use this influence and leave its mark on society. The substantial boost to the army's prestige once Germany discovered 'unity in the Prussian barracks', as Marx and Engels ironically noted, led to a greater weight being attributed to the barracks as a 'school of life', helping to anchor a programme of military education and training in civil society.[1]

Nevertheless, even under the Empire, the military was not totally immune from criticism. Although the army enjoyed what was virtually an extra-constitutional status, directly under the king/emperor as the armed forces' supreme commander, it was subject to the *Reichstag*'s budgetary controls, and in this way, at the very least, parliament had a chance to influence decisions in military policy and urge changes to be adopted. The press too repeatedly spotlighted deficits, malpractices and improprieties in the army and navy, giving the Imperial German armed forces more banner headlines than its predecessor had ever had: it was watched, judged, praised and reprimanded. Unwillingly, the military, as an organisation, found itself located in the social sphere, where rules, performances and communication structures were publicly analysed and debated. Simultaneously, it faced demands to substantiate and justify the way it defined its own mission, and even came under pressure to introduce modifications and alterations.

Within these parameters a lively military discourse arose comprising many diverse participants: soldiers and officers; journalists and politicians; social democrats, liberals and conservatives; and men and women. In what follows, I intend to examine both this discourse and the experiences of conscripts in the barracks, focusing on the primary concern of reconstructing the complex relations between the army and civil society as they became established in the second half of the nineteenth century – relations that proved to have a marked impact on both the social and political landscape, and were deeply embedded in the gender relations of the period. What, in Weber's sense, was the 'cultural significance' attributed to the military, and the experience of the military, in Imperial Germany? How far did these two aspects coin a particular *Weltanschauung* and personal identities? Which role did they play in building a nation internally, and how did they influence the new German national state's domestic integration? And how was this nation's military tint – or taint – affected by the army being born in a 'martial era', as Heinrich von Treitschke pointed out in the *Reichstag* in 1871, but then presiding over forty years of peace?[2]

1. Constitutional or Military State: Paving the Way in the Pre-Empire Years

Prussia's borders were not hermetically sealed against the constant search for other recruiting models and military structures that was so much an active part of daily political debate in the 'Third Germany' since the 1830s; criticising the military and suggesting reforms was just as popular in Prussia too, especially during the 1848 Revolution. As in Dresden or Karlsruhe, petitions presented in Berlin also called for a general armed citizenry (*Volksbewaffnung*), free elections of officers, and 'abolishing the standing army'. The concrete and radical nature of the criticism levelled at the prevailing situation in the military correlated strongly with the army's involvement in revolutionary events: when, on 18 March 1848, soldiers fired on demonstrators in front of the Berlin city palace, the official residence of the Hohenzollern royal family, it triggered days of bloody barricade fighting and incensed the citizens to the point where the king saw himself forced to withdraw the army from the city. In a simultaneous move, he granted permission for 'the forming of citizens' militias' (*Bürgerbewaffnung*), bowing to a request he had repeatedly received. Under the auspices of the local police superintendent, civilian militias were founded in all the Berlin districts. In no time, over 20,000 men had registered – primarily craftsmen and artisans, students and, at the behest of the interior ministry, civil servants. They were given weapons from the arsenal reserves and undertook to 'protect the city, the people and property'.[3]

Civilian militias formed in other Prussian cities too,[4] where they evolved in a way very similar to the Saxon or southern German organisations. Initially, there was considerable enthusiasm for the idea, especially among young men, with students or journeymen starting their own corps and extending the purpose of 'citizens' militias' to encompass revolutionary ideals. In contrast, their older comrades – usually settled civil servants, tradesmen and businessmen, often heads of a family – tended to interpret the militias' political task in a restrictive way, emphasising their role in securing order and maintaining peace. The members' motivation, though, rapidly evaporated when they were confronted with the gruelling reality of guard and patrol duties, while events such as the storming of the Berlin arsenal in June 1848 similarly played their part in eroding the trust in civilian militias and dampened the desire to join them.

The political discussion, though, took place in quite different areas. When, in 1848, the Berlin national assembly were considering a Law on Civilian Militias (*Bürgerwehrgesetz*), the majority of delegates assumed that militias would comprise 'the be-all and end-all of the entire military organisation', while even the conservatives showered praise on their 'moral force'. But integrating the 'military caste' within a 'general national defence force' (*Volkswehr*) was not simply an idea inspiring the myriad petitions driving parliamentary debate in 1848. It was equally present in many of the delegates' interpellations and motions, claiming that the 'former opposition between the people and the military' had had its day. According to Johann Jacoby, a democratic delegate, the regular army had to abandon its 'hostile attitude towards civilians', while 'in future the artificially created division between armed and unarmed citizens has to be abolished entirely'.[5]

However, Jacoby was less forthcoming on how this division was to be overcome. The *Landwehr*, applauded by many liberals, could no longer function as a role model since even this had fallen at the hurdle of 'merging the soldier and civilian estates'. Instead of preserving its civilian militia character, it had 'turned the citizen into an unarmed soldier'.[6] The military administration, though, considered that just the reverse had happened: the *Landwehr* had failed to measure up to military standards, an impression only intensified by the ambivalent experiences in the 1848 Revolution. Despite conceding that not many *Landwehr* soldiers had been 'found wanting' in 1848–9, their image persisted as 'unreliable cantonists' whose military deployment was severely handicapped by their civilian identity.[7] This picture also shaped the arguments in the 1850s and 1860s over restructuring the Prussian army and aligning it with interests in the changed foreign policy landscape.

As early as 1852, a group of ministers convened to consider whether the period of military service should be raised to three years again, after it had been cut to two years in 1833. The issue of funding, though, meant that the matter was initially dropped, but in 1854, as the conflict between the major European powers escalated into the Crimean War, Friedrich Wilhelm IV reintroduced the three-year term of service; despite Prussia's neutral status, it was extremely concerned to secure this neutrality by military means. Once the political tension eased in 1855, the finance and trade ministers, in particular, pressed the case for a return to a two-year period of service to avoid tax increases. Prince Wilhelm and the war minister countered this move, arguing that if one wanted an infantry consisting of soldiers and not merely 'drilled farmers', a three-year training period was the absolute minimum. It took that long 'to generate the totality of a soldierly nature in the army' and establish a basis for 'military order and discipline'.[8]

Debates in cabinet in 1855–6 on the three-year period of military service already presaged the conflict of opinion set to dominate the Prussian chamber of deputies after 1860, galvanising the public at large, fuelling a dispute over the constitution and only being resolved in the government's favour once Prussia had emerged victorious over Austria and the southern German states in 1866. This argument did not simply revolve around the length of military service and the military, economic and cultural consequences, but centred equally on the issues of *Landwehr* status and parliament's aspiration to employ its budgetary remit to influence decisions on military policy. In contrast to the southern German states' conscription laws, the 1814 Prussian conscription law had been passed entirely without the people or their deputies having any say in the matter, but when, in the 1860s, the Prussian government made moves to alter the structure of the army, they faced both mistrust in parliament and widespread political opposition.

In 1865, democratic delegates like Jacoby transformed the 'military question' into a fundamental 'question of liberty' with only two alternatives: 'standing army' or 'national defence organisation' (*volksthümliche Wehrverfassung*) – whereby they saw the former as bound to a 'pseudo-constitutional military state' and the latter as appropriate for a constitutional state under the rule of law. But while a 'military state' was a liberal and democrat nightmare, it was an object of veneration for the conservatives. Constantin Frantz or Hermann Wagener, for example, maintained that Prussia had always been a state where 'the spirit of discipline holds sway'; social structures and political institutions had become aligned with military goals and, they noted, given the current situation abroad – 'surrounded by rivals or enemies' – these needed to be similarly congruent in the future too.[9]

For liberals and democrats, the model held up as the antithesis of a 'military state' was the 'constitutional state under the rule of law'. Yet the latter too required some sort of army, and precisely those contemporaries hoping for a policy of national unity under Prussian leadership had no objections to Prussia strengthening its military arm. Nonetheless, they simultaneously called for 'warcraft' (*Kriegertum*) to be integrated into the constitutional framework of legal checks and controls, and not to regard it, as was the case in conservative circles, as virtually an extra-constitutional institution or, as Rudolf Virchow put it, a 'state within a state'. Views like these explain why the liberal-dominated chamber of deputies tenaciously exploited all the means at its disposal in parliament and the press to oppose the government's policy of presenting it with a *fait accompli* in military matters and, if need be, re-equipping and restructuring the army without any requisite legal basis.[10] It was not that parliament disputed the need to 'restructure military affairs' - in particular, it unanimously applauded the government's plan to apply the principle of universal male conscription, established since 1814, in a more thorough and 'even' way. After all, as late as the 1850s, previous practices resulted in nine out of ten men liable for military service being released from the draft, leading to widespread discontent, complaints and denunciations among the general public. There had been repeated calls for non-enlisted men to pay an 'army tax', although the population protested 'bitterly' against the idea of allowing any official buying-out of recruits, as was common in the southern German states and conceded to the Mennonites in Prussia until 1867.[11]

Against this background, plans for reorganisation that foresaw greater inclusion of recruits met with widespread support. The Prussian war minister, Albrecht von Roon, intended to enlarge the army, enlisting an annual 63,000 recruits instead of the 40,000 drafted at the time, spreading the 'burden' of military duty more equitably and making the system 'fairer'. Although the liberal parliamentary majority had no quibble with these plans, they took Roon to task for his suggestion of establishing a three-year period of service for the infantry and four years for the cavalry, effectively initiating a 40 per cent increase in the army's peacetime strength. The liberals and democrats remained adamant that the period of military service needed to be reduced, and even conservatives voted for a two-year military service to avoid the need for higher taxes.[12]

But aside from any economic considerations, political objections were becoming increasingly prominent. The premise that three years of service were needed to form the military 'spirit' met with some scepticism. After all, many delegates and citizens did not exactly revere such a spirit, and they continued to take issue with the army as representing an 'exclusive, special estate'.[13] In this context, they also reacted unfavourably towards the war ministry's declared aim of incorporating the *Landwehr* almost entirely within the regular army – with Roon's plans even finding little support among those contemporaries who rejected the democratic idea of militias or a national defence force, and believed an autonomous *Landwehr*, as originally envisaged by Stein, was no longer equal to the demands of the times. In 1862, like many others, Werner Siemens, successful industrialist and former lieutenant in the Prussian artillery, condemned the '*de facto* abolition of the *Landwehr* organisation'. In this way, the new army had cut 'any connection to the nation', and purely become a 'professional army' (*Soldatenheer*), which, furthermore, placed an 'intolerable' financial burden on the nation.[14]

The term 'professional army' was intended to be just as pejorative as 'military state': a professional army might have been efficient and combat-ready, but it hardly fitted into the constitutional discourse. Even in its previous structure, the Prussian army was far too 'soldierly' for many contemporaries, and, it was feared, any further reinforcement of the regular army at the cost of the *Landwehr* would substantially fuel the military 'caste spirit' – and in this context, the officers' courts of honour that provided institutional backing for the 'special honour' of the army were constantly cited.[15]

In fact, Prussian officers did indeed cultivate the notion of an elite class actively setting their own concepts of honour, discipline and order against the rules and customs in civil society. Criticism from military circles was equally vocal against the Berlin publicans' decision not to let armed soldiers onto their premises to prevent possible brawls with civilians, as it was against the 'dishonourable' resolutions passed by the Görlitz or Bielefeld Gentlemen's Clubs (*Ressource-Gesellschaften*) to subject officers to the balloting procedure for membership. Doubts harboured by affluent members of the upper middle classes about the wastefulness of an army that had not fought a war for decades were disdainfully parried with the assertion that the army 'is the *chief thing* and everything else is secondary, since without an army nothing else could even exist'.[16]

This awareness of 'estate' or 'caste spirit', fostered by many officers and taken exception to by many civilians, also spilled over into the troops. For example, in 1860 there was a clash in Minden involving four of the 'most peaceful citizens of this town' and three infantry soldiers. The former – two shopkeepers, a confectioner and a postmaster – were on their way to a choral society meeting when soldiers coming towards them forced them off the pavement. The men were determined not to be intimidated in this way. They restrained two of the soldiers and asked an army sentry, who was nearby, for assistance. He refused to help and, in the meantime, the third soldier, who had initially beaten a retreat, returned and set about the citizens with 'his bare sword' leaving one of them with his left cheek cut open. Such attacks where soldiers asserted their higher social standing were common, and quick to be reported in the press – 'partially in an extremely biased manner', as the Prussian interior minister indignantly noted. He appealed to the local authorities to 'apply the entire weight of their moral influence and the power entrusted to them by the law to reduce the instances of such excesses'; 'at the present time', he continued, this was 'an especially vital issue'. The civil administration found nothing to dispute in such a statement, but pointed out that the army bore the responsibility. The soldiers, more often than not, provoked the incidents and, as the Herford mayor commented in 1860, made 'all cordial relations between citizens and soldiers impossible'.[17]

The military authorities shrugged off such complaints – and promoted, as they did so, the soldiers' attitude of insolence to civilians. Soldiers were only too aware that under the protection afforded by their 'estate' and its 'spirit' they could take liberties with the civilian population and merely be reprimanded mildly, if at all. Military personnel were still subject to the law, falling, from 1845 on, under a military penal code and jurisdiction; but this, civilian critics maintained, was at the root of the 'perverted sense of honour and presumption of rank above the civil estate' that has 'repeatedly led to the most lamentable conflicts'. Moreover, they protested, such an approach contradicts the basic principle of equality before the law enshrined in the 1850 constitution, especially since the soldier 'is judged under a more favourable law than the citizen'.[18]

The military violated the principle of equality before the law in other ways too. Although the 'prerogatives of estate' were supposed to have been abolished, the officer corps persisted in the practice of largely recruiting from titled families. In the total population of Prussia, nobles may have accounted for less than 1 per cent, but in the officers corps they were grossly over-represented – even in 1865, 4,712 officers stemmed from the nobility, while the remainder of 3,457 came from the middle classes.[19] In 1860, in the cadet schools, the training ground for the majority of officers, the proportion of pupils from aristocratic backgrounds even peaked above the 70 per cent mark. This provided a firm buttress to mechanisms whereby the officer corps pre-selected its own kind, with major obstacles placed in the path of any middle-class hopefuls looking for an officer career, especially if they belonged to the Jewish or Catholic faith.

As a result, 'public opinion' was not entirely unjustified in seeing the cadet schools as the 'aristocrats' nursery garden', believing people of 'noble birth were principally favoured in the army'. The constant reproach was that the cadet schools systematically excluded the 'non-aristocratic element', leaving it only able to develop its potential in the *Landwehr*, though solely at the lower levels; and this view, in turn, influenced the liberal parliamentary majority's call for keeping the *Landwehr* as an independent military formation, since in this way they asserted the right of 'propertied' and 'educated' middle-class men to 'aspire to the officer's honourable rank and honorary privileges without being a professional officer'. If, on the contrary, the plans to absorb the *Landwehr* into the regular army were realised, its officers' relative independence would come to an end; even more than before, they would have to place themselves under the line officers' command.[20]

The stance taken by the liberal opposition, not surprisingly, received significant support from the middle class, with numerous petitions in their favour presented to the chamber of deputies by 'respected and settled men, to a large part also delegates chosen for the election of a deputy'.[21] In 1861, the Bielefeld parliamentary deputy Waldeck confirmed that 'hardly a man was elected' in the by-elections held in the western provinces 'who didn't say he was in favour of the two-year military service and keeping the institution of the *Landwehr*'. The 1863 celebrations for the 50th anniversary of the 'Prussian uprising' also paid due tribute to the *Landwehr* and its achievements. The general mood was such that even war minister Roon felt its influence. Though he still planned to bury the institution, he now intended to keep the name: 'The suggestion is not to abolish the name of the *Landwehr*. This may well seem to be inadvisable simply out of regard for the nation's historical conscience; it may be better, if one so chooses, to call the entire army the *"Landwehr"*.'[22]

In fact, Roon did not care about terms but content, and was quite capable of succinctly explaining how he planned to realise his aim – an expanded army, efficient and disciplined, led by an aristocratic officer corps and having sworn an oath of loyalty directly to the person of the king. In contrast, the liberals' concepts rested more on the pillars of pathos, invoked tradition and illusions: what had existed before ought to be kept, above all, the *Landwehr*, though less from conviction and more in memory of the old civilian militia army dream. The liberals were engaged in defending the civic military enclave, without seriously believing they could reform the entire military system from their increasingly marginalized position. Their case was not future-driven, drawing largely on retrospective arguments. The government, on the other hand, had far more precise notions about the coming challenges in military technologies and the army's tasks – and despite parliamentary opposition and the lack of a legal basis, these ideas were systematically put into practice in the early 1860s: the enlistment quota was increased by 50 per cent; the three-year military service period was kept; and the most recent groups of soldiers from the same recruitment year who were due to join the *Landwehr* were integrated instead into the regular army as reserve troops.

In this way, Roon's plans became accomplished facts. It seemed of lesser import that, at the same time, the government violated the constitution and bypassed the chamber of deputies' financial remit. This perpetual conflict was only finally laid to rest in 1866, after the reorganised and rearmed Prussian army had so brilliantly proven its value in the war against Austria and the southern German states. The case of liberal deputy Carl Twesten was indicative of the sea change: whereas in 1861, he was challenged to a duel by the head of the Prussian military cabinet for his critical remarks about the army, in 1867 he stood up to proffer his complete apology for the liberals' stance. On behalf of his national liberal colleagues, he said: 'We have fought this military organisation as unlawfully introduced and maintained. Since 1866, I believe that not only we, but the vast majority of the people, are now of the opinion that this organisation, however it may have been introduced, is firmly and irrevocably set, and can no longer be altered.'[23]

In its victory on the battlefield of Königgrätz, the Prussian army had not simply continued the heroic tradition of 1813–15; it had also cashed in the historical legacy of that era and placed national unity, the liberals' declared ideal goal, within grasp – and the greater the vanguard role taken by the army in achieving this unity, the more the critics of military reorganisation fell silent. Instead of admonishments to uphold the bequest of Scharnhorst, Gneisenau and Boyen, the heroes of the Prussian period of reforms under Stein and Hardenberg, large numbers of liberals now paid homage to the heroes of 1866: Roon, Moltke and Bismarck. In 1867, the liberal delegate Stavenhagen, previously one of the most vociferous opposition politicians, enthused that, to be fair, one had to admit that the successes of 1866 'went far beyond what one had hardly dared to dream or hope in 1813'.[24]

A critical attitude to the military, undampened by victory at arms, solely persisted in the democratic grouping and the social democratic movement, still in its infancy. Only here did the notion of a national defence force (*Volksheer*) survive – the idea formerly so prevalent and vital in the states comprising the 'Third Germany' – a notion resting on the twin columns of citizens' militias and the *Landwehr* gradually absorbing the standing army, making it superfluous. Reality, though, favoured the opposing model, with so-called civil formations absorbed everywhere into the line. Army reorganisations followed this pattern across Germany, whether in Prussia and, from 1867 on, the states encompassed by the North German Confederation, or in southern Germany. In the Franco-Prussian War of 1870–1, which was deliberately precipitated, this army structure then proved itself in a national baptism by fire.

2. Middle-class Arrangements: One-yearers and Reserve Officers

The Franco-Prussian War and the subsequent rapid founding of Imperial Germany afterwards fundamentally altered people's political consciousness. These two events were highly emotive, literally moving strong men to tears and, through an almost cathartic experience, leaving opposition supporters transformed into loyal proponents of Bismarck's power politics. But this was not simply a civic-minded citizenry, abhorring all manner of military force, suddenly adopting the guise of the Iron Chancellor's belligerent foot-soldiers overnight; rather, the ground for such a conversion had been prepared over years. The road down which the liberals rushed to embrace Bismarck and Prussian military policy in 1866–71 had a foundation based on two civil society traditions: affirming violent conflict as a means to achieving political ends, and the equally long-standing belief that citizens needed military skills for their own defence.

The liberals found it easy to identify with a new national state resting on proven military efficiency and strength, and cast aside their old reservations against the Prussian 'professional army'. The founding of Imperial Germany initially sounded the death knell for the citizens' swingeing criticism of aristocratic prerogatives in the army, and persistent calls for an autonomous civil-based *Landwehr*. While civilians in the *Vormärz* period had doggedly maintained that civic honour was at least on a par with military honour, in Imperial Germany they tended to acknowledge the latter's primacy and tried their best to participate in it. Despite chief of staff Moltke and Wilhelm I continually issuing warnings about middle-class aspiring officers whose origins and upbringing were foreign to the military ethos, in 1873 over 62 per cent of Prussian infantry lieutenants came from just such a background. Yet only in 1890 did Wilhelm II officially agree to ranking 'nobility of birth' and 'nobility of the mind' on a par, opening up the prospect of a military career to sons from those 'honourable non-aristocratic homes, where the love of king and fatherland, a warm sympathy towards the soldier's estate, and Christian morals are cultivated and instilled in the young generation'. The invitation was gladly accepted. In 1913 seven out of ten Prussian officers came from middle-class families, and were found mainly in the army service corps, navy and artillery. By way of contrast, nobility of birth predominated in the cavalry, guards officers corps, the higher officer ranks and the 'very good' garrisons.[25]

A regiment's social prestige was also affected by the number of nobles serving in it: non-aristocratic officers, for example, benefited from the reflected glory of being in a regiment with a high proportion of aristocratic officers, while, on the other hand, an aristocratic officer's prestige was reduced if he served in a regiment with too many middle-class officers. The niceties of status were a popular and frequent topic of conversation at Berlin court and town balls. Marie von Bunsen, born in 1860 and daughter of the liberal delegate Georg von Bunsen and his English wife, came out for her first season in the winter of 1877–8, shortly before she took her teacher's exam. At all the well-to-do upper-class houses she visited – whether the Bleichröders, Siemens, Behr-Behrenhoffs, or Mendelssohn-Bartholdys – a lieutenant, or more precisely, a lieutenant in the guards, was regarded as the most desirable dancing partner. The hosts' reputation as a ball venue hung on which regiment was found there: guards' officers were positively welcomed, while those from the navy, the engineers or the artillery regiments merely played 'walk-on parts'.[26]

Undoubtedly in Berlin, where the royal court played a central role, influencing middle-class houses and salons too, such intense 'regimental ranking' was particularly pronounced. Nonetheless, even in less eminent garrison towns, officers similarly enjoyed a prominent social standing and this was boosted considerably after 1871. Friedrich Meinecke, born in 1862, recalled how, in those days, a Prussian lieutenant passed through the world like 'a young god'.[27] Middle-class young men were becoming increasingly interested in sharing some of this glory; even if they did not pursue a professional officer's career, they could at least aspire to the rank of reserve officer and make do with the position of a 'demi-god', as

Meinecke termed it. This new position, created in the 1860s, replaced the old-style *Landwehr* officer. The reserve officer was part of the regular army, just like the new reserves themselves, comprising the three first age-groups of the former *Landwehr*. The reserve officer was subject to precisely the same expectations in terms of soldierly appearance and behaviour as the professional officer and, when in uniform, was required to obey the military code.

The one-year volunteers continued to provide the pool for producing reserve officers. They could conclude their period of service with an exam, qualifying them as a candidate reserve officer and then, after two eight-week exercise periods and further exams, the corps would decide whether it wanted to take on the aspiring officer or not. The conditions entitling young men to become one-yearers had hardly changed at all from the *Vormärz* period either. Proof of higher school education remained a key requirement, and they still had to pay for equipment and lodging themselves, which entailed a substantial outlay, although it varied according to the arm of the service chosen. In the infantry, for example, initial expenses for equipment amounted to 174 Reichsmarks, but, over time, a considerable number of extras were needed and care of the uniform itself required a sizeable investment. Lodging and subsistence were far from cheap either, with the one-yearers having to pay for accommodation and food themselves without receiving any pay whatsoever. Taken together, these expenses amounted to at least 300 to 400 marks per month, which even for mid-range civil servants represented a large sum – in those days, a senior executive officer in the highest salary bracket would have been earning around 8,500 marks a year.[28]

Nonetheless, financial considerations seem to have been no obstacle to enlisting as a one-yearer. Whereas in the 1840s, given his financial position, Wilhelm Lübke, an elementary school teacher's son, was happy to be classified as unfit for service, later writers described their profound disappointment at not being accepted into the armed forces. In Imperial Germany, elementary school teachers particularly did everything to become accepted as one-yearers; there was no longer any reason to be glad about the prospect of serving for only six weeks – an advantage dating from the *Vormärz* period. Instead, what was initially seen as a benefit steadily came to be viewed as a deficit tarnishing their social status. Apparently, after gaining the entitlement to one-yearer status in 1895, they readily accepted the high costs this involved.[29]

However, even in Imperial Germany, simply because young men had the formal educational requirements allowing them to serve only for one year and qualify as a reserve officer did not mean that they actually made use of the privilege, or could make use of it. Only one-third of those eligible as one-yearers went on to perform military service, while most were discharged as being physically unfit for service. Of those completing their one year, only every second recruit secured the sought-after certificate proving their aptness as potential reserve officers. A good third merely managed to reach the rank of reserve NCO, and 13 per cent were discharged as lance-corporals or without any promotion at all. The commission ruling on the aptness certificates consisted of battalion officers and, as a rule, they were extremely careful in the decisions they took, not only assessing the candidates' military knowledge but also – and primarily – evaluating their social and political suitability.[30]

In Prussia, around 5 per cent of the total group comprised Jewish one-yearers, but they stood almost no chance of passing this exam successfully, as Walther Rathenau discovered in the 1890s. Born in 1867 to a well-to-do Berlin family, Rathenau, later a liberal politician and Weimar foreign minister, was so inspired by his admiration for 'Prussianism' and the military atmosphere that he hoped to become a career army officer. However, despite the official policy on equal opportunities, he found Jews that were excluded from entering the professional officer career. Consequently, in 1891, he joined the Berlin Cuirassier Regiment of Guards for his voluntary one-year military service, and had a photograph taken of himself proudly wearing the uniform of a vice-sergeant major. But all the higher ranks were closed to him – as an unconverted Jew and a 'second class citizen' in Prussia at the time, he was not only blocked from a professional officer career, but was equally unable to obtain the entitlement to become a reserve officer.[31]

Max Warburg, the same age as Rathenau and a Hamburg banker's son, was also toying with the idea of an active officer career. In contrast, though, he served his voluntary year in Munich in 1888–9. Many Jewish one-yearers chose to serve in the Bavarian troops, since the officer corps there was reputedly more liberal and did not exclude Jews right from the start. In Warburg's case too, it proved to be a wise move: not only did he finish his year of service with a select regiment as an NCO, but, after completing his tasks in the requisite exercises, was even accepted as a cavalry officer candidate[32] – something generally denied to the majority of Jewish men serving in the Prussian military.

Despite knowing this, and against his better judgement, Willy Ritter Liebermann von Wahlendorf, born in 1863 in Berlin, was not deterred from serving his voluntary year in 1886–7 with a Strassburg Regiment of Lancers. He briefly shared the same desire to be an active cavalry officer as Rathenau and Warburg, but then consoled himself with the thought of passing through life as a reserve officer. Even though he knew this was practically unheard of in Prussia, he was prepared to trust to his luck – which in this case came in the form of family connections and his successes in a respected student corps. He also might have had in mind the example set by the three Bleichröder sons: they had managed to become reserve officers in the 1870s in nothing less than guards' regiments, despite their Jewish origins. Their father, though, was renowned as Bismarck's banker and could use the muscle of his excellent political connections. Liebermann was unlucky. His cavalry captain's anti-Semitic stance even denied him promotion to lance-corporal, and he ended his year of service as 'His Majesty's commonest commoner'.[33]

Ludwig Goldstein was more successful in the army than Liebermann. Goldstein, son of a Jewish master tailor and a Protestant mother, was born in 1867 in Königsberg. At the end of his year's service in 1890–1, he had at least been promoted to lance-corporal, and even went on to become an NCO in the reserves. 'There was no chance to climb any higher', Goldstein commented in his memoirs of 1936, in which his time in the army is cast in a thoroughly favourable light. Goldstein enjoyed being a soldier, and entered into it 'heart and soul'. He loved taking part in brisk exercises, hating it when they 'went at it lamely and listlessly', and all his life he 'remained grateful for the thorough military training and an education encompassing the entire person', which proved 'especially useful and necessary' for him as a 'weakly lad'.[34]

The training Goldstein experienced in building a tough and powerful physique ran counter to the stereotypical image of Jewish men as feeble, effete and physically unfit – a notion keenly underlined both by doctors and by the anti-Semitic press in the late nineteenth century.[35] This was the image that also pursued Victor Klemperer when he presented himself to the recruiting authorities in 1903. He had been born in 1881 into a Reform rabbi's family, and from his earliest childhood, like many boys, he felt drawn to the army, and dearly loved playing with paper and tin soldiers. He had watched the exercises of the Berlin grenadier regiments with pleasure, stood right in the first row at parades and devotedly listened to every kind of military music. Both his older brothers had been discharged as physically unfit at their mustering, and Klemperer too was persuaded that 'his back was a little bit hunched' and he would never be enlisted into the army. His joy was all the greater when, despite his short stature (he was only 166 cm tall) and slightly built body, he was passed as fit for service, with the army doctor saying, 'Though you have no muscles, you're completely fit and service will toughen you up.' The delight in not being 'physically inferior' and meeting the strict military standards of fitness outweighed all the other factors. Since he had already had himself baptized into the Christian faith, the 'route to a reserve officer [was] open' too, and he would not need to 'play the part of the Jewish one-yearer known from innumerable jokes'. Klemperer was then totally aghast to discover he had no role to play in the military at all – on entering the Halle Infantry Regiment he had been re-examined by a strict Medical Corps major who declared Klemperer's chest measurement insufficient. Completely downcast, Klemperer returned to Berlin with his pride in his presumed 'physical fitness' dented and his hopes of becoming a reserve officer utterly dashed.[36]

Without doubt, the relationship of Jewish men to the military was marked by a particular set of expectations and emotions. As the writings by Rathenau, Klemperer or Goldstein make only too apparent, the army virtually took on the role of a keystone in their civic and gender identity – a centrality significantly reinforced by the anti-Semitism prevalent in both the political and social spheres. Such anti-Semitic propaganda may not have sought to rehash the 1840s debates when the Prussian government had considered excluding Jewish men from military service and, consequently, from active citizenship, but it certainly could register some success in presenting Jews as poor patriots, seeking to dodge military service. Despite major protests and remonstrations from the Jewish population, this prejudice lived on and, even as late as 1916, was consciously used to fuel doubts over German Jews' feelings of national loyalty, precipitating the notorious 'counting of Jews' (*Judenzählung*) in the army. [37] In this context, many Jewish men attributed a supra-individual significance to serving in the army. They saw it as not only documenting their political and social belonging, but in addition as a particularly valuable 'ritual masculinising', locating them in a sphere clearly contradicting the prevalent stereotype of Jews as physically weak and feeble.

A similar reasoning strongly motivated some of the non-Jewish one-yearers too. For example, in 1877 Theodor Rocholl, a parson's son, hoped 'to be chosen with all my heart, as I always had very little good to say about the shirkers; it would have grieved me to have to go around stamped as a state cripple, and constantly stopped me from holding my head high'. [38] The year in the army, at least in retrospect, was often presented as bordering on a 'school of manliness' – an expression used by Professor Friedrich Paulsen in his popular standard work on German universities, which first appeared in 1902. Like many of his middle-class contemporaries, Paulsen also published memoirs of his youth, in his case in 1909, recalling his period of service in 1871–2 in a Berlin guards' field artillery regiment. Nearly forty years later, he duly praised his time there and though he largely managed to restrain himself from a romanticised glorification of this 'episode', he presented it very vividly and with great fondness. He found the gun practice 'particularly pleasurable', considering it 'exceptionally exciting'. For his officer's exam he had to lead a gun battery across open countryside and into a skirmish, and recalled the great enjoyment he found in 'mastering the movement of the mass of horses and troops'. Paulsen equally enjoyed taking part in field manoeuvres, too. This, he remembered, appealed to his 'animal needs': the fun of camping out, the 'inner satisfaction' of a simple meal and a bed in a hay-loft. With no regrets, he recalled 'how quickly one divests oneself of the civilised person's necessities, the serviette, knife and fork, and even cleanliness: the natural man lies directly under the skin'. [39]

Nowhere offered a better opportunity of acquiring such direct experience of human 'nature' than the mounted formations. Karl Alexander von Müller served in 1901–2 in Munich with the field artillery and, in his autobiography, focused particularly on the riding lessons 'and everything that goes with it'. He enjoyed the 'warm animal smell of the stable', brushing his horse down 'with curry comb and brush', and loved riding bareback with just a blanket. He portrayed Veronika, his horse, as 'a most delightful nimble little chestnut mare' with 'unpredictable moods' who he had 'almost fallen in love with'. When he had to leave Veronika behind at the end of his one-year service, he did it 'with a feeling of unfaithfulness'.[40] For middle-class men like Müller, raised in an urban environment, military service was generally the first chance to form such close relationships to horses, with or without the erotically tinged overtones. But even experienced riders relished the virile atmosphere in a cuirassiers' regiment, as did, for example, Werner Otto von Hentig. Born in Berlin in 1886, son of a lawyer and cabinet minister, Hentig especially enjoyed the sayings engraved over the stable doors: 'A good dog, a good horse is worth more than a hundred women' or 'best of all: a cuirassier is the ultimate man can achieve'.

Hentig appeared to have felt at ease in the world of the 3rd Cuirassiers in Königsberg in 1905, even if this was substantially different from the 'markedly intellectual and artistic atmosphere' at home. To begin with, he noted, 'it all seemed Greek to me'; 'it was all really surprisingly new: the strictest subordination to the orders of the NCOs in charge of training, stable duty attending to the royal Prussian service-horses, looked after more carefully and treated decidedly better than the men, the entire tone of talk in a world wholly new to me.' He found his period of service extremely physically demanding and the training exceptionally hard. In retrospect, though, he paid tribute to the 'military training and the horse' as an important 'educational factor' that had played 'too decisive a role' in his life for him to 'only have skimmed over it' in his memoirs.[41]

In the context of their memories of military service, many middle-class men talked of training and education and hence, intentionally or not, reproduced the official military discourse in Imperial Germany. Officer circles claimed that military service not only provided a professional training for a soldier's tasks, but offered complex character building. On starting their duties, the one-yearers learnt from their superiors that 'their period of service is a school of self-discipline, where they are to mature as men, capable of coping with the greatest hardships and learning to use the force of their iron will to watch over themselves'. School began with basic training, lasting around ten weeks, with drilling, rifle practice, athletics and service in the field, and only after this had been completed were the one-yearers put together with the 'normal' recruits and integrated into the companies. After the one-yearers had served for six months, they could then be promoted to lance-corporals, already taking over command of 'the men', and leading a squad. If they proved successful here, after three months more, they could achieve NCO status and leave the army as a 'reserve candidate officer'.[42]

Although the one-yearers had a 'special status' among the recruits from the very start, they were not supposed to be treated more leniently, and were to be 'made outwardly into a strapping soldier' as far as their 'physical constitution' would allow. In addition, they had to learn how to give commands, acquire a confident bearing, and prove their 'irreproachable conduct both on and off duty'. The Prussian first lieutenant Spohn, who fixed these standards in 1906, undoubtedly set exacting benchmarks and, as the superior officer, took pains to ensure they were rigidly adhered to. He rigorously punished any violation of the official regulations, whether it was reporting back late, or 'efforts to gain illicit relief from duty'. He was particularly infuriated by attempts to 'bribe' NCOs with money or goods to ensure a pleasanter day without guard duty, or less drill practice. In such cases, offenders were treated according to the motto: 'Men and soldiers are not born to a life of luxury, but only thrive on troubles and cares, hardships and renunciations.'[43]

Such admonishments indicate that officers were not always completely happy about having one-yearers in their regiment. The official line may have commended them as the jewel in the crown of the army, but in reality they faced reservations and scepticism from many superior officers. The one-yearers reputedly were spoiled and easily over-taxed, while their 'special status' appeared to pose a threat to discipline. Frequently, one-yearers dubbed their captain or cavalry captain a 'one-yearer-eater', recounting horror stories of their bullying and detailing the real 'grinding down' they had suffered at their hands during military service. Some NCOs too wanted to make the 'educated' pay and took delight in really 'putting them through it', testing the limits of their physical endurance.[44] Max Weber, for example, commenting on his military service in Strassburg in 1883, noted that 'we one-yearers do not get on at all well' with the captain, who mostly gave them the unpleasant duties and took particular pleasure in 'especially heartily chasing me around the barrack yard on my lame feet'. As it was, Weber painted his year of military service in the blackest colours. A civil servant's son, he had already discovered the pleasures of freedom in a student's life and the students' associations and, after enlisting, he did not mince words in his letters home to his parents. At the start, particularly, he complained bitterly about the ordeals he had to put up with, reporting how simply the 'physical exertions' on the parade ground were 'sometimes disproportionately huge for us one-yearers', let alone the demands made on field exercises with kilometre-long marches. They returned to the town 'with blisters on our feet, bloody torn hands, bruises all over, half-dead, drenched in sweat and water from puddles and, with a bit of luck, liquid manure, with the single pieces of our outfits hardly distinguishable from the filth', and in this way had obtained 'a foretaste of manoeuvres and war'.

Such descriptions were decidedly at odds with the idealised romance of manoeuvres complete with sweet-smelling hay and feasts of bread and bacon recalled in many of the one-yearers' memoirs. Such writers, though, tended to be older, looking back on a glorified military service set in the nimbus of youth's golden age, whereas Weber made no attempt to disguise what he had been through: dirt was dirt, pain was pain, and outrage experienced at the humiliation of having 'to listen to untold instances of insolence from the most wretched scoundrel' remained outrage. Although in his letters to his mother, in particular, Weber did try to use a lighter tone, he never attempted to hide his feeling that the 'fun side of military life' she had predicted had not yet materialised.[45]

But was Weber perhaps just the only one out of tune in the middle-class choir singing the army's praises? Might he not just have been especially critical or misanthropic, or perhaps tended to see things more blackly than others did? There is no evidence to support such a view. Instead, he seems to have been a quite normal one-yearer, neither especially 'slack' nor particularly keen, despite the scars from the students' fencing ground, neither overly patriotic nor expressly critical – but just as half-formed, vain and well-adjusted as the mass of his middle-class peers. Weber regarded his military service as a civic duty and an investment in his own personal future; with a lot of money, time and patience he gained the much-sought-after qualification as a reserve officer.

Perhaps, though, there were other reasons why Weber gave such a gloomy picture of his period of service. Undoubtedly, he intended to elicit a sympathetic reaction from his parents –first and foremost, forbearing and generosity. His mother and father both reproached him severely for his 'frivolousness' and his reckless extravagance. Weber had already spent considerable time and money on his involvement with the student *Burschenschaft* during his semesters at Heidelberg University, and his time in Strassburg appeared to be a more intense repeat of the same behaviour. His parents were displeased to hear of Weber's extravagant lifestyle and that his monthly allowance did not cover his costs. His indolence too was a thorn in their side. Instead of continuing with his studies alongside his military service, as they expected, he only attended a weekly lecture by Baumgarten, his uncle, and spent one afternoon a week in the university library. Even his letters were infrequent. Weber's justification lay in his picture of army life as unremitting drudgery which hardly left him time and energy for any intellectual pursuits: drilling, marching, weapons practice, roll-call, rifle cleaning 'and all those similar sorts of things, downright infuriatingly superfluous stuff' robbed him of 'every last trace of intellectual energy'.

Had Weber perhaps landed in an especially 'strict' regiment and, for this reason, found so much to report that was negative? If one compares his letters with the autobiographical texts of other one-yearers, such an objection does not seem very likely. Even in the often indulgent and glorified memoirs of old men, composed after a considerable lapse of time, one finds drudgery and corrupt NCOs too, just as much as physical privations. In addition, like Weber, almost all writers complained about the immense loss of time, the boredom and enforced idleness, which even at the end of an eventful and active civilian life, they still recalled as a torture and a waste. In a letter to his mother, Weber commented that 'even far worse' than the physical exertions was 'endlessly killing time' and 'the repetitions of any number of purely mechanical skills, not just a thousand times but a million times' which 'simply obliterated any power to think' and generated a 'dreadful apathy'.[46]

Paulsen, who had no problems either with 'duty' or 'discipline', also recalled the waste of time: 'The only thing I found distressing was waiting, the loss of time, hanging around superfluously, with no reason at all, and it remained the real cross to bear throughout that entire year.' The difference between Weber and Paulsen, between contemporary letters and later memoirs, was not so much in the negative experiences they both mention, but in the weight attributed to these experiences and their subsequent interpretation. While the 20-year-old Weber had a number of good reasons to present his military service to his parents as essentially a burden, sidelining the positive experiences, the 50-year-old Paulsen embedded his 'episode' into a unified, meaningful picture of his youth – a phase of development ending with his military service year, marking the transition into an adult life running down straight, coherent and defined lines, recording many challenges and dangers but even more successes, victories and triumphs through a conscious effort of will. The military service year had a key function in the logic underlying such male, middle-class retrospective résumés. It embodied all the adventures and freedom from cares and worries comprising the ideal of youth, while simultaneously preparing a man for the adult male's arduous existence, laden with responsibility. Consequently, it mediated those insights and experiences useful for male self-assertion. In this sense, in retrospect, Paulsen even found something positive in the 'waiting' and 'hanging around': 'Perhaps the soldier has to learn this too: standing ready for duty, without employment and without grumbling'.[47]

Moreover, for some one-yearers, the 'magic' exercised by the 'tremendous organism' of the army compensated for the 'paralysing mindlessness'. Müller, for example, enthused over the blissful 'feeling of being an active part of a vast body, marvellously trimmed for its purpose' and Paulsen thrilled to 'the power of an organised communal will', conveying a sense of well-being, trust and collective strength.[48] Furthermore, in their period of military service young men socialised into middle-class life could experience a feeling of relief from everyday burdens that was far from off-putting: there was no need to set a goal, or plan for the next day, or even think about the consequences of their actions. In 1908–9, the painter August Macke, whose work prospects seemed as precarious as his personal situation (his girlfriend was pregnant and a scandal was unavoidable), savoured his time in a Bonn infantry regiment to the full: 'There's something magnificent about only living for one's health for a whole year.'[49] And it was especially men like Macke, already bearing a responsibility for their lives and standing on their own feet in their professions, however uncertainly, who tended to celebrate their military service year as the crowning finale of their youth, or a reminiscence worth sharing. They even found something 'cosy' about standing guard duty, otherwise almost universally stamped as a wasteland of boredom and tedium: 'We have several bottles of good Mosel wine behind us. Next door at the inn, they're making music and singing', and the marches resembled enjoyable rambles: 'On the way, we stole apples from the trees and ate them as we were going along. In the evening, we arrived here in the village. From one wine pub to another until late in the night. The entire company slightly merry, with the lovely Mosel girls in our arms.'[50]

Alcohol and women – these two themes constantly run through the reports like a *basso continuo*. While some one-yearers may have already been experienced with both, especially those who had studied for several semesters and joined in life at the students' associations, others, like Müller, were largely unprepared for these aspects of army life. Shy, with a middle-class upbringing, Müller transferred directly from school to a Munich barracks in 1901, still uninitiated 'in sexual matters'. He found himself thrown 'headlong into the midst of the unreserved coarseness of a group of robust young men, whose thoughts, words and deeds after the pressure of duty could find no more desirable outlet than palpably erotic adventures'. It was common practice, among both the 'common soldiers' and the one-yearers, to 'initiate the regiment's last innocent childish ninny into the mysteries of Eros', and this was done by recourse to prostitutes. For the one-yearers, these were the 'invited young ladies' who appeared after dinner celebrating the prince regent's birthday, and for the troops, the 'common wenches' from cheap inns or the proverbial chambermaids, as immortalised in *Reigen*, Arthur Schnitzler's episodic play of 1896–7. In sexual terms, for many young men from 'a good background', their military service year seems to have been a time of transition and initiation.[51]

However, it was not only sexual experience that turned a youth into a man and an adult: another factor in this equation was the special attitude the army taught men to have to their own body. In their military service, men learnt to have bodies that were 'hard', disciplined and able to withstand privation. The army built on the groundwork of gymnastics at school with an incomparably greater rigour and single-mindedness. 'Training and developing physical strength' was one of the army's core educational goals, and the daily exercises, gymnastics and strenuous field marches, laden with heavy packs, all served this purpose.[52] Such a training was deemed especially essential for the one-yearers, often transferring directly from school or university to the drill yard, who were generally regarded as being 'weakly' and enfeebled.[53]

In addition to physical discipline and endurance, the army also taught one-yearers secondary virtues like 'learning to obey, orderliness and punctuality', which, many testified, were useful throughout their entire lives. But these young men did not merely learn discipline and subordination when under a superior's orders – after a few months, they were already allowed to give orders themselves, issuing commands to 'common soldiers' and exercising power, limited as it may have been. Müller recalled the 'manly feeling of testing your own powers, forcing others to act by your will, and taking up responsibility for others'.[54] Weber, who started his military service year in October 1883, took over the leadership of a squad in April 1884, similarly noting that he initially felt 'important'. At least his new rank put him in the pleasant position of not having to do athletics himself 'but only bawl out the others and correct them'. The downside, though, was having to live in the barracks with the soldiers for this period. As the senior of the room, he was responsible for ensuring the others were up punctually and tidied their beds, and had to oversee their washing habits and table manners, check their uniforms and make certain their wardrobes were neat. Any lapses in the squad were laid squarely at his door, and interpreted as a lack of a 'military perspective'. In this way, even the role of superior, which he had so enjoyed during the first few days, came to reveal a darker side, making Weber groan: 'It simply does make a difference whether you have to sleep in the same room with your men, etc. or first come across from home for every duty.' As a rule, one-yearers lodged in private quarters; occasionally, they rented an entire apartment, especially when they spent their leisure time together anyway.[55]

The amount of free time, and free space, enjoyed by one-yearers largely depended on the quality of their relations to the regiment's officers. This was not always harmonious, despite the evidence of Harry Graf Kessler's memories of his military service year with the Potsdam Lancers in the early 1890s. From the start, he recalled, he was drawn 'into the closest contact with the officers' corps' and came to know the military life 'in human terms, at its best'. With a circle of young ensigns and officers he read Nietzsche and debated 'literature and philosophy'. Naturally, he lived in private quarters and took his meals in the officers' mess. In other garrisons too, one-yearers were sometimes permitted to eat in the mess, although not together with the officers but in a separate room provided for the purpose. Where, as in the southern German town of Constance, officers and one-yearers both lodged in the same hotel opposite the barracks, a closer contact was virtually pre-programmed.[56]

But there were also officers who avoided such contact, regarding the one-yearers as somewhat dubious competitors, accusing them of unsuitability for the army. One could command their respect, as Weber learnt, by 'frequent duelling'. Similarly, it was exceptionally advantageous in career terms to belong to a students' corps, which guaranteed financial support and influence.[57] One-yearers invariably benefited from good relations with their superiors, and such connections loomed large in their letters and memoirs. In contrast, relations with the 'common' soldiers are hardly mentioned – if they appear at all, it is only as inferiors needing to be disciplined. Max Weber's cousin, Otto Baumgarten, was also promoted to squad leader after only a few months of service, and, in his view, the 'exigencies of duty' could often only be enforced by duress. It was advice he followed himself with 'a fellow from Upper Silesia, who put me in pretty pickle every day at roll-call, until I gave him a massive clip round the side of the head and recommended his room-mates give his scummy ears the same treatment'. Weber himself heartily regretted being allowed 'to learn this means of discipline but not to apply it' in teaching his subordinates 'military proprieties'. Everything else he had to say about the 'common soldier' fell under the headings of 'pilfering', alcohol consumption, sexuality, and 'often a dreadfully coarse use of language'. He commented that: 'It is worthy of note that they know how to find the right attitude towards the one-yearers without surrendering their dignity too much, yet without becoming too insolent.'[58]

It is not surprising that relations between these two groups were distant, considering the different status and privileges enjoyed by the middle-class young men in the army. The 'troops', though, got their own back by making the one-yearers regularly 'buy a round', while, retrospectively, former one-yearers emphasised how crucial and instructive their dealings with the 'common soldiers' had been. As Rostock businessman's son Adolf Langfeld commented, military service was the first time in his life he had come into closer contact with 'our population's lower classes' and gained 'an insight into their thoughts and feelings'.[59] Hardly anyone, though, spoke of having fostered 'cordial relations with all of his "brothers in arms", both one-yearers and three-yearers'.[60] The form of address similarly underlined the social gap, with the 'others' using the respectful *Sie* form to one-yearers (who also employed it with each other), while the 'common soldiers' used the informal *Du* form among themselves.[61]

The only time a cross-class young male community actually emerged was on manoeuvres when both groups turned out and camped overnight – portrayed by Macke in his usual colourful way:

> We are sleeping here on real straw-filled sacks, covered with two thick woollen blankets. There are always two beds, one over the other, and so closely packed together that we're like bees in a hive. In the mornings, when the hut-camp wakes, one sees how the blankets gradually come to life. People come crawling out from under them. Cold water is collected. Half-dressed, one walks out into the morning mist, or watches a magnificent red-tinged dawn break across the moorland. One sluices the other off with cold water, and we eat our army bread with good butter and honey, and then, with music playing, it's off past the high pines.[62]

In adopting this romantic view of army camp and adventure, Macke was directly borrowing from the topoi prevalent in youth movements and students' associations. However, both the students' associations and the back-to-nature organisations of the *Wandervogel* ('wandering birds') were socially exclusive and solely open to middle-class youth, while military service, no matter how non-universal, at least offered potential mixing across class boundaries. Despite the army recreating class boundaries in its own ranks, separating the 'good society' of those using *Sie* from the matey world of the familiar *Du*, it was still the only organisation in the whole of Germany that brought members of the working and middle classes, labourers, clerks and students together, rubbing shoulders with each other. The elite secondary schools (*Gymnasia*) or universities were middle-class preserves; the youth groups and professional and trade associations were similarly socially segregated. Only the army provided a sphere where men of roughly the same age but from different social backgrounds came together, in this case to join in preparing for the *casus belli*. Different personal sensitivities and career patterns may have disguised this meta-level 'patriotic' mission for a time, but it came back into focus from the vantage point of memory, at the latest.

In this sense, rather than the one-yearers' autobiographies merely underlining the army's function in binding social groups, they emphasised its political significance. Military service was the time when they learnt to see themselves as a part of a larger whole and subordinate themselves to it, a time reinforcing their 'patriotic disposition' just as much as their 'trust in the future'. Their feelings – proud of the army, proud of 'donning the king's colours' and proud of the prestige attached to their future state as reserve officer – seem to have been common to many one-yearers performing military service in Imperial Germany. Even Weber, whose letters spoke of quite different experiences, was determined to 'rise in rank' and reported to his father on the 'favourable' influence 'the German military' was exercising in Alsace-Lorraine on 'a foreign population adopting as negative an attitude as possible'.[63]

But the influence the 'German military' exercised on Weber's personal relations was at least as benign. All his life, he set great store by his status as reserve officer, and he even retrospectively attributed an important socialisation function to the period of military service itself. Apart from his active role in a Heidelberg students' association, he found being 'broken-in to resoluteness' as a prospective NCO played a decisive role in his overcoming the 'extensive inner shyness and uncertainty of my youthful years'.[64] In this respect too, army experience represented a rite of passage, marking the end of youth and the transition to life as an adult male.

3. Soldiers at the 'School of Manliness'

Those viewing their army service as a rite of passage also included the soldiers 'following the colours' for more than a year. Just as in the pre-Empire years, the vast majority of the troops in Imperial Germany – around 96 per cent – similarly comprised soldiers doing three years' continuous military service (and after 1893, only two years). Once discharged from the line army, they were on furlough under army reserve command for five years, then passed into the first *Landwehr* reserves for a further five years before joining the second *Landwehr* reserves and finally serving in the *Landsturm* (last reserves) until they turned 45 and all military obligations were completed. The actual active service load placed on the soldiers during this process varied considerably. Since the troops were never mobilised during the long decades of peace after 1870, no active service was required from the reserves and *Landwehr* reserves apart from one exercise period of 12–14 days. Active army experience, then, was largely limited to the training and practice blocks commonly completed when the men were 20 to 23 (or, later, 20 to 22).[65]

Three years – or even two years – was a long time for a young man who, as a rule, had finished school at 14 and either started an apprenticeship or gone into paid employment in agriculture, trade or industry. Furthermore, military service took such young men to live far from their familiar surroundings. Rural recruits were at the same time moving into an urban environment and, consequently, facing a doubly alien world, since even after their day's duty was done, they remained outside their known social context, practices and interactions. In these terms, the case of one-yearers was quite different. They were sons of respectable townspeople, used to an urban life, who frequently served in their home or university town and, as a rule, only had to be present in the barracks for a few hours a day. The 'common soldier' was not granted such privileges. Instead, he tended to experience the army as, in Goffman's sense, a total institution completely filling his life for a period of several years.

It is no surprise, then, that the transition into this institution was perceived as marking a major break in a recruit's own biography, and was staged accordingly. Collective leave-taking rituals are known from a variety of regions, revealing how vividly they impressed participants and observers alike. At Rottenburg in Württemberg, for example, the enlistees 'go around the village with their mates a day or two before they are due to enter the barracks, and demand a donation from their family and acquaintances. As they do so, either the drums are played or a bugle is sounded.' Frequently, even after 1890, they were also accompanied by firing guns, but this was, in the words of a report from 1899, 'recently forbidden'. The money collected was turned into a 'farewell drink', and if there was anything left, the young men took it with them 'into the barracks as money for provisions'. In addition, the enlisted recruits enjoyed 'special liberties' and were allowed to cut a figure at local festivities. A contemporary description in a folk life study noted that frequently 'those not required to serve or found unfit have to buy the recruits a drink'.[66]

The symbolic content in such rituals is easy to identify. The young men going to spend the next few years in the army provide an appropriately self-aggrandising setting for their departure, while the drums, bugles and gunshot give them a foretaste of what is to come. In the process, they make a racket that drowns out individual feelings of loss and fear. Military music on the drill ground or on the battlefield functioned to structure uniform movement and provide a point of orientation, but also to reinforce a feeling of strength and engender courage – and here, in a parallel custom, the beating drums, bugle calls and salvoes from the small Württemberg village drove out the future soldiers' worry and uncertainty. Furthermore, these sounds were also designed to cow those people staying at home. The young men occupied public space, filling it with a deafening noise, anticipating the power they would soon be able to exercise as armed soldiers. They were confronting the civilians with a pre-military presence, where the shape of this expression of force could certainly take on threatening forms – when asking for a 'donation', for example, was accompanied by shooting, it lost its childish innocence.

On the other hand, since such requests tended to be directed to family and friends, they testified to existing social bonds. The young men did not appear as highwaymen, but family members or the neighbours' son, who, before they finally packed their things and departed, requested provisions for their journey. Naturally, the whole procedure was given another touch by the men then investing the vast majority of the money collected in a drinking-bout at the local inn, where those leaving made their farewells to friends and peers staying behind. In this context, the 'donation' resembled a ransom or religious offering, where the civilians – especially those deemed unfit for service or not serving for other reasons – exchanged their freedom against cash, paying the young men symbolically, as it were, to leave their homes and take on the task of providing them with armed protection.

Furthermore, the subdued feelings most recruits experienced when starting off for the barracks were blunted by this extensive alcohol consumption. Spurred on by drinking in a group, they indulged in those 'excesses' that similarly belonged to the ritual of farewell but were less favourably looked on by the authorities and those directly affected. In 1869, the president of the Westphalian provincial synod complained to the government: 'As desirable as it may be that the young men subject to exercising their military duties should do so in a joyful mood and not in sadness, it nonetheless needs to be deprecated that especially on enlistment days, where one tempts the other, over-indulgence in brandy occasions excesses.'[67] Such excesses included damage to property and, occasionally, even physical assault –although such cases generally occurred on the march through neighbouring villages and not on the enlistees' home ground. Undoubtedly, such instances of assault could be put down to the group situation and the influence of alcohol, yet they also expressed an aggression against the civilians staying behind, from whom they recouped, as it were, the sacrifice of time, money and independence required behind the barracks' walls.

The more or less violent rituals involved in taking leave of familiar places had gender-specific connotations as well as social and generational ones. In some areas, for example, 'the girls looked down on' young men who had not served in the army. In Baden, one could recognise those at dances about to join up because they wore flowers instead of the usual plumes of coloured paper, and when they left their villages to join the garrison in the town, their rack-wagons were decorated with broad ribbons, prepared and attached by the village's young women. They also made a decoration of ribbons and artificial flowers for the recruits' hats, inspiring Wilhelm Hauff to write: 'When at last I must enlist / so lovingly and long she kissed / tied bright ribbons to my hat / and tearfully crushed me to her heart.'[68]

But the call to the colours did not only mean bidding farewell to sweethearts. It also signalled a leave-taking of childhood and youth – reflected in the evocative symbol of the colourful ribbons and flowers, contrasting sharply with the uniform the enlistee was to wear over the coming few years. The contrast was equally striking to contemporaries too, although such customs did not always meet with approval. In 1885, the daily *Dresdener Nachrichten* newspaper reported that decorating themselves with this 'tawdry frippery' was 'in the opinion of many, neither manly nor suited to the seriousness of the event. A German youth chosen to be enlisted in the German army ought not to get himself up in such baubles and trumpery.'[69] According to the author (and in 'the opinion of many'), the military service's masculinising effect ought to start directly with enlistment and not, as custom had it, when the enlistee first entered the barracks.

There was widespread agreement, though, both on the side of the enlistees and those staying behind, that army experience would alter the recruits' gender identity, transforming the 'youth' into a 'man'. The implications of such a view could be seen during the short periods of furlough, when the soldier, naturally in uniform, visited his home village. The privileged status he again enjoyed was most noticeably expressed in relations between the sexes. If soldiers visiting were especially valued as dancing partners, this did not merely underline their continued acceptance within the local community; it similarly emphasised their position as favoured husbands, free to choose a wife once they had been discharged without fear of being rejected. Their lives as young bachelors ended when they entered military service, and the army released them as men, not only capable of defending their fatherland, but also of protecting women and children.[70]

It was assumed, though never said, that they would also lose their youthful 'innocence' during military service and, in this sense too, become 'masculine'. However, official army reports make no mention of this aspect of masculine education. On the contrary, officers and writers on military affairs were at pains to present the army as a bastion of 'morality'. Garrison commanders forbade their troops to visit inns used by 'pimps' and 'disreputable women', attempting to persuade the landlords to choose their 'female staff' with care and limit them to 'the number required for serving at tables'.[71] They repeatedly warned the troops to refrain from 'licentiousness' and avoid intimacies with prostitutes, as 'repugnant' as it was 'injurious to the health'.[72] It was no coincidence that sexually transmitted diseases were mentioned. After all, in 1881, 35 out of 1,000 soldiers in the German army were being treated by army doctors for precisely this reason, a figure that steadily declined, partly due to the efforts of an intensive information campaign. Moreover, in 1912 the war ministry pointed out that 22 per cent of those suffering from sexually transmitted diseases had been infected prior to enlistment and, consequently, their illness could not be attributed to army life alone.[73]

In any case, the administration tended to treat any reproaches in this area in a rather dilatory manner. When, in 1910, the diocesan authorities for Freising, Munich, sent the Bavarian war ministry a soldier's note book that contained 'any amount of highly offensive, crude sexual descriptions', the ministry reacted with near indifference. As a courtesy to the diocesan authorities, who had discovered 'very many former soldiers in possession of such note books' and feared for their moral state, they notified troop commanders and army chaplains of the situation. However, there was to be no binding ruling on the matter. In the army's view, 'the men bring such things with them in from outside', and hence the schools and churches ought to deal with it 'before military service starts', adding: 'It's too late for such things in the army, which only has adults in its ranks, and furthermore it is less suitable here since this is a sphere where nature will always be the last thing that can be restrained.'[74] In this way, the army not only absolved itself from any responsibility but, in the same breath, clearly stated that it did not view the incident as a major problem. Young men needed to and ought to be free to let 'nature' take its course, especially during the years of their military service.

Not surprisingly then, the army did not enjoy the best of reputations when it came to 'moral conduct'. Far from demonstrating the 'right attitude', soldiers took back home with them the 'loose morals and lewd talk' they had picked up from 'their older fellow soldiers or even from some superiors'.[75] When Franz Rehbein, an agricultural worker from eastern Pomerania who served for three years in an Alsatian cavalry regiment in the 1880s, recalled barrack life, it was as 'a college of profligacy and immorality', where the curriculum offered 'obscene songs' alongside detailed lectures on brothel visits, presented with 'cynical directness'. Rehbein placed the blame on the humiliating treatment by superiors that drove all feelings of honour and modesty out of the soldiers, degrading them to 'animals'. Under such circumstances, it was only to be expected that 'we also lost all sense of propriety in sexual matters'. However, this interpretation appears over-simplistic. As a convinced social democrat, Rehbein had every reason to condemn the army and was at pains to unmask the 'glorification of militarism', revealing it as a mere 'fairy tale'. But his text reads as if he set out consciously to invert the military self-image: if the army claimed they developed honour and morals in recruits, Rehbein was determined to prove the opposite. In so doing, though, he falls into exactly the same simplifications – simply in a negative version – that he rightly saw propagated in those 'charming stories of soldiers'.[76]

In many cases, though, the notion of recruits entering the army as morally 'pure', 'modest' and 'untainted' youths sprang from the wishful thinking of parents and teachers; neither in the town nor in the countryside was pre-marital sex the tabooed topic middle-class moralists presented it as. Instead, autobiographical texts and military court files indicate that quite a number of young men had gained sexual experience prior to being enlisted, and some had been in 'firm' longer-term relationships, similar to a promise to marry.[77] But whether or not the recruits were already sexually initiated, their imaginations were normally no longer virgin, and songs, pictures and 'note books' all played their part in stimulating their fantasies. When, in 1912, a Bavarian rail dispatch agent accompanied his son on enlistment to Landsberg, he indignantly reported that all the other recruits spent their time in the packed train either 'cracking jokes' or singing 'highly immoral songs while their fellow recruits roared their approval'. A 'real Munich good-for-nothing' was even going round 'with a photograph from bench to bench. The accompanying howls of laughter made it easy to guess what it showed.'[78]

Of course, young men did not first discover their sexual appetite during military service, but the new situation did lend this drive a particular attitude and form. Since the recruit transport comprised many young men who had not met before, the sexual innuendo took on an unusual public form - and the Munich 'good-for-nothing' adroitly used this to his best advantage. In front of his enthusiastic audience, he played the role of the 'initiated', and, as the concerned father noted, declaimed 'highly offensive speeches, apparently learnt by heart' out of the compartment window, harvesting 'the rapturous applause of the others' for his performance. Here, sexuality became a communal experience, with 'immoral' language, laughter and applause as the ties binding the diverse individuals - and last but not least, it also addressed and expressed needs known and accessible to them all. Most likely, even those men who had just sadly bid farewell to their 'sweethearts', swearing to be eternally true, joined the 'coarse' lads in the choir - and quite possibly the dispatch agent's tearful son would have applauded with them if his father had not been there. Talking about relationships with women in crude imagery, often violent, induced an almost cathartic effect: apparently, reassuring each other that one 'could "use"' women sexually, and one could 'supply' it reinforced male self-esteem, shielding the young man against emotional dependency or bouts of sentimentality.[79]

Such behaviour simultaneously enhanced and upgraded that male primary group of which the young soldiers were going to be a part in future. Men were not only largely among themselves on the 'recruit transport' but, first and foremost, barrack life was similarly an almost women-free space. Official policy did not allow women even to set foot in the squads' quarters – rooms which could each sleep up to thirty recruits.[80] The only females permitted within the military compound were the wives and daughters of NCOs, and they generally lived in closed accommodation with their husbands and fathers. The vast majority of soldiers only came into contact with women, if at all, outside the barracks, either with an evening or Sunday pass. Yet even then, the soldiers remained primarily a male society: whether in the inns and pubs, flirting with the waitresses, or in dance-halls or brothels – everywhere the soldiers appeared in a group. And this gave them a point of orientation and a protection, but, in turn, demanded the kind of behaviour that prioritised a hearty ribaldry and left little room for tender feelings. Such behaviour did not only derive from the male barrack community, but also went to reinforce and sustain it. In this scenario, the superiors' role-model function, so prominent in Rehbein, had hardly any impact. If anything, it was the 'older' soldiers who had an influence.

In addition, the popular soldiers' songs underlined and confirmed such behaviour. Contemporaries were forever complaining that these songs were too racy, and did not keep within 'the bounds of good manners'. Military authorities may have promoted the publication of 'decent' song books but they could not prevent a parallel market developing for popular booklets, with a content often far removed from those 'decent' notions of innocence.[81] Yet even those songs without any explicitly risqué lines disseminated the image of a soldier that embodied a masculine ideal of a man who is strong and smart, yet gruff and ready to use force – and, moreover, implied these were precisely the qualities women found impressive and would open 'the door to [their] hearts'. But 'amorous glances' were quickly followed by 'lover's tears', since soldiers, as they themselves sang, were not just 'courageous and brave', but also footloose and fancy free. They were not made for faithfulness – or as an 1857 soldiers' song put it: 'Today it's Hetty, tomorrow's Betty, always new, that's how a soldier's true'.[82]

It hardly needs to be said that such messages are not to be taken at face value. The songs expressed projections, dreams and wishes. The reality, though, frequently looked very different. Soldiers might have celebrated a status without ties, yet this contrasted sharply with their everyday experience shackled to the strict rules of army service. Such an image of freedom, too, may have suppressed feelings of personal loneliness and the need for a fixed love relationship. The raw masculinity evoked in their songs had another function as well: it served as a protective shield against the homosexual temptations constantly present in the close confines of the squads' quarters. Admittedly, the sources (autobiographies, military publications, state and military court files) provide no direct references to this, and even the numerous handbooks and instruction manuals defining moral norms, and thus more or less, *ex negativo*, providing a chance to draw attention to possible lapses in behaviour, remain completely silent on this subject too. The 'common soldiers'' autobiographical texts, as a rule, also bypass the issue – with one exception. In his autobiography, Franz Bergg, a social democrat whose military service was spent in a Hamburg infantry regiment in the late 1880s, described how he was sentenced to join a fatigue party in a punishment squad based in Ehrenbreitstein, near Koblenz. He painted a picture of his time there in the darkest possible colours. In his account, he remarks that he 'frequently' noticed 'how soldiers unashamedly fawned on each other, shared one and the same footstool, and kissed like girls in love'. Bergg was amazed that no-one found 'the silly goings-on offensive', and this merely confirmed him in his belief that the 'militaristic society itself is to blame for the unnatural circumstances driving [people] to immorality'.[83] In his view, if the army kept soldiers imprisoned in a fortress, obstructing any 'natural' contact to women, it bore responsibility for the men taking refuge in 'unnatural' practices to satisfy their sexual needs.

The scanty sources available can give no indication of whether homosexuality actually occurred only in closed punishment blocks, created by the lack of other alternatives. No insights can be gained either from the existing court files. These may contain the details of numerous cases that fall under 'offences against morality', but they mostly cover (attempted) rape of women, sexual abuse of young girls or incitement to abortion. There are also many instances of soldiers being prosecuted in paternity suits or sued for alimony payments. All of these cases, though, demonstrate the soldiers' heterosexual activity; no official records provide evidence of homosexuality. Apparently it tarnished the military ideal of manliness in such a drastic and striking way that there was no desire even to mention it.

Without doubt, the soldiers' masculinity required confirmation by women. Their masculinity was shaped in an all-male environment, but had to assert and defend itself outside this space. This shows why the periods of leave were so important, whether a pass for the evening until the tattoo, for a weekend dance, or a visit home. In these leave periods, the soldiers could measure the success of their training in masculinity in the barracks by discovering whether it had made them more or less attractive. In addition, it offered soldiers a chance to measure themselves against their peers at home who had not enlisted and, according to official rhetoric, were not 'real men'.[84]

But how did women react to this canon of military thought? Autobiographical texts yield little information beyond the details of well-to-do teenagers' crushes on young lieutenants, and the apparent popularity of NCOs on the lower-class marriage market, though this had less to do with soldierly smartness and more with 'the candidacy for lifelong support' they carried 'in the pocket'.[85] In contrast, military court files paint an unremittingly negative picture, where the soldiers generally appear as aggressors trying to make the women sexually compliant, even against their will. At least, such cases undermined the popular widespread belief that soldiers always had the right key to open 'a girl's heart'. Rebuffed in their desires, they then sought to force an entry – at least, in the documented court cases. Where the skills learnt in the army's school of manliness failed to impress, physical strength and perseverance combined with the ever-present sabre provided effective reinforcements.[86]

On the other hand, though, these cases do not support the view that young women had a general fear of soldiers and, for this reason, avoided them from the start. They did not worry about having a soldier escort them home, valued them as dancing partners and were not averse to an erotic or sexual relationship, providing this respected their own wishes – and later such relationships might well have been given a formal blessing by marriage. Where numerous soldiers from rural areas remained in town rather than returning to their home villages, this may not merely have been because of the attraction of better wages but might also have been due to love relationships formed during their military service.

Although we have no evidence to indicate whether women really preferred soldiers as lovers or husbands, we can nonetheless speculate on the qualities they might have found particularly appealing. As future wives, perhaps they valued just those civilian virtues soldiers were taught in the army's school of manliness: after two to three years of military service, a man had learnt to be tidy, wash and fold his shirts, clean thoroughly, black his boots, mend the soles, and sew on buttons. Moreover, he could make his bed, clean up his wardrobe, and darn his socks. He knew how to stretch linen, was used to changing his underwear weekly, and taking a shower. He might even have learnt how to eat with a knife and fork and how to manage on his very basic pay.[87] The military aspect of his training then came into play where a women was not interested in finding a husband but was seeking a man for going out, dancing, or an erotic adventure. Reputedly, soldiers were not 'kill-joys' but cheerful company, living a carefree life in the barracks, never having to worry about a regular salary or career.[88] Young women could have been taken by their 'sense of fun' mixed with humour, and laced with a shot of dare-devilry, above all if they found little to be cheerful about in life and at work in their own circumstances as servants, factory workers or seamstresses.

The most obvious disadvantage, though, was a soldier's pay. Soldiers were chronically hard up, since their wages were extremely meagre and far below the money earned by their peers working in the factories or as day-labourers. In Imperial Germany, the troops received 2.20 marks every ten days, but this also had to cover their personal needs. They were given a warm meal at lunchtime in the barracks, coffee in the morning and evening, and 750 grams of bread a day; anything else beyond this had to be paid for themselves, including all the washing they had to have done. Financially, it was obvious that they were hardly able to 'live it up' or slip into the guise of the charming gallant. Quite the reverse – rather than paying the bills themselves, the soldiers often seem to have been supported by their 'sweethearts'.[89]

What particular skills or qualities, then, could have balanced out these deficits on the economic front? Undoubtedly, we should not underestimate the role played by the soldier's good looks, immortalised in any number of proverbs and sayings. The army's strict standards on fitness ensured that only the largest, strongest, straightest and healthiest men were actually enlisted, and their subsequent physical training enhanced these advantages. It was constantly noted that soldiers were physically more self-controlled, self-aware and self-assured than their non-military peers. They were self-confident in public and, especially out of the barracks, had to behave in line with the prescribed 'military proprieties'. They were not allowed to eat fruit on the street, nor carry a stick or umbrella, large market baskets or conspicuous packets. It was strictly forbidden to '*hook their arms* into those of female persons. Military personnel may lead ladies on their arm but are never to let themselves be led by the lady.' The uniform, of course, had to be kept perfect. Special emphasis was given to the shining buttons and the clean cravat which prevented 'anyone seeing the man's underwear under the collar'.[90]

Such instructions make only too clear how strictly regulated a soldier's appearance was, and how any influences from civilian life were screened off. Practices or objects designated as female were incompatible with the attractive outward appearance expected from soldiers. They may have cleaned, sewn and darned inside the barracks, but outside they presented themselves as sharp and smart men. Indeed, many grew beards in order to underline their masculinity.[91] In this context, the uniform was a particularly significant marker. It not only provided the soldiers with identical working gear, highlighting the mass and unified movement of military formations, but simultaneously clothed each individual in a way that peculiarly accentuated his own masculinity. Collars and cravats prevented any unauthorized glimpses of their underwear yet, at the same time, also forced the soldiers to adopt a particular posture, with a stretched neck and straight back. The uniforms were broad at the top tapering to a narrow shape around the hips, creating 'the illusion of a wasp waist and massive shoulders' and the impression that the soldiers in them were 'bursting with energy'. Many recruits complained that they were given worn and old uniforms, and needed to spend a lot of time and money making them presentable. But journeyman joiner Heinrich Georg Dirkreiter, performing his military service in 1886–7, found he made a sound investment when he bought a uniform on credit to be able to look 'smart' for his visit home, reporting that, above all, the 'parson's wife' could 'not get over the dashing looks and appearance of her former charge'.[92]

The uniform was also colourful – and this alone served to distinguish soldiers from civilians. Whereas, from the early nineteenth century on, civilian men's clothing experienced a growing trend towards dark, subdued tones, it was not until between 1907 and 1910 that the German army first adopted field grey uniforms. Previously, the soldiers had still dazzled with their conspicuous brightly coloured uniform jackets.[93] In military operations during wartime, this was remarkably impractical, marking the soldiers as highly visible targets, but in peacetime – and

Imperial Germany oversaw a forty-year period of peace – their colourful coats brought life into a grey world of male fashion, ensuring that the soldiers received the attention of civilians, and especially of women.

The uniform did not simply function as a valuable accessory in the civilian sphere. First and foremost, it clearly marked the wearer as belonging to the 'armed forces', and recalled their real 'profession' and the primary goal of military training and education: improving their dexterity in wartime skills. While this still covered the traditional values of 'manly discipline and valour', the range was being steadily extended to include the technical skills drilled into the soldiers during military service.[94] Nonetheless, this process generally continued to bracket off every dimension of war geared to active experience with violence: the soldiers were not expressly 'coached' in the act of killing. The result of being killed, on the other hand, was far more present, with every regiment mourning their dead heroes, erecting memorials to commemorate them, and having their names inscribed on lists in churches. It was not considered worth mentioning, though, that these men had not only been victims but also perpetrators, that they had killed and wounded others as well – and this was similarly omitted from the vast majority of stories centred around the adventure of war. Despite the cultural ban on killing being officially suspended in wartime, its impact continued unabated in both war memoirs and the preparation for war.

Consequently, only a minority of soldiers actually perceived their military service as a training to kill and use violence. In retrospect, Dirkreiter's comment on his three years in a Landau artillery regiment was: 'March pasts, military salutes, and guard duty – that was the be-all and end-all of our official daily duties.' When rifle practice started, he welcomed it as a change and a competitive sport, and, at the time, 'any humanitarian notions' never crossed his mind. The miner Franz Louis Fischer, who entered the army as a cavalryman in 1875, similarly viewed rifle training as a sport, an impression underlined by the regularly scheduled prize shooting matches. The rifle's technical details exercised a fascination too – fire power, range, speed of loading – but the fact that the wartime aim was not to hit a target but a real person was never addressed.[95] Against this background, the soldier's relationship to the force of arms was decidedly ambivalent. On the one hand, it was just this access to weapons and their legitimated use that marked soldiers as standing apart from civilians, and in particular women, yet when on duty weapons were presented more as an object of technical and sporting interest than as an instrument for killing. Each soldier came to know his rifle thoroughly, learning how to take it apart and reassemble it in seconds, to keep it perfectly clean, and how to shoulder and fire the gun. However, he was also instructed only to use weapons in special situations, under orders and with supervision. Rifle use was carefully regulated and monitored. After practice rifles were locked away and, under no circumstances, were to be used outside official duties.

The sabre was subject to another set of regulations. Even though it had long ceased to have any military value, all army personnel were required to wear a sabre, both within the barracks and, particularly, outside. When bicycles were introduced into the army, a special fitting was put on the handlebars to hold the sabre while cycling. Even when soldiers went for walks or into an inn, they never went without their sabre, and the only time they were briefly allowed to remove it was when dancing.[96] Even more than the uniform, the sabre offered a conspicuous and unequivocal symbol of the soldier as a potential warrior. After all, many other professional or social groups - railway employees, post office staff, prison warders, members of hunting or shooting clubs, and even student associations – all wore a uniform, or something closely resembling it. Carrying a weapon, though, was the exclusive prerogative of soldiers (and the police), who thereby participated in the state's monopoly of violence, and the right to use force in obtaining its ends.

However, the soldier's sabre was far from only having a symbolic character. It was also there to be used, and indeed, under certain circumstances, was actually required to be used. If physically assaulted, for instance, a soldier was obliged to use his sabre to defend himself: since the uniform and weapon clearly labelled a soldier as a member of the armed forces, a violent attack on his person not only injured his personal honour, but also that of the army and the army's supreme commander. Under military law, he was required to act 'prudently' and had no right to 'immediately cut down someone who had "jostled against" him'. In practice, though, the sabre was kept loosely in its scabbard, and it was left up to each soldier to decide for himself when and in which way his military honour had been besmirched.[97]

This area of interpretation was one where civilians and the army rarely saw eye to eye. While civilians repeatedly complained about the readiness of soldiers and officers to resolve conflicts with their sabres when the occasion arose, military personnel insisted on their right to be guided by their own notions of honour and discipline and 'not the views of people ... as far removed from [military] customs and thought as the earth is from the fixed stars'. It was conceded, though, that the general public also had the right 'to be protected against misuse by individuals of the right to bear weapons'.[98] When the government presented the Reichstag with a draft for a new military criminal code in 1872, it included provisions that allowed imprisonment when another's death or 'physically injury' arose from 'careless treatment of a rifle or munitions'. The Reichstag tightened the law further so that abuse of firearms was extended to cover all weapons, including the sabre, commonly employed in clashes with civilians, also allowing such offences to be punished with an increased term of imprisonment.[99]

Many soldiers enjoyed the power their uniform and weapon gave them. Dirkreiter, who entered military service in 1886, noted how he and his fellow soldiers were all 'proud of our uniform and special position over the "civilian pack"'"; these feelings compensated somewhat for the hardships in the soldiers' everyday lives.[100] Despite the young men having only temporarily ceased to run with the 'civilian pack' and having donned the king's colours, they seem to have been surprisingly quick in identifying with their 'special status'. Although this difference between 'us' and 'them' accompanied their period of active military service from the very first to the very last day, it did not mean suspending all relations to their former civilian lives. On the contrary, the men wrote letters (mainly asking for a 'mum's penny'), visited their hometowns 'on holiday', and sent photos. Similarly, they also gave some thought to the time 'afterwards' when they would rejoin the 'civilian pack'. Indeed, most soldiers kept a personal calendar, crossing off the days until they were to be discharged, and, much to the annoyance of superior army officers, many inns also kept what were called 'parole boards', listing the annual levees' remaining army service.[101]

4. The Regiment as a Family: The Potential and Limits of Military Comradeship

Nonetheless, the army's gravitational pull locked the vast majority of soldiers into its orbit, and mediated the awareness that they were something special. This cohesive force even survived beyond the end of military service, with the 'reserves' group photo showing the soldiers surrounded by their company, complete with officers and NCOs, providing a permanent reminder in civilian life of the 'hard but good years' they had spent in the army. Cohesion, though, was not only reinforced by outward symbols, such as the uniform or weapons, but drew its power equally from the 'inner transformation' and resocialisation the recruits experienced during their military service. As the former journeyman Michael Schwab noted in his memoirs, at the end of this time 'one felt a true citizen and a complete man'.[102]

However, such exalted feelings did not come cheaply. Nearly all autobiographical accounts contain reports of humiliations and personal abasement, mainly in the first year. The army approach followed precisely the same method used in all other 'total institutions' where, as Goffman has described, individuals are cut off from points of reference to their lives outside and prior to the institution. Immediately after entering the army, a process began with, in Goffman's terms, *trimming* and *programming*, *stripping* and *levelling*, leaving the newcomers devoid of their previous identity.[103] As the first step, newcomers had to surrender their civilian clothes before taking a bath and, finally, have their hair cut. Then, to make sure the new recruits were not bringing any illnesses with them, they were thoroughly examined by the army doctors. In the next phase, equivalent to Goffman's coding phase, the recruits' perfect and naked bodies then started on the complex procedures that were to 'transform the civilian into a member of the armed forces'. To begin with, they were issued clothes, and allocated a personal space in the barracks (a bed and a kit), although this had little individual character since every other recruit was being treated identically – and indeed this sensation of only being a part of a far larger entity was one of the key experiences in the entire period of service. Every action took place in the company of others, whether washing in the morning, showering, or even using the latrines. The lack of distinct spatially designated areas for work and non-work in the barracks was not radically different from the everyday civilian lives of farm labourers or urban apprentices, but even an urban factory worker in a working men's hostel would not have been faced with the constant pressure for community that a soldier had to endure for two or three years.[104]

In an attempt to reduce the pressure to conform inevitably generated by communalising military life, the army embedded the process within a special rhetoric designed to awaken a feeling of trust and familiarity. The message for the recruits was clear: the regiment was their new 'home', their 'family', where they could feel quite at ease providing they internalised the rules valid there. And just as in their family of origin, the army too had a clear division of roles. The company commander took over the role of the father, the ultimate authority, self-sacrificing in his care for his children, while the colour sergeant adopted the mother's role, responsible for day-to-day life, reprimanding and punishing where necessary to ensure orderly behaviour. In this scenario, the soldiers were the children, under the obligation to obey, love and respect their parents unquestioningly, and meet their siblings with fraternal and comradely feelings.[105] This metaphor of family gave the soldiers' new loyalties a tangible form enriched by an emotional content, teaching them that, from now on, their primary bond was to the troop and not their family of origin. During their military service, they were no longer the sons of their own mothers and fathers but acted as the king's 'children'. As such they could quite possibly be in a situation where they were expected to 'shoot down their own relatives, brothers, even parents', as Wilhelm II bluntly explained to recruits in the Potsdam regiment of guards in 1891, and such orders were to be followed 'without a murmur'. After all, when the Imperial German army was called out to 'suppress unrest, uprisings or strikes', the soldiers were not to 'ask who they had to turn their weapons on, but only what their duty demanded of them'.[106]

In order to give this bond with the new military family an emotional weight, and not merely appear as a duty, the army set great store by each regiment establishing a history to provide a point of identification for the recruits. Consequently, regimental history was narrated in arched gateways and on memorial plaques listing the names of regimental soldiers killed in battle. It was also disseminated as 'local history' in the soldiers' training lessons via oral accounts telling of battles, victories and heroic deeds. In Wilhelminian Germany, there was a major move towards regiments collecting these accounts in written form and, in this way, permanently fixing their own heroic legends.[107]

The most powerful incarnation of living regimental history was the regimental colours, an object of universal veneration, and a genuine totem in Durkheim's sense. Since, as military code prescribed, 'the flag is to be sacred' to every soldier, it was not only consecrated by a priest but presented to the regiment by the monarch, 'often embroidered by princesses'. When the recruit was sworn in, the regimental colours represented the person of the monarch, symbolic of his real physical presence. In this sense, the flag stood for a part of the king remaining constantly with the regiment, honouring and protecting it. This aspect took on particular significance in wartime; wherever the regimental colours flew, the nimbus surrounding the supreme commander was also present. The capture of the colours came close to a catastrophe, since the flag embodied the regiment's past history and was the guarantor for future deeds. The most dramatic war stories recounted how the regimental colours were rescued: the ultimate in bravery lay in tearing the flag from the enemy's hands, while the ultimate infamy consisted of deserting the colours in the hour of need. The colours were especially poignant if they bore the signs of victorious battle: blood-stains, and bands, buckles, iron crosses and silver rings around the flag pole bearing the names of dead regimental heroes engraved on them. To be sworn in on such a flag was an intensely emotive moment, when the recruit became one with the regiment's heroic past.[108]

Moreover, purportedly all were equal before the regimental colours, the soldiers just as much as the officers. Even the king paid his due respect to the flag: on ceremonial occasions, he followed the flag at the head of the accompanying company. This kind of performance gave every individual present the direct sensation of the army as a unified, closed body.[109] In this context, internal military hierarchies and borders dwindled into minor significance. The king relied on both the troops and the officers equally, and the highest general, just like any lieutenant or corporal, had to obey him. It displayed the army as a layered but homogeneous institution whose vertical command structures were supplemented and completed by horizontal relations of comradeship.

Under the broad idea of comradeship, the general staff officer was linked with the recruits, while the narrow concept only bound fellow soldiers of the same rank. These comradely relations, rooted in notions of similar 'family' status, could help soldiers cope emotionally with the unusual experience of communality and give it a positive reassessment. Unlike friends, messmates did not necessarily have to feel any great personal sympathies for each other. Friends sought and found each other but the messmate was assigned, with no need or chance to be chosen. This freed the relationship from any complex levels of communication, any exchanges on God and the world where commonalities were established and differences discovered, or any need to clarify misunderstandings. Similarly, it acted as a shield against reinterpretations and arguments. If friendship thrived on continuous and numerous signs of amity, comradeship managed without any elaborate support system. It was, in a certain sense, more practically based and robust: it was also more standardised, and hence clearer.

When officers explained to recruits what they understood by comradeship, they kept it short: the articles of war stated that no soldier was to leave his comrade 'in battle, in danger and in need'. Moreover, he had a duty to help him in 'permitted matters', living 'in harmony' with him and not initiating conflicts.[110] However, comradely support was not to go too far, and a distinct line was drawn where it crossed into tolerating, or even covering up for, criminal machinations. On the other hand, every officer was aware that comradeship might harm discipline and could be directed against superiors. Consequently, the military criminal code imposed severe sentences on any behaviour classified as 'mutiny' or 'military insurrection'. Any 'riotous assembly' leading to soldiers disobeying the instructions of an NCO or officer led to a punishment of several years' imprisonment, with soldiers stripped of their rank and demoted to the second class of soldiership – a kind of pariah existence with corporal punishment and fatigue duties.[111]

Anyone violating the laws governing same-level comradeship could expect to face tough sanctions too. Although theft was a particularly widespread problem, eroding trust between messmates and damaging the troops' 'morale',[112] living in such close quarters provided more than enough fuel for innumerable conflicts, supposed to be dampened by the call to soldierly comradeship. But this invocation of equal fellowship ignored and undermined the unofficial hacking order. This was swiftly established among the lower ranks, and could be most prominently seen in the example of older enlistees, with one or two years of service behind them. As experienced 'veterans', they could afford to boss about the raw recruits, demanding services and favours. They also enjoyed privileges that had considerable significance in the closed world of the barracks. Schwab, who served from 1894 to 1896 in an infantry regiment based in Bavarian Amberg, recalled how the 'best places' in the troops' main quarters naturally belonged to the old hands, who did their very best to 'make the recruits' lives an absolute misery. 'Dummy recruit-face', 'greenhorn' – those were the 'pet names' used to ridicule the young recruits' uncertainty and inexperience. Moreover, the 'older hands' expressed their superiority via physical violence that was applied in a near-ritual manner. For example, it was common for new recruits to be beaten up in their beds at night – an event the soldiers referred to as 'the barrack ghost came in the night and really wrapped them up proper'. It was a kind of initiation echoing similar practices in British boarding schools, signalising to the newcomer that existing hierarchies were already in place, and warning them not to try to rock the boat. On the other hand, it also presented the realistic hope that they could climb the hierarchy themselves and make others suffer the same humiliations.[113] Some soldiers, though, were unable to stand the pressure and deserted or committed 'suicide under the direct impression of the treatment they met with'.[114]

A hacking order similarly existed among those belonging to the same enlistment year and different branches of the services. Just as the army looked down on the navy, members of guards' regiments fancied themselves as better than any other soldiers; meanwhile, from their position on horseback, the cavalry belittled the footslogging infantry, and the artillery prided themselves on their technical know-how. Such general perspectives were further complicated by the specific regimental pride that frequently emerged in the contemptuous attitude towards other troop units. The appeal to comradeship was intended to counteract this since, despite any apparent differences, in the final analysis all regiments and all arms of the service were united in the same, unified body serving '*one* Kaiser'.[115]

But it was a service marked just as much by distinctions imported from the world outside as it was by the military's own homegrown varieties. The farmer's son with regular food parcels from home containing bacon, sausages and butter enjoyed a different status from the farmhand who had nothing to share and had to earn the extras to put on his bread by cleaning for better-off 'comrades'.[116] In contrast, those with a trade apprenticeship behind them could always profit from it, and the army was no exception to the rule. Almost everyone had some ability useful to others, even if it was only the commercial traveller's copperplate handwriting needed for his messmates' letters. Certain skills and possessions were of greater value than others, and, despite all the barriers the total institution erected, the signs of social prestige and cultural power valid outside the barrack walls continued to have their impact inside.

On the other hand, in the army, the force of hierarchies accepted without question outside could be softened, and their significance minimalised. Officers and fellow soldiers alike would look much more favourably on a factory worker handling his rifle efficiently and performing well on the drill ground than on a factory-owner's son who was clumsy and cack-handed – after all, if the company were given extra practice drill and treated harshly, everyone was affected.[117] Furthermore, although the army might not have completely neutralised socio-economic rankings, the organisational structures had substantially given them another gearing. NCO-level positions of command were obtainable by every halfway competent recruit, and even the former day-labourer might be granted the pleasure of chasing well-off and educated one-yearers across the parade ground.

It is harder to assess the role played by other civil sphere markers for cultural differentiation in the army. Church membership was a key issue in Imperial Germany, and denominational fault lines ran through the army too; the *Kulturkampf* – Bismarck's struggle against Catholic institutions, education and clergy in the 1870s – did not stop at the barrack walls. The Prussian army now paid Catholic army chaplains itself, their enlistment and discharge overseen by an army chaplain general with episcopal powers granted by the Pope at the request of the Prussian government, yet there was still sufficient fuel for recurring clashes – especially, for example, when a regiment's troops were drawn from cross-regional sources and hence contained mixed denominations, or when Catholic soldiers were stationed in Protestant areas and vice versa. Soldiers could only be officially required to attend their own denominational services; consequently, when Catholics from the Rhineland found themselves stationed in Protestant Lower Silesia, they merely stayed in the barracks when their messmates were ordered to attend the Sunday service. However, when major church parades were held to celebrate the birthday or name-day of the Kaiser or his wife Catholics were, as a matter of course, obliged to attend the Protestant service.[118]

The Prussian war ministry insisted that soldiers were directed to attend a Sunday church service at least once a month, despite the scathing criticism this ruling attracted in both the press and the *Reichstag*. However, disapproving voices were not only heard outside the army: while liberals were censuring this as an attack on the individual's right to religious freedom, many officers detailed to accompany the troops reacted on a more practical level. Their lack of enthusiasm for the task took the form of rarely trying to motivate the troops to attend church services voluntarily on their free Sundays, as they were supposed to. In many barracks, it was common for cleaning roll calls to be held on Sunday mornings, and there were even instances of drills fixed for that time, unleashing a hail of criticism from both the clergy and the civil sphere. Pastors complained about the violation of the strictures 'to keep the Lord's Day holy', while delegates in the regional parliaments felt called on to intervene, posing concerned questions about the officers' religious attitudes. In 1879, the Munich archbishop applied to the Bavarian war minister, deprecating the purposeful neglect of religious duties he had observed in the Catholic soldiers at the Munich barracks. On Sundays, he objected, 'only 144 men are ordered' to attend church' of 6,972 troops in total, and voluntary attendance similarly left much to be desired, giving rise to considerable concern over 'the most damaging effect' on their 'moral conduct'.

> Your Excellence is undoubtedly in agreement with me that all those who fulfil their duties to God and the Church conscientiously and faithfully also acknowledge the conscientious fulfilment of their duties to the King and Fatherland as their most sacred duty, and that religion and morality are just as much the highest good for every nation as they are the firmest and most well proven foundation for every state.[119]

Young officers, especially, appear to have been little impressed by such logic, and their superiors had to remind them just as often as the troops that their supreme commander had proclaimed religion to be the 'granite fundament on which soldierly virtues are created and the only support on which they rest securely'. Religious education is a 'part of the soldiers' military education', making the young man, not yet set in his character, 'more reliable, loyal and conscientious' in his duties. Moreover, it immunises him against the 'atheistic and socialist force of our days' - a force the army steadily found more threatening and wanted to fight arm in arm with the Christian church.[120]

However, in practice, this alliance does not seem to have worked overly well. According to 1896 statistics on churchgoing among the Munich garrison, only an average of 34 per cent of Catholic soldiers and NCOs attended services; in the same group, 23 per cent of Protestants attended.[121] From 1863 on, the Bavarian army no longer required soldiers to attend church services 'with the exception of celebrations for His Majesty's birthday and name-day', although special compulsory army services could be fixed.[122] But, unlike the Prussian practice, regular churchgoing for soldiers was based on a voluntary principle, which may explain the low figures in Munich – and, moreover, this 'dwindling' attendance tended to be more pronounced in major cities than in smaller garrisons. Apparently the majority of the troops in big cities, and seemingly Protestants more than Catholics, preferred to spend their Sunday mornings indulging in other activities.

There was a particular agenda underlying the Bavarian army's ruling on compulsory church attendance only for birthdays or name-days of the royal family, and otherwise merely sending a 'deputation from the body of the troops' to church, even on main religious feast days: it underlined how a soldier's religious practice was to be more explicitly bound to the ruling house than to the church. Rather than the key factor being the Catholic clergy's interest in the soldiers' religious education and monitoring, it was in fact the state's need to pad monarchic rule with a religious lining.[123] In contrast, in Prussia the king was not only sovereign but also the supreme Protestant bishop, structurally embedding the identity of church and state rule. As a result, the symbiosis in Prussia was far more pronounced than in Bavaria, whose clergy tended to turn more to Rome than Munich for guidance. Nonetheless, no matter how different the religious circumstances were in Bavaria's predominantly Catholic army and Prussia's mainly Protestant troops, they were agreed on one point: their army corps all considered themselves Christian. But what about the Jewish recruits?

Measures had already been taken to ensure that the religious needs of Jewish soldiers were respected: the swearing-in oath had been adapted to Jewish beliefs, and superior officers instructed to ensure, where possible, that Jewish soldiers were released from military exercises on the Sabbath and Jewish festivals. Similarly, Jewish men were never detailed to attend religious service, as the Protestants and Catholics were, since the percentage of Jewish soldiers in individual garrisons was too small (in 1907 only 0.3 per cent of troops belonged to the Jewish faith). Besides, there were no Jewish officers who could have escorted them to the synagogue.[124] On the material front, Jewish soldiers were not permitted to bring kosher food into the barracks, although they could apply to be released from joining in communal victualling and meals and eat in a 'Jewish boarding-house'. Since, in any case, the Jewish one-yearers saw to their own needs and ate outside the barracks, this ruling only applied to the 'common' soldiers. Moreover, the one-yearers tended to come from assimilated Jewish families and, consequently, were less likely to follow Orthodox ritual. This, however, was not the case for Jewish men serving two to three years, especially when they came from the province of Posen or a strongly traditional Jewish urban immigrant area such as Berlin's *Scheunenviertel*. For soldiers like these, following established Jewish ritual and rites, military service contained numerous obstacles and stumbling blocks.

Many superior officers were unsparing in their references to the soldiers' 'Jewish race', making them the butt of their jokes in front of the other troops.[125] Furthermore, the NCOs' stock phrases and expressions were littered with metaphors and images drawing on Christian tradition and implicitly excluding Jews. For example, Weber's sergeant major liked nothing more than drilling and exercising the troops for hours until they looked like 'the Mother of God in Treuenbrietzen'. In 1901, a captain calling on the troops to show greater religious tolerance did so with the words: 'We are quite simply Germans, and it's immaterial whether we are Catholics or Protestants.' In his terms, 'being religious' meant nothing more than adopting the 'Christian standpoint'.[126] At least such formulations were neither specifically directed against Jewish soldiers, nor obviously coloured with the undisguised anti-Semitic sentiment that became even more pronounced in Imperial Germany. Opinion in the Prussian officer corps was noted for frequently viewing 'immigrant Jews' as unreliable on national issues, cowards and potential traitors[127] – a clear limit to that comradeship so often invoked as a feeling transcending both the different arms of the services and religious faith.

The army was more successful in overcoming regional barriers to a common nationality. Of course, founding Imperial Germany did not automatically lead people to surrender their regional or individual state's identity in favour of a national consciousness. Instead, generating a shared group feeling required considerable sensitivity and a carefully orchestrated strategy in the administrative and policy areas to take the edge off the enmity between the various German 'tribes'. In this rhetoric, the 1870 war figured prominently, with high-ranking officers and politicians never missing a chance to highlight how the excellent cooperation between the northern and southern German troops had played a key role in the victory over France. In this way, the army presented itself as a role-model for the nation: in the civil sphere, union under the Kaiser should be infused with the same spirit that had been adopted by soldiers from Bavaria, Saxony, Baden and Württemberg and the other states when they all pulled together with Prussia in the military arena.

Yet great care was taken to ensure that the military structures respected the particular observances in each individual confederate state and preserved some of their specific features. In peacetime, for example, the Bavarian, Saxon and Württemberg armies remained under the chief command of their sovereigns, and only fell under the Prussian king and German emperor's supreme command in the case of war. Moreover, just as under the German Confederation, Bavaria formed two army corps, with, similarly, Saxony and Württemberg each forming a single corps of their own. Only those soldiers coming from smaller states were mixed with the Prussian body of troops, but even here the regiments were named after their region of origin. In this way, the Prussian army contained Oldenburg, Mecklenburg, Braunschweig, Anhalt, and Thuringia regiments, whose uniforms were decorated both with the initials and insignia of the local ruling house, and the regional state's arms.[128]

Since each army corps was assigned a specific recruitment area, the regiments were relatively homogenous. This general tenet of respecting regional origin and loyalties where possible was only consciously contravened in the Empire's western and eastern territories. Above all, recruits from the new Imperial province of Alsace and Lorraine were deliberately posted to other garrisons far away, while, conversely, the soldiers based in Metz or Strassburg were deployed from Berlin, Posen or Upper Silesia. In this way, the army gave a tangible form to their aspirations to be 'that most central and profound link' 'which was to be re-forged between the mother-country and her colony (*Tochterland*)'. This band, together with its 'assimilative influence and reconciliatory power', should not only embrace the 'soldiers from Holstein and Lithuania just as much as those from Bavaria' but ought specifically to include, first and foremost, those from Alsace and Lorraine. The hope was that given the chance to become more familiar with the 'German institutions and circumstances' during military service, the enlistees would take back with them the 'seeds of a German national sentiment' and it would root in the soil of their homelands.[129]

For those soldiers dispatched to places far away from their homes, military service offered an entirely new experience of geographical space. The majority of enlistees only knew their home villages or, at most, the nearest market town and, as a Prussian delegate delightedly observed in 1867, military service took them out of 'their little, restricted lives' and opened up a 'broad historical horizon', showing them 'a vast fatherland'.[130] Empire, nation, fatherland: these recruits were now able to give concrete form to such abstract concepts. In the army, they experienced directly how areas as disparate as East Prussia, the Rhineland, Baden and Schleswig-Holstein could all be united in one empire and, despite all their cultural differences, comprise one 'nation'. Such an experience did not preclude soldiers feeling there were differences nor prevent the reinforcing of ethnic stereotypes, ranging from the dirty Polish enlistee to the slow Mecklenburg soldier.[131] This, though, does not seem to have placed any lasting burden on the troops' everyday life, or their combat-readiness.

The polarities of urban and rural life appeared less absolute in the army, too. However, this process was tilted more to how garrison town life influenced rural recruits rather than the city dwellers' experience with the countryside and the people there while on manoeuvres. In garrisons, young men from 'the country' came into contact with messmates who had grown up in the towns, learnt other trades, did different jobs, and had other forms of sociability. They also came to know urban conditions personally – and particularly well if they were placed in private quarters. In any case, though, they learnt about the towns on their expeditions after duty and before the evening tattoo called them back to barracks. The city's attractions appear to have been so irresistible, and the material and cultural advantages so substantial, that many former rural enlistees remained even after their military service was completed. In 1901, an economist put the figures remaining at 'far larger than commonly estimated. One would hardly be mistaken in the assumption that lately only those have returned to the country who still have particular relationships there, or else own their own land, or will inherit such.' The others succumbed to the 'magic' of the city, above all, they fell under the spell of a 'more *remunerative livelihood*, generally not so strenuous, and mostly with regular pay and hours, as well as a *life richer* in some types of *enjoyments* and *pleasures*'.[132]

The knock-on effect from military service on urban population growth was anything but planned. In the context of an army that largely regarded itself as a bastion against modernising developments, it was more an irony of fate. The army may have been completely open to any innovations promising new technologies, weapons systems or logistics to heighten military efficiency, but when it came to any social or cultural process presumed to endanger its traditional patterns of social structures, order or discipline, it was ready to fight tooth and claw. Nonetheless, traces of the dramatic urbanisation and industrialisation processes changing the face of Imperial German society can also be found in the recruitment statistics: while soldiers before 1850 primarily came from rural areas, the post-1870 German army consisted largely, and in ever growing numbers, of troops who came from towns, earning their living as factory workers. The question, though, of precisely what statistical relationship existed between these two groups turned into a subject of fierce debate in the political and academic scene in the 1890s.

In 1897, the political economist Lujo Brentano released figures showing that, of all recruits conscripted into the army and navy between 1893 and 1896, 67 per cent – or more than two-thirds – came from areas predominantly involved in industry and commerce. His claim was met with a wave of disbelief. Numerous writers set about proving that Brentano had made a mistake in the way he had treated his statistical data, and posited the contrary hypothesis: only about one third of all recruits could be considered 'industrial'. The conflict that raged over these figures, an extremely emotional battle that received major press coverage, was not actually just about figures at all. It merely provided a stage for a political debate on whether Germany could be designated an industrial state, and what consequences this might have. While Brentano intended to show that a German industrial state need have no worries about its 'ability to defend itself' (*Wehrkraft*), proponents of an agricultural Germany underlined how crucial it was, especially in the military's interests, to protect and further German agriculture as 'the most durable power source driving our army'.[133]

Both sides criticised the statistical material on annual enlistments as inadequate, but if the data published by the war ministry for the *Reichstag* is subjected to a more dispassionate view, it supports both sides of the argument. It was difficult to disprove Brentano's claim that the troops were increasingly recruited from industrial areas. Given that a steadily growing proportion of the working population earned their living in the industrial and manufacturing sectors, as the 1882 and 1895 employment figures showed, and given that a majority of rural-to-urban inner German migrants tended to be young men, as the population statistics revealed, it was inevitable that industrial areas recorded a year-on-year upward trend in 20-year-old men liable for military service as listed in the muster-rolls and that this figure clearly exceeded the one in rural districts.[134] On the other hand, if one took fitness rates as the benchmark, then it was equally true that these were higher in rural areas than in industrial regions. The estates lying east of the River Elbe, for example, provided more recruits in proportion to their total population than was the case in industrial towns in Saxony, or in Westphalia and the Rhineland.[135] More detailed research by Georg Bindewald, published in 1901, supported this thesis, but proved at the same time that rural–urban differences ought not to be given too great a weighting. The 1892 claim by an anonymous author that, relative to their proportion of the population and in comparison to rural areas, industrial towns only provided a third to a quarter of the men able to be drafted turned out to be an extremely biased reading of the figures – even if it was one enthusiastically reported at the time.[136]

Nonetheless, such beliefs were, and continued to be, widely held throughout conservative circles, and many in the military tended to give them credence. Officers had particular reasons to prefer recruits from rural areas, repeatedly commenting that urban 'material' was 'ordinarily not easily malleable for army purposes', adding: 'Frequently the rising urban generation leaves the parental home early, and with it any potentially improving influence, and this combined with their own material independence often stamps them with a self-willed and unaccommodating spirit.' In contrast, in the country 'the simpler habits in work and life, the home influence, and family relations commonly incite and uphold notions of order and discipline, even when frequently without [the person's] knowledge'.[137] In other words, the farmers' sons, farmhands and day-labourers from the estates east of the River Elbe were less difficult to manage than the more self-assured factory workers, notorious for their disrespectful and glib manner. Since the regiments were less than keen to attract such unwieldy 'material' into the barracks, the military boards forming the relevant recruiting commissions applied especially strict selection and aptitude criteria. Consequently, the striking differences in fitness and suitability between East and West Prussian, Pomeranian, and Lower Silesian recruiting districts, on the one hand, and Berlin on the other are primarily a reflection of the officers' preferences.

Even so, manipulations of this sort could not totally invalidate the 'law' observed by Brentano and Kuczynski. The growth in the industrial population, and especially in the younger age groups, led to steadily growing numbers of recruits coming from just that dubious 'material', year after year. Faced with this challenge, the army reconsidered its approach and reasserted the educative task it had been entrusted with at the beginning of the nineteenth century. When this call to duty was initially pronounced, it aroused scepticism, if not antagonism, but the 1848 Revolution had shown, for the first time and across the board, the importance of grooming the soldiers' 'moral' character and not merely cultivating physical prowess. In Imperial Germany, the army introduced nothing less than a thorough and major educational campaign. Articles in the weekly *Militär-Wochenblatt*, published under the auspices of the Prussian war ministry and read by all officers, addressed with unfailing regularity the army's key significance as a 'school', underlining the officers' role as educators. There were also reviews of new books to help them in their task, a range of instruction or service training manuals designed to supplement the official army regulations that covered military training methods and goals in the narrower sense.[138]

Since the 1870s these regulations had been altered as well, much to the disapproval of older officers, but as the Prussian officer corps had grown and become younger in the wake of army reorganisation and enlargement, it had also undergone a generational change too, reflected, however subtly, in the training and exercise regulations. These rules emphasised the soldiers' greater independence and made clear that sheer drill and blindly mechanical training were not sufficient to ensure the individual flexibility needed in tactical operations. The army regulations published in the mid-1870s largely incorporated the 1847 Prussian directives, keeping the latter's drill standards. In contrast, the 1888 regulations, reacting to the introduction of the magazine rifle, marked a break with the past. The active service regulations effective as of 1900 similarly attributed a main role to the training of infantry soldiers 'to be riflemen acting independently and responsibly'.[139]

In 1900, the *Militär-Wochenblatt* boldly stated that the 'war in our day and age has to be fought by men'. But what did this mean? After all, only men had been engaged in fighting wars in the past too – though apparently other men than the ones needed in the coming twentieth century. Traditional drill and training could no longer meet the 'higher demands' modern warfare placed on the 'common man's intellectual development', the weekly continued, since although it might train 'unconditional and immediate obedience', 'corps morale' and 'an intense feeling of belonging', it failed to produce the 'high degree of independent action and insight' expected. On the contrary, it concluded, there was a great need for new forms of military training to engender just these qualities and, first and foremost, a more pronounced 'individualisation'.[140]

This paradigm shift answered two needs: firstly, it responded to the rapidly changing demands in the wake of developments in military tactics and weapons technologies. Secondly, it was a reaction to the type of recruits. Increasingly, the troops comprised urban workers and tradesmen, who brought with them the necessary 'intelligence and shrewdness' but behaved in ways that harmonised less well with the military 'spirit'. And as the numerous manuals and newspaper articles spelt out, this was precisely where the officers' 'moral' educative task began. Through the daily instruction sessions after physical drill, or in personal dealings with the recruits, these officers were then expected to accomplish the miracle of transforming young men, evermore headstrong, into soldiers, as disciplined as they were committed, ready to follow them into the field 'to victory or death'.[141] The soldiers' education had a second agenda, too: generating loyalty to the king and love of the fatherland, while immunising the troops against the 'forces of infamy and darkness'. According to an 1885 *Militär-Wochenblatt*, in this 'solemn age' such forces were already gnawing at 'the roots and essence of the state' – forces called 'liberalism', 'democracy', 'anarchy', and, first and foremost, 'socialism'.[142]

The army had already shown extreme concern about the 'socialist ethic' from the 1870s on. As the chief command of the 12th Saxony Army Corps noted in 1874, 'no signs of this disposition passing to the troops have been found anywhere', but they still felt compelled to call for 'swift and thorough action against this party undermining the very basis of the state'. It was an opinion shared by the Prussian war minister, who had agreed with Bismarck 'that redress in this matter appears to be imperative'.[143] However, even the 1878 anti-socialist bill could not prevent social democratic election pamphlets and materials finding their way into the barracks. For this reason, from the mid-1880s, recruiting commissions drew up lists of those recruits known as social democrats or suspected of having social democratic sympathies, and passed them on to the regiments, which then closely observed their new enlistees and carried out frequent 'wardrobe searches'. In 1894, the Prussian war minister issued a decree granting commanders the power to forbid their troops or NCOs 'any manifestation of revolutionary or social democratic sentiment, in particular by such proclamations, songs or similar demonstrations'. Moreover, no social democratic writings were permitted to be kept or distributed within the barracks.[144] Averting the danger of soldiers becoming infected did not stop at the barrack walls either; soldiers were forbidden to visit inns known as social democrat meeting points –in 1913, in Berlin, this ban covered 293 pubs.[145]

In a further move, the army intensified efforts to immunise soldiers against 'social democratic agitation' by providing the troops with the requisite schooling and instruction, emphasising values such as loyalty to the king, love of the fatherland and soldierly pride. In a parallel step, social democratic aims were condemned as 'utterly opposed to the army' and presented as directed against the monarchy and religion.[146] This view was an exact mirror-image of the answers given by recruits in a Silesian cavalry regiment in 1903–4 when an army doctor asked: 'What are social democrats?' The most common replies featured, for example, definitions like: 'they're the ones who don't want a Kaiser'; 'they don't believe in anything'; 'they want to get rid of everything, the church and the army'; 'they're against the law'; and 'they insult the German army'. The recruits appeared relatively well-informed about the social insurance system and their imperial benefactor, even though some were unable to distinguish between Wilhelm I and Wilhelm II. They had all heard of Bismarck, and the majority could list battles and generals from the 1870 war. Even if the gaps in the interviewees' knowledge caused the interviewer to blaze with indignation, they still knew a considerable amount when it came to those specific areas falling under the army's 'national education' programme. It was not necessary to read the papers regularly (which only one in four interviewees actually did), or know the name of the chancellor in office (which only a similar proportion knew), or know the difference between the *Reichstag* and a regional *Landtag* parliament (11 per cent), to be a loyal subject and reject the social democratic party.

However, the doctor's sample of recruits could hardly be considered representative for the army as a whole. The soldiers he interviewed all came from a cavalry regiment where, just like other regiments in this arm of the services, the majority of recruits came from rural areas. Out of a total of 174 interviewees, 147 had earned a living as unskilled agricultural labourers or agricultural tradesmen. The proportion of those enlisting voluntarily was strikingly high (44 per cent) and included greater numbers of German recruits (in contrast to Poles from Upper Silesia) than normal. Not surprisingly, this background was unlikely to be riddled with supporters of social democratic ideas. [147]

A different picture might have emerged if the interviewees had come from infantry regiments, since these comprised a majority of urban recruits and, quite possibly, even of factory workers. Social democratic policies and attempts to arouse public feeling primarily targeted the urban proletariat, and this group, in turn, provided the bulk of the party's members and voters. Even though the recruits were not yet old enough to vote and were not allowed to join a political party, they might well have been interested in and involved in politics. They would, after all, have had sufficient opportunity to listen to political debates or read social democratic newspapers prior to the start of their military service. Moreover, since the turn of the twentieth century, social democrats had been expanding their efforts to involve those under 18 years old in special youth associations – ostensibly non-political since joining political associations and taking part in political meetings was forbidden to people under 18. In 1900, the International Socialists' Congress in Paris called on social democratic parties 'to fight militarism by initiating youth organisations and education everywhere', adding that future recruits needed to be told what rights they had in the army, while flyers advised them to 'make the most extensive use of their right to complain' during their military service.[148]

Interestingly, these associations did not teach their members about the best ways to avoid military service altogether. It seems as if the social democratic movement was not merely content to combat 'militarism' from outside the barracks by blocking every allocation of funding in the *Reichstag*, but also wanted to penetrate the army's own inner sanctum. In 1885, the Prussian minister of the interior had advised fellow interior ministers in the other confederate states that the 'social democratic party has recently been advising those comrades selected to serve in the army to endeavour to use good conduct as a means to obtain the rank of lance-corporal and NCO in order to exercise a larger influence over their fellow soldiers or subordinates and make use of them in disseminating social democratic notions', and that enlisting voluntarily was intended to serve the same purpose.[149]

The army in Imperial Germany was too powerful for the SPD simply to ignore it; yet counteracting military influence required an exact map of the army's inner structure and action to disrupt it where possible. However, in contrast to the government's belief, this goal was not primarily achieved by winning soldiers over to the party. Instead, far more weight seems to have been placed on encouraging enlistees to detail negative experiences during military service, listing complaints and making them public – and it was a strategy that proved enormously successful. As early as 1894, Major-General von Schmidt noted that 'the treatment of soldiers [is] a very popular topic in the papers, for armchair politicians and at all manner of meetings', while in 1907 a lieutenant-colonel observed that 'any inappropriate treatment' creates a major stir and, 'today, thanks to the fuss created by the social democrats', leads to the story appearing 'in the papers'. He also took the opportunity to urge his fellow-officers, and the NCOs in particular, to avoid any 'mistake' since this only 'buttressed the social democrats, the internal enemy of the fatherland'.[150]

The *Reichstag* had also altered the original government bill to introduce tougher penalties for superiors who insulted, jostled and pushed, or beat their subordinates. The changes incorporated into the military criminal code foresaw long terms of imprisonment if such charges were proven. In a further move, the *Reichstag* added a supplementary clause making it a punishable offence for superiors not to pass on grievances lodged by their subordinates. In this way, they extended and secured the law on the right to complain anchored in the army statutes in the period prior to 1850; complaints, though, had to pass through official channels and be presented to the company captain.[151]

From the superior's perspective, grievances were an unpleasantly disruptive factor. As a rule, the company captain tended to cover up for his recruit officers and NCOs, only initiating an inquiry in exceptionally dramatic and notorious cases. Since presenting joint grievances was strictly forbidden, each soldier had to take a stand himself to prove that his superior's treatment had violated his person or his 'legitimate sense of station in life, his official privileges and prerogatives'. Simultaneously, it was intimated that he should not be over-sensitive, and he was told that such a step needed to be thoroughly considered: 'Not every little knock or primitive curse on the drill ground could be taken as an insult and a reason for a grievance.'[152] If all these warnings proved fruitless and the soldier was still determined to lodge a complaint, he could be absolutely certain he was not making himself popular with either the company captain or the immediate superior who triggered the grievance. In future, his behaviour on duty would be carefully watched, with merciless punishment for the smallest mistake, and any application for leave rejected out of hand.

Under such circumstances, many soldiers preferred not to make an issue out of maltreatment and did not lodge a complaint. In 1876, the Bavarian war ministry expressed its surprise that apparently many such 'misdemeanours' occurred 'without any grievance from the maltreated person' ever being submitted, and in 1888, while investigating an especially brutal case that took place over three years, it severely censured the fact that 'the majority of the troops were treated in a villainous manner but not one had the courage and confidence to lodge a complaint because of it'.[153] In 1891, a confidential decree by the chief commander of the Saxony Army Corps noted: 'Even violent acts performed in front of witnesses are not reported out of fear of being treated even worse.'[154] Consequently, maltreatment was often discovered via rumour or by chance, for example, when a soldier who had committed suicide left a farewell note pointing out the 'excesses' and 'coarseness'. On another occasion, deserters who had been caught stated in evidence that they ran away because they could no longer stand the 'grindingly harsh treatment'.

From 1900 on, many anonymous complaints typically ended with the threat: 'If this matter isn't looked into, it'll be made public'[155] – and here the social democrats were only too ready to help. Their party broadsheet delighted in printing such stories, seeing each case of a soldier's maltreatment as further exemplifying the army's cynical attitude and the scourge of 'militarism'. Such stories found their way into middle-class newspapers too – and every article published put the military administration under pressure. As early as 1887, the Bavarian war ministry informed the staff command units to inform it 'particularly of all cases of maltreatment in the press or that have come into public debate by other means ... in order to put the ministry into a position to assess such occurrences on the basis of the complete information available and, where necessary, to counteract a biased distortion and use of the facts'. The war ministries in Berlin, Stuttgart and Dresden also demanded an official report on every newspaper article about maltreatment so as 'to be able to give immediate replies to questions from parliamentary delegates about the case'. From the early 1880s, the *Reichstag* especially evolved into a popular forum to voice criticism of the military, with the social democrats, in particular, discovering that instances of maltreatment provided an abundant supply of ammunition for 'their political attacks on the army'.[156]

The cases that entered the public sphere, together with the internal reports the army chief commanders ordered at regular intervals,[157] reveal a picture diametrically opposed to the writings on education and the image presented in after-dinner speeches. Many companies were dominated by a degree of 'brutality and savagery' totally incongruent with either the notion of one single soldierly family or the much-lauded ethos of comradeship. The relatively rough and blunt way of dealing with each other common amongst the soldiers might have been justified by invoking a typically male use of 'gritty expressions', but over-zealous NCOs kicking and beating their subordinates apparently similarly shared a place on the everyday agenda. Since NCOs competed with each other over who had the best drilled company, they tended to deal harshly with any 'awkward' or 'obdurate' recruits – and with the recruits' officers primarily interested in the troops' active field skills and parade-ground performance, they, in turn, overlooked such incidents.[158]

Behind this wall of condoning silence, such monstrous instances of maltreatment and abuse occurred that they aroused indignation even in a society only hesitantly distancing itself from the ideals inherent in 'strict discipline' and the spirit embodied by the 'poisonous pedagogy' (*schwarze Pädogogik*). There were NCOs who forced an incontinent recruit to eat his own excrement; others rubbed 'boots too thickly covered with polish' into the faces of their subordinates or forced them 'to chew for four to five minutes on the toe parts of the dirty socks they had presented' at kit check. Some soldiers were beaten to a pulp because they did not move in the way prescribed. In contrast, the widespread disciplinary practice of cutting all the buttons off a uniform when one of them was loose appears to be nothing short of lenient and civilised.

While some of these punishments might be put down to sheer sadism and a superior's pathological character, the mass of cases punished for 'maltreatment' showed mere differentiations of degree from standard 'training measures', and were always justified by the claim that they strengthened discipline in the troops. If any single soldier proved incapable of attaining the training goals, the argument continued, or disturbed the overall impression, he would simply be 'trimmed' until he obeyed and fitted in properly. The recruits' officers and NCOs employed a system of delegating violence that underlined their own authority while simultaneously generating a communalising effect. By calling on their subordinates to 'all help together' in 'educating' one of their fellows they may not have created the sort of comradeship intended by the army statutes, but they did stimulate a community of perpetrators, who maintained a front of silence. As the confidential decree by the chief commander of the Saxony Army Corps noted in 1891: 'The same troops who had only recently been maltreated appeared a few months later accused of maltreatment themselves'.[159]

If the army tended to dub such incidents exceptions, large parts of the liberal public did 'not then consider the issue resolved'. In 1892, the *Reichstag*'s budget commission commented that the damage was 'more deep rooted, spreading throughout the entire army'. The various groups across the parliamentary spectrum saw different causes at play: conservatives pronounced on a general trend towards 'people reverting to savagery', while liberals bemoaned the 'mistaken notion of educating along caste lines' found in the training facilities for cadets and NCOs, and socialists blamed 'militarism'.[160] But whatever stand they took, the fierce debates raging on the military in Wilhelminian Germany throughout the print media and in parliament underlined one very central point. The army was increasingly in the public spotlight and subject to public monitoring and censure – no matter how little this was to the army's taste, and no matter how vehemently army circles struggled against it, constantly repeating that army duty and discipline practices concerned no-one but the king and emperor. But with the *Reichstag* empowered to vote on the military budget, the army had to live with parliament as a chamber debating issues it would rather have kept from the public gaze and away from the public sphere of influence.

And the more parliament debated military matters, the greater the pressure from the public became. While in the early 1870s, in the general euphoria about the army in the wake of the war, Bismarck had been able to talk delegates into agreeing on leaving large gaps between each ruling on the military budget, these periods became steadily shorter as the army upped its demands. A majority in the *Reichstag* rejected the army's express wish to have fixed long-term funding and, from 1890 on, peacetime troop size automatically linked to population growth. Moreover, the price parliament extracted for agreement on army enlargement in 1893 was the reduction in military service from three to two years – realising the old liberal goal they had failed to achieve in the 1860s.[161] The social democrats may have been alone in totally rejecting any approval of the budget estimate, but critical voices were heard repeatedly from both the liberals and the Catholic *Zentrum* (centre) party. The further the heroic era of the Wars of Unification (*Einigungskriege*) slipped into the past, the more the army's sacrosanct status became visibly tarnished. The military now had to provide reasons why it constantly needed more money and wanted to draft ever more recruits. It also had to vindicate itself against grievances and charges of abuse – and it had to defend its privileges.

5. *Liaisons Dangereuses*: The Military and Civil Society

Calls for introducing civil society practices into the army sphere (*Verbürgerlichung des Militärs*) were heard even in the years directly after Imperial Germany was founded. In 1872, for instance, liberal *Reichstag* deputy Eduard Lasker took a stand on moves to overcome the 'gap between the army and civil society point of view', citing the way the criminal code was applied in both spheres as a glaringly obvious example. He wanted to see 'civil society's peremptory demands' for equality before the law to become just as valid within the army context too – and throughout the entire Imperial Germany period, the liberal public's firm stance on this issue never wavered.

Precisely because the liberals also unequivocally accepted universal conscription, they were continually coming into conflict with the military's special rights and particularities. For instance, the liberals appeared quite willing to acknowledge that specific rules were needed in emergency situations, such as war. Neither did they have any objection to arming for war: they joined associations propagating comprehensive armaments programmes for the army and navy, and, at times, even sought to push through such policies against the government.[162] But liberals insisted that the soldier was and remained a member of civil society and, in peacetime, fell under civil law jurisdiction just like any other citizen. Even with the memory of Imperial Germany's birth vividly kept alive, and the early twentieth century witnessing a clear trend towards preparation for what Treitschke called a new 'encounter', the army was still increasingly seen as an institution needing to prove itself in peacetime. Public interest in the army was fuelled not least by the near doubling of peacetime forces from 422,615 in 1875 to 794,319 in 1914. If hundreds of thousands of young men disappeared into the barracks annually, with a fifth to a quarter of all young men born in any given year subjected to military 'discipline', it is no surprise that the public were concerned to cast light on the internal affairs of such a powerful and inclusive institution.[163]

The concern was not *that* life was different in the barracks but *how* it was different. The army's aspiration to educate its soldiers was generally welcomed, especially since its training curricula perfectly reflected (lower) middle-class ideals – after all, what mother or father did not want their sons to develop qualities like order, cleanliness, punctuality and obedience? When the Munich-based Anna Mayr wrote to the Bavarian war minister in 1906, complaining about her unreliable and violent lover, her suggestion was 'it would be a good thing to be able to dispatch someone like that into the army'.[164] However, trust in the army's virtue was not fathomless. A belief in strict military discipline did not necessarily preclude distrust over the army's efforts to keep its internal affairs to itself and block off any outside influences. With soldiers incapable of finding a collective voice in the army or escaping from it – except by deserting or suicide – the public sphere recognised a pressing need for monitoring what was happening there.

But, of course, the army did not share the civilian standpoint. While outside the barracks concerned parents were worried about their son's health and liberal politicians pointed to deficits in civil rights, inside the barracks the prime interest centred on the soldier's ability to function optimally. The individual was unimportant; it was the troop alone that counted. The soldier was simply viewed as the smallest link in a long chain, only able to withstand pressure if it was perfectly forged. In this smelting process, the individual's sensitivities were of little interest – an infantryman's sore and blistered feet were only relevant in as far as they restricted his ability to march. But civilians could only reconcile themselves to the cold logic of inherent necessity to a certain extent. Even in Imperial Germany society, allegedly so utterly compliant in military matters, such views did not go unchallenged.

The military could rely on the stable power axis linking the army with the monarch and the armed services' guaranteed extra-constitutional status, but it could no longer afford to simply ignore the increasingly vociferous criticism in parliament, the press, associations and societies. It went on the attack, developing counter-offensives and pursuing them in a number of different political arenas. The war minister in the *Reichstag*, with conservative delegate support, formed one strand of this movement, defending the army's right to its own concepts of discipline and honour, justified increasingly by an appeal to their functional nature. The administrative sector provided a second strand, working to reduce friction in everyday affairs and seal off weak spots. But the army's counterattack had one other crucial element. In contrast to other total institutions such as monasteries, convents, hospitals or orphans' homes, the military was not content just to reinforce internal structures and seal off outside access. Instead, to put it dramatically, it claimed to be legitimately entitled to shape civil society in its own form. As far as the military was concerned, it was not one institution among many, but the model on which all others should be based.

Consequently, while liberals and (social) democrats were busily hoping to bridge the much-deplored 'gap' between the civil and military sphere by introducing civil society practices into the army, the military was arguing for just the opposite. But before it could hope to obtain agreement on moves to militarise civil society, the army needed, first and foremost, acknowledgement of its extensive educative skills, and, secondly, support for them. One constant refrain in the army's argument highlighted how military training left a mark on the soldier's life long after military service had finished. A man who had 'served' could easily be spotted in later civilian life, and the values he had learnt provided a 'physical and moral' counterweight to all 'unhealthy, effete, or material influences'. In Imperial Germany, the image of civil society as ill and frail found widespread resonance among officers, allowing them to see their mission not only as to train and educate soldiers, but also to save and heal 'the entire nation' infected by 'egotism, hedonism, and chronic laziness' and the 'infectious bacteria' of socialism.[165]

In this view, rather than soldiers merely leaving the army as citizens loyal to the crown, they acquired virtues 'of incalculable value' in civilian life. Their investment in resolutely learning to carrying out orders, thriftiness in managing their pay, and the moderation and perseverance needed to master the wear and tear of military service would be repaid in full by the benefits accruing in their everyday work and home lives. The sense of order and propriety taught in the army would be of benefit later too – and what was more, as Major Menzel reminded his readers, this salutary training programme also inculcated the duty to apply these virtues to the welfare of the fatherland.[166] In 1907, 400,000 copies of Menzel's book *Dienstunterricht des deutschen Infanteristen* (Instruction for the German Infantryman) were in circulation. It is, of course, hard to say how far his advice, or the advice from other similar writers, was really taken to heart. It seems that at least the injunction to reserves urging them to join a veterans' association bore fruit, presenting them as the perfect way 'to cherish ideals such as love of the fatherland and loyalty to the king and to hearten oneself in these beliefs'. By 1903, the *Kyffhäuserbund*, the umbrella organisation of German veterans' associations, could already boast more than 2 million members in over 24,000 associations, with annual growth of around 500 associations and 50,000 members recorded by the Prussian state association alone.[167] When one considers that, in contrast to military service, membership was voluntary and not obligatory, these figures become even more remarkable. From the turn of the century, the military expended ever greater energies in supporting veterans' associations, both morally and organisationally, yet it had neither the authority nor the means to command discharged soldiers to join. Nonetheless, by 1913 membership had reached nearly 3 million – and hence can be considered a clear statement on the strength of a widespread bond with the military.

The immediate post-1870 period saw a mass of veterans' associations being founded by soldiers with active service experience, as a living memorial to heroic deeds. As time went on, growing numbers of army reserves and *Landwehr* reserves joined who had never seen war themselves, so that, for example, in 1908 only 15.5 per cent of members were veterans.[168] The veterans' associations' statutes clearly delineated their primary purpose as 'maintaining and exercising love of and loyalty to the emperor and Reich, to the sovereigns and our closer native state', and 'reinforcing and raising national consciousness'. They also fulfilled social functions at least as important: financial support for members in need and beery get-togethers after work. The veterans' association provided a vehicle for carrying male comradeship from military or active service over into civilian life – as was common practice in places in Baden, where it marched at the head of the procession when a member married, and gave his coffin the last honours on its way to the grave.[169]

The close link between the veterans' association and the army was shown in a variety of ways, including the symbols of weapons, military headgear and uniforms – the latter given to the soldiers as their final outfit when they were discharged. But this bond was demonstrated, first and foremost, by the flags, and approval for them, granted by the *Landrat* as the regional representative of the king, frequently led to acrimonious disputes. Once the flag had been presented, it was regarded as the association's most valuable possession and jealously guarded. Inauguration was conducted in an atmosphere of religious awe and marked the 'association's fairest festival', starting with divine worship and ending with a ball in the evening, placing the veterans' association right at the heart of local events. The authorities, religious and worldly, civil and military, all paid their respects, while it was feted by other veterans' associations and 'patriotically minded clubs'. Women were present too. As the members' wives, sisters and daughters, they had prepared colour-belts or sashes. The ceremonial procession was headed by 'maidens of honour', bearing the flag to the place where the inauguration was due to begin, where they gave an introductory prologue. As young girls, they had put ribbons around the recruits' hats, and later, as married women, they decorated the veterans' association colours and danced at the ball.[170]

Apart from the major celebratory act of inaugurating the colours, the flag's special significance became primarily apparent during patriotic celebrations, such as Sedan Day, marking the German victory over the French in 1870, or on royal birthdays, when the association colours took pride of place leading the local procession. A further mark of privilege for the veterans' associations came in the shape of an invitation from the chief command to participate in the annual parade in honour of the emperor's birthday, where they were allowed to line the emperor's route; veterans' associations similarly figured prominently in any visits the emperor made to their district. Their own event calendar was taken up with association fetes, complete with military parades, ceremonies held at veterans' war memorials, or military concerts and dances. In town or village life, the veterans' associations were all-pervasive and yet, at the same time, were unusually socially inclusive. In comparison to the local traditional shooting clubs which charged a high membership fee, particularly in urban areas, the veterans' associations offered factory workers and day, agricultural and hired labourers an organised forum in a space outside classical social hierarchies and fault lines.[171] Moreover, the privileged position enjoyed by the veterans' associations on 'patriotic' occasions was especially attractive – easily leaving even prominent citizens' clubs and associations lagging behind. When it came to love of the fatherland and loyalty to the throne, the veterans' associations were in a class of their own.

Naturally, this did not necessarily imply that all members were ardent monarchists or even conservatives – many may have rated the social capital derived from association membership far higher than any (lip) service paid to patriotism. Indeed, the numerous conflicts over association members' political loyalties, and above all their relationship to the SPD, illustrate only too well that patriotism did not need to be equated directly with unquestioned loyalty to the ruling authorities. In the Catholic Rhineland, for instance, some veterans' associations apparently valued the affinity to the Catholic *Zentrum* party more than the love of the Kaiser enshrined in the association statutes and proclaimed in their veterans' journal, even if that meant taking a stand against the government's military bill in the 1893 *Reichstag* elections. The 1903 election too, where the SPD won nearly one third of all votes, generated 'a not entirely ungrounded suspicion that even veterans' association members have voted for the social democrats'[172] – for the umbrella veterans' organisation, nothing short of a sacrilege.

The veterans' associations were, after all, supposed to be 'bastions against social democracy', their statutes expressly excluding SPD members from joining and strictly forbidding association members from promoting the party's 'aspirations by word or deed' – which, naturally, also included voting for them. Just as the soldiers were actively warned of the dangers of the SPD during their military service, the reserves and *Landwehr* reserves were encouraged to form a 'solid wall' holding back the 'red flood': from 1907 on, when soldiers completed their military service, they were handed a flyer calling on them to join a veterans' association; from 1909 on, local command units made lists of all reserves available to the veterans' associations; and in 1911, the Prussian war minister urged all general commands to spare no efforts in making recruits aware of the veterans' associations during their military service, strongly recommending that they join later.[173]

Such massive state promotion indicates how much the ruling authorities trusted the associations and how far these had been successful in working against social democratic 'attempts at infiltration'. And, in the early days of the movement, such attempts had indeed occurred. Above all, in the 1870s, social democrats had joined veterans' or military associations in vast numbers. In 1878, 'a part of the members' in all Saxon associations were considered to be believers in 'socialist sentiments', remaining demonstratively seated when the call went up to toast the king. In many places, social democrats even founded their own veterans' associations, with statutes that were, as the Saxon war minister reported to his Prussian counterpart in 1874, 'totally harmless' although providing a 'cloak' under which social democrats could engage in 'propaganda for their party'. The Saxon war ministry certainly took the danger seriously, since they refused to continue selling their old stock of rifles from army arsenals to the military associations and limited permission to carry arms to the guard of honour firing the salute at a fellow association member's funeral. This restrictive attitude – also noted by the Prussian war ministry – was only abandoned in 1909. Apparently, by then the incriminating 'suspicious elements' had left the associations.[174] This may indeed have been the case: after all, by the 1890s, at the latest, the social democrats had positively encouraged their members and supporters to leave veterans' associations. In 1909, they distributed broadsheets in a major campaign warning discharged soldiers of the associations and their 'murderous patriotism'. Apparently, this action was 'not always without effect', as the Prussian war minister noted two years later, and actually set some obstacles to membership.[175]

On the other hand, there were many social democrats who did not support the official party line on the incompatibility between the party and veterans' associations: a frequently heard comment was 'We are soldiers and social democrats, and both of them heart and soul'. Consequently, many remained in the veterans' associations, continued to pay membership fees and kept their political opinions to themselves. The concern over lifting the demarcation between the party and the veterans' associations was one they did not share, and their living rooms might well have contained pictures of Wilhelm I, Moltke and Bismarck next to portraits of Bebel and Liebknecht, Marx and Lassalle.[176] In any case, vast numbers of party members and adherents were unable to find their own military service reflected in that 'descent into hell' so dramatically described by Bergg or Rehbein. As Paul Göhre reported in 1891 from Chemnitz, both young and old social democrats were proud of their regiments, 'happy' to look back on their period of service, telling 'charming stories about manoeuvres', and passing their reserve troop photographs around.[177] Even social democrat functionaries expressed an understanding for how young men 'take their place with a certain pride in the cogs of this mechanism, so impressive in its own way'. In 1907, August Bebel was lauding the German army as an organisational 'masterpiece', while the Bavarian war minister was extolling social democrats as being among the best type of soldiers, commenting that 'thanks to the discipline characteristic throughout the social democratic party', there was 'no complaint' against them.[178]

However, this did not mean the SPD had toned down its criticism of the army as a bulwark of 'militarism'. Even moderate social democrats continued to condemn 'the unnecessary drill, the grindingly harsh treatment of soldiers, the sealed officers' caste, and the definition of the army as a power instrument maintaining the propertied classes' ascendancy over the unpropertied'. Yet in the same breath, they demanded 'universal training in military skills' as a 'necessary element in preserving the nation, which our party manifesto expressly acknowledges'. And indeed, the call for 'universal military skills' (*allgemeine Wehrhaftigkeit*) did appear as early as 1875 in the Gotha Programme, when various socialist groupings met to form a single German democratic socialist party. According to Wilhelm Liebknecht, this was 'something so much taken for granted' at the time 'that it does not need to be discussed any further'. When the SPD was preparing its new programme in 1891, though, there was more to say on providing a new rationale for the 'old demand'. Nonetheless, Liebknecht did little more than indicate the need to emulate the Swiss model, where the young men in every village were 'trained in all the skills needed in military service', call for its introduction and point out how it would 'reinforce defensive power' in Germany too.[179]

Even in later years, the social democrats never denied it was necessary to have a defensive force, claiming national independence was only viable where nations were 'capable of defending themselves'. It was a principle they saw as equally applicable to Germany, as Gustav Noske made clear in 1907 in the *Reichstag*, saying: 'It is our desire that the entire German nation is interested in the military institutions needed to defend our fatherland.' But Noske did not offer any further description of such 'institutions', and the party programme at the time only mentioned in passing the commitment to having 'a national defence force (*Volkswehr*) replace the standing army'.[180] This, of course, appealed to the military authorities about as much as the proletariat's revolutionary concept of the fatherland found in social democratic thought. Undoubtedly, when, in 1911, the Prussian war minister numbered 'maintaining a strong and joyful national feeling when on furlough' as among the 'vital conditions' for the army, he was harbouring quite another notion of 'national sentiment' than the social democratic party leadership.[181]

At the same time, such comments do make apparent how far the army was dependent on a social environment that endorsed its existence and corroborated its assertion of hegemony. The task of creating this surround devolved not only onto the veterans' associations, but was equally shared by those numerous other organisations formed in Imperial Germany furthered or approved of by the military, such as the associations for one-yearers and reserve officers founded in the post-1870 period. As a rule, the local level commanders were responsible for ensuring the reserve and *Landwehr* reserve officers developed a coherent group feeling and came together for social events. However, to start with, in many instances, the initial initiative came from the officers themselves. In Augsburg, for example, in 1872 a *Landwehr* officers' club was formed to cultivate 'comradeship' and offer a forum for lectures and talks as further military training.

A similar association founded in Stuttgart swiftly distanced itself from any 'parliamentary forms' inherent in the association concept behind such organisations by disbanding and then reforming as an 'officers' corps'. The trigger for this change came from the experience of the Munich officers' association, started in 1879 as a 'private club', which recorded steadily dwindling attendance at evening meetings despite two-thirds of the local *Landwehr* officers being members. Reorganising the association under local level *Landwehr* commander leadership and 'along more military lines' ushered in a turn-around in the club's fortunes: wearing uniforms became obligatory, and regular attendance was required at the fixed monthly lectures. In 1899, even with formally voluntary membership, nearly 90 per cent of all reserve officers had joined, providing the civilian businessmen, architects, doctors, lawyers, professors, bankers or engineers a chance to listen to lectures on 'the German infantry attack' or 'the military application of balloons'.[182]

From the army perspective, reserve officers had a pivotal role to play both in wartime, compensating for the lack of professional line officers, and in peacetime, as an 'active agent for all of the army's interests'. With 'one foot in the army system, and the other in the general population', they could function as mediators – though naturally only in one direction.[183] Rigid customs systems and immutable honour structures posed an effective obstacle to any threat of reserve officers importing civil notions back into the army. Despite the strict criteria already applied in sorting officer recruits, and their subsequent co-option, the military wanted to be absolutely sure that the majority of middle-class reserve officers would obey the rules of conduct prescribed by the military for the social and political context.

The military could be reassured by the high status enjoyed by reserve officer commissions, one of the most coveted marks of distinction available for middle-class men in Imperial Germany. Most one-yearers applied for it, and were enormously disappointed when judged unsuitable on military, political or social grounds. It seems, though, that the high costs involved in obtaining a commission paid off. Adolf Wermuth, for example, recounted how his appointment to the high-ranking civil service post of Reich commissioner in 1887 was due to 'the quality of being a lawyer – and a reserve officer', since the Kaiser had been looking for a civil servant who had 'also learnt the conduct of an officer'.[184] And in addition to any material advantage, many men were especially keen on the 'elevation in rank' the commission brought with it, a pride even expressed in private life, as when, in 1880, the lawyer Ernst Bassermann donned his full dress reserve officer's uniform to propose to his future wife.[185]

Nonetheless, identification with the title of reserve officer did not push all civil sphere interests completely into the background. Local level commanders, or the relevant clubs, organised further military training events, but many men appear to have been less interested in them than their commanders would have liked. They seem to have been similarly glad that work commitments frequently prevented them from attending the regular obligatory meetings. Moreover, they were extremely reluctant to follow the call to join the local veterans' association and take over leading positions on the board. Superiors were constantly reminding reserve officers of their duty to join the veterans' associations, the 'army of the king in civilian dress', urging them to take on an active role there, making them 'into crystallisation points of a positive way of thinking, loving the fatherland and loyal to the king'. It was a duty, as a former local level commander put it in 1894, which should be considered as 'arising directly' from the reserve officer position,[186] and though, in the end, numerous reserve officers bowed to this logic, most of them never joined the veterans' associations at all.[187]

The reason for this reluctance appears to have been principally related to social status concerns. At least, the military administration was forever reprimanding reserve officers for their unwillingness to mix with 'fellow soldiers' from lower social classes – apparently, they placed little value on a comradeship which had been extremely tentative at the time of their one-year service, and which, in civilian life, was even more problematic. The lawyer or factory owner might have sympathised in theory with the notion of cultivating a comradely relationship with a day-labourer or even an employee from his own factory in the same veterans' association, but the strains such an involvement would have entailed left the argument severely weakened on the practical level.[188]

Instead of spending hours in the veterans' association, monitoring the levels of patriotism, reserve officers preferred conviviality in a socially homogeneous group. They not only expressed their monarchist feelings by voting for the right (conservative or national liberal) party, but also by meeting for dinner to celebrate the emperor's birthday.[189] One other benefit from such events lay in the chance they provided to bring together leading figures in society and the army, where the intimate male atmosphere facilitated settling disputes, curbing animosities, and, in addition, developing business networks. Aside from these 'men's evenings', 'ladies' evenings' were similarly popular, where female companions were permitted to attend 'in correct evening dress'. Furthermore, the *Landwehr* level officers' corps regularly organised dances and balls where 'festive patriotic performances' showed 'how the warrior's estate has always honoured women in all changes throughout history'.[190]

The women were also honoured in their absence, sometimes in jocose male humour ('the greatest power of women is – the power to swoon!'), and sometimes in a mood more sombre and tinged with pathos. Such occasions did not only make the polarity of the former one-yearers and reserve officers' gender concepts transparent, but also clearly expressed their uncertainties in the face of the contemporary women's emancipation movement. As one speaker making a toast declared in 1906, women may attempt 'to increase their influence in all areas of life and compete with men', but one sphere remains firmly closed: 'participation in military matters'. The speaker continued:

> I am certain no-one can better heal the severe wounds war inflicts than the soft and gentle hand of a woman; neither do I doubt in the slightest that there are exceptional points of attraction between the lovely eyes of a young lady and the enamoured glances of a youthful warrior. But the horrors of war are too dreadful for a woman's tender nerves, and the exertions of a campaign too great for their delicate bodies.

Yet despite this, women were not excluded completely from military affairs – if they taught their sons, the future 'warriors', a 'fervent patriotism', then 'the victory is already half ours'.[191]

The gender language employed here was simultaneously inclusive and exclusive. Inclusions were posited where the issue was discussed on the large scale, using collective terms like people, nation and fatherland – it went without saying that women were also a part of the German *Volk*, or the German nation, and that the fatherland similarly included them as well. The state too, that 'purely *male* being', could not manage without women, requiring at least their mediative services as wives, mothers, daughters and sisters. Women could even attain the absolute pinnacle of honour for some of their contributions: just as Friedrich Wilhelm III awarded the official *Luisenorden* medal to patriotic women, his son presented the coveted 'war medal' (*Kriegsdenkmünze*) in 1871 to 'women and maidens' who had actively helped in field hospitals, and just as the soldiers presented with the Iron Cross could hang a 'commemorative plaque' in their living rooms with their names engraved on it in gold letters, so the female holder of the *Verdienstkreuz* medal awarded for services rendered to her country could also purchase a 'handsome drawing-room print' to leave to 'future generations' as a memento.[192]

In this sense, women had many opportunities to demonstrate their ties to the state, nation or fatherland, and their contribution took on an especially symbolic form if they embellished the veterans' associations' flags with fine needlework, or led the ceremonial procession on the day the colours were inaugurated. Imperial Germany did not widen the spectrum of such inclusion mechanisms, which were generally already tried and tested, dating from the period of the wars against Napoleon and reactivated during the 1848–9 Revolution, although it did draw them together more within an organised framework. This process, for example, saw the creation of the patriotic women's associations (*Vaterländische Frauenvereine*), established in 1866 in the wake of the 'German war', and an institution that, by the outbreak of the First World War, could boast nearly 600,000 members. The associations' primary remit focused on promoting voluntary nursing, but gradually became extended to embrace a broader profile of welfare and caring without, however, abandoning the key *leitmotifs* of 'love for the fatherland and loyalty to the king'. The women involved were largely drawn from the middle classes, citing their membership of state and nation, and the 'social and national duties' this entailed, as the reason for their show of commitment.[193] Such an ethos of duty received support from the highest levels, with the empress and regional sovereign princesses taking over positions as chairs of the organisational board or patrons. But the women's sense of national duties stopped far short of ever seeking to include military or wartime service among their tasks. On this point, women and men agreed: using weapons to defend the state, nation and fatherland was and remained an exclusively male domain.

Despite this agreement, the after-dinner speaker mentioned above addressing his fellow soldiers in 1906 still felt a need specifically to mention women's exclusion. The reason behind this, though, related directly to the women's political emancipation movement at the time, which had sparked an extremely fierce and acrimonious debate. The vast majority of feminist movement associations had adopted, in a variety of different ways, the cause of women's franchise, but found, across the board, no middle-class based political party ready to support them. Left needing to justify this rebuff, these parties were only too happy to resurrect the argument Carl Welcker had developed in the 1830s linking franchise and military service: women could not vote on political matters since they were unable to fight in wartime, and hence did not perform military service.

A leading figure in this discourse in Imperial Germany was Heinrich von Treitschke, who propounded the male character of politics and war, constructing a political and historical context underlining the link between them. In his lectures and writings, the state is defined as a quasi-military institution, 'the public force for offence and defence'. The core of this force lay in 'the appeal to arms', which distinguished the state from all other forms of community; since women were not allowed to bear arms, they were in a position to neither understand nor to shape the life of the state. 'Government ... must be backed by armed men', but armed men 'do not like taking their orders from a woman'.[194] This line of argument based exclusion from political participation on the premise of exclusion from military duties and the right to bear arms – and as Imperial Germany came to rank military service ever higher until it became the 'crown of all civic duties', this biologically and culturally based link seemed to gain even more weight. With the value attributed to citizens of the state determined by whether they had served or not, women found themselves pushed into a political backwater.

The underlying logic behind this stance proved especially frustrating for women attaching an importance to political rights in themselves and who, unlike members of the patriotic women's associations, were not merely satisfied with fulfilling social and national duties. As early as 1874, the Berlin writer Hedwig Dohm pointed out the inconsistency of many men enjoying political rights despite never having been in the armed services, adding that women too would be dying for the fatherland when they tried to 'give birth to fill the gaps torn by the sword and bullet in the ranks of people'. Besides, she noted, one could rate female nursing in field hospitals as 'a patriotic deed equivalent to the merit of men in military service'.[195] It was a view similarly shared by Louise Otto, from 1865 president of the German Women's Association (*Allgemeiner Deutscher Frauenverein*) and, in contrast to Hedwig Dohm's individualism, intensively preoccupied with the organisational means needed to strengthen and bind the elements in the female emancipation movement. She too held up the example of women's 'patriotism' in the 1864, 1866 and 1870–1 wars, pointing to their donations, welfare work and nursing tasks as contributing to victory. This was indeed deserving of recognition, she continued – but not solely in the form of 'medals and awards'. Instead, women should be granted a 'self-assured and legally based participation' in the state and society. Neither was there any question of such participation being founded on extending 'skill with arms' (*Wehrhaftigkeit*) to women. As far as Otto was concerned, women were unequivocally on the side of peace.[196]

However, the notion of a female peace mission gave rise to conflicting views even in the middle-class women's movement, which, proportionally, contained no higher density of committed pacifists than the minority found in the rest of German society. The German Women's Association also supported the government's programme of expanding the fleet, and advocated the right of the German Reich to maintain independence through military means. The German Women's Navy League (*Flottenbund Deutscher Frauen*) left even fewer doubts about its support for Wilhelminian international policy goals and the potential military consequences they might entail. When formulating its founding statutes in 1905, the organisation deliberately omitted any statement embracing a welfare remit, refusing to spend their donations on such 'trivialities'. Similarly, the German Colonial Society Women's League (*Frauenbund der Deutschen Kolonialgesellschaft*), founded in 1907, was no stranger to the concept of Germany's cultural mission being strongly rooted in its military clout.[197]

These associations, including the *Vaterländische Frauenvereine* with their large membership base, may have represented an organised body of women's power to confront the military, yet despite occasionally criticising over-zealous military aspirations to dominance, they showed no inclination to fundamentally contest the military's general position. Undoubtedly, the middle-class women's movement contained many voices, along with Louise Otto's, concerned with the dangers of 'militarism' and underlining its negative impact on the 'female element' – as, for instance, when Helene Lange took a stand against the convention of duelling enshrined in the military code of honour, and not only drew on those arguments shared with male critics, but contested the supporters' position on the grounds that the 'patriarchalism' manifest in duelling denigrated women. Similarly, when the German League of Women's Associations (*Bund Deutscher Frauenvereine*) presented a petition calling for soldiers to be given lessons in hygiene and instructed on the health dangers deriving from 'intemperance and immorality', they were not so much concerned with the men's physical well-being as with their own as (future) wives.[198] However, in principal, they accepted the need for a strong, combat-ready army just as much as they accepted a division of tasks ascribing men military duties and weapons skills, and keeping women away from them.

Dissention from the women's movement only became openly voiced when the military's assertion of exclusivity was applied as a logical tool to derive women's further exclusion in the political and social spheres: women's movement members could see, for instance, no logical reason why not performing military service should prevent them from enjoying full citizenship. Instead, their rallying cry was 'equal but not the same', emphasising the equivalent value of women's duties, from the educative task in motherhood to voluntary welfare work and nursing in wartime. In this process, the women's movement even debated 'obligatory social service' (*soziale Dienstpflicht*), to be organised along the same lines as male conscription.[199]

Ironically enough, this frenetic search for parallels left the asymmetry between male conscription and a female service year exposed even more starkly. While the women's voluntary year of social service, depending on schooling and class background, could provide preparation for a woman's later roles as housewife or social welfare worker, the core of the obligatory period of military service did not correlate at all with common male roles at work or in the family. Despite all the efforts made to ascribe a civil 'added-value' to the time in barracks, its genuine purpose was to train young men for the uncommon scenario of war. The military skill learnt was, in essence, how to kill – and this hardly had a place in civilian life, and was precisely what gave it that unique aura, an equal mix of fear and awe.

Maintaining this aura, though, required discrete but impressive staging. Performances occurred everywhere in Imperial Germany, and the message appears to have been convincingly conveyed. After all, where possible, the military had to present itself in its most attractive colours if it planned to realise its influence on civil society, and ensure lasting societal acceptance, admiration and cooperation. The violent, martial core was needed, but had to be somewhat toned down – and the army showed considerable ingenuity in mastering the challenge. Their most effective public performances took place as parades and musical events, and both their success and sustained effect can be seen, not least, in autobiographical texts. Hardly a memoir written by contemporaries of the Wilhelminian era, whatever their gender or class, fails to mention military parades or music, and always with a positive connotation. The military were similarly aware of the aura engendered by such a public performance and expended considerable energies in perfecting it further. The emperor's parades, the jewel in the crown of the troop reviews held annually since the 1870s, were far from being a private dialogue between the supreme commander and his men. Instead, they provided a staged event to present the army, and later the navy as well, to a large section – and cross-section – of the general public: an audience of men and women, children and adults, workers and clerks, civil servants and serving girls.

Though forms of appropriation varied, and the recipients' attention favoured different elements, the total impression was never anything short of overwhelming. This was an institution presenting itself as equally powerful and elegant, sombre and light-hearted, homogeneous and yet varied: the closed ranks marching past the Kaiser in formation and stretching their legs in a single, uniform movement expressed a primeval power, tamed by discipline, yet with the potential for aggression still distinctly perceptible. The sabres, rifles and bayonets may have been left at their side, but it did not need any great imagination to envisage them being used in battle. In contrast to later military parades where the technology of weaponry took centre stage, Imperial Germany's military parades accentuated the physical presence of troops and officers, an effect the colourful uniforms underlined. The message to be conveyed was that the army's strength lay in the men's physique, their vitality and youth, their smart posture and sharp precision.[200]

Military theorists and training officers were well aware that the parading soldiers' goose-step was not a decisive factor in winning wars, but it provided that highly artificial spectacle the public apparently loved to see: soldiers marching, legs flicked out in a swift single movement and heads neatly snapping round to salute. Such a display appeared best suited to remove the army from the everyday world, heighten their powerful particularity, and create that feeling of grandeur in the audience. The soldiers' non-civilian guise was absolutely obvious; they appeared as a different species of human being and man, embodying a masculinity peculiar to their status, yet still signifying something wider. Just as the Kaiser taking the march past combined military and civil functions in his personal union of supreme commander and royal sovereign, so any number of men in the crowds watching the troops similarly bridged these two spheres by displaying their military socialisation in civilian life. Such men were reserve and *Landwehr* officers or members of veterans' associations, preserving and prizing the manliness they had gained in the army, or at least the outward signs of it. In this way, even after being officially disbanded from the reserves at 45, men could continue to give themselves a certain resolute and virile touch, participating in the appeal of the active soldier – strength, suppleness and youth.

This cross-generational bond did not only become apparent at parades or military musical events. Many autobiographical texts recount how moved a father or grandfather was when looking at his sons or grandsons about to be enlisted – and the emotion was all the greater if the son was to serve in the same regiment, forming a kind of military genealogy closely binding the male family members, allowing the father and grandfather to recount their stories of service to set the mood for the new draftee's future conduct in the army.[201] Moreover, the young recruits could already draw on their own experience of the army gained as young children. Soldiers belonged to everyday life in garrison towns, and even in villages or in towns without any garrisons one commonly came across soldiers on holidays or quartered there during exercises.

Moritz Bromme, a signalman's son born in 1873, recalled growing up in Schmölln, Saxony, and how soldiers appeared there on manoeuvres in the early 1880s. The children were let off school and 'stood gaping open-mouthed, unable to see enough of this resplendent spectacle – after all, we'd never seen anything like it before'. Undoubtedly, inspired by their experience, they turned to playing the usual children's army games, where the boys equipped themselves with both wooden and real sabres, and pistols with real gunpowder.[202] In the nineteenth century, such items regularly belonged to the boys' standard toys – and indeed were often given to them as presents when still very young. For instance, Wilhelm von Kügelgen, born in 1802 and son of a well-known painter, was given 'a small wooden musket, dagger and trumpet' for Christmas when he was 2, and after receiving a 'sweet little crossbow' when he was 3 his mother proudly commented on how he was so eager to use it and tried so hard when 'shooting at the target'. In addition, lead and tin soldiers were extremely popular at that time, and used to re-enact eighteenth- and nineteenth-century battles. Ludwig Goldstein, for example, born in 1867 in Königsberg and a master tailor's son, had more than 1,000 figures, which he sent off on parades, manoeuvres and battles.[203]

This military ethos was then completed by the requisite clothes young middle-class boys wore in the nineteenth century. Boys had been put in military clothes long before the sailor suit became *de rigeur*, reflecting the intense enthusiasm for the naval fleet in the later years of Imperial Germany. In 1868, Gabriele Reuter's mother, 'like all Prussian mothers', was dressing her four young boys in grey officers' greatcoats with red collars and soldier's caps,[204] and many parents additionally supported their children's paramilitary or pre-military involvement, though for a wide variety of reasons. Records exist documenting lads' brigades as early as the 1840s, especially in southern Germany, where pupils, students, young shop staff and commercial clerks took part in rifle practice and military exercises, but it was the democratic movement in the 1850s and 1860s that took up paramilitary education as a core concern. From the 1870s on, the social democrats too expressly endorsed a 'military youth training' connected to school gym lessons.[205] They saw this providing a basis for a Swiss-style militia, while gym teachers and athletics clubs regarded it as a chance to upgrade the status of their work. However, the war ministry firmly rejected the suggestion of cutting the military service period of athletics clubs' members by one year on the grounds they were already physically fit. Army chief of staff Count von Moltke left no doubt about his serious objections to such initiatives, warning against the 'overrated games with guns and exercises': real military training had to be left to the army itself.

While Moltke aimed at preserving the army's monopoly on military training, Heinrich Stürenburg, philologist and *Landwehr* officer, had other concerns in mind when, in 1879, he spoke out just as vociferously against 'militarising' education. In his view, 'Our civic life [needs] to be kept as free as possible from any further interference by the martial life, so fundamentally different from it in design and purpose.'[206] Yet in the first decades of Wilhelminian Germany, both of these positions – the weight given by the middle class to a fundamentally civic thrust in culture and society, and the army's internal disquiet over a watered-down military training – led to a front forming against the various and varied calls for military youth training, effectively blocking any moves towards it. In this process, teachers, particularly, had a key role to play. Their professional self-interest already aligned them directly against any mixing of military and civilian cultures, and they rejected educational goals heavily biased towards military needs. There may have been some overlap between a 'soldier's training' and a 'school education', as the educational theorist Ernst Roloff conceded shortly before the First World War, mentioning specifically 'civic spirit', 'comradeship' and 'obedience', yet, nonetheless, in contrast to the army, the school had to 'adequately allow for the forming of character and educating to self-responsibility', and take the individuality of each pupil seriously.[207]

Even in a military-friendly Imperial Germany, maintaining this essential and basic distinction remained very much a present concern, as is witnessed by syllabi at the elite *Gymnasium* secondary schools, and schools' inspection and annual reports. Harry Kessler recalled from his years at the Hamburg Johanneum school in the 1880s how a young teacher might occasionally play the reserve officer and seek to emulate their strident tone, and the duty to defend the fatherland was assiduously debated in final year exam essays and discussed in innumerable speeches marking special events, usually with reference to the classical world or the Wars of Liberation. In addition, pupils were delighted to take part in ceremonial national parades as flag-bearers, or go target shooting on class-trips. However, those teachers 'loudly lauding keenness and patriotism' were well down in the popularity stakes, and national and military matters were only a minor item on the schools' everyday agenda. In any case, the *Gymnasium* curricula focused far too much on Latin, Greek and the German classics for military associations to play more than a marginal role.[208]

Similarly, the elementary level schools for children until 14 did not present a unified picture of an education orientated towards military drill and jingoism – which, naturally, did not exclude teachers taking pains to kindle respect for the exploits of great wartime leaders and the deeds of major army figures. The turn of the century, too, appeared to usher in a phase where military-style conduct seemed to have increasingly 'wandered from the barracks into the schools', with older teachers especially criticising younger colleagues who, in the classrooms, acted 'like an officer in front of the troops', making the children 'march up and down the school yard two-by-two, in the proper army way'.[209] Such tendencies may have been rooted in the more intensive contact elementary teachers had with the army after 1900, after, in the 1890s, teachers' organisations had made efforts to ensure their members could enjoy one-yearer status. In this case, the argument ran that teachers with military experience and reserve officer commissions would be 'a valuable connecting link between the school and the army'.[210] But even if this forecast proved correct in part, the success in militarising elementary schools ought not to be overrated. The military journals themselves clearly testify to the limits of such success; many complained about the quality of recruits provided by elementary schools, not only bemoaning insufficient education in 'national' matters, but, despite the gym lessons, deficits in physical skills.[211]

Educationalists countered these claims with the argument that what children learnt in elementary school they forgot in the six years between school and military service, and suggested two ways of closing this gap: either extending the period of schooling, or shifting the military element forward. When the introduction of any obligatory further school training fell victim to the struggle between the various ministries over contradictory concepts and areas of competence, the idea of a military youth training gathered impetus after 1900. In contrast to the 1870s, when neither the army nor civil instances were willing to offer active support to such an idea, it now met with widespread approval. The crucial change in the army's stance came as a reaction to political developments in France. The French government had initiated a broad militarising of male schoolchildren via their *bataillons scolaires*, and additionally successfully encouraged numerous youth organisations to include military physical training programmes in their syllabi by creating the *brevet d'aptitude* diploma.[212] A further impulse towards such changes was provided in the shape of the British Boy Scout movement, founded by Lieutenant-General Sir Robert Baden-Powell. In 1909, inspired by Baden-Powell's idea, a group of young officers in Munich founded the *Wehrkraft* association with the explicit aim of toughening up secondary school and former elementary school pupils, making them fit for the army with a set of gym and athletics exercises, hikes and rifle practice. With Bavarian war ministry support, the association founded sixty-two local groups within only three years, and, in 1913, the main Munich group alone could boast 1,400 pupils.[213]

In contrast to the lads' brigades (*Jugendwehren*) in Berlin and northern Germany, the Bavarian version followed the Boy Scout model in highlighting the competitive and playful nature of its Sunday leisure activities. Their main target group comprised precisely those young apprentices and workers identified by educationalists, social policy makers and officers as a potential problem needing to be resolved, and experience had shown they were not overly taken with the lads' brigades' standard diet of marching practice and drill. The spectre of a morally abandoned, socially uprooted and politically malleable urban youth was found everywhere, and many places considered the 'young men problem' as 'the most demanding of all modern problems'.[214] Binding these young men in organisations appeared to be a sensible way of resolving the problem and protecting the young men from 'brutalisation and temptation'.

The main organisations concerned did not only include the *Pfadfinder* (the German equivalent of the Scouts) and denominational youth groups, but also athletics and sports clubs. The military-style boys' brigades and defence associations, on the other hand, played a relatively minor role in terms of numbers, though they were able to extend their influence somewhat.[215] The notion of giving organised male youth groups a stronger national and military flavour without imposing a 'military training' in the narrowest sense had been steadily gaining ground since the turn of the century. The Central Committee to Promote National and Youth Games (*Centralausschuß zur Förderung der Volks- und Jugendspiele*), founded in 1891, and primarily numbering teachers, educational board members, politicians and administration specialists among its members, decided to instigate a 'Committee to Promote Military Skills through Education' (*Ausschuß zur*

Förderung der Wehrkraft durch Erziehung), which urged schools and clubs to toughen up young men both physically and mentally with a special set of physical exercises, games and marches so that they would prove 'later, to as high a degree as possible, suitably fit for military service'. The committee forcefully rejected the French notion of *bataillons scolaires*, though, or the Swiss-style youth militia. It was a stance able to rely on support from the majority of officers, who similarly warned about any 'direct transfer of military forms and exercises into youth education'.[216] However, an indirect influence was actively sought, and was also endorsed by the Prussian ministry of culture, education and church affairs which, in 1911, advised that, in the context of leisure activities for young people, 'everywhere, with utmost care, though without creating any great stir outwardly' steps were taken to toughen up the young men for the military and educate them in a national spirit.

The majority of youth associations hardly needed such advice. They had already developed the requisite practices themselves. The Catholic youth associations prepared its members – in 1914, close to 300,000 – for the patriotic duty of military service, while the Protestant youth groups, with around 150,000 members, played the war and outdoor exercises card to augment their appeal against the rapid spread of soccer clubs. The German Society of Gymnasts (*Deutsche Turnerschaft*), with nearly 200,000 14- to 17-year-olds in 1913, similarly had never left any doubts that they rated their exercises not least as an investment in male youths' physical fitness for military service and their readiness to defend their country. The German Boy Scouts League (*Deutscher Pfadfinderbund*), founded in 1911 and two years later boasting 60,000 members, acknowledged the national aspect of its educational task, just as did the Bavarian Defence Association (*Bayerischer Wehrkraftverein*), emphasising the importance of their members becoming hardened physically and mentally. The main point of reference running through all of these organisations was confirmed by them joining the German Youth League (*Jungdeutschland-Bund*), founded in 1911 with massive government support.[217]

Nonetheless, Gustav Wynekens, the driving force behind the middle-class *Wandervogel* back-to-nature movement, was far too radical in his criticism of the German Youth League when he accused it, in 1913, of 'overheated nationalism', claiming they were 'militarising' German youth and inculcating a spirit of 'military absolutism and national servility'. He had overshot the target on two counts: firstly, by overestimating the League's ideological influence and the propaganda impact of the central administration and, secondly, by underestimating the desire of each individual organisation in the League to maintain its own independence. Their activities may well have been 'patriotic' and shown distinct military traits, but these were not the dominant elements. Even in the defence associations (*Wehrkraftvereine*) in the narrowest sense, comprising only 9 per cent of the entire League membership, military practices such as drill, uniforms, weapons and rifle practice did not play a major part.[218]

It would, hence, be exaggerated to read these intensive efforts to provide structured leisure activities for youth as a general and widespread militarisation of society. No doubt, the army ensured that its interest in 'reinforcing patriotic sentiment and military feelings in youth' was fostered and, certainly, the majority of youth associations and clubs were happy to import some military practices, yet the national youth associations' degree of inclusion remained limited: even with more than 700,000 members shortly before the outbreak of the First World War, they only represented a fifth of all male youths. Moreover, the vast majority of youth group leaders came from the teaching professions – except in defence force groups – and were not primarily interested in promoting that enthusiasm 'for the military' and 'joy in soldiering' among male children and youths that was, allegedly, naturally inherent. The group leaders were, in fact, far more likely to see themselves principally as social workers. In the process of providing societally acceptable bonds and activities for an urban city youth exposed to a range of potentially damaging influences, they were simply utilising performances and forms that exercised a proven integrative force: comradeship, the romance of camp fires and the direct experience of nature. The gymnastic, camping and tracking skills acquired in this process might also have had a military application, but this did not exhaust their possible uses.[219]

Neither were soldiers, generals and naval officers the only figures embellishing the contemporary canvas of heroes presented to young male children and youths in the various clubs and associations, or in schools and youth literature. Adventurers, scientists and inventors also had their place there, as did, in the context of denominationally linked milieus, missionaries and successful doctors. Middle-class boys' playrooms did not solely contain lead and tin soldiers, but also chemistry sets, building blocks and toy train sets.[220] Consequently, the claim that male children and youths in Imperial Germany were oriented exclusively or even primarily towards military ideals and conduct hardly appears viable. Undoubtedly, military matters played a role, especially since every growing lad knew he had to reckon with being enlisted into the army or navy when he turned 20. The military's omnipresence in everyday life too, in parades, army orchestra concerts, manoeuvres and garrison guards, contributed to a perception of the army as an accepted part of the everyday landscape and, to a large extent, a respected societal institution.

In this instance, the German context differed substantially from that in Great Britain, where despite the steady growth in recruitment numbers recorded by the National Service League, universal conscription did not exist and the army was considerably less visible than on the continent. In France, however, developments ran parallel to the German experience. The Third Republic's enthusiasm for military parades, festivals and military music was on a par with that in Germany, and in addition, the degree of inclusion in military and paramilitary organisations was much greater. In Germany, the proportion of recruits was kept lower thanks to a higher birth rate, while France's smaller population led to stricter enlistment criteria, with a much larger proportion of the corresponding age group actually serving.[221]

In both states, though, the institution of universal conscription meant that the army had a profound influence on civil society, and this began with the basic form of administrative organisation to implement conscription. After all, the local districts had an obligation to compile the muster-rolls, the keystone for a continuous, countrywide gathering of data on the population. Since the muster-rolls recorded the details about all the young men in an area, and were compared with the birth registers, this gave the authorities an instrument enabling them to gain an exact overview of all the men born and resident in the local parishes and districts. In addition, the annual recruiting procedures allowed a reverse information flow from military concerns to civil administrative practices. The commissions dealing with recruiting, temporary exemption and exemption from service comprised officers and civil servants, and needed to reach joint decisions. Civil society considerations and military aspirations had to be balanced one against another, although in cases of disagreement the military-civil commission weighting ensured the military standpoint would prevail. The military and civil agencies cooperated on the legal and police service levels too, with civil authorities not only helping the military to identify social democrat recruits, but also providing details on whether any individual recruits to be mustered had a criminal record or were known for disciplinary problems. The military authorities, in turn, informed the local police if a soldier received a court sentence while in military service. Local authorities also had access to the conduct report, produced when soldiers were discharged from active military service and passed into the reserves or *Landwehr*, listing all the court and disciplinary penalties imposed during this period. Employers, too, asked to see the conduct reports, and in this way obtained an exact picture of a job applicant.[222]

The civil society, then, and the military were closely connected in many different ways during the nineteenth and early twentieth centuries – and this applies structurally to all those states with universal conscription where, in contrast to states with voluntary or professional armies, interfaces and overlaps between the military and civil sphere became established. This led to options of either civil society becoming militarised and/or the military being subjected to civil society influences. Both directions can be observed in the European conscription systems from the early nineteenth century on with, on the one hand, civil sphere values and concepts of rules influencing the military, as seen in the upgrading of educational qualifications, the civil influence in restructuring the military criminal code and the waning dominance of the aristocracy among active officers. On the other hand, the military perspective gained ground in civil society, primarily through specific

forms of demeanour and socialisation practices that found expression in the value
attached to one-yearer entitlement and reserve officer status, the attraction in the
veterans' associations' organisation, and the enthusiasm among many young men
for spirited war and soldier games.

How strong such civil society influence or militarisation actually was in practice
varied in line with specific temporal and spatial factors. In Germany, the monarchist
constitution and the close alliance between the king and the army undoubtedly
generated a greater readiness in civil society to adopt military forms. Furthermore,
the successful wars, imbued with national significance, heightened the army's
prestige, generating not only respect for it but also pride – a re-evaluation first
given a major new impetus in Prussia, after the wars against Napoleon in 1813–15,
before the even stronger and more pervasive status gains for the army and, above
all, the officer corps from the campaigns of 1864, 1866 and 1870–1, which were
read as wars of national unity. Such status gains were no doubt higher in Prussia,
able to preen itself with an active vanguard role in building the German national
state, than in Bavaria or Württemberg, but, despite initial resistance, the same
movement gradually gripped the southern German states too.

Nonetheless, even in Germany, the pride in the national army and its successes
on the battlefield did not automatically imply either uncritical admiration or, at
its most extreme, unbridled veneration. The institution of conscription placed
the army so much at the heart of civil society, directly affecting every family
with growing sons, that it also became subject to dissenting inquiry and public
monitoring, with parliament and the press both developing into vigilant watchdogs
over military practices, and quite capable of baring their teeth if needed. The
harsh criticism voiced over maltreatment of soldiers, officer caste conceit, and
attacks by soldiers on civilians convincingly show that the army did not have a
completely free hand. In this context, the '*Hauptmann von Köpenick*' case, so
often cited as a prime instance of how prevalent submissive military sentiment
was in Imperial Germany, threw the limits of acceptance into clear relief in 1906,
with contemporaries too ridiculing the farcical nature of the spectacle, denying
it showed any general tendency whatsoever or, even worse, revealed some sort
of representative character.[223] The case concerned Wilhelm Voigt, a journeyman
shoemaker, who, wearing a second-hand captain's uniform, took over a group of
armed soldiers, and ordered them to the local town hall, where he wanted to help
himself to the local authority's cash funds. In one particular aspect, his idea was
exceptionally realistic and convincing: he was in control of a group of soldiers who
would use their weapons on his command. It was precisely this threat of force,
more implicit than explicit, that gave Voigt the power to keep the civilians under
his control. The weapons were a reminder that military and civilian personnel
were not at all on an equal footing. Even if the use of weapons militarily was
governed by strict rules and disciplinary measures, the weapon stood out as the

principal symbol differentiating soldiers from civilians, and publicly expressing their unique status and specific functions.

This was indeed the crux of the relationship between the military and civil society in states with universal conscription. Society agreed to equipping its young men deemed fit for army service with weapons and training them in their use. Theoretically, the weapons were to be directed, first and foremost, against an external enemy, but on the practical level they could equally well be used against any 'inner enemy'. Even unused, the weapons still endowed their bearers with an authority, and at times a power, which the soldiers never would have enjoyed in their civilian lives. The weapons endowed them with the status of men, giving them a feeling of superiority over their non-army peers and, not least, making them able to demonstrate this superiority in their relationship to women. The aura of this armed, soldierly masculinity even clung to them after the weapons had been surrendered, and found institutional reinforcement through the veterans' associations. However, this did not completely overshadow all competing notions of masculinity or imply that military ideals had cast all civic moral values in their own image. It would be vastly over-exaggerated to claim that the military triad comprising violence, discipline, and the readiness to sacrifice one's own life was the hegemonial cultural model determining gender roles in the late nineteenth and early twentieth centuries. Nowhere were only soldiers and officers accepted as real men, or considered the sole male role-models, neither in Imperial German society, nor in the French Third Republic, let alone Great Britain or Austria-Hungary; nowhere did men lose the right to vote or marry because they had not performed military service.

Nevertheless, the correlation between the weight a society places on national identity and the likelihood of it ascribing a high status to military qualifications is more than just coincidental. Where patriotic or even nationalistic values gained greater acceptance, good citizens became distinguished less by their economic or cultural services and more by their ability and readiness to use weapons to defend their country. Aggressive nationalist stances and scenarios depicting national threats were standard fare in nearly all European countries before the First World War, providing an initial kick-start to a momentum upgrading military-style models and reinforcing the military as the accepted norm for, in Paulsen's words, the 'school of manliness'.

Given this connection between nationalism and the military, civil society could ease cultural objections to the military apparatus of violence and the army's socialisation practices. If the purpose of this apparatus was to secure the rights to a national existence, then it was also acting in the civic interest – and this allowed the citizen to exchange his hat for a military cap, spiked helmet or, after 1916, steel helmet, without doubting his own intelligence, morals or credibility, accepting war as a 'citizen's duty', as Ernst Jünger sarcastically remarked in 1922.[224] Under the banner of defending one's country, military and civil values and practices turned out to be compatible, and perhaps even complementary. In the same way that military writings never tired of emphasising the value of a military education for members of the reserves, so no lesser figures than former wartime combatants from the 1860s claimed that even as soldiers they had remained citizens.[225] The concrete experience of killing or maiming others, though, remained screened off, neither appearing in their memories of war or military service, and if such aspects were included at all, they only appeared in the context of violence suffered. The victim perspective culminated in a cult of war memorials, maintained by the military with the keen assistance of civil authorities and citizens, immortalising the army's services in the person of its fallen soldiers.[226]

This 'blind spot' in the soldiers' memory and their conceptual horizon again indicates the cultural limits imposed on the symbiosis between military and civil society, proposed and promoted by so many contemporaries, even those at opposite ends of the political spectrum. Apparently, the core logic behind the military – exercising physical force and killing enemies – could not be transferred without a break into the canon of civil society's values, although the latter had no objection to semantic embellishments using the metaphors of war, sacrifice and victory, or applying this martial language in areas removed from the military sphere. Indeed, youth literature in the late nineteenth and early twentieth centuries is riddled with precisely such images. Without exception all the role models and heroes were victorious, martial figures, whether it was the doctor combating illness and defeating bacteria, the businessmen fighting for new products and markets, the socialist workers' leader calling for all forces to unite in the struggle against capitalism, the polar researcher, undaunted by death, intractable in the face of all the inner and outer challenges in his contest with snow and ice, or the ingenious inventor overcoming all the misunderstandings and obstacles preventing technical progress. Some may have died in service to their chosen field, but they then became heroes of science, technology, or revolutionary ideas.

But death was not the real horror lurking behind the heroic and selfless struggle. The real horror was actively killing others and the training for it. This is rarely the theme of personal or collective memories precisely because it had no place in public and private culture, and it was precisely because it was made taboo that the majority of the pre-1914 population could continue to believe in a relationship between the soldier and citizen, the military and civil society, that may at times have been strained, but was in essence harmonious. It was this that allowed war to be portrayed not as a collective act of coordinated individual violence, but as the heroic sacrifice of a particular person. This too made it so easy for the many volunteers to answer the call to serve at the front – and explains why they were so utterly disappointed, disgusted and despairing when their preconceived ideas crumbled against the force of an impersonal violence. August Macke has provided us with an impressive example of this illusion and its destruction. Full of youthful enthusiasm, he had completed his military service in 1908–9 and, in the same spirit, he travelled to France in August 1914. The first few letters he wrote to his wife echoed the one-yearer's language; he felt as if he was involved in some military exercise, massive, exciting and adventurous. But his tone rapidly changed: 'After a gruesome battle yesterday, my fondest wishes to you all, my dears. We won but suffered heavy losses ... Heavens, we prayed in the night. Half our battalion is gone.' Macke himself died in action in September 1914. It is not known how many French soldiers he had killed by then.[227]

Notes

1. *Marx-Engels-Werke*, vol. 17, p. 269. The phrase 'school of life' derives from Claß, *Strom*, p. 13.
2. *Stenographische Berichte*, vol. 1, 1871, p. 600.
3. Obermann, *Flugblätter*, p. 66, 111; Wolff, *Revolutions-Chronik*, vol. 1, primarily pp. 15 ff., 243 ff., 289, 329 ff.; Hachtmann, *Berlin*, pp. 234–59, 586–96.
4. Lüdtke, "*Gemeinwohl*", pp. 289–90; Pröve, 'Partizipation', and also *Republikanismus*, pp. 370 ff.; Seyppel, 'Köln'.
5. *Stenographische Berichte über die Verhandlungen der zur Vereinbarung der preußischen Staats-Verfassung berufenen Versammlung*, vol. 2, Berlin 1848, Quotes from pp. 929, 931; on the conservative attitudes, see the patriotic association's stance in Wolff, *Chronik*, vol. 3, p. 379.
6. *Stenographische Berichte* 1848, vol. 2, p. 931.
7. *Preußische Landwehr*, pp. 103 ff.;
8. GStA Berlin-Dahlem, Rep. 151 IC Nr. 2456: Protokoll des Ministerconseils dated 9.6.1855; Finanzminister dated 31.10.1855; Protokoll der Kommission dated 13.11.1855; Votum des Kriegsministers dated 8.8.1856.
9. *Stenographische Berichte*, vol. 2, 1865, pp. 1229–30. (Jacoby); vol. 2, 1866, p. 1028 (Wagener); *Sammlung sämmtlicher Drucksachen*, vol. III, 1863, Nr. 130, p. 11; Rosenberg, *Publizistik*, vol. 1, pp. 14–16, 164–5; vol. 2, pp. 516–18.
10. Rosenberg, *Publizistik*, vol. 1, pp. 134–5; *Stenographische Berichte*, vol. 1, 1865, p. 640; vol. 2, 1865, p. 1341; Biefang, *Bürgertum*, Chapter 4.
11. *Stenographische Berichte*, vol. 5, 1860, pp. 1486–7; vol. 1, 1860, p. 96; enlistment figures to 1854 from Dieterici, *Mittheilungen*, pp. 329–30; 1855–8

from Engel, 'Resultate', p. 71; GStA Berlin-Dahlem, Rep. 151 IC Nr. 2456: anon. Berliner dated 13.11.1859; Jacob Jaeger dated 7.12.1859; Baumgarten dated 25.2.1860; Rosenberg, *Publizistik*, vol. 2, pp. 501–2; Engel, *Resultate*, pp. 81 ff., 181 ff.; Jolly, 'Militärsteuer'; *Stenographische Berichte*, vol. 5, 1860, p. 1482 (*Petitionen westpreußischer Bürger gegen das Mennoniten-Privileg 1860*).

12. *Stenographische Berichte*, vol. 1, 1860, p. 96; StA Detmold, M1 Pr Nr. 307, 308: Landratsberichte 1861/2.
13. *Stenographische Berichte*, vol. 3, 1861, p. 1399; vol. 5, 1860, pp. 1240 ff.
14. Rosenberg, *Publizistik*, vol. 2, pp. 480–1, 509–10.
15. *Stenographische Berichte*, vol. 2, 1863, p. 1149; vol. 3, 1863, Aktenstück Nr. 107, p. 656; Frevert, *Men of Honour*, pp. 53 ff.
16. *Militärische Blätter*, vol. 1, 1859, pp. 36–40; vol. 5, 1861, p. 40, 178–9; vol. 8, 1862, p. 21.
17. StA Detmold, M1 IC Nr. 298: Mindener Oberbürgermeister dated 15.11.1860; Interior minister from 29.8.1860; Herforder Bürgermeister dated 8.6.1860.
18. *Sammlung sämmtlicher Drucksachen*, vol. IV, 1862, pp. 36–41.
19. *Stenographische Berichte*, vol. 2, 1865, p. 1238.
20. *Stenographische Berichte*, pp. 1333–5; vol. 1, 1861, p. 1405; *Sammlung sämmtlicher Drucksachen*, vol. 6, 1860, p. 25.
21. *Stenographische Berichte*, vol. 5, 1860, pp. 1481 ff. The petitions supporting the government were signed by members of conservative associations, but in addition, and also primarily, by men from the 'lowest estates'.
22. *Stenographische Berichte*, vol. 1, 1861, p. 1402 (Waldeck); Roon, *Denkwürdigkeiten*, p. 555. On the festivities of 1863 cf. the *Landrat*'s reports in StA Detmold, M1 Pr Nr. 309.
23. *Stenographische Berichte*, vol. 1, 1867, p. 31.
24. *Stenographische Berichte Norddeutscher Bund*, vol. 1, 1867, p. 280.
25. Demeter, *Offizierkorps*, pp. 16–7, 21, 26–7; Messerschmidt, 'Armee', pp. 106–7; Deist, 'Armee'; Endres, 'Struktur', pp. 296–7. In the other German states, the proportion of aristocrats in the 1860s already stood at only 42% (Saxony) and 30% (Bavaria) (Demeter, *Offizierkorps*, pp. 30 ff.).
26. Bunsen, *Welt*, pp. 49–50, 53–4; Wilke, *Erinnerungen*, pp. 86 ff.; Strätz, *Schwert*, pp. 52–3; Schlötzer, *Jugendzeit*, pp. 268–9.
27. Meinecke, *Katastrophe*, p. 25, and also *Erlebtes*, pp. 109 ff.; Lübke, *Lebenserinnerungen*, p. 60, 148–9; Delbrück, *Lebenserinnerungen*, vol. 1, p. 122; Ritter, *Staatskunst*, vol. 2, pp. 117–31.
28. Menzel, *Infanterie-Einjährige*, p. 41; Weber, *Jugendbriefe*, pp. 76–137; John, *Reserveoffizierkorps*, pp. 56–7.
29. Lübke, *Lebenserinnerungen*, p. 148; Fürstenberg, *Lebengeschichte*, p. 27; Wallraf, *Leben*, p. 66; John, *Reserveoffizierkorps*, pp. 91 ff.; Roloff, *Lexikon*, Column 677–9.

30. *Stenographische Berichte Reichstag*, I. Legislaturperiode, III. Session 1872, vol. 1, 1872, p. 272; John, *Reserveoffizierkorps*, p. 57, 148 (for the five-year period 1906/10). In Prussia between 1860 and 1865 only 10% of all men entitled to enter the army actually did so, and of these around 45% left the army with the requisite permission to become a reserve officer, and 13% with the reserve NCO qualification. 36 % received no promotion (Engel, 'Institut', pp. 248–9, 255). Simply being given an 'aptness certificate' did not automatically entail being awarded the desired rank. In the Bavarian army, for example, although nearly 43% of all one-yearers left the army in 1906 as 'aspiring officers', in the following years only 43% of them – around 18% of all one-yearers from the 1906 intake – actually received the reserve officer status (John, *Reserveoffizierkorps*, p. 155).

31. Rathenau, *Schriften*, vol. 1, pp. 192, 207, 188–9. In Prussia between 1880 and 1910 no Jew was even promoted to officer rank, and in the same period, no volunteer one-yearer of the Jewish faith was awarded a reserve officer's commission. Converted Jews had better chances. (Hecker, *Rathenau*, p. 38; John, *Reserveoffizierkorps*, pp. 150–220; May, *Militärstatistik*, p. 8).

32. Warburg, *Aufzeichnungen*, p. 10; Rumschöttel, *Offizierkorps*; John, *Reserveoffizierkorps*, pp. 154 ff.

33. Stern, *Gold*; Liebermann von Wahlendorf, *Erinnerungen*, pp. 57, 60–1.

34. GStA Berlin-Dahlem, HA XX, Handschrift 7: Dr. Ludwig Goldstein, Heimatgebunden. Aus dem Leben eines alten Königsbergers, Königsberg, 31.10.1936, vol. 2, pp. 64–5.

35. Gilman, *Rasse*, pp. 181 ff.; Hödl, *Pathologisierung*, pp. 167 ff.

36. Klemperer, *Curriculum*, vol. 1, pp. 5, 101, 348–9, 352–3.

37. Angress, 'Army', and also *Militär*.

38. Rocholl, *Malerleben*, p. 59.

39. Paulsen, *Universitäten*, p. 471, and Paulsen, *Leben*, pp. 178–82.

40. Müller, *Gärten*, pp. 212–13.

41. Hentig, *Leben*, pp. 12–15.

42. Menzel, *Infanterie-Einjährige*, primarily pp. 19–44; Spohn, *Einjährig-Freiwilligen*, p. 28.

43. Spohn, *Einjährig-Freiwilligen*, pp. 15–16, 19, 22, 27 ff., and 32–3.

44. *Stenographische Berichte*, vol. 1, 1872, p. 270; Gennrich, *Erinnerungen*, pp. 21–4; Müller, *Gärten*, p. 211.

45. Weber, *Jugendbriefe*, quotes pp. 77, 82–3, 90, and 96–8.

46. Weber, *Jugendbriefe*, pp. 90–1.

47. Paulsen, *Leben*, p. 179; Baumgarten, *Lebensgeschichte*, pp. 43–8.

48. Müller, *Gärten*, pp. 214, 218; Paulsen, *Leben*, p. 181.

49. Macke, *Briefe*, p. 18. His views were similar to Gennrich, *Erinnerungen*, p. 22; Körner, *Erinnerungen*, p. 51; Kühlmann, *Erinnerungen*, p. 53; Spielhagen, *Finder*, vol. 2, p. 8; Wille, *Traum*, p. 17.

50. Macke, *Briefe*, p. 192; Weber, *Jugendbriefe*, pp. 127, 129.

51. Müller, *Gärten*, pp. 214, 216–17; Arthur Schnitzler, Reigen und andere Dramen, Frankfurt 1978, pp. 69 ff.; Baumgarten, *Lebensgeschichte*, pp. 45–6.

52. HStA Stuttgart, E 286, Nr. 33: 3rd Battalion Commander dated 14.9.1866.

53. Wille, *Traum*, pp. 17–18; Weber, *Jugendbriefe*, p. 91; Gennrich, *Erinnerungen*, p. 22; Föppl, *Lebenserinnerungen*, p. 96; Langfeld, *Leben*, p. 61; Schott, *Künstlerleben*, p. 63; Grube, *Jugenderinnerungen*, pp. 322, 327; Claß, *Strom*, p. 13.

54. Kaun, *Leben*, p. 22; Bosse, *Jugendzeit*, p. 279; Langfeld, *Leben*, p. 62; Binding, *Leben*, p. 113; Müller, *Gärten*, p. 219.

55. Weber, *Jugendbriefe*, pp. 109, 119, 89; Menzel, *Infanterist*, pp. 52–3.

56. Kessler, *Gesichter*, p. 324; Kruse, *Vergangenes*, p. 75; Kühlmann, *Erinnerungen*, p. 49; Niemeyer, *Lebenserinnerungen*, p. 98.

57. Weber, *Jugendbriefe*, pp. 100, 120.

58. Baumgarten, *Lebensgeschichte*, pp. 45–6; Weber, *Jugendbriefe*, pp. 116, 108, 104.

59. Müller, *Gärten*, p. 211; Weber, *Jugendbriefe*; Bosse, *Jugendzeit*, p. 288; Lubarsch, *Gelehrtenleben*, p. 22; Langfeld, *Leben*, p. 58 (Langfeld served in 1874–5 in Rostock).

60. Exceptions are: Kaun, *Leben*, p. 22; Claß, *Strom*, p. 13.

61. Menzel, *Infanterie-Einjährige*, pp. 36 and 43.

62. Macke, *Briefe*, pp. 184–5.

63. Müller, *Gärten*, p. 213; Langfeld, *Leben*, p. 62; Weber, *Jugendbriefe*, p. 129; Paulsen, *Leben*, p. 181.

64. Marianne Weber, *Max Weber*, p. 80.

65. Menzel, *Infanterist*, pp. 164 ff.; *Militär-Wochenblatt*, Nr. 43, 1900, Columns 1045–7; Jany, *Geschichte*, vol. 4, pp. 286–7; *Handbuch zur deutschen Militärgeschichte*, vol. V, 1968, pp. 49 ff.

66. *Beschreibung*, p. 174; Bächtold, *Soldatenbrauch*, p. 11; Gestrich, *Jugendkultur*, p. 122.

67. StA Detmold, M1 IC Nr. 299: Präses Dr. Albert dated 15.3.1869; *Militär-Wochenblatt*, Nr. 7, 1914, Column 130–31; Bromme, *Lebensgeschichte*, pp. 209 ff.

68. Bächtold, *Soldatenbrauch*, p. 11; Meyer, *Volksleben*, pp. 238–9; Transfeldt, *Wort*, p. 1; Severing, *Lebensweg*, vol. 1, p. 65. [The Hauff original reads: '*Als ich zur Fahne fortgemüßt, / Hat sie so herzlich mich geküßt, / Mit Bändern meinen Hut geschmückt / Und weinend mich ans Herz gedrückt*'.]

69. HStA Dresden, Kriegsarchiv, Nr. 1011: Dresdener Nachrichten dated 20.3.1885.

70. Meyer, *Volksleben*, p. 240.

71. HStA München, Abt. IV, M Kr 2501: Münchener Kommandantur dated 10.2.1894; Neuburger Regiment Commander dated 19.12.1898.

72. Schmidt, *Erziehung*, p. 17; Menzel, *Infanterist*, p. 47.
73. *Militär-Wochenblatt*, Nr. 17, 1913, Columns 372–3; Engel, 'Gesundheit', p. 210; Ingenlath, *Aufrüstung*, pp. 212 ff.
74. HStA München, Abt. IV, M Kr Nr. 2323: Note dated March 1910; Communication dated 23.3.1910.
75. *Militär-Wochenblatt*, Nr. 105, 1895, Column 2632; Meyer, *Volksleben*, p. 240.
76. Rehbein, *Leben*, pp. 192–3.
77. HStA Stuttgart, M 33/1 Bü 59 b; M 1/7 Bü 125a; Bromme, *Lebensgeschichte*, pp. 110–11, 215 ff.; Gestrich, *Jugendkultur*, pp. 131 ff.
78. HStA München, Abt. IV, M Kr Nr. 2822: Bahnexpeditor Kümmerle dated 4.10.1912.
79. The expressions are direct quotes from remarks made by the soldiers. They are similarly taken from the military tribunal files mentioned above.
80. This did not exclude women occasionally being smuggled in and 'used for sexual intercourse', as in 1873 in Freiberg in Saxony (HStA Dresden, Kriegsarchiv, Nr. 1009: Communication dated 15.6.1873).
81. Schmidt, *Erziehung*, pp. 132 ff.; *Militär-Wochenblatt*, Nr. 105, 1895, Column 2634; Spohn, *Erziehung*, p. 72; Göttsch, "Soldat".
82. Göttsch, "Soldat", pp. 138, 150–1. (Song texts) [*Heute Jettchen, morgen Bettchen, immer neu, Das ist Soldatentreu.*]
83. Bergg, *Proletarierleben*, pp. 148–9.
84. Rehbein, *Leben*, p. 169; Menzel, *Dienstunterricht*, p. 35; *Militär-Wochenblatt*, Nr. 108, 1887, Column 2368; Beiheft 1906, pp. 236–7; Nr. 16, 1910, Column 362.
85. Reuter, *Kinde*, p. 161; Schumacher, *Schulmädel*, pp. 22–3; Niese, *Gestern*, p. 134; Silling, *Jugenderinnerungen*, p. 28; Meyer, *Lebenstragödie*, p. 67; Hasenclever, *Erlebtes*, pp. 35–6.
86. HStA Stuttgart, M 33/1 Bü 59b: Judgement dated 29.9.1910; M 1/7 Bü 125a: Judgement dated 9.10.1893.
87. Menzel, *Infanterist*, pp. 52 ff. and Menzel, *Dienstunterricht*, pp. 46 ff.; Albert, *Jugenderinnerungen*, p. 14; Schwab, Erinnerungen (HStA München, Abt. IV HS 3432).
88. Schmidt, *Erziehung*, p. 133; HStA München, Abt. IV, HS 74: Hauptmann (a.d.) Karl Pleitner, Vorträge zur militärischen Pflichtenlehre 1875–86.
89. Göttsch, "Soldat", p. 138; Menzel, *Infanterist*, pp. 60–6; Spohn, *Erziehung*, p. 59; Schwab, *Erinnerungen* (HStA München, Abt. IV HS 3432); Enters, *Welt*, p. 73.
90. Menzel, *Infanterist*, pp. 126, 139; HStA München, Abt. IV, Militärgerichte Nr. 6402: Standortkommando Konstanz, ca. 1917; M Kr. Nr. 2322: Bavarian war minister from 26.10.1895 on *Haltung und Anzug der Mannschaften außerhalb der Kaserne (The Troops' Conduct and Dress outside the Barracks).*

91. Gestrich, *Jugendkultur*, p. 124; Wilke, *Erinnerungen*, p. 96.

92. Wilke, *Erinnerungen*; Schwab, *Erinnerungen* (HStA München, Abt. IV HS 3432); Rehbein, *Leben*, pp. 174–5; Fischer, *Arbeiterschicksale*, p. 115; Dirkreiter, *Geschichte*, vol. 1, p. 338; Grube, *Jugenderinnerungen*, p. 331; *Militär-Wochenblatt*, Nr. 66, 1893, Column 1712; Brändli, 'Offiziere', pp. 201 ff.

93. Stein, *Symbole*, p. 109.

94. Rathenau, *Schriften*, vol. 1, p. 199.

95. Dirkreiter, *Geschichte*, vol. 1, pp. 305 and 315; Fischer, *Arbeiterschicksale*, pp. 125–6; Langfeld, *Leben*, p. 59; Binding, *Leben*, p. 114.

96. Menzel, *Infanterist*, p. 139; HStA München, Abt. IV, M Kr Nr. 2322: Communication dated 16.11.1892.

97. Henseling, *Kriegsartikel*, p. 46; HStA Dresden, Kriegsarchiv, Nr. 1009–11, 1255.

98. *Militärische Blätter*, vol. 1, 1859, pp. 36–7.

99. *Stenographische Berichte*, vol. 2, 1872, Anlage Nr. 122, p. 567.

100. Dirkreiter, *Geschichte*, vol. 1, p. 298.

101. HStA München, Abt. IV M Kr 2501: Note dated 11.10.1898, exchange of letters dated 29.9, 6.10, 16.10 and 19.12.1898.

102. Schwab, *Erinnerungen* (HStA München, Abt. IV, HS 3432); Göhre, *Monate*, p. 119; Schulz-Oldendorf, *Briefe*, p. 24; Könenkamp, 'Entlassungsbräuche', pp. 62 ff.

103. Goffman, *Asylums*, see primarily p. 16, 119–20.

104. Dirkreiter, *Leben*, vol. 1, p. 272; *Militair-Wochenblatt*, Nr. 58, 1875, Column 1151; Nr. 40, 1879, Column 702; Nr. 96, 1879, pp. 1695–6.

105. Menzel, *Dienstunterricht*, p. 39; Estorff, *Anleitung*, p. 65; Spohn, *Erziehung*, p. 21; *Offizier*, pp. 89–90; *Militär-Wochenblatt*, Nr. 77, 1890, Column 2370; Nr. 69, 1903, Column 1706; Nr. 70, 1903, Column 1730; Briefe, p. 68; Rehbein, *Leben*, pp. 178–9, 193–4, 203; Bergg, *Proletarierleben*, pp. 124, 127, 131.

106. Fricke, 'Rolle', p. 1299; Gillhaußen, *Eideshart*, p. 90.

107. Strätz, *Schwert*, p. 88; *Militär-Wochenblatt*, Nr. 16, 1890, Columns 483–4; Nr. 77, 1890, Column 2370–2373; Schmidt, *Erziehung*, pp. 126 ff., 151–2.

108. Henseling, *Kriegsartikel*, pp. 28 ff.; Estorff, *Anleitung*, pp. 2 ff.; Gillhaußen, *Eideshart*, pp. 19 ff. The French flags captured in the Franco-Prussian War were exhibited as war booty in the Berlin Arsenal; looking at them filled young female visitors, like Gabriele Reuter, 'with a frightening awe' (Reuter, *Kinde*, p. 171).

109. Rehbein, *Leben*, p. 205; Göhre, *Monate*, p. 118.

110. Estorff, *Anleitung*, pp. 76 ff.; Henseling, *Kriegsartikel*, pp. 21 ff.

111. *Stenographische Berichte*, vol. 2, 1872, Anlagen Nr. 5, pp. 10–1.

112. HStA München, Abt. IV, M Kr Nr. 2322: Kriegsministerium dated 28.4.1888; Dirkreiter, *Leben*, vol. 1, pp. 274–5; HStA Stuttgart, Militärarchiv, M 1/7 Bü 125a; M 33/1 Bü 59b.
113. HStA München, Abt. IV, HS 3432: Schwab, *Erinnerungen*; Dirkreiter, *Leben*, vol. 1, pp. 297–8; Spohn, *Erziehung*, p. 21; HStA Stuttgart, Militärarchiv, M 1/7 Bü 69: Judgment dated 3.11.1911.
114. HStA München, Abt. IV, M Kr Nr. 11099: decree dated 22.2.1912; Bavarian Kriegsministerium dated 13.3.1912; HStA Stuttgart, Militärarchiv, M 1/7 Bü 125a: Judgment dated 15.11.1898; M 33/1 Bü 59b: Judgments dated 17.3.1903, 3.2.1909 and Strätz, *Schwert*, p. 62.
115. Menzel, *Infanterist*, p. 139; Menzel, *Dienstunterricht*, p. 41; Estorff, *Anleitung*, p. 81; Strätz, *Schwert*, pp. 68–9.
116. *Briefe*, p. 69.
117. HStA München, Abt. IV, M Kr Nr. 11099: Decree dated 28.1.1911; Bergg, *Proletarierleben*, p. 116.
118. In 1907, 67. 6% of the troops and NCOs were Protestant, and 83% of the officers, compared to 61.7% of the total population (May, *Militärstatistik*, p. 5); *Militärische Blätter*, vol. 28, 1872, pp. 181–4; HStA München, Abt. IV, M Kr 2500: Provisions for Garrison Service (*Garnisondienst-Vorschrift*) from 1892, §28 and §29.
119. HStA München, Abt. IV, M Kr Nr. 2499: Exchange of letters dated 12.3. and 21.4.1875, 6.7 and 23.8.1879, 6.11.1881; Nr. 2500: Pfarrer Denzinger from 15.9.1910.
120. *Militär-Wochenblatt*, Nr. 100, 1888, Columns 2066–71; Fricke, 'Bündnis', pp. 1388–94.
121. HStA München, Abt. IV, M Kr Nr. 2500: Statistic from 23.5.1896.
122. HStA München, Abt. IV, M Kr Nr. 2499: Kgl. Verordnung dated 8.8.1863; Generalmajor v. Weinrich dated 25.7.1878; Bischöfliches Ordinariat Augsburg dated 25.10.1878; Provisions for Garrison Service (*Garnisondienst-Vorschrift*) dated 1892; M Kr Nr. 2323: Decree dated 20.1.1896.
123. Blessing, *Staat*, primarily Chapters 4 and 5.
124. HStA München, Abt. IV, M Kr 2500: Prussian war minister from 3.9.1909, 8.3.1911, 3.10.1913.
125. *Allgemeine Zeitung des Judenthums*, Year 44, Nr. 51, 21.12.1880, pp. 810–11. Estimates put the proportion of Jewish one-yearers at around 30% of all Jewish soldiers in 1907, and 45.8% in 1913. The comparable figures for Protestants and Catholics in 1907 were 2% and 1.5% respectively (May, *Militärstatistik*, pp. 8–9).
126. Menzel, *Infanterie-Einjährige*, p. 22; Weber, *Jugendbriefe*, p. 78.
127. *Militärische Blätter*, vol. 4, 1861, p. 186; Angress, 'Army'; John, *Reserveoffizierkorps*, pp. 150 ff.

128. Menzel, *Infanterist*, pp. 74 ff., 374 ff.
129. *Militair-Wochenblatt*, Nr. 1, 1873, pp. 3–7; Strätz, *Schwert*, p. 61; Weber, *Jugendbriefe*, p. 127.
130. *Stenographische Berichte*, Norddeutscher Bund, vol. 1, 1867, p. 422.
131. Weber, *Jugendbriefe*, pp. 96, 108; Langfeld, *Leben*, p. 58.
132. Bindewald, 'Wehrfähigkeit', pp. 563–4; Vogl, *Jugend*, pp. 8, 17. On similar developments in France, see Weber, *Peasants*, pp. 301–2.
133. Landwirthschaftsrath, *Bedeutung*, pp. 13, 21; Brentano/Kuczynski, *Grundlage*, pp. 10, 32–3.
134. Brentano/Kuczynski, *Grundlage*, p. 10; Engel, 'Noch einmal Resultate', p. 180.
135. Brentano/Kuczynski, *Grundlage*, Tab. p. 89; Landwirthschaftsrath, Bedeutung, Tab. p. 92; Bindewald, 'Wehrfähigkeit', p. 577.
136. *Vermächtnis*, pp. 11, 23, 30–1; Brentano/Kuczynski, *Grundlage*, pp. 43–8; Landwirthschaftsrath, *Bedeutung*, p. 24; Vogl, *Jugend*, p. 11.
137. Landwirthschaftsrath, *Bedeutung*, pp. 30–1; Bindewald, 'Wehrfähigkeit', pp. 184–6; *Militär-Literatur-Zeitung*, Nr. 4, 1900, Column 109; *Militär-Wochenblatt*, Nr. 29, 1911, Column 636.
138. Hoenig, *Mannszucht*, p. 209; Gregory, *Jahre*, pp. 64, 73.
139. *Militair-Wochenblatt*, Nr. 34, 1875, Columns 697–8; Nr. 18, 1879, Columns 323–31; Nr. 44, 1882, Columns 865–75; Nr. 13, 1887, Columns 261–72; Nr. 58, 1889, Columns 1243–8; Nr. 5, 1891, Columns 113–18; Nr. 98, 1902, Columns 2597–8; Nr. 15, 1900, Column 364; Briefe, pp. 23 ff.
140. *Militär-Wochenblatt*, Nr. 13, 1887, Column 272; Nr. 2, 1900, Column 21; Nr. 91, 1902, Columns 2409–17; Nr. 98, 1902, Columns 2595–2601; Nr. 107, 1902, Columns 2836–9; Nr. 4, 1903, Columns 82–90; *Briefe*, pp. 51 ff.
141. Bindewald, 'Wehrfähigkeit', p. 185; Vogl, *Jugend*, p. 22; *Militär-Wochenblatt*, Nr. 4, 1903, Column 83; Nr. 13, 1887, Column 263; Nr. 1, 1889, Columns 9–12; Beiheft 1906, pp. 205 ff.
142. *Militär-Wochenblatt*, Nr. 108, 1887, Column 2371; Nr. 15, 1885, Columns 310–11; Beiheft 1888, pp. 67–92; Nr. 138, 1907, Column 3142.
143. HStA Dresden, Kriegsarchiv Nr. 1436: Police report dated 16.1.1874; Generalkommando dated 1.2.1874; Prussian war minister dated 4.3.1874.
144. HStA Dresden, Kriegsarchiv Nr. 1438; Nr. 25001: Leipzig Regimental Commander dated 20.11.1894 and on Prussia StA Detmold, M1 IC Nr. 35–37, M2 Bielefeld Nr. 456; for Württemberg HStA Stuttgart, Militärarchiv M 11 Bü 13; M 33/1 Bü 6 and 7.
145. HStA München, Abt. IV, M Kr Nr. 2501: Berlin register dated 28.6.1913; on the association prohibition HStA Dresden, Kriegsarchiv, Nr. 1255: Exchange of correspondence dated 18.6.1888, 31.1.1890, 30.8 and 2.9.1891, 15.12.1892; Höhn, *Sozialismus*, vol. 3.

146. HStA München, Abt. IV, M Kr Nr. 2501: Bavarian Kriegsministerium dated 6.2.1904; *Militär-Wochenblatt*, Beiheft 1888, pp. 67–92; Nr. 15, 1885, Columns 307–12; Nr. 94, 1887, Columns 2048–50; Nr. 108, 1887, Columns 2367–71; Nr. 30/31, 1901, Columns 815–18, 842–6; Nr. 68/69/70, 1903, Columns 1669–75, 1705–12, 1728–31; Nr. 27, 1906, Columns 597–602; Nr. 53, 1906, Columns 1262–5; Nr. 123, 1906, Columns 2833–841; Nr. 138, 1907, pp. 3139–46; Spohn, *Erziehung*, p. 37.
147. Rodenwaldt, *Aufnahmen*, pp. 7, 41 ff.
148. Fricke, *Handbuch*, vol. 1, pp. 316 ff., 454 ff., 463; Stargardt, *Idea*, pp. 91 ff.
149. StA Detmold, M 1 IC Nr. 35: Prussian interior minister dated 31.5.1885; HStA Stuttgart, Militärarchiv M 11 Bü 13: Stuttgart interior ministry dated 15.10.1885 and 7.11.1894. In 1896, the Berlin war ministry took a recent incident as a reason to issue a pointed reminder to command authorities that 'people whose social democratic sentiment is established prior to being enlisted are not to be promoted on principle during their active military service. Given the brief time available, and the rule of good conduct as soldiers adhered to by social democrats, it seems impossible to reach a secure judgement on whether such men have undergone a fundamental change in their way of thinking or whether this is only temporarily assumed' (HStA München, Abt. IV, M Kr Nr. 2323: Communication dated 5.3.1896).
150. Schmidt, *Erziehung*, p. 82; Spohn, *Erziehung*, pp. 13–17.
151. *Stenographische Berichte*, vol. 2, 1872, Anlagen Nr. 122, primarily pp. 563–4, 808; Henseling, *Kriegsartikel*, pp. 51 ff.
152. Schmidt, *Erziehung*, pp. 115–18; Henseling, *Kriegsartikel*, p. 52; Estorff, *Anleitung*, p. 60.
153. HStA München, Abt. IV, M Kr 11099: Kriegsministerium dated 3.5.1876 and 15.6.1888.
154. HStA Stuttgart, Militärarchiv, M 1/7 Bü 69: *Frankfurter Zeitung* dated 1.2.1892, pp. 1–2. This decree was 'not for publication' but leaked to the SPD, who printed it in *Vorwärts* before other newspapers followed suit. It created a major stir and was also debated in the *Reichstag* budget commission (HStA Stuttgart, Militärarchiv, M 1/7 Bü 69: Report by Kriegsrat v. Horion dated 5.2.1892).
155. HStA München, Abt. IV, M Kr Nr. 2821: Letter dated 4.9.1901, and Nr. 2822; HStA Stuttgart, Militärarchiv M 1/7 Bü 69; *Militär-Wochenblatt*, Nr. 9, 1896, Columns 263–9; Füllkrug, *Selbstmord*, p. 94. While socialist and the Catholic *Zentrum* party politicians saw the typical army maltreatment at the root of the high suicide rates among soldiers as compared to civilians, Ursula Baumann has suggested that 'better record keeping and the efficiency of the means chosen' pushed the rates up: soldiers tended to use guns far more often than civilians did (Baumann, *Recht*, pp. 269–70).

156. HStA München, Abt. IV M Kr Nr. 2322: Communication dated 13.11.1887; HStA Dresden, Kriegsarchiv, Nr. 25004; Sächsischer Militärbevollmächtigter in Berlin, Nr. 164; HStA Stuttgart, Militärarchiv, M 1/7 Bü 69: Exchange of letters dated 8, 11, 13, 21. 2.1893.

157. HStA Stuttgart, Militärarchiv, M 1/7 Bü 69: Württemberg war minister from 24.5.1912; Exchange of letters dated 16.7 and 8.11.1873, 6.7.1874; HStA München, Abt. IV M Kr Nr. 11099: Bavarian king from 22.3.1877; Written exchange dated 10.2.1874, 30.7.1910, 28.1.1911, 20.7.1912.

158. HStA München, Abt. IV M Kr Nr. 11099. Nürnberger Eskadronchef dated 23.10.1891 and Kriegsministerium dated 15.6.1888 and 21.10.1912; HStA Stuttgart, M 1/7 Bü 70: Judgement dated 3.11.1911.

159. HStA Stuttgart, M 1/7 Bü 69: Decree dated 8.6.1891 and other examples; Bü 70: judgement dated 3.11.1911; Kriegsministerium from 21.2.1893; M 1/ 4 Bü 717 and M 1/7 Bü 70; Wiedner, 'Soldatenmißhandlungen'.

160. HStA Stuttgart, M 1/7 Bü 69: Kriegsrat v. Horion from 5.2.1892.

161. Jany, *Geschichte*, vol. 4, pp. 268–9, 289–90, 326 ff.; Förster, *Militarismus*, primarily pp. 28 ff.

162. *Stenographische Berichte*, vol. 1, 1872, pp. 94, 98; Wette, *Militarismus*, pp. 97–114, 115–27; Chickering, "Wehrverein"; Coetzee, *Army League*; Eley, *German Right*.

163. Becker, *Bilder*; Dülffer, *Bereit*; Jany, *Geschichte*, vol. 4, pp. 270, 326.

164. HStA München, Abt. IV, M Kr Nr. 2821: Communication dated 20.2.1906; Gregory, *Jahre*, p. 41.

165. *Militär-Wochenblatt*, Nr. 15, 1885, Column 310; Beiheft 1888, primarily pp. 72 ff.; Beiheft 1906, pp. 236–7. Also see Bergg, *Proletarierleben*, p. 110.

166. Heyberger, *Kamerad*, p. 5; *Militär-Wochenblatt*, Nr. 31, 1895, Column 836; Nr. 49, 1911, Column 1123; Menzel, *Dienstunterricht*, pp. 188–9; Gillhaußen, *Eideshart*, pp. 13–14, 90; Albert, *Jugenderinnerungen*, pp. 3–9, 14–15, 25–6.

167. Westphal, *Kriegervereinswesen*, p. 11; Saul, "Kriegerbund", pp. 95, 159.

168. *Militär-Wochenblatt*, Nr. 120, 1908, Column 2829; Rohkrämer, *Militarismus*, Chapter II.; Zimmermann, "*Wall*".

169. Westphal, *Handbuch*, p. 111; Meyer, *Volksleben*, p. 240; Albert, *Jugenderinnerungen*, p. 32.

170. Westphal, *Handbuch*, pp. 36–7, 45 ff.; Saul, 'Kriegerbund', pp. 102–3; *Beschreibung*, p. 179.

171. Siedenhans, 'Vereinswesen'; Friedeburg, 'Klassenidentität'.

172. Henning, 'Kriegervereine', p. 448; Westphal, *Kriegervereinswesen*, p. 13.

173. Westphal, *Kriegervereinswesen*, p. 7; Saul, *Kriegerbund*; Zimmermann, *Wall*, pp. 192 ff.; *Militär-Wochenblatt*, Nr. 74/75, 1895, Columns 1875–0,

1891–6; Nr. 28, 1896, Columns 765–71; Nr. 113, 1905, Columns 2577–80; Nr. 109, 1908, Columns 2567–70, Nr. 120, 1910, Columns 2804–7.

174. HStA Dresden, Kriegsarchiv, Nr. 1436: Exchange dated 16, 26, 28.3.1874, 9.7, 16.7, 10.9.1874; Nr. 1437: Exchange dated 11.10 and 2.12.1878, 13.3.1879; Nr. 1445: Kriegsministerium dated 7.4.1875. For Prussia, see Saul, *Kriegerbund*, p. 129.

175. Saul, *Kriegerbund*, pp. 119, 152, 159.

176. Bromme, *Lebensgeschichte*, pp. 71–2; Göhre, *Monate*, pp. 122–3.

177. Bergg, *Proletarierleben*, p. 105; Göhre, *Monate*, pp. 118 ff.; Bromme, *Lebensgeschichte*, pp. 184, 189, 219; Wieber, *Leben*, p. 10; Fischer, *Arbeiterschicksale*, pp. 113, 121; Enters, *Welt*, p. 73.

178. Heine, 'Militarismus', p. 917; Ritter/Tenfelde, *Arbeiter*, pp. 731 and 742.

179. Heine, 'Militarismus', p. 912; Protokoll 1875, pp. 4, 36; Protokoll 1891, pp. 5, 348–9.

180. Protokoll 1891, p. 5; Bebel, *Heer*, pp. 43 ff.; Groh/Brandt, *"Gesellen"*, pp. 116 ff.

181. Saul, *Kriegerbund*, p. 152.

182. HStA München, Abt. IV, M Kr Nr. 11504: Exchange dated 19.12.1872; Statut u. Motive des Stuttgarter Vereins; Rechenschaftsbericht der Münchener Gesellschaft 1883; Note dated 8.12.1899; Zirkular des Bezirkskommandos dated Oct. 1902.

183. Goltz, *Volk*, pp. 50–1; *Militär-Zeitung*, Nr. 12, 1894, p. 126; Nr. 15, 1886, p. 171.

184. Wermuth, *Beamtenleben*, pp. 70–1; Föppl, *Lebenserinnerungen*, p. 95; Wille, *Traum*, p. 18.

185. Gall, *Bürgertum*, pp. 405, 558; Braun, *Ostpreußen*, p. 48; criticism in Kehr, 'Genesis'.

186. *Militär-Zeitung*, Year 17, 1894, pp. 127–8; Year 13, 1890, pp. 299–302.

187. In 1895, 73.1% of the chairmen of local associations of war veterans were officer rank (reserve or *Landwehr*), and in 1913 86.9%. In contrast, in Bavaria in 1913, of 157 local chairmen only 12 were reserve or *Landwehr*, which Saul attributes to the lower level of pressure from official circles (Saul, *Kriegerbund*, pp. 97, 109–10).

188. *Militär-Zeitung*, Year 13, 1890, pp. 299–302; Year 17, 1894, pp. 127–8; Roloff, 'Kriegervereine', pp. 133–4.; Westphal, *Kriegervereinswesen*, pp. 22–3.

189. *Militär-Zeitung*, Year 13, 1890, p. 302; Köhler, *Lebenserinnerungen*, pp. 11–12; Lubarsch, *Gelehrtenleben*, p. 92.

190. *Militär-Zeitung*, Year 19, 1896, pp. 9, 629; Year 15, 1892, p. 103.

191. *Die Schnur*, Nr. 35, 1905, p. 496; Nr. 39, 1906, p. 547; Nr. 43, 1907, p. 623.

192. Frevert, *"Mann"*, pp. 61 ff.; *Die Schnur*, Nr. 43, 1907, p. 623; *Militär-Wochenblatt*, Nr. 27, 1906, "Zum 27. Februar"; Nr. 74, 1871, p. 520: Decree dated 22.5.1871; Nr. 19, 1872, p. 179–80; Nr. 33, 1872, 33, 1872, p. 527.

193. Süchting-Hänger, "Helferinnen", pp. 131, 133; Daniel, 'Frauenvereine'; Quataert, 'Women's Work'; Misch, *Geschichte*.

194. Treitschke, *Politik*, vol. 1, pp. 32–3, 39, 252–3; English quotes from Treitschke, H.v., *Politics*, New York, 1916, vol. 1, pp. 22, 29–30, 252; Paulsen, *System*, p. 263; Frevert, *"Mann"*, pp. 119 ff.

195. Dohm, *Emancipation*, pp. 171–3; Bebel, *Frau*, p. 340; Honegger, *Ordnung*, p. 223.

196. Otto, *Frauenleben*, pp. 163–7, 185 ff., 256–7; Planert, *Nation*, pp. 113–30.

197. Schaser, 'Women'; Chickering, "Gaze"; Wildenthal, *German Women*.

198. Lange, *Kampfzeiten*, vol. 2, pp. 92–100; *Neues Frauenblatt*, Year 4, Nr. 40, 7.10.1900, p. 784.

199. Dammer, *Mütterlichkeit*; Schaser, 'Women', pp. 260 ff.

200. Vogel, *Nationen* and 'Gardisten'; also see Vogel, "Revue".

201. Bromme, *Lebensgeschichte*, pp. 11–16; Goldstein, *Heimatgebunden*, vol. 1, pp. 22–3 (GStA Berlin-Dahlem, HA XX, HS 7); Bode, *Tage*, pp. 38–9; Bernstein, *Kindheit*, p. 41. The cross-generational link in military service was something underlined by the working-class Carl Fischer, born in 1842, who was classified as not fully fit and consequently not enlisted: 'I felt as if I'd been put under the greatest curse there was. All my uncles were soldiers and I wasn't allowed to go.' (*Denkwürdigkeiten*, T. 1, p. 123); Wolff, *Leben*, p. 269; Schwab, *Erinnerungen* (HStA München, Abt. IV, HS 3432).

202. Bromme, *Lebensgeschichte*, pp. 48–9, 46; similarly in Heck, *Lebensbeichte*, p. 18.

203. Kügelgen, *Lebensbild*, pp. 103, 120; Scholz, *Weisen*, p. 56; Goldstein, *Heimatgebunden*, vol. 1, pp. 44 ff. (GStA Berlin-Dahlem, HA XX, HS 7); Klemperer, *Curriculum*, vol. 1, p. 5; Breysig, *Tagen*, pp. 6–7; Mommsen, *Vater*, p. 23; Marx, *Erinnerungen*, pp. 23–4, 40; Budde, *Weg*, pp. 198 ff.

204. Reuter, *Kinde*, pp. 79–80.

205. Bebel, *Heer*, pp. 50 ff.; Biefang, *Bürgertum*, pp. 179–80.

206. Stürenburg, *Wehrpflicht*, pp. 28–9, 42.

207. Roloff, *Lexikon*, Columns 680–1.

208. Kessler, *Gesichter*, pp. 132, 134; Graf, *Schülerjahre*, pp. 42, 73, 89, 172.

209. Roloff, *Lexikon*, Column 681.

210. John, *Reserveoffizierkorps*, p. 93.

211. Rodenwaldt, *Aufnahmen*, pp. 61–2; *Militär-Wochenblatt*, Nr. 1234, 1906, Column 2831.

212. Ingenlath, *Aufrüstung*, pp. 116 ff., 130 ff.

213. Bothmer, *Jugend*, pp. 71, 46; Obermayer, *Wehrkraftbewegung*, p. 18.
214. *Militär-Wochenblatt*, Nr. 150, 1910, Column 3516; Nr. 39, 1900, Column 990.
215. *Militär-Wochenblatt*, Nr. 107, 1901, Column 2838; Fricke, *Handbuch*, vol. 1, pp. 454 ff.; vol. 2, pp. 1099 ff.
216. *Militär-Wochenblatt*, Nr. 107, 1901, Columns 2838–40; Nr. 80/81, 1909, Columns 1831–1835, 1859–1862; *Handbuch der deutschen Bildungsgeschichte*, vol. IV, 1991, pp. 505 ff.
217. Saul, 'Kampf', pp. 113 ff.
218. Wyneken, 'Militarisierung', pp. 204, 208; Saul, 'Kampf', pp. 121–3, 141.
219. Bothmer, *Jugend*, pp. 49 ff.
220. Frevert, 'Herren'; Budde, *Weg*, pp. 201–2.
221. Strachan, 'Militär'; Jahr, 'British Prussianism'; Best, 'Militarization'; Ingenlath, *Aufrüstung*; Vogel, *Nationen*.
222. *Militär-Wochenblatt*, Nr. 3, 1855, p. 12; 1861, p. 91; StA Detmold, M1 IC Nr. 24: Generalkommando dated 4.6.1896; Dirkreiter, *Leben*, vol. 1, pp. 277–8.
223. Ziemann, „Hauptmann".
224. Jünger, *Kampf*, p. 56. This highly decorated First World War volunteer and veteran poked fun at this idea of war, ridiculing the *Volksheere* as well as a 'military expression of democracy'; as far as he was concerned, there were only 'two sorts of soldiers: the mercenaries and the volunteers'.
225. Becker, *Bilder*, pp. 189 ff., 350 ff.
226. Koselleck/Jeismann, *Totenkult*; Mosse, *Fallen Soldiers*; Geyer, 'Kriegsgeschichte'.
227. Macke, *Briefe*, p. 330 (1.9.1914).

–5–

The Twentieth Century: The (Ex-)Soldier as Citizen

When the First World War ended in 1918, it left 7–8 million dead and around 20 million wounded. The first mass war in Europe had cost the lives of more than 2 million men in the German forces alone, with a further 4.2 million left permanently marked as war invalids. The Great War, as contemporaries dubbed it, not only showed the immense destructive power of the modern weaponry introduced from the late nineteenth century on, but also showed how well soldiers had been trained both to use these weapons and to withstand the stress of combat. After forty years of peace, the military had been able to prove how highly efficient it was, whether in terms of technical, organisational or 'moral' prowess.

All the countries involved, including Britain and the USA, had employed conscript armies to fight the war – and this was precisely why the politicians and army general staffs had been able to carry on for so long and with such persistence. At the same time, conscription had united the combat and home front, forging and maintaining the link between them. With wartime service obligatory for young men, older women and men felt the call of a similar duty; the result was civilian and military mobilisation reaching heights unknown previously in Europe.

In Germany, total mobilisation was followed by near-total demobilisation. The provision in the Versailles Treaty proscribing conscription, only permitting Germany a small, professional army, was adhered to until 1935, when the National Socialists reintroduced universal military service for young men as a part of their overall strategy paving the way to the Second World War, where the drive to mobilise and release destructive forces was even greater than in the First. In 1945, with the Third Reich politically in ruins and the German military totally defeated, the Allies insisted on comprehensive German demilitarisation. Although Germany then experienced a military lull, with no professional or conscript army for ten years, both German states already began establishing new armed forces in the early 1950s, each backed and supported by their respective system of aligned states. In the process, both invoked the ghost of Prussian tradition, and both appealed to the guiding notion of the 'citizen in uniform' – but both the uniform and the citizenship concepts in the two German states were radically different, only becoming identical in the wake of German reunification in 1990.

As this brief overview has indicated, the draft continued into the twentieth century unabated, with only minor interruptions. Conscription made it possible to gather armies of millions and fight wars with them, unleashing a destructive energy no nineteenth-century contemporary could ever have imagined conceivable. But conscription in the post-Second World War world presided over forty years of peace without influencing civil society nearly as much as in Wilhelmine Germany. After the First World War, British politicians feared an indissoluble bond existed in Germany between conscription and social militarisation, yet the Federal Republic of Germany (FRG) gave the lie to their concerns since, despite rearming, there was no second flowering of that 'militarism' the Allies had planned to uproot in 1918 and 1945. At the other end of the spectrum, the emphatic stance taken in 1949 by liberal politician Theodor Heuss, the first West German President, labelling conscription 'the legitimate child of democracy', does not stand up to closer historical examination either – and in his case, one might have thought he would have taken to heart the lessons taught by the experience of the Nazi period and the example given by the British and American approach.[1]

But where is the place between, or beyond, 'militarism' and 'democracy' occupied by male conscription in the twentieth century? And what was conscription's relationship to the waves of militarisation and demilitarisation that coined German history in various phases? What impact did military socialisation processes have, how strongly did they shape gender images and, finally, how close was the link between civic spirit and military service, or civil society and the apparatus of violence? These are the questions we will concern ourselves with in this chapter.

1. The Post-First World War Years: Militarisation without Military Service

When the Allied Powers met in the various Paris suburbs during 1919 to dictate the terms of peace to Germany, their concerns ranged from territorial concessions and economic reparations to military and social policy. France, in particular, insisted on broad German disarmament as a means to protect its own security interests. Looking for ways to restrict effectively the '*militarisme allemand*', they wanted the German army reduced from the 800,000 men before the war to only 200,000, with military service limited to one year. In contrast, the British believed German militarism could only be uprooted by abolishing the conscription army. In their view, conscription led to a militarisation of the population, awakening their 'martial instincts', while only a professional army could, in the final analysis, be controlled and directed within the democratic process. In the end, the British position won out and the Treaty of Versailles stipulated a future German professional army of 100,000 men.[2]

The post-1918 German government, a majority coalition of the MSPD social democratic party with their partners, the Catholic *Zentrum* party and the left-of-centre liberal DDP (*Deutsche Demokratische Partei*), were certainly not totally averse to this provision. The first government in the Weimar period had already proposed abolishing 'forced conscription', partly for tactical reasons and partly as a reaction to the general anti-war mood sweeping the country. The law on forming a provisional *Reichswehr* army, passed in February 1919 with support from the right-of-centre liberal and conservative DVP (*Deutsche Volkspartei*), had distanced itself, 'for technical reasons', from reinstating conscription, which was, in fact, still technically in force. Instead, it foresaw the recruitment of existing volunteers and the merging of volunteer groups already existing under a single supreme command, providing them with a binding set of disciplinary standards.

In making this move, the government was facing up to a reality that had taken increasingly dramatic forms since the end of 1918. On the one hand, the old army formations were being disbanded in the demobilisation process, and all politicians agreed it was unlikely any new conscription orders would be obeyed since the majority of soldiers returning showed no inclination whatsoever to continue wearing their uniforms, yet, on the other, the problems confronting the new Weimar Republic – the eastern border conflicts and the near-civil war conditions in Berlin and some other cities – underlined the pressing need for a reliable army, working in support of the government, providing an efficient and effective instrument of power capable of, as the law founding the army phrased it, 'protecting the Reich's borders, ensuring the validity of government provisions, and maintaining law and order internally'.[3]

Initially, the government had fallen back on the Free Corps and volunteer units for the key tasks guaranteeing stability. These paramilitary groups had formed from the rump of the old army and not only fought, like private armies, in East Prussia, the Baltic provinces, Upper Silesia and on the Czech border, but were also employed against revolutionary movements within Germany. Despite the Free Corps' involvement in numerous violent outrages and attacks on civilians, and the searing criticism this provoked in the National Assembly and the left-wing press, the Weimar government, with no other viable alternative, stuck to its policy of supporting these groups. The Army Law (*Wehrgesetz*) in spring 1919, though, set out to bind the Free Corps' units into a fixed command and disciplinary structure, with the duty of protecting the government 'appointed by the people'. Moreover, once the Weimar constitution had been formally adopted, they had to swear an oath of loyalty on the constitution – a radical departure from the pre-war years, and one that many of the troops and officers incorporated from the old army only reluctantly accepted.

In addition to the volunteer paramilitary groups integrated into the *Reichswehr*, in 1919 many cities and villages had armed local citizens' defence groups

(*Einwohnerwehren*), whose activities were coordinated by the interior ministry. They saw themselves as middle-class and farmers' self-defence units, exercising police functions; and in this way, they drew directly on the tradition of civilian militias and security organisations (*Sicherheitsvereine*) in the early nineteenth century.[4] These local groups comprised around 1 million men, mostly former soldiers, who, though primarily supporting counter-revolutionary measures, kept themselves away from any direct major military operations. Instead of functioning as a mobile unit combating the working-class movement, in line with the central directorate's wishes, they contented themselves as a rule with guard duties in their local district and scaring 'Spartacus sympathisers' in industrial areas.[5]

The temporary volunteer units (*Zeitfreiwilligenverbände*) were more active. These units similarly comprised large numbers of war veterans, including many student 'militias', and were mobilised against attempted working-class uprisings. Access to weapons was not confined to the right of the political spectrum; the radical left also attempted to utilize the institutional vacuum in the immediate post-war period for its own ends. However, since many war veterans with socialist leanings, in particular, rejected the creation of any paramilitary formation, social democratic self-defence units never really got off the ground.[6] It is no surprise, then, to find the social democrats, together with the left-of-centre liberals and parts of the Catholic *Zentrum* party, as the most vociferous political groups calling for disarming and disbanding paramilitary units as an issue of pressing concern. Under the threat of imminent civil war between 1919 and 1921, the notions of a general national defence force long cherished by the (social) democrats lost all political viability, despite being briefly revived in the December 1918 workers' and soldiers' councils. Implementing the SPD's programme of 'major educational ideals ... in the military sphere too' was postponed indefinitely.[7]

The Allies similarly had no interest in Germany having either militias or a 'general defensive capacity'. In fact, the Versailles terms prohibited any military training or activity undertaken by social institutions or associations, and the Inter-Allied Military Commission of Control insisted on the local citizens' defence groups disbanding and all military and civilian associations being disarmed with the exception of the *Reichswehr*. By 1921, with millions of weapons surrendered, the goal of social demilitarisation had largely been attained.[8] At the same time, the *Reichswehr* had reduced military manpower, cutting army numbers under Allied pressure from the 400,000 men in spring 1919 down to 100,000.

Measured in terms of the extremely high degree of militarisation in the early months of the Weimar Republic, Germany found itself steadily moving into civil society relations from 1921 on. The local citizens' defence groups had been disbanded and disarmed, and the Spartacists and workers' and soldiers' councils had been defeated. The Free Corps and voluntary paramilitary units had either been incorporated into the *Reichswehr* or dissolved. The First World War's immediate legacy of military mobilisation and the wave of domestic political unrest and violence flooding the country in its wake seemed to have been halted. The experience had been new to Germany, but the state had reasserted its control over violence as a state monopoly, though it appeared neither to be permitted to use it, nor want to use it.

Many contemporaries, however, were unhappy with these measures – primarily the rightist middle-class and nationalist parties. From the start, they had left no doubts where they stood on forced disarmament, and they were similarly vocal in calls for a speedy return to a large conscription army. The social democrats, for their part, eyed the professional army sceptically, with some in the party even rejecting it outright. Rather than any quibble with the size, though, they feared that 'in the longer run' a 'mercenary troop' could easily become a 'reactionary tool'. In their view, a conscript army's high recruit fluctuation blunted such a danger.[9] As a result, social democrats put considerable effort into creating a social mix in *Reichswehr* troops and officers, and binding them to the Weimar Republic by their oath on the constitution. In a further move, they ensured the Weimar constitution also abolished those special rights enjoyed by the Imperial German army: officer corps' courts of honour were dissolved, and plans made for lifting the jurisdiction of military courts – the goal of liberals and left-wing groupings for years – leaving soldiers, at least in peacetime, subject to the same criminal law as civilians. In so doing, they revoked the legal basis for an essential differentiation between citizens and soldiers, laying to rest an issue that had generated so much heated and acrimonious debate in Wilhelminian Germany.

This innovation, fiercely opposed by the conservative and nationalist parties, might have left the new professional army 'closer to the citizen' than the Imperial German conscript army, but in political terms it remained, if anything, 'removed from the citizen'. The Wilhelminian prohibition forbidding active soldiers from attending political meetings, joining political associations and voting remained in force in the *Reichswehr*. In the Weimar Republic's polarised political landscape, both the civil government and the army chiefs of staff considered it wise to keep the troops out of party political infighting. In 1930, the Leipzig supreme court noted that: 'It is an impossibility for the German armed forces [to have] lieutenants travelling around campaigning, for whichever party.'[10]

Many officers found such restraints irksome. They had nearly all been socialised in the old army structures, often finding the new republican military not to their taste and the required oath on the constitution frequently at odds with their own political sympathies. Despite the efforts made in the early years of Weimar to pro-mote former NCOs to officer ranks, the officer corps remained largely drawn from a social elite. In 1932, more than 70 per cent of all *Reichswehr* officers came from families of officers and high-ranking civil servants, and nearly 24 per cent could show aristocratic origins. Such a mix of officers could hardly be expected joyfully to embrace service in a 'socialist republic' and accept a social democratic Reich president as a Kaiser *ersatz*. Nonetheless, many officers learnt to see themselves as 'non-political soldiers', putting their energies into forming the *Reichswehr* 'into a disciplined, capable troop again'.[11]

And the new army structures bode well for such efforts. First of all, unlike its predecessor, the *Reichswehr* was a national institution. In the general process of strengthening the national-level institutions in the Weimar Republic, the previous confederate state army structures were replaced by a centralised organisation and command system. There may still have been troop contingents drawn from particular *Länder* and traditional regional bonds maintained, but many regiments were now mixed, underlining the army's new status as a national state-level institution following a set of unified guidelines.[12] Secondly, the composition of the troops facilitated their training in 'martial efficiency'. Young male volunteers, aged between 17 to 21, signing on for twelve years, could be treated in a completely different way from conscripts leaving the barracks again after one or two years. As General von Seeckt emphasised in 1921, the aim was 'no longer repeatedly to train annual levees of recruits in a brief, limited time, but instead direct education and training far more of the individual, developing their abilities and skills to the utmost'. In this way, a 'military training' could reach a 'far higher level' than in the old army, with the corps morale similarly profiting from a professional army's continuity and solidarity.[13]

Yet from the military's perspective, the *Reichswehr* also had serious drawbacks. Numbers and arms had been frozen at the lowest levels conceivable, with the once 'vast school of the army', as von Seeckt put it, only comprising an infinitesimally tiny proportion of the male population. With army numbers radically cut, the monarchist aura dissolved, its social allure tarnished, and its major national educational task aborted, the army tried to present itself as a genuine 'people's army' (*Volksheer*), but all the rhetorical attempts to lift the opprobrium attaching to a professional army could not hide its loss of status and prestige – a loss profoundly felt in the officer corps. Besides, the army also found its functions limited: it hardly seemed feasible for an army of this size to defend the country's borders, the primary task for any national military force. Furthermore, Germany saw itself technically lagging even further behind its neighbours since under the terms of the Versailles Treaty it was allowed neither an air force nor submarines, nor was it allowed to import weapons and war materials.

To cope with these deficits, the *Reichswehr* soon started sidestepping the Versailles provisions. The Allies and some civil authorities may have been watching suspiciously, but nonetheless secret rearmament took place from 1923 on, and covered far more than just cooperation with the Soviet army on the technical and manpower levels. It was a process involving innumerable 'civil' officers', regimental, and soldiers' associations which the *Reichswehr* provided with weapons, equipment and trainers, extending the groups of those ready and willing to defend the 'fatherland' far beyond the ranks of its own troops.[14] They had two preferred partners: the veterans' associations, with a massive 2.2 million members in 1922, rising to 2.8 million in 1930, and particularly the paramilitary veterans' association *Stahlhelm, Bund der Frontsoldaten e.V.*, named after the steel helmets worn in the war. This organisation had been founded directly after the war ended and, by 1924, had nearly 150,000 members, all with experience of active service at the front, with a further 110,000 men joining in 1925, once this stipulation for membership was lifted. They formed a reservoir the *Reichswehr* could draw on indiscriminately.[15]

The conservative governments in the Weimar Republic sought to play down such trends towards militarisation, claiming that groups like the *Stahlhelm* only wanted to replace those things the old army had provided for 'serving girls', namely '1. Military music, 2. Uniform, 3. Kisses'.[16] No doubt there was a grain of truth in such observations, since the attraction and homogeneity of many paramilitary associations derived not least from the way they portrayed themselves in public. Their regimented appearance, reinforced by their standardized uniforms, in parades and demonstrations created an aura of power and invincibility not only for the 'serving girls' – actually few in number in the Weimar Republic – but, above all and most importantly, for their own particular clientele. As a 1924 comment on the *Stahlhelm* noted, the organisation provided a stage for those upstanding men proclaiming their 'faith in power, masculinity and the struggle against all that was rotten and ailing'; instead of following the republican zeitgeist, it went on, cringing and crawling, and bowing and scraping, members of the *Stahlhelm, Jungsdeutscher Orden, Wiking-Jugend*, veterans' associations or the SA (*Sturmabteilung*) were demonstrating masculine toughness and decisiveness, 'courage' and 'enthusiasm' for their cause.[17]

The enthusiasm for military drills and march-pasts was most marked among the young association members without any direct war experience. The SA too, (re)formed from 1926 on as the National Socialist's paramilitary arm, was best able to keep the mood of the masses of young men entering its ranks after 1930 under control by organising sports festivals, manoeuvres and rifle practice. It was similar in the left-wing organisations, especially the communist 'Red Front' (*Rotfrontkämpferbund*), which also attracted a high proportion of very young men – and even the social democratic *Reichsbanner Schwarz Rot Gold*, founded in 1924, increasingly adopted military or paramilitary forms to attract new members.[18]

In election and propaganda campaigns, the flags, uniforms, bands, and march-pasts impressed not only the public, but first and foremost the participants. They conveyed a feeling of unity, strength and security, an effective counterpoint to the experience common among many young men especially, of personal instability, social disintegration and economic fears about the future. The key active military practices did not solely have a symbolic function, but were found across the board in nearly all of the youth movements at that time, from youth organisations in the Catholic *Zentrum* party or the right-of-centre liberal DVP, to the nationalist DNVP's *Bismarckbund*. Rather than being limited to a single world-view, the rituals and practices in this work with young men all shared the same combination of strict hierarchical command structures with regimented dress codes, disciplined march-pasts with flags, roll-calls before the colours and camping out on field exercises – and this was even widespread throughout the non-party-aligned youth organisations too.[19]

In fact, the political message does not actually seem to have been the key motivating factor in the young men's decisions to join the various different military-style groupings. Instead, the main attraction appears to have been the promise of a male communal experience centring on the twin poles of defence and fighting skills – and consequently, the politically oriented youth groups tied to political parties normally counted far fewer members than the corresponding paramilitary youth wings. Apparently, the young potential members targeted by, for example, the *Reichsbanner*, *Stahlhelm*, or other veterans' associations, had little interest in the specific party's policies, and were equally unmoved by the war experience that had played such a central role in bringing the original membership of these organisations together. If anything, the only topos they adopted came from trench warfare, where a troop was viewed as overcoming class warfare and generating awareness of a 'national community' (*Volksgemeinschaft*) that minimised all social and political differences, and could bind its members across these divides. Such memories of trench-war camaraderie lived on, occupying a firm place within the political rhetoric of the 1920s and early 1930s, and were accompanied by vivid images of the civil war in the immediate post-1918 period.

The primary explanation, though, for the high degree of societal militarisation in the final years of the Weimar Republic lies in the young generation's specific socialisation and their status fears. The main factors here were twofold: firstly, many young workers, employees, students and university graduates were either already unemployed or facing a situation where they could not find suitable work; secondly, and equally importantly, the period was marked by cultural insecurity, accompanied by a break with traditional gender relations and ways of organising life. Many contemporaries considered the dramatic changes in the appearance of young women, their growing presence and visibility in public and commercial life, as not only shocking but even revolutionary. In contrast, young men's gender image, particularly, appeared fragile and uncertain, without the world of work or educational institutions offering any fixed point of orientation. Even the military, that benchmark of masculine standards in the pre-war years, was unable to compensate their loss.

Under such circumstances, paramilitary organisations promised help and recompense, using a language, appearance and types of exercise guaranteeing men a future in their fighting cohorts, protected and strong. This ethos was at its most blatant in the conservative and NSDAP groups, but similarly ran through the *Reichsbanner* and the communist Red Front, where both organisations cultivated overtones of masculinity. This was an area defined as a women-free zone, and anxious to remain as such; women might have been welcome as party members, but the men insisted on remaining exclusively among themselves in their combat units.[20]

Even if it was sceptical about the paramilitary associations' parades and flag march-pasts, and dubious about their military value, the *Reichswehr* still had to rely on unofficial troops for assistance – and consequently was left no choice but to acknowledge the role paramilitaries could play as support troops. The Versailles provisions had left the *Reichswehr*'s hands tied, unable to pursue its self-declared goal of making the Reich's male population 'combat-ready' (*wehrhaft*), and ready to be quickly mobilised if needed. Yet realising such aims was only viable with the defence associations' help. With foreign policy concerns preventing any reintroduction of the draft and plans for a state-organised pre-military training for youths unrealisable in practice, paramilitary associations appeared ideal multipliers, maintaining male youths' 'will to fight' outside any official military structures, and pointing them into a direction favoured by the ruling power politics.[21]

The public sphere, though, eyed such calculated reciprocal instrumentalisation with considerable distrust. The SPD particularly, fearing the loss of the military's neutrality, heavily criticised *Reichswehr* and *Stahlhelm* cooperation, while middle-class circles viewed the delimiting of military violence with disquiet, not least because of the link to political extremism, regarded by many contemporaries as harbouring the risk of destabilisation. In 1925, for instance, concerned voices warned of how the military and political 'civic' education of youth, so firmly in army hands before the war, was steadily being placed in the hands of 'seditious' and 'subversive' movements which 'consider utter destruction as an essential prerequisite to creating a new world'.[22] Such a description did not only fit the communists, but applied equally to *völkisch* (nationalist) groups taking a radical stand against existing political structures and even advocating overthrowing the Weimar Republic by force.

In fact, neither the Red Front nor the National Socialist SA were worried about foreign and security policy issues since their perceived opponents were not found outside Germany's borders, but inside the state itself. Nonetheless, both paramilitary organisations had discovered the difficulty of trying to push through their goals via an attempted *putsch*; and despite the militant followers at their disposal, who were perfectly prepared to use violence, outnumbering any forces the *Reichswehr* could muster, their strategies avoided any direct confrontation of military strength, concentrating their energies instead on a political struggle. The increasing brutality of this struggle since the 1920s, with election meetings ending in mayhem and fist fights, and brawls a normal part of political demonstrations, was not simply a sign that those parties considered force a suitable means in political debate, or that they could draw on the requisite resources: it also acted to cement inclusion and the associations' inner structures. This could be seen in a variety of techniques, not least the language of self-defence, which all sides favoured equally: one did not attack opponents, but merely defended oneself against attacks from others; one did not use violence, but only reacted to the violence used by others. A myriad of speeches, stories and songs evoked and invoked sacrifice and heroic courage, creating rituals of solidarity and a climate of group cohesion, lending the movement new energy and unity.[23]

Every war had set up an interpretative model where military violence was portrayed as passive suffering, with the active perpetrator portrayed as the victim; and the paramilitary associations in the Weimar Republic borrowed from this very same image. Although these groups advocated decidedly anti-civil society attitudes, they generally stopped short of lauding the use of violence for violence's sake, although this did not preclude some of their activists experiencing or enjoying the sort of nihilism so vividly portrayed by Ernst Jünger in his post-war writings. The younger the men were, and the less experience they had, the less moral or political resistance they could offer to such a stance. Yet even so, this attitude never received any official blessing. Rhetoric across the political spectrum decried violence as an end in itself, merely allowing that force might be necessary as a means to an end, but then only defensively, and never as intentionally planned aggression.

But in the everyday political reality, it was hardly possible to distinguish between defensive or aggressive violence, victim or perpetrator. When political groups appeared as an organised mass of men, prepared to use force, this could be understood either as a challenge or as a defensive measure, serving to quell one's own fears as much as to intimidate the opponent. The readiness, prevalent on all sides, to perceive the other as the aggressor, was itself a manifestation of the dynamic inherent in such confrontations, which were so difficult to control. Furthermore, this testified to the weight of a political propaganda denouncing opponents as enemies, even disputing their right to exist, without evoking any reprimand from constitutionally enshrined political institutions, or having any negative consequences at the ballot box. With political thought militarised in this way, the political arena was reduced to categories of war, and spoke of victory and defeat, overpowering enemies and annihilating them. In such a political discourse, the civil process of debate, seeking consensus and negotiation had no place, and compromise was impossible.[24]

In the final analysis, the self-destruction of the political sphere and discourse led to the failure of the Weimar Republic. The roots of Weimar's militarisation process did not feed on front-line experience in the First World War, but in the conflicts over domestic policies and law and order issues that surfaced during the war years, and continued and intensified in the initial post-war period. Paramilitary associations and their martial parades had not initiated the erosion of civil political forms and accepted patterns of debate, even if they reinforced and orchestrated the process; they were an expression of a politics holed and sinking, but not its cause. Despite their numerical strength, the party militias to be found in the milieus on the right and extreme left remained an insignificant military factor and limited in their power to integrate and unify: after all, the republican *Reichsbanner* could boast far more members than the *Stahlhelm*, SA and communist combat units combined.

Furthermore, the figures specifically for young men in organisations show the vast majority were not involved in paramilitary associations but had joined sports and soccer clubs.[25] Of course, these clubs were not isolated from the trends shaping the 1920s and early 1930s either, which also embraced an ideal of masculine decisiveness and resolution, and demanded discipline and self-determination. Nonetheless, sport followed another logic than the army and war; its object was competition in a game, testing each other's strength, but not gradually wearing down opponents and then liquidating them. Apparently, most young men were content to assert their 'manliness' in competition in sport and the *Körperkultur* (physical culture) movements prominent at the time. They would have had difficulty in underwriting the idea that 'the basic nature of man [is] primarily fulfilled by a soldier's estate'. Consequently, despite the efforts of the *Reichswehr* and the paramilitary organisations, rather than the soldier being the measure of all things male in the Weimar Republic, the ultimate ideal was the sportsman.[26]

2. Soldiers and *Volksgenossen*: The Escalation of Violence under the Nazis

From 1933 on, this ranking was turned upside down. Once the National Socialists had legally attained power and formed a government, they used their position to stamp their political goals and vision of a new order on every area of society, destroying any alternative models. Their internal 'enemies', whether social democrats, communists, liberals, Jews, pacifists or feminists, had no chance to develop an alternative stance and publicly express their views, and their organisations either underwent the process of 'coordination' (*Gleichschaltung*), or were destroyed, with their members physically threatened, persecuted, or forced into migration. At the same time, the new government hastened to inject institutions with the key specific National Socialist concepts intended to shape and inspire the entire population – and for men, this entailed a primary self-definition as soldiers, where evolving a martial spirit and developing 'military virtues' ranked as core concerns.

After 1933, the discourse of soldierly masculinity, clearly discernible during the National Socialists' early 'years of struggle' (*Kampfzeiten*), grew steadily more inclusive and more dominant. In this, they adhered to the precept announced at the very inception of the National Socialist programme in Hitler's *Mein Kampf*: men were to be trained as soldiers from their earliest childhood. Schools were only to shoulder a part of this task; the rest devolved onto youth organisations, with the army as the last stage, applying the final finishing touches. But sports clubs and students' associations were also expected to play their part in transforming men into soldiers, as was the Labour Service (*Arbeitsdienst*), already established in 1931. In the end, the only institutions outside this combined effort to train men as soldiers and transmit the ethos of combat were the family and the Christian churches; they alone presented a different set of values to the emerging male generation.

Actually, the stress given to youth military training by the National Socialists was nothing new, and merely followed a long-standing tradition. The early nineteenth century too had witnessed plans to include military training in the curriculum for boys, and later the democrats and SPD had called for similar measures before the German Youth League (*Jungdeutschland-Bund*) took on young men's pre-military training shortly before the First World War. Such training seemed to have a new urgency in the Weimar Republic, since there was no conscripted military service to reinforce the skills learnt, while any universal school of 'military capability' foundered on the rocks of foreign policy concerns, domestic policy mistrust and demarcation disputes over areas of competence. Even the National Governing Board for Youth Fitness (*Reichskuratorium für Jugendertüchtigung*), founded in 1932 specifically with this remit and active *Reichswehr* officer support, never managed to go beyond merely recommending outdoor athletics and exercise camps, but fell short of ordering compulsory participation.[27] When the National Socialists came to power, this voluntary approach soon changed.

National Socialism's vehemence in trying to impose its own *Weltanschauung*, its zeal in 'coordinating' social institutions, and the destructive energy it unleashed, spun it away from accepted areas and into entirely new orbits. The Nazis may have cited formal links to the initiatives in the early 1930s, but strait jacketed these into a unified ideology, subjecting them to far more rigid controls. By 1936, 60 per cent of all children and adolescents belonged to the Hitler Youth, and by 1939 membership was compulsory; male youths aged between 10 to 18 received a training shaped by military forms and ideals, learning not only the principle of order and obedience, but march-pasts and march steps, and all types of military sports, including field exercises and rifle practice. Military influence similarly shaped the six-month period of labour service for young men, made obligatory in 1935. Labour service conscripts were even dubbed 'soldiers of labour'; they lived in camps, subject to rigorous discipline and a strict hierarchy. Moreover, this notion of service formed a conceptual link to the military, with labour service placed on a par with conscription: both were service for the 'national community' (*Volksgemeinschaft*), and a selfless act stemming from an inner conviction without need for any financial remuneration. Both marked the rite of passage for a young man from mere *Reichsangehöriger* to the full citizenship of *Reichsbürger*, but also leading to the status of *Volksgenosse* (national comrade) as a member of the racially-based 'national community'.[28]

As National Socialist politicians and ideologues never ceased to emphasise, military service was the crowning glory in this progression. Hitler commonly drew on his own front line experience in the 1914–18 war, portraying the soldier's estate as the pinnacle of achievement, although he had a second agenda too. Rather than wanting to revitalise the old adage, popular since the nineteenth century, of the army as the 'training school for the entire nation', Hitler's eulogies to the martial male German were inspired far more by his own ambitious foreign policy goals. He needed a strong, efficient army, backed by an unrelenting rearmament programme, to reverse the result of the 1914–18 war, regain 'political power' and push for territorial expansion. Clearly, such aims required conscription, and its reintroduction had in fact been on the NSDAP agenda since 1920. A professional, voluntary army would never have reached the proportions Hitler needed to turn his massive expansion plans into reality.[29]

The *Reichswehr* contained many who received his ideas with open arms. Although they were initially sceptical about the National Socialist government, their reserve evaporated once Hitler had instituted the army as the second pillar of the state, next to the NSDAP, and underlined its position through shrewd political manoeuvring and status-enhancing symbolic practices. The officers' other concern was the SA, which had grown phenomenally since 1930, numbering 3.5 million after absorbing the *Stahlhelm*, veterans' and regimental associations in 1933. But once the 'Night of the Long Knives' of June 1934 had left the SA effectively neutralized, the question of whether Hitler would leave the monopoly of violence with the army seemed resolved in the army's favour. This shift in military power, though, did not solely benefit the *Wehrmacht*; it also levered the SS into a powerful position. Their strictly organised troops, firm believers in the Nazi world-view and under almost monastic structures, claimed to be concentrating on internal policy and policing tasks; the small elite body they comprised appeared to pose no real threat to army provenance as the mass-movement SA had done.[30] Furthermore, the military's energies were increasingly channelled into the high-pressure rearmament programme and intense war preparations that took on ever clearer contours after, at the latest, 1936.

National Socialist policy on war preparations had long called for conscription to be reintroduced, despite its being prohibited under the Versailles Peace Treaty. The announcement of imminent draft legislation was made in March 1935, with the new Army Law coming into force only two months later, signalising the intention that 'once again, from now on, safeguarding the honour and security of the German empire [is entrusted to] the German nation's own strength'. The National Socialists justified this move by reference to France's armament plans, where military service had just been extended to two years, while army minister von Blomberg cited the Prussian military reformer Scharnhorst in the *Völkischer Beobachter* Nazi newspaper, invoking the defence of '*Lebensraum*' (living-space) as the 'free man's most noble right', reminding readers that 'the German *Volk* had always seen conscription as the irreplaceable *school of the nation*, the school of discipline, and comradeship, and the practical expression of the national community'.[31] Firmly resting his case on premises of defence was designed to appease Allied objections to this flagrant breach of Versailles, and simultaneously dispel any reservations the broad German public might have had.

Yet despite the waves of propaganda sweeping the media, the new law left many unconvinced, and some even totally opposed. The exiled SPD noted in its reports on Germany in 1935 that, with the exception of *Stahlhelm* and veterans' associations' members, no 'genuine enthusiasm' for the draft could be found anywhere. Although support was especially forthcoming in 'middle-class circles', it continued, welcoming the move as a foreign policy coup and an expression of the government's political resolve, with the older generation glad to see 'young people being kept on a tight rein', learning 'order and discipline', the 'young people' themselves were more ambivalent. Some could hardly wait to don their army uniform, while others 'moan because they are expected to do military service after already doing labour service'. Few of them, though, seem to have shared the fears aroused in many older people of a link between rearmament and conscription feeding a possible new war. Apparently, many young men saw war as an 'inevitable act of fate' and had no hesitation about 'thoroughly preparing for it inwardly'.[32]

Spread through public media channels and institutions, the propaganda message of military prowess (*Wehrhaftigkeit*) specifically addressed this group. Despite the message being adapted to fit Hitler's official protestations of peace, it was couched in terms of war to come. The three key words here were *Kampf, Opfer* and *Gemeinschaft* – struggle, sacrifice and community. In the 'heroic struggle', fought not only outwardly, but inwardly with himself, the German male was to 'glimpse the ultimate principle of life'; he was not only expected to deal with the enemy of the *Volk* harshly, but also to carry on a similarly 'determined struggle' in the battle to overcome his 'personal flaws, especially gentleness and over-exaggerated sensitivity'. Making a 'sacrifice for the *Volk*' was then the 'highest honour' for the 'combat-ready fighter', and this sacrifice was demanded not to attain the single individual's happiness, but to benefit the 'welfare of the whole' – and this led to community, the third word cited by every NS teacher and functionary: 'National

Socialist education will always be a schooling to community, as has long been practised in the SA and the HJ [Hitler Youth].' Its 'ultimate form' was found in conscripted military service, above all, in the comradeship of 'fellow fighters' and, consequently, the very zenith was reached with 'comradeship in war', eulogized as the perfect form of the '*völkisch* (national) community'.[33]

These three words comprised the prism refracting the National Socialist state's concept of a person into the patterns of how its male citizens should behave. It was further reinforced by the NS party and the *Wehrmacht* (the post-1935 *Reichswehr*), both seemingly taking a unified stance on these issues, identifying themselves in the discourse of service to the *völkisch* state, and affirming the 'same fundamental military approach'. Where the party perceived itself as the 'German nation's prime teacher of political concerns', the army was its 'school for soldiers' and 'sole arms bearer'; where the party asserted the notion of a 'political soldiership', the *Wehrmacht* set itself the educative task of producing 'not merely well-trained fighters and masters of arms, but a man conscious of his national identity (*Volkstum*) and his general duties to the state'. To cite war minister Blomberg from 1935, this training of youths naturally took place 'in the National Socialist spirit and following the will of the commander in chief'.[34]

Conservatives at the time might have thought the *Wehrmacht* would provide an effective check to the NS party but the reality, though, after this open avowal of what Blomberg called the 'community of will' (*Willensgemeinschaft*), looked very different. In fact, the exiled SPD reported in June 1935 that the 'vast majority of the population' regarded 'the introduction of conscription as an advance' since 'it would lead to the brown uniforms [SA] disappearing from the public sphere'. Many believed the *Wehrmacht* was 'not so strongly bound to the party line as the hordes under the thumb of Hitler's party bosses', and appeared to provide 'greater security' than that 'brown mob'. Although such views might be taken to imply underlying opposition to the National Socialist regime, there were almost identical criticisms expressed by the SA itself: 'They all feel that their time of glory is over, they have been neutralised, and will be put under Prussian drill, where only the Prussian officer matters.'[35]

However, such assumed crass differences between the *Wehrmacht* officer and the NS fighter faded steadily into insignificance as acceptance of National Socialism became widespread among Prussian officers with, from 1934 on, their swearing-in ceremony including a personal oath of absolute obedience to Hitler. The *Wehrmacht* might have been concerned about preserving its own sphere of independence, constantly complaining of interference from lower- and mid-range party officials, welcoming the dissolution of the NSDAP's army policy office (*Wehrpolitisches Amt*) and the army law stipulation suspending party membership for active soldiers, but it also assiduously supported the basic tenets behind National Socialist leadership, wore the swastika on its steel helmets, uniforms and headgear, introduced the 'comradely greeting' (*kameradschaftlicher Gruß*) for all party affiliations, and dispatched troops to take part in national party rallies and other party events.[36]

Moreover, the *Wehrmacht*'s readiness to fulfil tasks in the party's racist programme also indicates how its concern centred on organisational control, and not on distancing itself from the National Socialists' political standpoint or worldview. Its contribution to 'a National Socialist education for the young German man' inculcated the soldier's belief in belonging to a superior race, and the duty to defend it. For this reason, soldiers were admonished never to buy from Jewish shops nor have anything to do with Jews privately; neither were they to marry a woman of 'non-Aryan descent'. Furthermore, the 1935 Army Law only allowed men of 'Aryan descent' to perform military service and be promoted in the army.[37] Non-Aryans, and above all, Jews, were excluded from this 'honorary service for the German *Volk*'.

They were 'liable for service' and had to appear at the mustering, but were then transferred to an 'on furlough' status; 'service at arms', the 'principal part of military service', was not open to them – since this should 'be and remain the prerogative and honorary privilege of the German men belonging to the *Staatsvolk*'.[38] In propounding such views, National Socialism had shifted the borders of exclusion into new realms, locating them far beyond any earlier efforts at exclusion, or provisions regulating it, in the nineteenth or twentieth century. From 1933 on, anti-Semitism, long present in the officers' corps, was established as a ruling principle and rigidly applied throughout all the Third Reich's institutions and organisations. It was not to be expected that the army would prove an exception to the rule and yet the Jewish population saw it as an especially dramatic signal of their general disenfranchisement and humiliation. From the Jewish perspective, the struggle for acceptance from the late eighteenth century on had come to focus on military inclusion, with equality in conscription symbolising civic integration. Even in the Weimar Republic, the national association of Jewish front-line veterans (*Reichsbund jüdischer Frontsoldaten*) had energetically countered numerous attempts to defame Jews as anti-national shirkers, but with one stroke of the legislative pen, the National Socialists made short shrift of any such argument. While Imperial Germany had at least allowed converted Jews the chance to become reserve officers, the National Socialist policy rejected any such compromise. From now on, the only thing that counted was 'race' and 'blood'.[39]

When, in 1935, the Nuremberg Laws excluded Jews from Reich citizenship, they spelled out a principle already applied in the Army Law passed a few months earlier. From 1933 on, Jews had already been removed from all public and civil service posts, but the Army Law provisions prescribed the far more radical and comprehensive step of denying Jews citizenship altogether. 'The Jew', it bluntly stated, 'cannot perform active military service', a move that left Jews permanently ostracised. The force of such anti-Jewish legislation can be gauged better if one bears in mind the prestige attaching to the military under the National Socialists, and how fervent were the calls for every young man to dedicate himself, actively and personally, to military skills and proficiency in them. By excluding Jews from an all-encompassing German male community centred on combat, struggle, sacrifice and service, they could neither be comrades in war or peace, nor a part of the 'community of fate binding the German *Volk*', leaving them both defenceless and dishonoured.[40]

As anti-Semitic propaganda and policies grew more vitriolic, Jewish exclusion from the *Wehrmacht* became more relentless. Applications submitted appealing to the few exceptions allowed under the Army Law were simply no longer processed after 1936, and, especially after the war had started, cases of 'mixed Jewish race' (*jüdische Mischlinge*) were treated far more rigidly too. Under the original legislation, they had been obliged to, and entitled to, perform military service, just like 'people of ethnic German origins', but could not be promoted. From 1940 on, though, men whose 'blood' was 50 per cent from 'Jewish origins' could no longer become soldiers, and were to be discharged immediately if they had already been enlisted. Hitler personally decided on any exceptions to this rule, and granted the last one in 1942. The only 'mixed Jewish race' soldiers allowed to remain in the *Wehrmacht* were those classified as 'second degree *Mischlinge*' (with one Jewish grandparent); these alone were considered worthy of 'being absorbed into the German people', even occasionally being promoted.[41]

The National Socialist's fervour in drawing absolute external boundaries to exclude those banished on racial grounds from the '*Staatsvolk*' was paralleled by the energies invested in removing barriers within the *Volk* itself. National Socialism's credo in social policy maintained that the racially defined 'national community' had no classes or castes, and the *Wehrmacht* particularly was expected to be living proof of this tenet. If the army wanted to be 'a national and social crucible to shape the new German man', then, as Hitler put it in 1934, it had to avoid its former 'lordly arrogance' at all costs. In his view, officers should not erect barriers against their troops, but meet them on a comradely level. It was a view underlined in a secret order issued by von Blomberg in 1934, calling for the 'idea of the national community to infuse our social life. There is no justification for prejudices based solely on origin and education'. He went on to remind particularly those new officers appointed in the wake of *Wehrmacht* expansion to free themselves from any such notions and, instead of vaunting military qualifications, bring with them the requisite racial awareness and National Socialist attitudes.[42] Established officers too received reminders that comradeship did not only stop with the rank of lieutenant, but ought to be extended to the troops, who all deserved the same comradely treatment. Recruits, they were told, should not be 'ground down', but 'schooled' and 'led'; their personal honour was not to be disgraced by crude swearwords or, in the worst case, maltreatment. As the 'Duties of German Soldiers' announced in 1934, comradeship provided a basis for that 'unbreakable combat community' (*Kampfgemeinschaft*) of 'Führer and troops', vital for any 'major achievements', either in war or in peace.[43]

Imperial Germany had repeatedly experienced calls for this sort of comradely concern, and the Weimar Republic *Reichswehr* had aspired to something similar, yet under National Socialism the image of comradeship bridging class boundaries became a core icon. Rather than just being immanent in calls for 'communal use before personal use' or putting the *Führergedanke* into practice and submitting to leadership, it infused an attitude that acknowledged the primacy of 'achievement' and blocked any other channels of promotion. Such moves appeared essential given that the soldiers recruited into the *Wehrmacht* after the end of 1935 represented quite another 'sort' from their fathers or grandfathers who had served in the Imperial German army; as many officers confirmed, these new recruits were not only more critical and aware, but had also been far more politically shaped. After all, they had already passed through the ideological and mental 'training' of the HJ and Labour Service and had learnt to reject any class and caste notions in favour of the racial boundary defining the German 'national community'.[44]

To meet the challenge of, as Foertsch put it, 'exemplifying National Socialism' convincingly, the *Wehrmacht* even voluntarily agreed to forego one Prussian military institution existing between 1813 and 1918: the one-yearer volunteer service. In 1925, Hitler's eulogies on the traditional army and the place allocated to it in a programme of national education already noted that 'the one-year voluntary arrangement might be the only flaw'. Ten years later, the one-yearer status was excluded from the Army Law, which instead established a unified period of service for one year, increased to two years from 1936; the former privilege derived from education and property was abolished, and all recruits treated equally. This move simultaneously left greater freedom for upward mobility inside army structures. In contrast to the pre-1918 situation, where reserve officers had exclusively been recruited from middle-class one-yearers (no longer needed in the Weimar period), the Third Reich accepted anyone 'with a good military training' as a reserve officer, providing they were of 'Aryan descent' and could prove their 'financial affairs were in order'; candidates no longer needed to show they had attended the higher school grades, as in Imperial Germany.[45] In this way, the National Socialist *Wehrmacht* established more genuinely egalitarian or 'socialist' structures than its predecessor.

Although various moves buttressed officer status, for example, reintroducing military jurisdiction and keeping the courts of honour established under the Weimar Republic, officers were simultaneously exposed to greater political pressure and felt the party's mistrust towards them. After the Second World War broke out in 1939, the NSDAP demanded more from officers than mere pledges of loyalty. Instead, every officer had to acknowledge National Socialist beliefs unconditionally – an approach culminating in the appointment, after March 1944, of so-called National Socialist conduct officers (*Führungsoffiziere*) attached to all troop commanders, responsible for intensifying political indoctrination both in the troops and the officers, and creating 'a closed and unshakeable National Socialist combat community'.[46] This was not the only way in which the traditional boundaries between the troops, NCOs and officers were made less rigid. The conduct officer was a clear snub to the line officers' function as 'teachers of the proper political will', while in a parallel move, the social barriers to officer status were being dismantled and the very status itself prised from its accepted elitist milieu.

In this way, the *Wehrmacht* came close to fulfilling its expected task of symbolising the 'national community' in its military form. The army met the demand to be socially inclusive too, as from autumn 1935 on increasing numbers of young men received their call-up orders, with 2 million recruits passing through the *Volk*'s 'school of masculinity' by the time the Second World War started. At the end of the war, 18 million had been called up. The rapid increase in losses during and after 1943 completely exhausted all the reserve forces. With more than 2 million soldiers being enlisted in 1943 alone and another 1.3 million in the second half of 1944, demand vastly outstripped the supply from any year's intake. This increasingly led the military to resort to age-groups with no previous direct military experience, whom the SA first 'toughened up' by training military sports. Steadily younger age-groups were also enlisted. When war started, draftees had to be twenty years old or older, but by 1943–4, teenagers of 17 were already being called-up. The initial age limits gradually dissolved at both ends of the scale as the war fronts closed in on German territory, with the final reserves consisting of the *Volkssturm* (people's militia) with men between 16 and 60, and boys drawn from the ranks of the Hitler Youth.[47]

But whatever age they were, those called up were always male; fighting was considered too onerous for women. In 1940, it was noted that female active participation in combat aligned 'so little with a woman's particular nature, character and abilities' that it was better not to involve them; moreover, training female battalions would 'certainly not increase ... the army's combat strength'. This view was confirmed by the *Wehrmacht* supreme command in 1942, explicitly reiterating that: 'The "female soldier" is not in keeping with our National Socialist idea of womanhood'.[48] But this attitude was far less rigid than it seemed to be in the 1920s and early 1930s, and even though in *Mein Kampf* Hitler only hit on the idea of giving women the task of being soldiers' mothers, the spectrum of potential female roles had in fact widened considerably. Most girls had voluntarily joined the Hitler Youth before 1939, when membership for them became compulsory – a year that also saw Labour Service being made obligatory for young women too. After 1941, the service term was extended by six months, and tasks were expanded beyond the standard work on the land to cover munitions factories, hospitals or military and civil administrations, where women were often employed in areas far removed from their so-called 'nature-specific' jobs: Hitler's 'total war' left no space for those ideological niceties propounded in speeches by armchair politicians.[49]

But it did not lead to the gender borders being entirely eroded either; after all, one major National Socialist project had been directed towards preserving and fortifying them. The *Wehrmacht* might have counted nearly half a million women among its numbers in 1943–4, but this was still only a twentieth of the entire army strength. Moreover, army commanders had been instructed to avoid at all costs moves that might lead to the 'militarisation of women'. In keeping with Hitler's dictum, even in the military women had to be given jobs reflecting their 'female nature' and treated accordingly; on the other hand, men in army service ought to be immunised against any 'softening or effeminising'. Ensuring women were given 'suitable' tasks was relatively easy when they were working in field hospitals, offices or for the telephone services, but was more tricky when they were deployed to assist on anti-aircraft guns. Nonetheless, even as late as March 1945, the supreme army command affirmed the basic principle that women and girls should not generally 'be called on to use firearms in the battle against the enemy' – although this principle was not necessarily enforced if women volunteered for the work.[50]

On the home front, women's deployment was voluntary too, until 1943. Since the start of the war, the Nazis had been calling for women to take over traditionally male jobs to allow the men to go to the front, a stance already indicated by the wording of the Army Law, which stated that, in the case of war, 'every German man and German woman' had the duty of 'serving the fatherland'. There followed further provisions in 1938, 1939 and 1941 detailing exactly how this duty was to be realised, but they never came into force. Just as in the First World War, no-one doubted that men were liable to take on official duties – but the political implications of expanding this policy to women made the National Socialists hesitant to broaden its application. Hitler, primarily, believed that the morale and stamina of his troops would be bolstered, encouraging their perseverance and doggedness, if they knew their wives and families were well cared for, and not burdened with additional duties. Given this context, it was no surprise Hitler preferred to use millions of 'non-Germans' as forced labour, and also allowed numerous exceptions and possible appeals when women's registration was finally introduced in 1943–4.[51]

Not surprisingly then, although the concept of service, along with 'struggle' and 'sacrifice', stood at the very heart of the NS ideology, it meant something different for men and women. There was a common basis, where both genders had their role within the 'national community', but their service cashed out in different ways. Women's service was located, first and foremost, in their own family. There, serving the *Volk* meant blessing their husbands with a happy home life and producing and raising children for Hitler's state. In contrast, men's service was both more abstract and yet more direct. In military service, but equally in the Labour Service, their service directly benefited the 'national community', giving visible expression to the much-vaunted tenet of 'communal use before personal use'. A man's efforts were not measured against the benchmark of personal interests or individual rights, but against the duty of benefiting the *Volk* or 'nation'. Individual rights rested on a 'racially determined membership of the German people', and this imposed the duty of 'community-related' agency, and each person's active affirmation of their status. Under Hitler, the 'liberally-predetermined' term 'citizen' was frowned on, replaced by the national comrade (*Volksgenosse*), only attainable by first fulfilling 'the duties of a national comrade to the national community', and submitting oneself to the 'discipline of shared service'.[52]

The resolute de-individualising and 'normative comradeship' inherent in such 'national honorary service' were echoed in the rituals and ceremonies around it. Imperial Germany had sought to transform army entry into a performance, but they never came close to Nazi bombast, where enlistment into the *Wehrmacht* became a staged event, utilising arcane symbols of communal, *völkisch* experience. Being sworn-in took on the character of a 'communal' ceremony, one a recruit was expected to remember forever, representing 'the major event of his life', where he vividly experienced both 'national unity' and how he merged, as an individual, with the 'national community'. Drum rolls accompanied heavy guns and pyramids of weapons to form the backdrop for the oath, and it was considered especially impressive to be sworn in 'in the darkness, lit by torches'. The features of the recruits were hardly discernible in the half-light as they recited the oath, and those whose fathers had fallen in the First World War stepped forward to place their hands on the adjutant's sabre; a gesture testifying how their fathers' legacy lived on in the sons' generation. Distributing the recruits' weapons was similarly embedded in a ceremonial form, with suitable music to underscore the drama of the event.[53]

In this sense, the Third Reich went far beyond the borders of Imperial Germany's military tradition in a number of ways. Of course, the National Socialists borrowed Wilhelminian military traditions, both formally and rhetorically, reinstigating the personal bond between the soldier and the supreme commander, in this instance Hitler, returning to conscription and a military criminal code, reviving reserve officer status, re-accentuating the army's significance as a site of male education, and reformulating the military as an embodiment of national *völkisch* unity. Yet it represented a marked break with the past in the organisation of command structures, and especially in the ideological content given to military service – and both trends were crucially important in the Third Reich's new kind of internecine war.

This sort of war required innovations in three main areas. Firstly, there was the need for a centrally organised structure. The *Wehrmacht* had inherited a central structure from the *Reichswehr*, but it had only existed in Imperial Germany during the First World War. Under the Nazis, it was tightened further when the *Wehrmacht*, along with many other Reich institutions, was brought under a strict, centralised control system. The desire to want all the reins of power in Berlin similarly led to the *Land*'s status as an independent political unit being revoked.

Secondly, Hitler, as the army's supreme commander, steadily absorbed greater areas of competence in decision-making and influence, leaving the military leadership largely disempowered from, at the latest, 1938. In contrast to the First World War, with what one might call a military dictatorship by the supreme army command, the Second World War saw the 'political soldier' Hitler setting the guidelines for his generals, and giving them direct orders. Since the NS state was designed from the start for war and battle, it would be absurd to maintain that Hitler steered by the lodestar of a 'civil policy', subsuming the 'trade of war' under 'statesmanship' (in Ritter's terms). The most obvious difference between Wilhelminian Germany and the Third Reich lies precisely in the way the political sphere was infused by the military and vice versa. To talk of 'militarism', as the Allies did in the post-1945 years, assumes, in purely semantic terms, a border between the military and political spheres. However, they overlooked the fact that, for the National Socialists, this border had long been entirely dismantled.

Thirdly, the characteristic National Socialist notion of a 'political soldiership' had a direct influence on military service and the experience of individual soldiers and officers. In contrast to Imperial Germany, military service in the Third Reich was not the first experience a young man had of performing a social and political service for his *Volk* or nation. Military service was certainly considered the jewel in the crown of the *völkisch* and nationalist canon of duties, embedded in the requisite ceremonies, but those young recruits in the light of the flaring torches ready to step forward and perform their 'honorary service' had, as a rule, already passed through other institutions (HJ, Labour Service) where they had acquired both practical paramilitary skills and National Socialist beliefs. By being integrated into a chain of institutions, sharing similar views, military service took on a characteristic political and ideological tint. In comparison to 1871–1918, with officers' corps training the troops to be loyal to the king, love their fatherland, and obey the laws, the National Socialists' educational programme – which the army also had to adhere to – was both more comprehensive and, at the same time, more exclusive. In addition to political enemies, its primary concern was to fight 'racial' enemies, denying them any chance of conversion – indeed, denying them the right to exist at all.

Under the National Socialist *Wehrmacht*, wars were fought with soldiers and officers holding other political beliefs and values than in the Imperial Germany army. Convinced of their 'racial superiority', the National Socialist troops fought, in particular on the eastern and south-eastern fronts, against *'Untermenschen'* (subhumans), and treated them accordingly. In the final analysis, the unprecedented brutalisation of the *Wehrmacht* on the eastern front and in the Balkans can be attributed, in particular, to the long-term and determined indoctrination of this racist ideology. It was this that helped officers and soldiers transgress previous standards and principles governing the use of military force, carrying out orders that made a mockery of all ethical norms and rules of international law, and it was this racist ideology that even transformed the murder of Jewish civilians, men, women and children, into a legitimate act of war: they may have been unarmed but were nevertheless classified as partisans, members of an 'organised world Jewry', an 'enemy' that had allegedly declared war on National Socialist Germany. And for this reason, they could be called to account.[54]

3. Post-war Germany: From Disarmed to Rearmed State

In 1945, such logic found itself completely at odds with the Allied charges against Germany for having engaged in a criminal, aggressive war, requiring suitable punishment. The last edition of the army report (*Wehrmachtsbericht*), dated 9 May 1945, may have claimed that, after 'nearly six years of heroic struggle', every soldier could 'lay down their weapons, honourably and proudly', but the Allies took a profoundly different view in the immediate post-war years. Allied protocols and directives spoke of German 'Nazism' and 'militarism' destroying world peace, needing to be eliminated forever – a policy aim requiring not only a far-reaching programme of denazification and re-education but the complete 'demilitarisation' of the country: industrial disarmament, a complete moratorium on any rearmament, disbanding and dissolving the army, and bringing suspected war criminals to trial. At the Nuremberg war crimes trials, leading National Socialist officials were prosecuted along with high-ranking officers, and even if the international tribunal found itself unable to condemn the army general staff and supreme command as a criminal organisation, the court left no doubt about their opinion that *Wehrmacht* members 'actively participated in all these crimes, or sat silent and acquiescent', and consequently could not escape personal responsibility.[55]

Although tens of thousands of officers and common soldiers were tried in the post-war years, the public sphere quickly embraced the legend of a 'normal' war and an 'innocent' German army. Despite this belief being fuelled by the Nuremberg trials' collective acquittal of the army as an organisation, and high-ranking generals excusing their actions publicly in autobiographical tracts, it derived, first and foremost, from the general readiness of the population to see themselves primarily in the victim role – victims of Hitler and National Socialism, victims of the war, victims of displacement and victims of bombing raids on German cities.[56] Soldiers, especially, tended to adopt this victim status, giving it a centrality, both actively and passively, in their perception of themselves: first sacrificing themselves for their *Volk* before then falling victim to the foreign power. Political considerations, too, made it seem reasonable to remove any blanket ascription of guilt to the *Wehrmacht* as such, and avoid any equation of the military with 'militarism'. Such concerns, though, had less to do with a desire to salvage the individual honour of any particular *Wehrmacht* members who had not taken part in war crimes, such as shooting Soviet commissars, liquidating hostages, or murdering Jewish civilians, and much more to do with the overall long-term goal of (re)building armies in eastern and western Germany to be integrated into the East's and West's military blocs, where they were supposed to help each respective bloc pursue its Cold War aims.[57]

In contrast to the First World War, this time the Allies insisted on Germany's complete demilitarisation, leaving the dual founding of the western Federal Republic of Germany (FRG) and the eastern German Democratic Republic (GDR) as decidedly 'civil' affairs. Neither the FRG nor the GDR had their own army, relying on the Allied troops stationed on either side of the German–German border to secure their territory externally, and guarantee their statehood. This accorded not only with the occupying powers' remit but harmonised with the mood among the public at large. As SPD politician Carlo Schmid put it in 1946, 'We never want to send our sons into the barracks again!' – a view prevailing far into the 1950s, with most Germans rejecting any moves to remilitarise. When the first post-war West German Chancellor Konrad Adenauer commissioned a small group of former *Wehrmacht* officers in 1950 to debate moves to possible rearmament, they despondently noted a continuing lack of '*military will* (*Wehrwille*) in many circles', with the humiliations of the previous five years 'systematically undermining' any 'notions of defending the country', leaving the population without any 'assertive will'. But, they continued, it was time to stop 'maligning the German soldier', and called on both the western Allies and the FRG government to issue a full declaration of honour and initiate 'moves to change public opinion abroad and at home'; only in this way, they claimed, could the FRG release the '*military power* (*Wehrkraft*)' that was 'definitely present in the German people' and use it 'to fill the major gap in the European Atlantic defence'.[58]

The declaration of honour soon became reality. In 1951, the supreme commander of NATO forces, General Eisenhower, let it be known that he had rethought his 1945 position that 'the *Wehrmacht* and the Hitler gang were all the same', and undergone a change of heart: 'The German soldier fought bravely and honourably for his homeland.' In 1952, Adenauer stated his government's position to parliament:

We recognize all those of our countrymen who in the framework of high soldierly traditions fought honourably on land, on sea, and in the air. We are convinced that the good name and the great achievement of the German soldier, despite all aspersions of past years, still lives and will remain alive in our people. It must be our task, and I am sure that we shall solve it, to blend the moral virtues of the German soldier with democracy.[59]

Adenauer, borrowing the diction of the last army report, built a bridge from the old *Wehrmacht* to the new Bundeswehr; it was one that would be crossed by many ex-*Wehrmacht* officers in the years to come.

Ex-*Wehrmacht* members were active too in the GDR (whose government issued no such declaration of honour), helping set up the *Nationale Volksarmee* (NVA). Although the East German socialist-communist party, the SED, and the GDR government officially clung to an image of the *Wehrmacht* as an organisation of 'reactionary militarism', and an 'instrument of criminal leadership', they nonetheless energetically integrated former professional and reserve officers into newly formed 'national armed forces' structures, but they ensured that important commanding positions always remained firmly in the hands of trusted SED members. In a further move, the GDR's founding of the National Democratic Party (NDPD) in 1948 created a political pool to receive former *Wehrmacht* soldiers, offering them a chance to become actively involved in 'constructing a new Germany' and thereby combining national and socialist notions in a new way. The NDPD were then the main driving force behind the 1952 amnesty law, ratified by the GDR parliament, lifting all special political regulations on *Wehrmacht* officers.[60]

In West Germany too, the FRG government put out similar integration signals, responding to the vociferous demands made by veterans' associations. In parliament, the centrist liberal FDP party was especially active in taking up their cause, linking the building of what Erich Mende called the 'new *Wehrmacht*' to a comprehensive 'psychological' and material rehabilitation of the 'old' one.[61] It was an argument that touched a sore point, even if their general stance rejecting any blanket ascription of guilt, including cases of proven war crimes, clearly overstepped the mark and led them into political isolation. Nonetheless, if the Federal government actually intended to set up a 500,000 strong army in the near future, as it had indicated, it needed to incorporate the requisite numbers of officers and NCOs, and these could only be drawn from old army personnel. It would take some years before they would be able to find commanders and troop leaders trained in the 'new ethos'.

But whatever ethos it was, old or new, many contemporaries felt they were ridden over roughshod by this volte-face in military policy, viewing it with undisguised scepticism when they saw that the same politicians who had vehemently called for an unarmed state in 1949 were now equally vociferous in their pleas for remilitarisation. The sudden swing led some commentators to claim that this indicated the resurgence of previously repressed military leanings, but it was, in fact, driven purely by the logical pursuit of political interests. From no later than the start of the Korean War in 1950, it was obvious that, from at least the US, British and Soviet perspective, the East–West confrontation had replaced the original denazification and de-militarisation leitmotifs in Allied policy on Germany. In both East and West Germany, the transformation from defeated to ally took place under the shadow of security policy concerns. In this way, re-militarisation in both German states was, on the one hand, a condition of their political empowerment while, on the other hand, the price for that power was being bound tightly into the respective western or eastern blocs, with their systems of pacts and alliances.[62]

In 1954, with the signing of the Paris treaty, the Federal Republic became a sovereign state with the right to an independent defence and foreign policy. It simultaneously accepted limits to its armaments autonomy, agreeing not to stockpile A, B or C weapons, or set up its own armed forces general staff. In additional provisions, the Federal Republic agreed to place its army under NATO supreme command in cases of crisis or conflict, allow NATO liaison officers to inspect all military institutions and operations, and have NATO states' troops stationed on its territory. Irrespective of these provisions, the Allies continued to maintain contingents of occupying forces on West German territory to safeguard their previous 'rights and responsibilities in relation to Berlin and Germany as a whole'.[63]

Establishing the Federal Republic's Bundeswehr over the coming years was a process embedded within this thoroughly complex network of international treaties where FRG sovereignty gains were subject to a closely knit system of international controls. It was a process accompanied by domestic difficulties that were nearly greater than the ones in the foreign policy arena. Although the 1953 elections left Adenauer and his centre-right coalition with a massive two-thirds majority and theoretically sufficient backing to push through any necessary changes to the constitution's Basic Law (*Grundgesetz*) without opposition support, the key difficulty did not lie in the parliamentary chamber. Outside, large union factions had joined women and youth groups and the Protestant church to form a front at best sceptical, and at worst directly opposed to the government's main security policy guidelines. At the start of 1955, before ratification of the German sovereignty and NATO treaties, 'leading figures in public life' made their way to the Frankfurt *Paulskirche*, symbol of national unity and liberty since 1848, to protest against moves towards establishing German armed forces on either side of the Iron Curtain, arguing that this remilitarisation would 'extinguish the chance of reunification for an indefinite time and reinforce the tension between East and West'.[64] In the end, the left-of-centre SPD echoed the same argument in their refusal to back the Paris treaties in the parliamentary ratification process. It was a line they maintained throughout 1954–6, resisting legislation designed to pave the way for the new Bundeswehr. SPD support only came for one provision, guaranteeing 'the armed forces would never again become a state within a state'.

Government policy advocated transferring ultimate command and authority to the defence minister, or the Chancellor in case of war, ensuring that 'the civil power of the parliamentary government' had primacy and preventing the sort of constellation found in the Weimar Republic after 1926 when high-ranking officers and state presidents colluded in setting military policy goals without recourse to government or parliamentary consent. Parliamentary controls over the military were strengthened too by ceding board of inquiry rights to the parliamentary defence committee. The SPD were especially vocal in calling for measures to ensure constitutional rights were observed in the Bundeswehr as well. This led to the post of parliamentary commissioner for the armed forces being created, on the Swedish model, despite major reservations from the ranks of the ruling CDU. The commissioner's task was twofold: firstly, to function as a direct recipient for soldiers' complaints and, secondly, to monitor carefully whether constitutional rights were being respected.[65] Politicians across the spectrum spoke in unison of this starting 'a new chapter' in the history of army–state relations in Germany. But the completely new extent of parliamentary controls and powers to intervene found some claiming the institutionalised 'mistrust' shown towards the 'German soldier' had gone decidedly too far.

Criticism was also voiced over the plans being drawn up for a new kind of soldier under the direction of Wolf Graf von Baudissin at the 'Internal Structure' department in the *Dienststelle Blank* – later the ministry of defence. For some, his principles represented an intervention into the army's traditional model that was at least as radical as the new parliamentary control mechanism.[66] Baudissin's department favoured a concept of the Bundeswehr's internal structure that took the notion of 'citizens in uniform' as their basic guideline. The choice of terms was shrewd, harking back to the *soldat citoyen* or citizen-soldier image that was so much a part of the French and Prussian military reformers' vocabulary in the late eighteenth and early nineteenth centuries, a historical reference intended to assuage those warning of an abrupt break in army tradition and the impossibility of rebuilding the military without the requisite 'awe for traditional role-models'.

But it was not actually too clear which traditions from Prussian and German military history could have been reinstated in the 1950s as a link to the past, since there appeared to be a pronounced dearth of suitable candidates. The new democratic tenor in post-war West Germany would hardly have embraced the Imperial German army ethos or Roon's military structures let alone Weimar's *Reichswehr* or Hitler's *Wehrmacht*. The only viable potential link was rooted in the Prussian period of reforms, with Scharnhorst and Gneisenau as their guiding lights. Unfortunately, though, these two seminal figures had to be shared with a crowd of admirers. It seemed as if everyone concerned with military policy down the years had borrowed these names to vindicate their own stance, from Roon to Moltke, Seeckt to Blomberg and Hitler – and the GDR was even doing the same. Besides, the analogy between 1807 and 1945 could not be stretched too far. After the complete military, moral and political collapse of Germany, there was not going to be any new 1813 and 'war of liberation'. The Bundeswehr was not supposed to be established against the (western) Allied victors of the Second World War, but with them, embodying just those political values the Allies had fought for.

Consequently, as Baudissin elaborated in 1955, the model of the soldier, in a virtually self-referential move, was justified by appealing to the system he was to protect. As a 'citizen in uniform', a soldier was entitled to exactly the same rights as the ones he had to defend outwardly, above all, active and passive franchise, the rights to information and free expression of opinion, and the rights of free association and petition. This was a radical break with all previous army incarnations, where those rights for soldiers had been suspended to keep political quarrels out of the barracks. In future, given the new, constitutionally enshrined respect for political parties and civil political debate being encouraged as a desirable practice, troops engaging in party political discussions were no longer doing something considered 'indecent'. Just as a citizen's political majority did not stop at the barrack gates, so the 'moral value system' guaranteed in the constitution continued to have binding force in the army too; it was the lodestar for every soldier's actions, even for his duty to obey orders.

The issue of obeying orders also firmly broke with the past. The new model soldier was to be moulded around different command practices than those inherited from earlier German army structures. This move signalled a clear distance to the *Wehrmacht*'s 'acting under binding orders' provision, retrospectively invoked by so many army personnel to excuse their own participation in war crimes; it simultaneously paid tribute to those army members involved in the 1944 July Plot against Hitler and, in the face of stiff resistance from many former *Wehrmacht* officers, integrated Stauffenberg and the others involved into the founding moment of Bundeswehr tradition. They might have broken their army oath when they set out to kill Hitler, but in doing so they showed themselves true to that 'moral principle' Baudissin was positing as central in 1955. This principle was supposed to be equally apparent in soldiers' watchfulness against any 'totalitarian' tendencies, i.e., not seeing the enemy as a person, perceiving them as 'the ultimate evil', making moves to 'peace utterly impossible'. This stance simultaneously implied a different conception of war: since 'absolute war could not be humanised', every viable political means had to be employed to avoid it. Wars of aggression were, in any case, 'totally out of the question' and, in reviewing the Second World War and the future nuclear potential, Baudissin felt the 'reality of modern warfare' made it impossible to 'continue thinking in ways staked out in the nineteenth century, seeing war as a long-hoped way "of proving oneself", or an accepted method for states to resolve tensions between them'.

Moreover, the 'citizen in uniform' notion embodied a different relationship between superiors and those under their command, replacing the Wilhelmine 'father' and 'immature children' image with the idea of working together as 'partners'. However, as Baudissin was quick to point out, this did not mean discussing and negotiating orders and commands as 'partners' – there was no place in the army for 'parliamentary processes'. Nonetheless, 'democracy as a way of life' should also be present inside the barrack walls, expressed in an approach as cooperative as possible, limited forms of co-responsibility in the troops, and the avoidance of harsh treatment.

This sort of description makes it clear what a spectrum the notion of '*Innere Führung*' had to bridge – the idea of leadership combining military tasks with upholding constitutional rights, and resolving any conflicts between them. It not only had to reassure critics from within the military, who saw discipline as an immutable element in military force, warning against any moves to water it down, but also to quash the widespread belief that democracy and the military were poles apart, underlining the new army's potential for democratic processes. For this reason, no mention whatsoever was made of special or exclusive military rights, or any reference to reviving courts of honour, or a military criminal code. In Baudissin's view, the armed forces did not aspire to 'any autonomous education for soldiers' any longer, or set themselves up as the absolute model of social education, as in Imperial Germany. The army was not to be the 'school for the nation'. Instead, the 'nation and the state' were to be the 'school for the armed forces'.[67]

Baudissin's ideas were far ahead of his time. Even in 1969, right-of-centre CDU Chancellor Kurt Georg Kiesinger, speaking to the German Federal Armed Forces Association (*Bundeswehrverband*), praised the army as the 'nation's major school for our young people', dismissing the tenet of *Innere Führung* in the same breath as an 'old cliché'. High-ranking generals also sharply criticised Baudissin's ideas, branding them 'unmilitary' and claiming they might have been suited to dispelling the reservations against the new German army commonly found in the domestic public sphere, but that they could hardly be expected to play a role in day-to-day military business – as the parliamentary commissioners for the armed forces in the 1960s were to learn only too well.[68]

The officer and NCO mix was one principal cause behind the adherence to traditional training and leadership styles. In the Bundeswehr, for example, at the end of the 1950s, over 80 per cent of the nearly 15,000 professional officers had already served in the *Wehrmacht*. They had been brought up in the 'spirit of National Socialism', and even if they had officially foresworn it, their concepts of military efficiency and soldierly duties inevitably drew on their pre-1945 experience. Reformers had imagined the troops receiving a thorough re-education, but this was never implemented, either for those newly enlisting, or those who had already joined the federal border guard (*Bundesgrenzschutz*) in 1951 and were later absorbed into the Bundeswehr. It was a situation guaranteed to result in tension between the idea of '*Innere Führung*' and the reality of the early Bundeswehr. In 1956, SPD military expert Fritz Erler was already warning in parliamentary debate of rushing the rebuilding of the army and thereby enhancing the 'political dangers', since in the end 'the army's ethos and attitude towards democracy depends on how the commander and lower-commander corps are composed'.[69]

Erler's criticism was primarily directed at the scale of planning, though he also doubted whether it was wise to rebuild and rearm the West German military at the accelerated rate adopted after 1956, which, as it turned out, left the administration and infrastructure totally unable to cope. The government had set itself the goal of establishing a 500,000-strong army from the ground up within three years; by the end of 1956, less than a seventh of the envisaged force had enlisted, and all were volunteers – making it only too clear to everyone involved that existing recruiting methods would never produce these ambitious target figures. Even the revised estimate for a 350,000-strong army in six years could only be achieved if agreement was reached to reintroduce 'the citizen's duty to defend their country'.[70]

Consequently, the quantitative logic was well to the fore when the government introduced a law on conscription in the German parliament in 1956. However, the SPD opposition remained unconvinced. They had already spoken out against disarmament, and were vehemently opposed to a large conscription army both for political reasons and because they believed that this was the wrong strategy and tactic to follow in military policy. Firstly, they considered the political and human 'alienation' experienced in East and West Germany would only become more extreme if a conscription army were set up on either side of the Iron Curtain – and the GDR would be certain to follow suit if the west played the conscription card; secondly, the era of conventional mass armed forces was over, replaced by a military doctrine based on the atomic deterrent theory; and thirdly, technological advances in the military sector increasingly required longer-serving, well-trained soldiers, and such concerns were already built into the navy and air force recruitment plans. In view of this, they rejected reintroducing the draft, favouring instead a small highly specialist voluntary force as a practicable solution in line with actual needs.[71]

This step marked a radical break in the SPD's traditional line on military policy. Ever since the 1860s they had advocated local militia forces, or people's defence forces, concepts assuming widespread military inclusion for the entire male population. They had long rejected any standing, or 'mercenary', army as undemocratic and uncontrollable. The policy shift in 1956 can best be explained by their opposition role and the stand they had taken against integrating West Germany militarily into the western Allies and the rearmament this would entail. They also believed in the viability of democratic control over a professional army, established under precisely those military structures they had helped vote into law. Now, in contrast, they saw the conscription army as posing a threat to an individual's right to freedom, and significantly 'drawing people under state control'. Moreover, the SPD was jockeying for position in the run-up to the 1957 election. With surveys revealing large sectors of public opinion against the draft, the SPD's promise to abolish it if voted into office clearly smacked of electioneering.[72] But it was a strategy that did not pay off. In the wake of the landslide victory for the ruling CDU, returned with an absolute majority, the SPD abandoned its resistance to conscription and returned to its traditional roots.

In 1956, the CDU had unswervingly followed the chancellor's line, rushing the Conscription Law through parliament, and being roundly condemned for it in the press and major public groups including the unions and the church. This did not prevent the CDU from celebrating a benchmark victory the following year, indicating how little the issues of remilitarisation and conscription really figured in voters' priorities. Given the threat of Soviet intervention, a fear revived only too vividly by the crushing of the Hungarian uprising that same year, the main SPD argument of conscription inhibiting or complicating German reunification came to sound slightly hollow. With only a twelve-month period of service coupled with low call-up quotas, the initial objections to conscription were dampened too.[73]

On 1 April 1957 the first draft of nearly 10,000 men, all born in 1937, entered the barracks, selected from the 15,000 mustered by the end of 1956. Of these, only 0.3 per cent had appealed against military service as conscientious objectors, making use of the right enshrined in the Basic Law. Despite the substantial rise in conscripts for each draft year, this proportion only rose slightly, and was still below 1 per cent of all young men mustered in the mid-1960s. This figure only changed drastically after political issues became a major concern for 1960s youths, with the student movement, the *Notstandsgesetze* (emergency laws in reaction to the Red Army Fraction's terrorist acts) and the Vietnam War all fuelling protests and social conflicts. As the number of conscientious objectors first passed the 10,000 mark in 1968, politicians across all parties warned against 'misusing' the basic right to refuse military service. Political anger was also vented over the increasing numbers of young men moving to West Berlin to avoid the draft, since the city's special status was not subject to West German conscription law, and this led to stricter controls and punishments for draft dodging.[74]

Conscientious objectors had a range of reasons for not wanting to serve. Initially, the motives primarily related to a Christian upbringing, but 1967 marked a watershed where steadily growing numbers of conscientious objectors cited political rather than religious grounds to support their case. In such instances, they had to show that their objections were not 'determined by the situation', but were actually of a 'fundamental' nature. This definition had already fuelled a violent debate in the Bundestag in 1956, with the CDU pushing through a narrower reading than the one favoured by the opposition SPD. Even if no parliamentarian officially protested against the constitutionally guaranteed right to refuse military service, its legitimacy was still viewed in completely different ways. The social democrats, for instance, praised it as expressing the state's readiness to step back in prescribing such decisions, pointing out that it would be a 'bad sign' if, after the experience of the last war, there were no conscientious objectors among those mustered – although these arguments only left the CDU shaking their heads in disbelief.[75]

The CDU similarly resisted the SPD proposal to change the name of the *Ersatzdienst* (alternative civilian service) for registered conscientious objectors into *Zivildienst* to give this service its 'own vindication' in semantic terms too. In 1969, the CDU defence minister Gerhard Schröder noted military service was really the 'normal' service, and therefore *Ersatzdienst* had to remain an exception requiring individual justification. This logic was echoed by the constitutional court in 1978 when it overturned legislation introduced by the SPD–Liberal coalition to grant both forms of service more or less equal status. The law had abolished the requirement for conscientious objectors to justify their stance personally before a board, a complex and frequently inquisitorial process, replacing it with the right to submit only a written declaration, *de facto* offering the enlistee the choice between military and civilian service. The constitutional court judges found in accordance with the primary status of military service in principle, rating the civilian alternative only as a secondary obligation, deserving a suitably 'onerous' form. Although the legislation then introduced in 1984 was more restrictive than the 1977 law, it still represented a major step forward in liberalising conscription when compared to the previous practices; in this instance, the conscientious objector had to submit a letter, explaining the reason for refusing to serve, and a subsequent decision was then taken on the merits of the individual case.[76]

If we compare the evolution of military policy in the FRG and the GDR, the most marked and essential difference emerges in the constitutionally enshrined right to conscientious objection, and its liberal form dating from the later 1970s on. At first glance, it seemed as though both states were following similar paths, though observing each other closely and commenting on each other's decisions. In security policy, particularly, a kind of 'feedback loop' quickly became established where one state's action was justified as a reaction to what the other did. For example, when the GDR set up its armed forces in 1956 and integrated them within the Warsaw Pact military alliance of Soviet bloc powers, it justified these measures by pointing to the events unfolding in the FRG. Conversely, the West German government argued that the steps to build up a federal border guard from

1950 on – later an important source for Bundeswehr personnel – came in response to the GDR's decision to set up a *Kasernierte Volkspolizei* (billeted police force), the predecessor to the NVA. It goes without saying that both sides, despite such reciprocal moves, were keen to present their own policy as defensive and peace-loving and the other's as aggressive warmongering.[77]

Such a negative delimitation, though, was problematic where both states invoked shared tradition. As mentioned above, neither the FRG nor the GDR wanted to do without the services of former *Wehrmacht* officers, nor could they manage without them. In East Germany's case, the official line stressed the officers' complete change of heart under socialism, and was accompanied by a policy of generally leaving them lower down the command chain. But both states also laid claim to the positive legacy of the Prussian military reformers in the early nineteenth century. Here, while the FRG borrowed the American model for their uniforms, harvesting criticism from many 'traditionalists', the GDR affirmed the tradition more radically by dressing its soldiers in uniforms matching those in the old army perfectly in colour, cut and shape, a symbol giving this national tradition an outwardly visible form – apparently unconcerned that, both at home and abroad, the former style of uniforms, boots and goosestep evoked unpleasant associations with the National Socialist *Wehrmacht*.[78]

Both states also experienced resistance at home to their moves towards rearmament. In the GDR, it may not have been possible to express such opposing views, either within parliament or through extra-parliamentary channels, but they nonetheless led to the start date for conscription being postponed until after the Berlin Wall was built in 1961. One year later, in 1962, the first conscripts entered the NVA (National People's Army) barracks, five years after the draft was reintroduced in the FRG. At 116,000 men in 1963, the East German army was smaller than the Bundeswehr's 400,000 in absolute terms, but was larger in proportion to the population. In the mid-1970s, there were 110 members of the armed forces for every 10,000 GDR citizens, compared to only 80 in West Germany. In other words, many more from a particular age-group were drafted in East Germany than in the FRG.[79]

One further difference in the GDR came from copying the Soviet model, although at the same time it was continuing National Socialist ideals: the emphasis on paramilitary links and institutions, found especially in the '*Kampfgruppen der Arbeiterklasse*' (fighting units of the working class). These were established after the 17 June 1953 unrest, and fell under the interior ministry's remit. By 1962, they numbered around 350,000 men aged between 25 to 60, supposed to smash 'counter-revolutionary actions' and ensure 'inner security'. From 1952 with the founding of the *Gesellschaft für Sport und Technik*, which was directly under defence ministry control, young people between 14 to 24 had already been provided with a pre-military education in outdoor sports, shooting and map reading. The youth associations such as the *Thälmann-Pioniere* and the FDJ (*Freie Deutsche Jugend*), incorporated army sport exercises into their brief too, while pupils at school were also taught about the army and its tasks. In 1978, this duty was formally enshrined in legislation requiring all pupils in the 9th and 10th grades (14- to 16-year-olds) to attend lessons providing basic pre-military knowledge.

This broad-based cross-gender militarisation of children and young people in the GDR realised one of the classic SPD aspirations from the nineteenth century, but without establishing a militia defence force and implementing the second stage of the old SPD reform programme. In fact, the NVA was anything but a rather loose militia built around decentralised structures – a model which, by the way, found equally little support in the FRG. Instead, it was a strongly centralised army with a relatively long, eighteen-month period of service. Rather than the pre-military training directed at creating the potential for militia-like structures, it was intended to 'help shorten and ease the young man's route to becoming a soldier', as GDR defence minister Heinz Hoffmann constantly stressed, and generate a 'potential for quickly establishing military combat collectives'.[80]

East Germany was not only highly militarised in comparison to West Germany but also to other socialist states, indicative of the GDR's pressing need for security (and its feeling of insecurity), and how it felt insufficiently protected despite the national and international armed forces stationed there. While the FRG relied on the democratic process of debate, prosperity and mass consumption to secure the loyalty of its citizens, the GDR primarily endeavoured to achieve the same by arming its citizens ideologically and binding them into institutions. On the back of highly pervasive foe images and the implied need for ready defence against an opponent constantly poised to invade, the GDR focused almost obsessively on military organisation and strength as the top priority – and this was not only prevalent in the army, but the entire population was supposed to identify themselves with this organisation as well and the duty to join in a general, combat-style programme for the 'socialist defence of the country'. This programme included political education intended to awaken pride in the 'socialist fatherland' and engender an 'ineradicable hatred for the enemies of socialism and peace'. In 1984, an 'advice booklet' for 18-year-old NVA recruits defined these 'concrete enemies' more precisely as:

Not only the masters of monopolies and banks, who commission the aggression, not only the NATO generals, who plan the armed attack on socialism and test it in manoeuvres. Your enemies are also the mercenaries of imperialism, incited to anti-communism and drilled for a war of aggression. Whatever language they speak, whether German or English, whatever uniform they wear, whether that of the Bundeswehr or any other imperialistic army, whether voluntarily or involuntarily in the pay of imperialists, and whatever class they come from – anyone serving imperialism by carrying arms, acting at their behest, is our enemy.[81]

The NVA used this kind of indoctrination to power a policy of ideological confrontation already on the wane in the Bundeswehr after the late 1960s. The need for West Germany to set clear anti-communist borders might have marked West Germany's early years, and generated a loyal echo in the army, but as the state found growing stability in domestic and foreign policy concerns, it was a motif that steadily became sidelined. When Georg Leber, SPD defence minister, officially abolished the Bundeswehr's emotionalised image of East Germany as an enemy, he was reflecting those national and international developments accompanying moves towards 'détente' and 'ideological disarmament' in the early and mid-1970s. The GDR however, did not follow suit, electing instead to erect massive barriers to any such tendencies, particularly within the military sector.[82]

The NVA's strong politicisation, with officers and soldiers almost entirely either SED party and FDJ members, indicated the degree to which the GDR attached a crucial significance to a loyal party-line army backing internal and external security. This key role was reflected in the NVA's prominence at all political events and celebrations, parading their military strength. With the support of political and educative measures, soldiers and officers could enjoy relatively high social status, even though, given the longer service and shorter periods of furlough compared to West Germany, the GDR military was more removed from civil society. Constantly in uniform and trimmed to a military bearing, their outer appearance also set them more obviously apart from civilians than their West German counterparts, who tended to travel home on leave in their normal clothes and, from the early 1970s, could keep the hairstyles or beards popular in civilian life. However, it would be wrong to imagine that this cultural and geographic distance between the GDR military and society inevitably generated a basic alienation between them. Any such gap was constantly filled by official propaganda and education boasting 'unity between the people and its soldiers' and stressing the 'pride and respect ... with which the citizens meet their sons in uniform' – after all, they were protecting peace and the socialist fatherland; consequently, their service, simultaneously 'a right and an honourable duty', was 'worthy of the highest honour'.[83]

Indeed, for that reason all young men were expected to perform military service; in contrast to West Germany, the GDR did not acknowledge any right to refuse military service on grounds of conscience. Only after the church, theological faculties, and the East German CDU party had forcefully called for moves to allow conscientious objection did the GDR pass an amendment in 1964 permitting those refusing military service on religious or similar grounds to opt for what was called a 'construction unit' (*Baueinheit*) under NVA command, and serve without bearing arms. This, however, was also considered on a par with 'military service', although of a 'special kind', as indicated by the shovel symbol on the army uniform's epaulettes. Moreover, there was no legal right to this substitute military service. It was merely offered as a 'concession granted by the socialist state' out of 'consideration' for an individual's conflict of conscience.[84] Such formulations reflect how far military service in the GDR was geared to state interests – and hence the degree to which it continued in the spirit of Imperial Germany and the National Socialism era. The individual did not have any fundamental right to refuse this 'honorary duty' and, as Carlo Schmid put it in 1956, act against a '*raison d'état*'; instead, the army was held up as a civic duty and civic honour, and the individual was denied any chance of performing any obviously civilian service in a civilian institution.

4. Civic Spirit and Gender Politics: The End of Conscription?

In West Germany too, from 1956 on, the state was entitled to require young men to 'serve in the armed forces, in the federal border guard or in a civil defence association' – a provision still in force in today's reunited Germany. Every young man is liable for this duty, since complete refusal to serve in some form is disallowed. In other words, male German citizenship tacitly implies the duty of contributing to the defence of the state – and the debate over dual citizenship for Germans in the 1990s indicated just how this duty is linked to citizenship's legal status, with a main argument against dual citizenship in Germany resting on the claim that conscription requires a choice, unequivocally and permanently, for *one* state, and *one* nationality.

But is conscription really a core duty of a state's citizens? Or, to put it another way, is the citizen's relationship to 'his' state determined principally and primarily by his readiness to bear arms to defend it? By enshrining the right of every citizen to refuse armed war service, hadn't the constitution already acknowledged that such a stance was itself subject to doubt? And what about the citizenship status of women, with no such duty imposed on them to start with – are they then second-class citizens?

Such questions lead us directly to the heart of the ongoing debate on whether to keep or abolish the draft, a feature of the reunited Germany from the early 1990s, and common in other European countries as well. However, these questions also lead back to the history of conscription, both recent and distant, which this book has tried to (re)construct. Given this longer timeline, the economic, security policy and military strategy aspects dominating the present debate recede, leaving space for political considerations addressing gender relations and violence, as well as notions of citizenship and national integration.

When the Basic Law, the provisional constitution for the Federal Republic of Germany, was discussed in 1948, the men and women involved were primarily concerned to protect the inviolability of human dignity from state interference. In establishing this prime aim, they were taking into account the historical line of a distorted development, discernible in the nineteenth century and culminating in the Third Reich. In 1933, the traditionally state-centred stance pervading Prussian-German society had taken a dramatic turn, with jurisprudence and political practice devaluating the individual in favour of a racially defined 'national community' and its state forms. The emphasis this placed on citizens' *duties* over the vastly lower rating given to their *rights* underwent an about-turn after 1945, with the Basic Law mainly concerning itself with rights and hardly at all with duties.[85]

This appears to have undergone an ostensible change of focus with amendments to the Basic Law and the passing of a Military Service Law in 1955–6, although since a conscript had the right to refuse military service on grounds of conscience, the individual's rights were still ranked above 'reasons of state'. Even if, against the political backdrop of the 1950s and 1960s, the conscientious objector option tended to be discredited as abnormal and a bad exception to a good rule, with correspondingly few men making use of their right, Article 4 Section 2 of the Basic Law unswervingly maintained the primacy of the individual's civic right to refuse military service on grounds of conscience over the civic duty of taking up arms to defend the country. Moreover, the concrete form given to this right facilitated a civil definition of service as a duty that was radically removed from the state domain and embedded in the societal area. In contrast to the GDR's arrangement for service without a rifle, the FRG 'civil substitute service' was not performed in unarmed Bundeswehr units, but in civilian institutions taking society as a principal reference point, and not primarily oriented towards the state and its territorially determined existence. The 'Zivi', nicknamed after the non-military *ziviler Ersatzdienst* (officially called *Zivildienst* from 1973 on) neither defended the state's borders nor prepared to rebuff military incursions into the state's territory; instead, he helped in hospitals and old people's homes, or later in environmental protection or other areas acknowledged as for the 'public good'. In other words, he was performing a service directly benefiting society and buttressing it in crucial areas.

Over the last few decades, 'civilian service' (i.e., non-military service) has become significantly more common. Although even in the 1970s, when many reforms were introduced, this was still supposed to be an 'onerous' and 'unpleasant alternative' to military service, its evolution since then has set other accents. For a start, the numbers of young men opting for civilian service have been steadily increasing; by the end of the 1990s they reached near parity with the figures for those serving in the military.[86] Secondly, society has witnessed a growing trend towards positively evaluating the decision to refuse military service, and the corresponding respect for this stand. While the logistical problems created by the rapid growth in conscientious objectors in the late 1960s made it hard to find suitable places for them, many institutions have now become used to drawing on a growing pool of potential short-term helpers. Two-thirds of all 'Zivis' now work in care facilities for the elderly, the ill, and people with disabilities, where they are firmly planned into work schedules; without their help, many social care and aid programmes would not be able to function.[87]

Many areas of German public opinion have gradually come to realise that young men performing civilian service are serving society more usefully and meaningfully than their peers in the barracks and on the drill grounds. This trend has aroused the anger of the conservative press and politicians over a number of years, both raging against an insidious erosion of values and beliefs and insisting that civilian service is 'always worth less than military service in real terms'. After all, they argue, the soldier is getting ready to 'risk his own life for others', while the 'Zivi' shies away from this danger. But young people especially are no longer reached by claiming that 'Zivis' are less masculine than soldiers because they are doing 'female' tasks instead of learning masculine weapons' skills; now, the military no longer enjoys the same hegemony it had in the nineteenth and early to mid-twentieth century when it was the undisputed 'school of masculinity'.[88]

This image was still prevalent even as late as the 1950s and early 1960s, when large parts of the population continued to believe in the armed forces as an institution teaching genuine masculinity. A 1956 Federal Government memorandum cited comradeship, sport and physical fitness, and a valuable 'training for life' as reasons for choosing military service. Research carried out in the same year into whether 'today's youth' needed the army to teach it 'orderliness and decency' revealed 63 per cent of women and 55 per cent of men agreeing – from respondents aged 30 to 60-plus across all social classes and political affiliations, even among SPD supporters who made no secret of their objections to reintroducing the draft.[89] Two reasons might explain why the percentage for women was significantly higher: firstly, amid the constant lamentations about a post-war 'family crisis' in Germany, women's belief in their own maternal pedagogical skills may have been shaken, and with many fathers killed in the war, or physically weakened by it, mothers no doubt could feel relieved to think their sons were under the 'firm hand' of the army. The second reason relates to the motif of women's interest, in principle, in men made more 'manly' through military service, a motif which constantly recurred from the nineteenth century on, although it is not possible to determine whether it really existed concretely and empirically or not. It was commonly believed, though, that the army taught men maturity, responsibility, self-discipline and reliability, and even how to be orderly and sew on shirt buttons – all qualities suiting them to be viable husbands and heads of a household. Furthermore, the conscripts gained a demeanour considered genuinely male. They had a self-assured bearing and correct posture, creating an aura of strength, resoluteness and invulnerability. Here, as the polarity of everything soft and female, uncertain and tender, they offered themselves as protectors of women in all their alleged gentleness, tenderness, insecurity and defencelessness.

Even in the second half of the twentieth century such paradigms constructing masculinity and femininity as crude polarities, simultaneously signifying and mutually determining each other, still enjoyed a certain credence. In 1962, for example, the *Junge Welt*, official broadsheet for East Germany's FDJ socialist youth organisation, printed a drawing, shortly after conscription was introduced there, showing, next to a man in uniform, a modern young woman with short hair and a stylish dress, mouthing prettily: 'Well, really, darling brother, I hardly would have known you – you've become a real man! When I think what a gangly, silly thing you used to be. One thing's for sure: my "Mr Right" will have to have visited the same school – our *Volksarmee*.' The GDR magazine *Frau von Heute* similarly presented its readers with a thoroughly positive picture of NVA soldiers in the 1960s, portraying them as the protectors of women and children.[90] Even if such images should not be taken at face value, the fact that they were thought suitable to be used as propaganda suggests they were not entirely wide of the mark of the conceptual horizon and expectations in their female target audience.

In contrast, it is noticeable how reserved the media were in West Germany in dealing with the topic of the 'military'. For example, *Brigitte*, West Germany's highest circulation women's magazine in the 1960s, hardly contained any articles about soldiers and the Bundeswehr. If anything, the articles that appeared tended to take a sceptical view of the army, warning of a 'brutalisation' effect.[91] In this instance, the pendulum had swung back in the other direction: rather than borrowing from the classic gender-stereotyping repertoire, reaffirming the soldier as a symbol of masculine manliness, defender of the feminine woman, he became a man imbued with the potential to generate fear, threatening not only women but the entire civil society and its culture.

The Bundeswehr reacted to these reservations and worries by referring to the key principles of '*Innere Führung*', stressing how soldiers were trained in a far more civil spirit than armies in the past. The 1957 training guidelines, though, still invoked the same traditional set of military values transmitted from the nineteenth century: 'A soldier's training aims specifically at creating resoluteness in defence, obedience and conscientiousness, bravery and chivalry', while 'the soldier has to be robust and resilient, ready to suffer deprivations and be harsh to himself'. Nonetheless, a great emphasis was placed on describing military training as merely one part of that general education the recruit could expect to receive as the citizen of a democratic state: 'This includes, first and foremost, schooling [soldiers] to become aware of preserving personal dignity and political co-responsibility.' Educating a recruit to become a soldier and a citizen was supposed to be compatible – not in the pre- and anti-democratic traditions requiring the soldier/citizen to subordinate himself to 'authority' or the 'national community', but in active political participation, both in the army and outside, where he could play a role in shaping democratic principles.[92]

The declared aim of integrating the armed forces' social practice and normative system into society had an effect on the image of masculinity it then disseminated. Baudissin had already warned against showing 'improper harshness' in training, and over-stressing the drilling needed. He countered internal army criticism of this 'tender trend' with the argument that the Bundeswehr could not detach itself from those 'libertarian principles' shaping West German society. Admittedly, these principles had less impact of everyday military life in the 1950s and 1960s than politicians claimed in their public speeches, but complaints by conservative officers such as Brigadier General Heinz Karst in 1967 on the loss of 'masculinity' in the troops, condemning the 'widespread practice of wearing civilian clothes' when not on duty as 'civilianising' and eroding soldierly 'group solidarity', indicates that they did indeed play a certain role. In the 1970s particularly, a decade marked by the SPD drive to reform, they then experienced a renewed impetus.[93] In the GDR, conscious steps were taken to ward off the danger of 'civilianising' soldiers, with the NVA's training style drawing strongly on 'Prussian' traditions, until the army was finally disbanded in 1990 in the wake of German reunification.

The Bundeswehr, in contrast, pursued another route, despite massive resistance from within the armed forces.[94] At its inception, it had been entrusted with the task of minimising barriers to civil society, and expected to remove, as far as possible, those that existed – and, over the long term, it had succeeded extremely well. Whether the West German army wanted to or not, it had to accept that the classic notions of a male, military identity aroused little echo, either in the barracks among recruits, or outside the barrack walls. Conversely, the armed forces saw themselves forced to tolerate civilian 'trends' in informal youth culture. The Bundeswehr's attempt to counter old prejudices and attract new, young officer recruits utilized preferences and tendencies already present in post-war society, cashing in on the appeal of technology, sports and a team spirit. The army's deployment in emergency work in natural catastrophes too could be seen as maximising the potential for a positive public image, positioning the army as a solidly integrated part of society.[95]

However, those features needed for the army's genuinely military remit proved incapable of generating such widespread acceptance and agreement. As the policy of rapprochement and détente pursued from the 1970s on began to bite, increasing the West German population's sense of security and leaving the threat from the 'East' seemingly tamed, criticism of military institutions or armaments spending hikes became ever more vocal. The peace movement in the 1980s and the collapse of the communist bloc in 1989–91 only further fuelled doubts about whether a personnel-intensive army, equipped with sophisticated weaponry, was needed at all – and, far from removing such doubts, military deployments since the 1990s have only intensified them. They may have offered an impressive statement on the military's right to exist as such and put paid to nearly all calls for abolishing the armed forces altogether, but they have also triggered a lively debate on the role of the military in the twenty-first century, raising questions not only about its functions, but about the structures and size it ought to have to fulfil them.

The military operations in the Balkans and Central Asia have given German society a clear and painful reminder of why an army 'actually' exists: not just to threaten violence to intimidate an enemy, but also to use violence if the initial show of force does not deter. What military personnel viewed as a proud demonstration of military capability, a sort of professional coming out, alarmed and divided the civil sphere. After fifty years, the return to martial violence came as a shock, even though the violence was only transmitted via the TV screens, without directly affecting one's own state territory.

This shock seemed so dramatic in Germany, more so than in other European states or the USA, because of Germany's specific historical experience. In Germany, the Second World War and its consequences left a mark on the relationship to the military that was fundamentally different from the Allied states. When Germany broke with its militaristic past, this represented a calculated political act, radical and profound, above all in West Germany. It entailed a massive loss of status for officers, who had to come to terms with being just one professional group among others and were additionally confronted with the task of explaining why their cost-intensive sphere of activity was necessary at all. For the general public, the press, political parties and associations, the army was an object of disinterest and distrust – and this attitude followed exactly those reservations expressed by civil parliamentarians in Baden, Bavaria or Württemberg in the first half of the nineteenth century about their 'standing armies'. The national pride many French felt towards their *Force de Frappe*, or that was widespread in Britain during the Falkland crisis or first Iraq war, had no counterpart in Germany, where such feelings, if they existed at all, were linked to a soccer team or car brand, rather than the Bundeswehr. In Germany, an army was viewed as necessary, given the lack of viable alternatives, but was then expected to follow strictly those rules set by the political sphere. Any refusal to do so resulted in public scandals, clearly expressing a latent mistrust in the armed forces' ability to adhere to democratic forms and practices.[96]

Furthermore, the institution of conscription itself has marked the relationship between the army and civil society in (West) Germany now, and in the past, by more tension than, for example, in the USA or Britain. Drafting tens of thousands, if not hundreds of thousands, of young men every year awoke an interest in the general public in what went on behind the barrack walls. While the first generation of parents viewed the army's traditional claim to educate positively, later generations were far more sceptical, especially the 'white' age-groups without any military experience of their own. The public sphere took careful note of how young men were treated in the army, how their superiors dealt with them, and the attitudes conscripts brought back – and openly criticised all of them. In contrast, the armed forces in Britain and America moved in a less transparent area, sealed off from society. Since in this case transmitted military structures were based on voluntary enlistment, with, after a brief interim phase during the Second World War period, a volunteer army reinstated in the 1960s, the public sphere was accustomed to seeing the military functioning as a specific and relatively autonomous area, and accepted it as such: what happened there lay outside the sphere of general interest.[97]

It is precisely this gap, though, that seems to have enabled Britain and America to accept the particular logic underlying the armed forces and their real purpose in a more pragmatic and less emotional way (with some exceptions such as, for example, the Vietnam war era). In those countries, there is no question of the army's principal role centring on driving licence provision, sports competitions, or repairing river-bank dams threatened by flooding. Such secondary skills are not at the heart of the recognition and legitimisation of their armies' existence, which instead rests squarely on their ability to exercise politically sanctioned violence, and do so as professionally, effectively and efficiently as possible. Consequently, public reaction is more subdued when the apparatus of violence is employed, without any of the moral overtones regularly recurring in the debate in Germany. Conversely, one might well argue that just such impassioned discussions over the use of physical violence to kill others are, by definition, a part of a civil society. Precisely a society which banishes violence from its internal structures and relations and gives absolute primacy to the violence-free self-organisation of its members has repeatedly to engage in the process of critical debate to restate the conditions and aims validating the use of other benchmarks in regulating its foreign affairs. In this sense, one could argue, conscription stands as a constant reminder, focusing public attention on that institution where state-authorised means of violence are concentrated.

Yet the history of conscription shows that it does not lead *per se* to a critical attitude towards violence and the military, or to reflection on it. The frequently cited quote from Germany's first post-war president, Theodor Heuss, claiming that conscription is 'the legitimate child of democracy', does not apply to Germany; quite the reverse, in fact, since conscription there tended to inhibit democratic processes, rather than supporting them, well into the twentieth century. As a duty constructed on a state basis, and demanded by the state, it certainly helped to fix and formalise the relationship between the state and the citizen conscript – but this had nothing to do with participation in civil society. One might even claim that the German fixation on the prominent role of the state, reinforced by conscription, was not compatible with the establishment and expansion of civil society cooperation and communication processes. The militarily formed 'state citizen' suffocated the 'civic citizen' committed to civil society tasks. If conscription was regarded as the 'crowning glory of all civic duties', other expressions of 'civic values and public spirit' were squeezed out and found themselves occupying less respected and honoured rankings. In theory, this scale was only overturned at that moment when the 1949 Basic Law recognised the right to conscientious objection and the 1956 legislative allowed a civilian 'alternative service' that took into account social institutions and interests. In practical terms, military and civilian service were supposedly placed on an equal footing in the 1980s, at the earliest, but this still remains, in fact, a bone of contention.

But conscription in Germany did more than simply block the development of a socially oriented civic spirit, it also fixed gender relations so they forcefully resisted the modernist drive to dynamic changes in the social, economic and cultural sectors. Conscription embodied a norm conceived of at a time when the notion of a radical gender difference enjoyed widespread validity and power, and transmitted this norm unchallenged into the early twenty-first century, an era when all other areas had long rid themselves of any similar precept. For around a hundred years, women in Germany have been able to access educational institutions and professional careers still closed to them in the nineteenth century. When Imperial Germany fell, it took with it those barriers previously separating women from political status in the civic sphere. In 1918, the argument collapsed completely for political rights as a dependent condition of military duties, that reciprocal trade-off buttressed by all parties and press organs drawing on middle-class support. Women were granted the franchise without having to defend the fatherland with a rifle in hand.

Yet political empowerment did not put an end to the armed forces as an exclusively male domain. Even in the GDR conscription was a purely male affair, although the GDR pursued a far more rigorous policy of gender equality than in the FRG, and the 1968 GDR constitution expressly imposed the duty of defending the country on 'every citizen'. In West Germany too, when parliament debated introducing the draft in 1956, it similarly exempted women. They could voluntarily join the Bundeswehr, preferably as telephone operators and secretaries, and were later even allowed to train as officers in the music and medical corps, with the first woman promoted to a general's rank as medical corps head in the German air force in 1994. However, even if women actually wanted combat service, this was not permitted – a ruling only changed in 2000 after the European Court of Justice intervened.[99]

This ruling echoed the nineteenth-century world-view, according to which women, in principle, comprised the unarmed sex, while men were, in principle, armed. This concept has only changed gradually, against stiff resistance from both men and women, but gender equality in bearing arms takes the ground from under other gender images linked to a male monopoly over weapons: the idea that women need men to protect them from other men's aggression, or the belief that, by nature, women are – and have to be – more peace-loving than men. In this respect, after the entire architecture of gender polarity has largely collapsed, at least officially, in the worlds of work, science, academia, education, culture and politics, this step to gender equality sees the last stone in the foundations removed.

The military has also lost its status as purely male space, first and foremost in the combat units, which it preserved so carefully and for so long. This change only came about because society no longer acknowledged the military's claim of creating a special kind of masculinity in this male space. Surrendering this gendered exclusivity only became feasible after the 1960s had produced clear challenges to a specific military concept of masculinity, rooted in toughness and violence, which lost value and attractiveness against other male images propounded in youth culture, technology, sports, and the context of motoring.

At present, conscription's male exclusivity is similarly under debate. Even if the European Court of Justice ruled in 2003, on pragmatic grounds, against a case questioning the male nature of conscription, the principle of exclusivity seems hard-pressed to appear viable. If women are to be excluded from combat service because they have to be 'protected from danger in case of war', they could easily be recruited to perform unarmed service in the military – which they have been allowed to do for years on a voluntary basis. Not requiring women to perform military service, though, suggests that reservations about a female draft are not logically consistent, and are, simultaneously, concerned with more basic and specific issues. Public debate in this area has shown there was, and is, a principled aversion, justified in anthropological terms, to involving women actively in violence directed at killing others. Furthermore, there is a reluctance, quite in the nineteenth-century tradition, to force women into a personal relationship of service to the state without being able to provide a logical legitimisation for it.

Feminists too, who discovered this theme in the 1980s, were also divided in their opinions, with some arguing for universalising the draft as a part of a programme for radical gender equality, while others rejected such moves, claiming women's emancipation was impossible in principle without removing given 'patriarchal' structures. Yet others took a pragmatic stance, calling for gender equality in other social institutions and work areas before tackling gender equality in conscription, and, finally, others again pointed to the innumerable services women had already provided free for society, reasoning that men could easily be left to perform their military and civilian service on their own.[100]

As yet, the final word has not been spoken either in the gender policy debate over male conscription, or in security and socio-political policy discussions on whether a draft is needed at all. Nonetheless, indications suggest that Germany too will move towards a professional army. Those arguments supporting a downsized, professional army comprising long-term volunteer recruits – which already make up the vast mass of Bundeswehr personnel – might well gain force and conviction as the political and social objections to this move are increasingly overcome. The history of conscription presented in this book can play a part here, since it shows, for example, that the claim that a conscript army is easier to control by political means actually has no basis in historical fact in Germany. In the Weimar Republic, the *Reichswehr* did not operate outside parliamentary control because of the structures inherent in professional armies, but because there were deficits in the political control and communication processes. Similarly, the British and American experience supports the view that professional armies can indeed be incorporated into the democratic process and subjected to political control mechanisms.

Conversely, developments in Germany demonstrate the lack of any direct link between democracy and conscription. When conscription was introduced in the early nineteenth century, democracy was a theoretical notion with, as far as the ruling classes were concerned, a revolutionary ring to it. Rather than Imperial Germany's move, in 1871, to extend the Prussian conscription system to all confederation states reflecting some idea of promoting democracy, it merely applied a convention of, as Treitschke put it, a 'martial era'. Hitler, too, by reintroducing conscription in 1935, was laying the keystone for policies leading to the Second World War, not realising any belief in the democratic process. The GDR, equally, could hardly be described as a democratic country when it reintroduced the draft in 1962. In other words, in contrast to other neighbouring western European states, in Germany the symbiosis between democracy and conscription has not been the rule, but an exceptional instance within historical development.

On the socio-political front, too, the result of conscription has, at best, been ambiguous. One can indeed say with a considerable degree of certainty that Imperial Germany's army, in its own way, accelerated the development of, and helped shape, an inner national sentiment. Marx and Engels's comment in 1870 that Germany found unity in the Prussian barracks did indeed have a prophetic touch, beyond any relevance it had at the time. Victory over France not only provided the foundation for a unified German national state (without Austria), but the army proved itself to be a 'school for the entire nation', in a social sense as well, combining men from a range of social and regional origins and religious beliefs under the rule of a common curriculum that transformed them into a homogeneous whole. In the army, the 'nation', previously a relatively abstract term in the vocabulary of liberal-democratic citizens, became tangible, a personally experienced concept, laden with vivid and intense emotions. This shaping of an inner national sentiment in the barracks, though, had nothing to do with basic liberal or democratic principles. The nation experienced and shaped in the armed forces was one that remained sworn, by obedience and discipline, to the state or king as father of the nation and its supreme commander; it was subordinated to his command and bound to unconditional loyalty, without ever being allowed to, or able to, constitute itself independently. The ideal citizen expected to emerge from the Wilhelminian army was neither liberal nor (social) democratic; he was a vassal, obedient, politically conservative and ready to pass on these values to his children.

Without doubt, the FRG had very different notions of citizenship in mind when it planned the birth of the 'citizen in uniform'. The topos of the army as the 'school for the entire nation' never revived either, although it was regularly cited by conservative politicians well into the 1960s. Soon afterwards, though, Chancellor Willy Brandt's scathing remark that the 'school of the nation' is not the army but, in fact, the school finally sealed the fate of the army's representative and pedagogical aspirations. Such claims may have been common before the First World War, and have undergone a resurgence with National Socialism, but they had no place in the new West German society. A nation defining itself as a democratic civil society did not need military integration as a support, or the armed forces as a focus of identity. The barracks, as a place where a nation was trained and cohesion constructed, had served their time.

Notes

1. Lutz, *Krieg*, p. 101.
2. Salewski, *Entwaffnung*, p. 17, 31–2; Temperley, *History*, vol. 2, p. 128.
3. Wette, 'Erfahrungen', p. 97; *Reichs-Gesetzblatt*, Jg. 1919, pp. 295–298; *Stenographische Berichte*, vol. 326, 1920, pp. 295–319, 322–342; *Handbuch zur deutschen Militärgeschichte*, vol. VI, 1970, pp. 56 ff.; Bessel, *Germany*, pp. 69 ff.
4. Beutel, *Bürgersoldaten*, p. 5; Bucher, 'Geschichte'; Diehl, *Politics*, pp. 32–8, 55–67; *Stenographische Berichte*, vol. 330, 1920, pp. 3578–9, 3582.
5. *Stenographische Berichte*, vol. 326, p. 315; Ziemann, *Front*, pp. 394 ff.; and "Fronterlebnis", p. 68; Schumann, 'Einheitssehnsucht', pp. 92–3.
6. Herbell, *Staatsbürger*, pp. 245 ff.; Rohe, *Reichsbanner*, pp. 29 ff.; Ziemann, "Fronterlebnis", p. 61; Zimmermann, *Wehrpolitik*, p. 72; Diehl, *Politics*, p. 32.
7. Carsten, *Reichswehr*, pp. 26–7; Sten. *Berichte*, vol. 326, p. 308.
8. Salewski, *Entwaffnung*, pp. 120–77.
9. *Sten. Berichte*, vol. 326, p. 297, 299; vol. 327, p. 856; Vol. 330, p. 3528. The party programmes of the DDP (1919), DNVP (1920) and NSDAP (1920) called for a return to universal conscription (Treue, *Parteiprogramme*, pp. 122, 136, 158).

10. Demeter, *Offizierkorps*, pp. 303–5.
11. Demeter, *Offizierkorps*, pp. 53, 56, 307.
12. Carsten, *Reichswehr*, pp. 193 ff.
13. Demeter, *Offizierkorps*, pp. 298–301; Kroh, *Erziehung*, pp. 17 ff.
14. Abenheim, *Bundeswehr*, p. 21; Zimmermann, *Wehrpolitik*, pp. 212 ff.; Elliott, 'Kriegervereine'; Bramke, 'Funktion'; Geyer, 'Organisation', pp. 42, 76 ff.; Carsten, *Reichswehr*, pp. 240 ff.
15. Berghahn, *Stahlhelm*, pp. 55 ff., 85; Ziemann, 'Kriegserinnerung', p. 366; Mommsen, 'Militär'.
16. Berghahn, *Stahlhelm*, p. 61.
17. Schumann, 'Einheitssehnsucht', p. 104.
18. Bessel, *Violence*, pp. 47 ff., and 'Militarismus', pp. 208 ff.; Ziemann, 'Kriegserinnerung', pp. 369, 394–5; Mallmann, *Kommunisten*, pp. 193 ff.; Schuster, *Frontkämpferbund*; Rosenhaft, *Fascists*, pp. 149 ff., and 'Gewalt', p. 246; Opitz, 'Sozialdemokratie', pp. 275 ff.; Rohe, *Reichsbanner*, pp. 96 ff.
19. Krabbe, *Zukunft*, pp. 61 ff., 103 ff., 154, 180–1; Zimmermann, *Wehrpolitik*, pp. 300 ff.; *Handbuch der deutschen Bildungsgeschichte*, vol. V, pp. 46 ff., 100 ff.
20. Ziemann, 'Kriegserinnerung', p. 375; Berghahn, *Stahlhelm*, pp. 33–4; Götz v. Olenhusen, 'Jungstahlhelm'.
21. Geyer, *Aufrüstung*, pp. 87 ff., 234–5, and 'Organisation', pp. 50–1, 99.
22. Frauenholz, *Entwicklung*, p. 23; *Sten. Berichte*, vol. 391, 1927, pp. 8580 ff.
23. Rosenhaft, *Fascists*, pp. 128 ff. and 'Links'; Behrenbeck, *Kult*.
24. Rohe, *Reichsbanner*, pp. 110 ff.; Weisbrod, 'Gewalt'.
25. Krabbe, *Jugend*, p. 9; Götz v. Olenhusen, 'Jungstahlhelm', p. 150 estimates only around a quarter of all the male youths in organisations in 1932 belonged to a paramilitary association.
26. *Der Große Herder*, 4th Edition, vol. 7, Freiburg 1933, Column 1545–5; *Handbuch der deutschen Bildungsgeschichte*, V, pp. 53–4, 100 ff.; Zweig, Welt, pp. 78–9, 88, 113; Zimmermann, *Wehrpolitik*, pp. 303 ff.; Vogelsang, *Reichswehr*, pp. 231, 286–7.
27. In 1933, the SA took over the National Governing Board and the pre-military training of those age-groups that had never experienced battle themselves (dubbed the 'white' years of birth) (Messerschmidt, *Wehrmacht*, pp. 26–7). The SA retained its remit to train military sports even after the Night of the Long Knives in 1934 (Domarus, *Hitler*, vol. I, p. 490).
28. Oertzen, *Grundzüge*, p. 127; Bennewitz, *Wehrerziehung*, pp. 14 ff.; Schoenbaum, *Revolution*, pp. 83 ff.; Keim, *Erziehung*.
29 Vogelsang, *Dokumente*, p. 435.
30. Wegner, *Soldaten*; see also, Wegner, 'Anmerkungen'.

31. Wagner/Röder, *Wehrpflicht*, p. 11; Goebbels, 'Klarheit und Logik', *Frankfurter Zeitung*, Nr. 144, 19.3.1935, pp. 1–2; Generaloberst von Blomberg, 'Die deutsche Wehrpflicht', *Völkischer Beobachter*, 20.3.1935, pp. 1–2.

32. *Deutschland-Bericht*, vol. 2, 1935, pp. 275–82, 409–12, 527–31, 667–9.

33. Haegert, 'Nationalsozialismus', pp. 21, 23.

34. Absolon, *Wehrmacht*, vol. III, p. 11; Oertzen, *Grundzüge*, pp. 32–3; *Völkischer Beobachter*, 24.5.1935 (Frick).

35. *Deutschland-Bericht*, 1935, pp. 668, 281.

36. Messerschmidt, *Wehrmacht*, pp. 48 ff., 93 ff.; Foertsch, *Wehrpflicht-Fibel*, pp. 37, 39.

37. Messerschmidt, *Wehrmacht*, pp. 70, 74–79; Foertsch, *Wehrpflicht-Fibel*, pp. 52–3.

38. Dietz, *Wehrgesetz*, p. 116.

39. Dunker, *Reichsbund*; Caplan, 'Männlichkeit'; Müller, *Armee*, pp. 57–61, 189.

40. Fischer, *Wehrpflicht*, p. 131; Heckel, *Wehrverfassung*, T. 1, pp. 97 ff.; Wette, 'Ideologien', pp. 200 ff.

41. Dietz, *Wehrgesetz*, pp. 114–18; Absolon, *Wehrgesetz*, pp. 117–20.

42. Absolon, *Wehrmacht*, pp. 9–12; Demeter, *Offizierkorps*, pp. 57–8, 320–1. Between 1935 and 1939 the number of army officers rose from 3,858 to 21,760, until May 1944 to 47,788; the reserve officer group rose from nearly 50,000 (1939) to 126,000 in May 1944 (Kroener, 'Weg', pp. 652–3).

43. Absolon, *Wehrmacht*, p. 11; Altrichter, *Wesen*, pp. 217–18.

44. Foertsch, *Wehrpflicht-Fibel*, pp. 33, 35 ff.; Bennewitz, *Wehrerziehung*, p. 23.

45. Hitler, *Kampf*, p. 307; Fischer, *Wehrpflicht*, pp. 126–7; Scholz, *Wehrpflicht*, pp. 60–1.

46. Demeter, *Offizierkorps*, pp. 309–11; Messerschmidt, *Wehrmacht*, pp. 216 ff., 422 ff.

47. Absolon, *Wehrgesetz*, pp. 152 ff.; Holm, *Wehrpflicht*, pp. 173–4; Gersdorff, *Frauen*, p. 55–6; Wette, 'Erfahrungen', p. 103; Deist, 'Aufrüstung', pp. 497 ff.

48. Resch, *Stellung*, p. 12; Gersdorff, *Frauen*, p. 62.

49. Frevert, *Women*, pp. 207 ff.

50. Gersdorff, *Frauen*, pp. 62, 74, 72; Kundrus, 'Geschichte', p. 721; Hitler, *Kampf*, p. 308; Foertsch, *Wehrpflicht-Fibel*, pp. 32, 80, 94–5.

51. Frevert, *Women*, pp. 222 ff.; Gersdorff, *Frauen*, pp. 49–56; Kundrus, *Geschichte*, pp. 731–2.

52. Fischer, *Wehrpflicht*, pp. 128, 138–42; Heckel, *Wehrverfassung*, p. 101.

53. Altrichter, *Wesen*, pp. 145–51; Stein, *Symbole*, pp. 104–5.

54. Bartov, *Front*, Chapter 3, and *Army*, Chapter 4; Kühne, 'Gruppenkohäsion'; Heer/Naumann, *War of Extermination*.

The Twentieth Century

55. Wette, 'Bild', p. 295; Kleßmann, *Staatsgründung*, p. 353; Meyer, *Soldaten*, p. 708. [English quotation from *Trial of the Major War Criminals before the International Military Tribunal*, vol. XXII, Nuremberg: 1948, p. 523]

56. Messerschmidt, in Heer/Naumann, *War of Extermination*, p. 381–99; Lockenour, *Soldiers*.

57. Wettig, *Entmilitarisierung*; Thoß, *Volksarmee*.

58. Gebhardt, 'Militär', p. 82; Rautenberg/Wiggershaus, "Denkschrift", pp. 168–70; Jacobsen, 'Rolle'.

59. Wettig, *Entmilitarisierung*, pp. 400–1; Abenheim, *Bundeswehr*, pp. 44 ff.; Large, *Germans*, pp. 114–15; *Bundestags-Berichte*, 1. Wahlperiode, 3.12.1952, p. 11141; Frei, *Vergangenheitspolitik*, pp. 77–8 [Translation of Adenauer's statement from the Armed Forces Journal International website].

60. Stumpf, 'Wiederverwendung'; Wenzke, 'Erbe', pp. 1113, 1120, and 'Wege', pp. 220 ff.; Danyel, 'Erinnerung', p. 1142; Hass, 'Bild'.

61. *Bundestags-Berichte*, 2. Wahlperiode, 132. Sitzung, 6.3.1956, pp. 6851 ff.; 159. Sitzung, 6.7.1956, pp. 8790–1; Frei, *Vergangenheitspolitik*, pp. 195 ff.; Jahn, *Wehrbeitrag*, pp. 166–71.

62. *Bundestags-Berichte*, 1. Wahlperiode, 16.12.1949, pp. 734–42; Wettig, *Entmilitarisierung*; Schubert, *Wiederbewaffnung*; Large, *Germans*, Parts 2 and 3; *Anfänge*, vols. 1 and 2.

63. Bald, *Militär*, p. 21; *Anfänge*, vol. 3. The Allies' reserved rights were only finally repealed in 1990 when both German states were unified.

64. Jahn, *Wehrbeitrag*, pp. 200 ff.; *Anfänge*, vol. 2, T. 2; vol. 3, T. 2; Doering-Manteuffel, *Katholizismus*, T. 3; Stoehr, Phalanx.

65. Vogt, *Militär*; *Bundestags-Berichte*, 2. Wahlperiode, 132. Sitzung, 6.3.1956, pp. 6845 ff.

66. Ebd.; Abenheim, *Bundeswehr*, pp. 56 ff.; *Anfänge*, vol. 1, pp. 777 ff.; vol. 3, pp. 853 ff.

67. Baudissin, 'Leitbild', pp. 28–32, 37; Large, *Germans*, pp. 176 ff.; Abenheim, *Bundeswehr*, pp. 92 ff., 104 ff., 134 ff.

68. *Süddeutsche Zeitung*, Nr. 154, 28./29.6.1969, pp. 1–2; Bald, 'Wehrmacht', pp. 396 ff.; Abenheim, *Bundeswehr*, pp. 113 ff., 168 ff.

69. Bald, 'Kameraden', pp. 51–5; Wettig, *Entmilitarisierung*, pp. 357 ff.; *Bundestags-Berichte*, 2. Wahlperiode, 159. Sitzung, 6.7.1956, p. 8780.

70. *Bundestags-Berichte*, 2. Wahlperiode, 176. Sitzung, 5.12.1956, p. 9757; Rautenberg, Bundeswehr, pp. 138 ff.; Anfänge, vol. 3, pp. 514 ff.

71. Anfänge, vol. 3, 519 ff.; Jahn, *Wehrbeitrag*, pp. 122–3; *Bundestags-Berichte*, 2. Wahlperiode, 159. Sitzung, 6.7.1956, pp. 8772 ff.

72. *Bundestags–Berichte*, 2. Wahlperiode, 159. Sitzung, 6.7.1956, p. 8781; Klotzbach, Weg, pp. 356–62; *Anfänge*, vol. 3, pp. 535 ff.

285-

73. After the Berlin Wall was built, the draft service period was increased to 18 months before being reduced in 1973 to 15 months, and to 12 months in 1991. The proportion of those drafted was initially rather low, since in the early years of the Bundeswehr the need for conscripts remained well below the numbers available from years with high birth rates: for those born in 1939, only 29% were drafted from those found fit when mustered, although this figure rose to reach 90% of the age-group born in 1946. Moreover, under a policy of 'equality in conscription', governments from the early 1970s have also been drafting the large group of those ranked unfit when mustered (comprising, in 1960s around 35% of all conscripts), using them for 'fixed tasks'. In 1980, the proportion of those fit for service when mustered was 76.5%, and in 1984 this figure reached nearly 82% (*Weißbuch 1970*, pp. 63–68; *Weißbuch 1985*, p. 246).
74. Meier-Dörnberg, 'Auseinandersetzung', p. 107; Bald, *Militär*, pp. 122–3. As the numbers applying rose (from 2777 in 1964 to 33,792 in 1972) the number rejected also increased; in 1964, 93% of the applications were granted, while in 1970 this figure fell to only 48% (*Verteidigung*, p. 258). *Süddeutsche Zeitung*, Nr. 154, 28./29.6.1969, p. 2; Krölls, *Kriegsdienstverweigerung*, pp. 85 ff., 242 ff.
75. *Anfänge*, vol. 3, pp. 526 ff.; Lutz, *Krieg*, pp. 48 ff., 75, 79 ff., 101 ff.; *Bundestags-Berichte*, 2. Wahlperiode, 159. Sitzung, 6.7.1956, pp. 8819, 8853.
76. *Bundestags-Berichte*, 2. Wahlperiode, 159. Sitzung, 6.7.1956, p. 8827; *Süddeutsche Zeitung*, Nr. 154, 28./29.6.1969, p. 2; Bald, *Militär*, pp. 120–1; *Entscheidungen*, vol. 48, pp. 127–206; *Gesellschaft*, p. 13.
77. Wettig, *Entmilitarisierung*, pp. 294 ff., 310, 335–6; *Anfänge*, vol. 3, pp. 920 ff., 1138 ff.; Wenzke, 'Kaderarmee', pp. 212 ff.; Diedrich, *Dienste*, pp. 339–69.
78. *Bundestags-Berichte*, 2. Wahlperiode, 132. Sitzung, 6.3.1956, p. 6851–2; Abenheim, *Bundeswehr*, pp. 65, 85, 102; Wenzke, 'Erbe', p. 1134; Stein, *Symbole*, pp. 112, 175, 185–6; Backerra, NVA, pp. 255–68; Herbell, *Staatsbürger*, pp. 499 ff.
79. Wenzke, 'Wehrpflicht', pp. 123 ff.; *Verteidigung*, p. 465; Studiengruppe Militärpolitik, *Volksarmee*, pp. 7, 61; *Wehrpflicht*, pp. 12–13.
80. Hoffmann, *Landesverteidigung*, pp. 63, 123; *Wehrpflicht*, p. 50; Studiengruppe Militärpolitik, *Volksarmee*, pp. 100 ff.; Kabel, *Militarisierung*, pp. 46 ff., 156 ff.; Diedrich, *Dienste*, pp. 169–99, 281–337; Bald u.a., *Volksarmee*, pp. 75–90; *Anfänge*, vol. 3, pp. 515 ff.
81. *Vom Sinn*, pp. 32, 50; Hoffmann, *Landesverteidigung*, p. 122; Studiengruppe Militärpolitik, *Volksarmee*, pp. 124–5; Herbell, *Staatsbürger*, pp. 12–13.
82. *Verteidigung*, pp. 266–7; Bald, *Militär*, pp. 150–1; Thoß, *Krieg*, pp. 233–4.

83. *Vom Sinn*, pp. 92, 13–14, 27; Kabel, *Militarisierung*, pp. 131 ff.
84. *Wehrpflicht*, pp. 16–17; Studiengruppe Militärpolitik, *Volksarmee*, pp. 155 ff.; Diedrich, *Dienste*, p. 445. West German employer associations and the Bundeswehr were opting for similar structures when they called for non-combat units in the Bundeswehr and rejected the legistation on conscientious objectors as too liberal (*Gesellschaft*, pp. 49–50).
85. Stern, *Staatsrecht*, vol. 3.2, pp. 995 ff., 1013 ff.; Hofmannn, 'Grundpflichten', §114.
86. *Entscheidungen*, pp. 148–9, 153–4. The proportion of conscientious objectors in each year's intake rose in the 1990s to more than 40%. Since at present around 20% of a given age-group is found not fit for service at the mustering, the balance between those doing military and civilian service is more or less equal (*FAZ* v. 14.5.1994, 2.2.1996).
87. Bartjes, 'Zivildienst', pp. 131, 133. In 1974, demoscopic research showed that 60% of respondees thought every conscript ought to be able to choose freely between military and civilian service; in the 16–29 age-group this figure was 80% (*Allensbacher Jahrbuch*, vol. 6, p. 106). The figure for those asked whether they thought civilian service was a 'more important service' for society than military service rose between 1980 and 1990 from 23% to 48%; conversely, the proportion of those ranking military service as more important fell from 24% to 10% (*Allensbacher Jahrbuch*, vol. 9, p. 1058).
88. Lutz, *Krieg*, p. 49; *FAZ* from 18.4.1994, Leader article p. 1; Birckenbach, *Gewissen*, p. 120; Lippert, 'Lagefeststellung', pp. 12 ff.
89. *Anfänge*, vol. 3, p. 523; *Der Spiegel*, Nr. 20, 16.5.1956, p. 16; Noelle/Neumann, *Jahrbuch*, pp. 304, 307–8; on similar attitudes in the GDR Bald et al., *Volksarmee*, p. 160.
90. Kleßmann, *Staaten*, p. 367; Kabel, *Militarisierung*, pp. 110 ff.; *Frau von Heute*, 3.3.1961, p. 7; 20.10.1961, p. 6.
91. *Brigitte*, Nr. 24, 1961, pp. 70–71.
92. Schubert, *Sicherheitspolitik*, vol. 2, pp. 389–90.
93. Baudissin, 'Leitbild', pp. 33, 35–6; Schubert, *Sicherheitspolitik*, vol. 2, pp. 407–17; Kutz, 'Militär', pp. 293 ff.; Abenheim, *Bundeswehr*, pp. 184 ff.
94. The Prussian traditions in the NVA not only included provisions requiring the uniform to be worn on furlough, or keeping the goosestep at military parades; the GDR military criminal code was far more directed towards sealing off the military than the FRG military criminal law which only covered certain offences specifically related to the troops, and which in peacetime fell under the jurisdiction of civil courts. In contrast, cases under the GDR military criminal code were heard in front of a military court, in a way reminiscent of the situation in Imperial Germany. Regulating appeals were similarly dealt with as internal military matters, while in West Germany, creating the parliamentary

commissioner gave such processes an essentially civilian touch. (*Wehrpflicht*, pp. 28 ff.; Kabel, *Militarisierung*, pp. 145 ff.; Diedrich, *Dienste*, pp. 461 ff.).

95. Brockmann, 'Militär'; Abenheim, *Bundeswehr*, p. 183; Birckenbach, 'Wehrdienst', pp. 205 ff.

96. Kühne, 'Soldat', pp. 347 ff.

97. Spiers, *Army*; Bond, 'Experience'; Strachan, *Army*, and also Strachan, *Politics*; Kirkpatrick, 'Entscheidung'; Chambers II, *To Raise*; and *Draftees*.

98. For a more complex definition of citizenship compare Walzer, *Obligations*, Parts 1 and 3; Thompson, *Citizen*; Shklar, *Citizenship*; Kerber, *Right*.

99. *Wehrpflicht*, pp. 10–11; Deutscher Bundestag. Ausschuß für Rechtswesen und Verfassungsrecht, 16. Ausschuß, Stenographische Protokolle, 106. Sitzung (6.2.1956), pp. 2–12; 110. Sitzung (20.2.1956), pp. 3–10.

100. Ibid.; Seifert, 'Gender'; Kraake, *Frauen*, Chapters 3 and 5; Albrecht-Heide/ Bujewski-Crawford, *Frauen*. On the discussion in the USA see Jones, 'Ranks'.

Bibliography

I. Archives

Geheimes Staatsarchiv (GStA) Berlin-Dahlem
Bundesarchiv-Militärarchiv Freiburg
Nordrhein-Westfälisches Hauptstaatsarchiv (HStA) Düsseldorf
Nordrhein-Westfälisches Staatsarchiv (StA) Münster
Nordrhein-Westfälisches Staatsarchiv (StA) Detmold
Sächsisches Hauptstaatsarchiv (HStA) Dresden
Bayerisches Hauptstaatsarchiv (HStA) Munich
Hauptstaatsarchiv (HStA) Stuttgart

II. Journals and Periodicals

Allgemeine Militär-Zeitung, ed. Gesellschaft deutscher Offiziere und Militär-beamten, Leipzig/Darmstadt, vols 1–77, 1826–1902.
Militärische Blätter, in Verbindung mit Mehreren ed. R. de l'Homme de Courbiere, Berlin, vols 1–30, 1859–1873.
Militair-Wochenblatt (from 1877: *Militär-Wochenblatt*), Berlin, vols 1–126, 1816–1942.
Militär-Zeitung. Organ für die Reserve- und Landwehr-Offiziere des Deutschen Heeres, Berlin, vols 1 ff., 1878 ff.
Die Schnur. Zeitschrift der Vereinigung ehemaliger Einjährig-Freiwilliger, Kampfgenossen von 1864, 1866, 1870/71, Berlin, vols 1 ff., 1896 ff.

III. Printed Sources

Abbt, T., 'Vom Tode für das Vaterland (1761)', in: F. Brüggemann (ed.), *Der Siebenjährige Krieg im Spiegel der zeitgenössischen Literatur*, Leipzig, 1935, pp. 47–94.
Actenstücke für die Deutschen, oder Sammlung aller officiellen Bekanntmachungen in dem Kriege von 1813, vols 1 and 3, Dresden, no date.
Noelle-Neumann, E. (ed.), *Allensbacher Jahrbuch für Demoskopie 1974–1976*, vol. 6, Vienna, 1976.

Bibliography

Noelle-Neumann, E. (ed.), *Allensbacher Jahrbuch der Demoskopie 1984–1992*, vol. 9, Munich, 1993.

Albert, R., *Wie ich flügge wurde. Jugenderinnerungen eines Arbeiters*, Stuttgart, 1916.

Altrichter, F., *Das Wesen der soldatischen Erziehung*, Oldenburg, 1935.

Arndt, E. M., *Zwei Worte über die Entstehung und Bestimmung der Teutschen Legion; Was bedeutet Landsturm und Landwehr?* (1813), ND Berlin, 1988.

Arndt, E. M., *Grundlinien einer teutschen Kriegsordnung*, Leipzig, 1813.

Bächtold, H., *Deutscher Soldatenbrauch und Soldatenglaube*, Straßburg, 1917.

J.B. Basedows Elementarwerk, ed. T. Fritzsch, vol. 1, Leipzig, 1909.

Baudissin, W. Graf v., 'Das Leitbild des zukünftigen Soldaten', *Die Neue Gesellschaft* 2 (1955), pp. 26–37.

Baumgarten, O., *Meine Lebensgeschichte*, Tübingen, 1929.

Bavaria. Landes- und Volkskunde des Königreichs Bayern, vol. 4, 2. Abt., Munich, 1867.

Bebel, A., *Die Frau und der Sozialismus*, reprint Frankfurt, 1976.

Bebel, A., *Nicht stehendes Heer, sondern Volkswehr*, reprint Leipzig, 1989.

Bennewitz, G., *Die geistige Wehrerziehung der deutschen Jugend*, Berlin, 1940.

Bergg, F., *Ein Proletarierleben*, Frankfurt, 1913.

Bernstein, E., *Von 1850 bis 1872. Kindheit und Jugendjahre*, Berlin, 1926.

Beschreibung des Oberamts Rottenburg, ed. Kgl. Statistisches Landesamt, vol. 1, Stuttgart 1899.

Beyschlag, W., *Aus meinem Leben*, Halle, 1896.

Biefang, A. (ed.), *Der Deutsche Nationalverein 1859–1867. Vorstands- und Ausschußprotokolle*, Düsseldorf, 1995.

Bindewald, G., 'Die Wehrfähigkeit der ländlichen und städtischen Bevölkerung', *Jahrbuch für Gesetzgebung, Verwaltung und Volkswirtschaft* 25 (1901), pp. 521–80.

Binding, R., *Erlebtes Leben*, Frankfurt, 1928.

Bode, F., *Glückliche Tage*, Kassel, 1942.

Bodelschwingh, E. v. (ed.), *Leben des Ober-Präsidenten Freiherrn von Vincke*, Part 1, Berlin, 1853.

Bosse, R., *Aus der Jugendzeit*, Leipzig, 1904.

Bothmer, R. Graf v., *Jugend und Wehrkraft*, Munich, 1911.

Boyen, H. v., *Erinnerungen 1771–1813*, Berlin, 1953.

Bräker, U., 'Lebensgeschichte und natürliche Ebenteuer des armen Mannes im Tockenburg (1789)', in U. Bräker (ed.), *Werke*, Berlin, 1966, pp. 83–281.

Braun, M. Freiherr v., *Von Ostpreußen bis Texas*, Stollhalm, 1956.

Brentano, L. and Kuczynski, R., *Die heutige Grundlage der deutschen Wehrkraft*, Stuttgart, 1900.

Breysig, K., *Aus meinen Tagen und Träumen*, Berlin, 1962.

Briefe über Rekruten-Ausbildung. Von einem Kavallerieoffizier, Berlin, 1892.

Brockhaus, R. (ed.), *Aus den Tagebüchern von Heinrich Brockhaus*, vols 1 and 2, Leipzig, 1884.

Bromme, M. Th. W., *Lebensgeschichte eines modernen Fabrikarbeiters* (1905), Frankfurt, 1971.

Bunsen, M. v., *Die Welt in der ich lebte 1860–1912*, Biberach, 1959 (1929).

C.v.W., *Denkschrift den Antrag des achten Provinzial-Landtages der Provinz Preußen, die Vermehrung der Wehrhaftigkeit des Volkes betreffend*, Berlin, 1848.

Claß, H., *Wider den Strom*, Leipzig, 1932.

Das Volk braucht Licht. Frauen zur Zeit des Aufbruchs 1790–1848 in ihren Briefen, Darmstadt, 1970.

Delbrück, R. von, *Lebenserinnerungen 1817–1867*, vol. 1, Leipzig, 1905.

Deutscher Landwirthschaftsrath, *Die Bedeutung der landwirthschaftlichen Bevölkerung für die Wehrkraft des Deutschen Reiches*, Berlin, 1902.

Deutschland-Bericht der Sopade 1934, reprint Frankfurt, 1980.

Devrient, E., *Aus seinen Tagebüchern. Berlin-Dresden 1836–1852*, ed. Rolf Kabel, Weimar, 1964.

Dieterici, F.W.C. (ed.), *Mittheilungen des statistischen Bureau's in Berlin*, vol. 8, Berlin, 1855.

Dietz, H., *Das Wehrgesetz vom 21. Mai 1935 und seine Ausführung*, Dresden, 1936.

Dirkreiter, H. G., *Die Geschichte meines Lebens*, 2 vols, no place, no date.

Dittmar, W., *Die Heeres-Ergänzung*, 2nd edn, Magdeburg, 1851.

Dohm, C. W., *Ueber die bürgerliche Verbesserung der Juden*, 2 vols, Berlin, 1781/1783.

Dohm, H., *Die wissenschaftliche Emancipation der Frau*, reprint Zürich, 1982.

Domarus, M., *Hitler. Reden und Proklamationen*, vol. 1, Munich, 1965.

Dowe, D. (ed.), *Berichte über die Verhandlungen der Vereinstage deutscher Arbeitervereine 1863 bis 1869*, reprint Berlin, 1980.

Dowe, D. (ed.), *Protokolle und Materialien des Allgemeinen Deutschen Arbeitervereins (inkl. Splittergruppen)*, reprint Berlin, 1980.

Ehrenberg, F., *Der Charakter und die Bestimmung des Mannes*, 2nd edn, Elberfeld, 1822.

Ellrodt, F. W. v., *Ueber Zweck und Einrichtung des Bürger-Militairs der freien Stadt Frankfurt*, Frankfurt, 1823.

Engel, E., 'Resultate des Ersatz-Aushebungsgeschäfts im preussischen Staate in den Jahren von 1855 bis mit 1862', *Zeitschrift des Königlich Preussischen Statistischen Bureaus* 4 (1864), pp. 65–84.

Engel, E., 'Noch einmal Resultate des Ersatz-Aushebungsgeschäfts und die Militärdienst-Steuer', *Zeitschrift des Königlich Preussischen Statistischen Bureaus* 4 (1864), pp. 173–86.

Engel, E., 'Die Gesundheit und Sterblichkeit der königl. Preussischen Armee in dem 18jährigen Zeitraum von 1846 bis mit 1863', *Zeitschrift des Königlich Preussischen Statistischen Bureaus* 5 (1865), pp. 193–237.

Engel, E., 'Das Institut der einjährig Freiwilligen in der preussischen und norddeutschen Bundesarmee', *Zeitschrift des Königlich Preussischen Statistischen Bureaus* 9 (1869), pp. 241–259.

Engels, F., *The Prussian Military Question and the German Workers' Party*, trans. Barrie Selman, International Workingman's Association.

Enters, H., *Die kleine mühselige Welt des jungen Hermann Enters*, 2nd edn, Wuppertal, 1971.

Entscheidungen des Bundesverfassungsgerichts, vol. 48, Tübingen, 1979.

Estorff, E. v., *Anleitung zum Unterricht über Fahneneid, Kriegsartikel und Berufspflichten*, 4th edn, Berlin, 1902.

Ewald, J. L., *Der gute Jüngling, gute Gatte und Vater, oder Mittel, um es zu werden*, vol. 2, Frankfurt, 1804.

F., Elisabethe v., *Frauensteuer an der Wiege des wiedergebornen Vaterlandes*, no place, no date.

Fischer, C., *Denkwürdigkeiten und Erinnerungen eines Arbeiters*, ed. P. Göhre, vol. 1, Leipzig, 1904.

Fischer, F. L., *Arbeiterschicksale*, Berlin, 1906.

Fischer, W., *Die Deutsche Wehrpflicht, ihre Rechtsgrundlagen und ihre Rechtsnatur*, Ph.D. Tübingen, 1938.

Foertsch, H., *Wehrpflicht-Fibel*, Berlin, 1935.

Fontane, T., *Von Zwanzig bis Dreißig. Autobiographisches*, ed. O. Drude, Frankfurt, 1987.

Föppl, A., *Lebenserinnerungen*, Munich, 1925.

Frank, J. P., *System einer vollständigen medicinischen Policey*, vol. 2, Vienna, 1786.

Frauenholz, E., *Die Entwicklung des Gedankens der allgemeinen Wehrpflicht im neunzehnten Jahrhundert*, Munich, 1925.

Freiherr vom Stein, *Ausgewählte politische Briefe und Denkschriften*, ed. E. Botzenhart and G. Ipsen, Stuttgart, 1955.

Freiherr vom Stein, *Briefe und amtliche Schriften*, ed. W. Hubatsch, vols 2 and 3, Stuttgart, 1960/1961.

Freund, I., *Die Emanzipation der Juden in Preußen*, 2 vols, Berlin, 1912.

Füllkrug, G. F., *Der Selbstmord. Eine moralstatistische und volkspsychologische Untersuchung*, Schwerin, 1919.

Fürstenberg, C., *Die Lebensgeschichte eines deutschen Bankiers, niedergeschrieben von Hans Fürstenberg*, Wiesbaden, 1961.

Gennrich, P., *Erinnerungen aus meinem Leben*, Königsberg, 1938.

Gerhard, D. and Norvin, W. (eds), *Die Briefe des Barthold Georg Niebuhr*, 2 vols, Berlin, 1926/29.

Gesellschaft und Verteidigung, Bonn, 1978.

Gillhaußen, G. v., *Eideshart und treufest. Ein Freund und Führer in aktiver Dienstzeit wie im Beurlaubtenstande*, 2nd edn, Berlin, 1907.

Gleim, B., *Was hat das wiedergeborne Deutschland von seinen Frauen zu fordern?*, Bremen, 1814.

Goebel, K. and Wichelhaus, M. (eds), *Aufstand der Bürger. Revolution 1849 im westdeutschen Industriezentrum*, Wuppertal, 1974.

Göhre, P., *Drei Monate Fabrikarbeiter und Handwerksbursche*, Leipzig, 1891.

Goldammer, P. (ed.), *1848. Augenzeugen der Revolution*, Berlin, 1973.

Goltz, C. Freiherr v. d., *Das Volk in Waffen. Ein Buch über Heerwesen und Kriegführung unserer Zeit*, Berlin, 1883.

Goos, B., *Erinnerungen an meine Jugend*, Hamburg, 1907.

Graf, A., *Schülerjahre*, Berlin, 1912.

Granier, H. (ed.) *Berichte aus der Berliner Franzosenzeit 1807–1809*, Leipzig, 1913.

Gregory, M. Freifrau v., *Dreißig Jahre preußische Soldatenfrau*, Brünn, 1944.

Grube, M., *Jugenderinnerungen eines Glückskindes*, Leipzig, 1917.

GutsMuths, J. C. F., *Gymnastik für die Jugend*, Schnepfenthal, 1793.

GutsMuths, J. C. F., *Turnbuch für die Söhne des Vaterlandes*, Frankfurt, 1817 (reprint 1973).

Haegert, W., 'Nationalsozialismus und Allgemeine Wehrpflicht', *Wehrfreiheit. Jahrbuch der Deutschen Gesellschaft für Wehrpolitik und Wehrwissenschaften* (1935), pp. 20–5.

Hansen, J. (ed.), *Rheinische Briefe und Akten zur Geschichte der politischen Bewegung 1830–1850*, vol. 1, reprint Osnabrück, 1967.

Harkort, F., *Die Zeiten des ersten Westphälischen (16.) Landwehrregiments. Ein Beitrag zur Geschichte der Befreiungskriege 1813–1814–1815*, ed. W. Köllmann, Hagen, 1964.

Hasenclever, W., *Erlebtes. Erinnerungen 1857–1871*, Arnsberg, 1987.

Heck, L., *Heiter, ernste Lebensbeichte. Erinnerungen eines alten Tiergärtners*, Berlin, 1938.

Heckel, J., *Wehrverfassung und Wehrrecht des großdeutschen Reiches*, vol. 1, Hamburg, 1939.

Heim, E. L., *Tagebücher und Erinnerungen*, Leipzig, 1989.

Heine, W., 'Wie bekämpfen wir den Militarismus?', *Sozialistische Monatshefte* 2 (1907), pp. 911–18.

Henseling, W., *Die Kriegsartikel mit Erläuterungen*, 4th edn, Berlin, 1902.

Hentig, W. O. von, *Mein Leben – eine Dienstreise*, 2nd edn, Göttingen, 1963.

Bibliography

Heyberger, J. (ed.), *Der Kamerad. Ein Lesebuch zur Unterhaltung und Belehrung für bayrische Soldaten*, Munich, 1872.

Hitler, A., *Mein Kampf*, Munich, 1933.

Hoenig, F., *Die Mannszucht in ihrer Bedeutung für Staat, Volk und Heer*, Berlin, 1882.

Hoffmann, H., *Sozialistische Landesverteidigung. Aus Reden und Aufsätzen 1970 bis Februar 1974*, Berlin, 1974.

Huber, E. R. (ed.), *Dokumente zur deutschen Verfassungsgeschichte*, 2 vols, Stuttgart, 1961/1964.

Hummel-Haasis, G. (ed.), *Schwestern zerreißt eure Ketten. Zeugnisse zur Geschichte der Frauen in der Revolution von 1848/49*, Munich, 1982.

Jäger, E., *Das Militärwesen des Königreichs Württemberg*, Stuttgart, 1869.

Jahn, F. L., *Deutsches Volkstum* (1810), ed. F. Brümmer, Leizpig, no date.

Jahn, H. E., *Für und gegen den Wehrbeitrag. Argumente und Dokumente*, Cologne, 1957.

Jenaczek, F. (ed.), *Ferdinand Lassalle: Reden und Schriften. Aus der Arbeiteragitation 1862–1864*, Munich, 1970.

Johanning, C., *Vorgänge zwischen Militair und Civil in Bielefeld*, Leipzig, 1847.

Jolly, L., 'Die Militärsteuer oder das Wehrgeld', *Zeitschrift des Königlich Preussischen Statistischen Bureaus* 9 (1869), pp. 319–30.

Jünger, E., 'Der Kampf als inneres Erlebnis (1922)', in E. Jünger (ed.), *Sämtliche Werke*, 2. Abt., vol. 7, Stuttgart, 1980, pp. 11–103.

Kaun, H., *Aus meinem Leben*, Berlin, 1932.

Kessler, H. Graf, *Gesichter und Zeiten. Erinnerungen*, Frankfurt, 1988.

Klemperer, V., *Curriculum Vitae. Jugend um 1900*, 2 vols, Berlin, 1989.

Köhler, H., *Lebenserinnerungen des Politikers und Staatsmannes 1878–1949*, Stuttgart, 1964.

Körner, O., *Erinnerungen eines deutschen Arztes und Hochschullehrers 1858–1914*, Munich, 1920.

Krafft, *Dienst und Leben des jungen Infanterie-Offiziers*, Berlin, 1914.

Kroh, O., *Erziehung im Heere*, Langensalza, 1926.

Kruse, F., *Vergangenes und Gebliebenes. Lebenserinnerungen eines preußischen Beamten*, Eschwege, 1967.

Kügelgen, H. M. v., *Ein Lebensbild in Briefen*, 8th edn, Stuttgart, 1922.

Kügelgen, W. v., *Bürgerleben. Die Briefe an den Bruder Gerhard 1840–1867*, ed. W. Killy, Munich, 1990.

Kühlmann, R. v., *Erinnerungen*, Heidelberg, 1948.

Lange, H., *Kampfzeiten*, vol. 2, Berlin, 1928.

Langfeld, A., *Mein Leben. Erinnerungen*, Schwerin, 1930.

Liebermann v. Wahlendorf and W. Ritter, *Erinnerungen eines deutschen Juden 1863–1936*, ed. E. R. Piper, Munich, 1988.

Lubarsch, O., *Ein bewegtes Gelehrtenleben. Erinnerungen und Erlebnisse, Kämpfe und Gedanken*, Berlin, 1931.

Lübke, W., *Lebenserinnerungen*, Berlin, 1893.

Macke, A., *Briefe an Elisabeth und die Freunde*, Munich, 1987.

Marx, A. B., *Erinnerungen*, Berlin, 1865.

May, R. E., *Konfessionelle Militärstatistik*, Tübingen, 1917.

Meinecke, F., *Erlebtes 1862–1901*, Leipzig, 1941.

Menzel, M., *Der Deutsche Infanterist*, 4th edn, Hofgeismar, 1894.

Menzel, M., *Der Infanterie-Einjährige und Offizier des Beurlaubtenstandes. Ausbildung und Doppelstellung im Heer und Staat. Ein Lehr- und Lernbuch, sowie treuer Ratgeber für Einjährige etc., Reserve-, Landwehr-Offiziere, für jüngere Linien-Offiziere, für Fahnenjunker und Fähnriche*, 5th edn, edited by Eckart v. Wurmb, Berlin, 1901.

Menzel, M., *Dienstunterricht des deutschen Infanteristen*, Berlin, 1910.

Meyer, E. H., *Badisches Volksleben im neunzehnten Jahrhundert* (1900), reprint Stuttgart, 1984.

Meyer, G., *Die Lebenstragödie eines Tagelöhners*, Berlin, 1909.

Misch, C., *Geschichte des Vaterländischen Frauen-Vereins 1866–1916*, Berlin, 1917.

Mohl, R. v., *Lebens-Erinnerungen 1799–1875*, vol. 1, Stuttgart, 1902.

Mommsen, A., *Mein Vater. Erinnerungen an Theodor Mommsen*, Munich, 1992.

Müller, K. A. v., *Aus Gärten der Vergangenheit. Erinnerungen 1882–1914*, Stuttgart, 1958.

Neuendorff, E., *Geschichte der neueren deutschen Leibesübungen vom Beginn des 18. Jahrhunderts bis zur Gegenwart*, vol. 1, Dresden, 1930.

Niemeyer, V., *Lebenserinnerungen eines Siebzigjährigen*, Berlin, 1937.

Niese, C., *Von gestern und Vorgestern. Lebenserinnerungen*, Leipzig, 1924.

Noelle, E. and Neumann E. P. (eds), *Jahrbuch der öffentlichen Meinung 1957*, Allensbach, 1957.

Nostitz Drzewiecki, H.C.F. v., *Die Communalgarden des Königreichs Sachsen, in ihrer Entstehung, gesetzlichen Begründung, Organisirung und gegenwärtigen Gestalt*, Dresden, 1832.

Obermann, K., *Flugblätter der Revolution. Eine Flugblattsammlung zur Geschichte der Revolution von 1848/49 in Deutschland*, Berlin, 1970.

Obermayer, H., *Die Wehrkraftbewegung*, Munich, 1914.

Oertzen, K.L.v., *Grundzüge der Wehrpolitik*, 2nd edn, ed. Hermann Foertsch, Hamburg, 1938.

Otto, L., *Frauenleben im deutschen Reich. Erinnerungen aus der Vergangenheit mit Hinweis auf Gegenwart und Zukunft*, Leipzig, 1876.

Pappenheim, A. v., *Militairische Fantasieen über Heerbildung, Heerverfaßung und was auf das Soldatenwesen Bezug hat*, vol. 1, Augsburg, 1831.

Paulsen, F., *System der Ethik mit einem Umriß der Staats- und Gesellschaftslehre*, 3rd edn, vol. 2, Berlin, 1894.

Paulsen, F., *Die deutschen Universitäten und das Universitätsstudium*, Berlin, 1902.

Paulsen, F., *Aus meinem Leben. Jugenderinnerungen*, Jena, 1909.

Pfister, A., *Deutsche Zwietracht. Erinnerungen aus meiner Leutnantszeit 1859–1869*, Stuttgart, 1902.

Pockels, C. F., *Der Mann. Ein anthropologisches Charaktergemälde seines Geschlechts*, vol. 1, Hannover, 1805.

Preuss, Eduard, *Die höheren Aufgaben des jungen Offiziers für Armee und Volk*, Munich 1906.

Die Preußische Landwehr in ihrer Entwicklung von 1815 bis zur Reorganisation von 1859, Berlin 1967.

Protokoll über die Verhandlungen des Allgemeinen Deutschen sozial-demokratischen Arbeiterkongresses zu Eisenach am 7., 8. und 9. August 1869, Leipzig, 1869.

Protokoll des Vereinigungs-Congresses der Sozialdemokraten Deutschlands, abgehalten zu Gotha, vom 22. bis 27. Mai 1875, Leipzig, 1875.

Protokoll über die Verhandlungen des Parteitags der Sozialdemokratischen Partei Deutschlands. Abgehalten zu Erfurt vom 14. bis 20. Oktober 1891, Berlin, 1891.

Rathenau, W., *Gesammelte Schriften*, vol. 1, Berlin, 1918.

Rehbein, F., *Das Leben eines Landarbeiters* (1911), Hamburg, 1985.

Reil, J. C., *Diätetischer Hausarzt*, vol. 2, Frankfurt, 1791.

Die Reorganisation der Preußischen Armee nach dem Tilsiter Frieden, 2 vols, Berlin, 1862/66.

Resch, I., *Die Stellung der Frau im neuen deutschen Wehrrecht*, Ph.D. Marburg, 1940.

Reuter, G., *Vom Kinde zum Menschen. Die Geschichte meiner Jugend*, Berlin, 1921.

Riesser, G., *Gesammelte Schriften*, ed. M. Isler, 3 vols, Frankfurt, 1867.

Ringelnatz, J., *Gesammelte Werke*, vol. 6, Berlin, 1983.

Rocholl, T., *Ein Malerleben. Erinnerungen*, Berlin, 1921.

Rodenwaldt, E., *Aufnahmen des geistigen Inventars Gesunder als Maßstab für Defektprüfungen bei Kranken*, M.D., Halle, 1904.

Rönne, L. v., *Das Staatsrecht der Preußischen Monarchie*, vol. 2, 4th edn, Leipzig, 1882.

Roloff, E. M. (ed.), *Lexikon der Pädagogik*, Freiburg, 1914.

Roloff, G., 'Die Deutschen Kriegervereine', *Preußische Jahrbücher* 85 (1896), pp. 124–34

Roon, A. v., *Denkwürdigkeiten aus dem Leben des Generalfeldmarschalls Kriegsministers Grafen von Roon*, vol. 2, 5th edn, Berlin, 1905.

Rosenberg, H., *Die nationalpolitische Publizistik Deutschlands vom Eintritt der Neuen Ära in Preußen bis zum Ausbruch des Deutschen Krieges. Eine kritische Bibliographie*, 2 vols, Munich, 1935.

Rotteck, C. v., 'Gemeingeist', *Staats-Lexikon*, 2. Aufl., Bd. 5, Altona, 1847, pp. 514–22.

Rotteck, K. v., *Stehende Heere und Nationalmiliz*, Freiburg, 1816.

Scheel, H. and Schmidt, D. (ed.), *Das Reformministerium Stein*, 3 vols, Berlin, 1966/1968.

Schlötzer, L. v., *Aus der Jugendzeit*, Dresden, 1938.

Schmidt, G., *Charlotte Perthes. Das Lebensbild einer deutschen Frau (1794–1874)*, Gotha, 1929.

Schmidt, P. v., *Die Erziehung des Soldaten*, Berlin, 1894.

Scholz, B., *Verklungene Weisen. Erinnerungen*, Mainz, 1911.

Scholz, G., *Die Allgemeine Wehrpflicht in Deutschland und in der Welt*, Hamburg, 1935.

Schott, W., *Ein Künstlerleben und gesellschaftliche Erinnerungen aus kaiserlicher Zeit*, Dresden, 1930.

Schubert, K. v. (ed.), *Sicherheitspolitik der Bundesrepublik Deutschland. Dokumentation 1945–1977*, 2 vols, Cologne, 1978/79.

Schubert, W. (ed.), *Der Provinziallandtag der Rheinprovinz von 1841, 1843 und 1845*, vol. 5, Vaduz, 1990.

Schulz-Oldendorf, W., *Briefe eines Rekruten an seine Mutter*, Berlin, 1913.

Schumacher, T., *Vom Schulmädel bis zur Großmutter*, Stuttgart, 1900.

Schumacher, T., *Was ich als Kind erlebte*, Stuttgart, 1901.

Severing, C., *Mein Lebensweg*, vol. 1, Cologne, 1950.

Silling, M., *Jugenderinnerungen einer Stettiner Kaufmannstochter*, Greifswald, 1921.

Spielhagen, F., *Finder und Erfinder*, vol. 2, Leipzig, 1890.

Spielhagen, F., *Erinnerungen aus meinem Leben*, Leipzig, 1911.

Spohn, *Die Einjährig-Freiwilligen, Offizier-Aspiranten der Reserve und Offiziere des Beurlaubtenstandes aller Waffen. Ihre Bedeutung für die Armee und ihre Ausbildung*, Berlin, 1906.

Spohn, *Die Erziehung des Soldaten für seinen Beruf in Krieg und Frieden*, Berlin, 1907.

Stenographische Berichte über die Verhandlungen der zur Vereinbarung der preußischen Staats-Verfassung berufenen Versammlung, 3 vols, Berlin, 1848.

Stenographische Berichte über die Verhandlungen des Preußischen Abgeordnetenhauses (o.ä.), (inkl. sämmtl. Drucksachen; Anlagen), Berlin 1860 ff.

Stenographische Berichte über die Verhandlungen des Reichstags des Norddeutschen Bundes, vol. 1, Berlin, 1867.

Stenographische Berichte über die Verhandlungen des Deutschen Reichstags, Berlin, 1871 ff.

Stenographische Berichte über die Verhandlungen der Verfassungsgebenden Deutschen Nationalversammlung, Berlin, 1920.

Stenographische Berichte über die Verhandlungen des Reichstags, Berlin, 1921 ff.

Stenographische Berichte über die Verhandlungen des Deutschen Bundestages, Bonn, 1949 ff.

Strätz, R., *Schwert und Feder. Erinnerungen aus jungen Jahren*, Berlin, 1925.

Stürenburg, H., *Wehrpflicht und Erziehung*, Berlin, 1879.

Temperley, H. W. V. (ed.), *A History of the Peace Conference in Paris*, vol. 2, London, 1920.

Thorwart, F. (ed.), *Hermann Schulze-Delitzsch´s Schriften und Reden*, vol. 3, Berlin, 1910.

Transfeldt, W., *Wort und Brauchtum des Soldaten*, 5th edn, Hamburg, 1959.

Treitschke, H. v., *Politik. Vorlesungen*, ed. M. Cornicelius, 2 vols, 2nd edn, Leipzig, 1899/1900.

Treue, W. (ed.), *Deutsche Parteiprogramme seit 1861*, 4th edn, Göttingen, 1968.

Vaupel, R. (ed.), *Die Reorganisation des preußischen Staates unter Stein und Hardenberg*, vol. 1, Part 2, Leipzig, 1938.

Verhandlungen der Ersten und Zweiten Kammer der Stände-Versammlung des Großherzogthums Baden (o.ä.), Karlsruhe, 1822 ff. (with protocol and supplemental booklets).

Verhandlungen der Württembergischen Kammer der Abgeordneten, Stuttgart.

Ein Vermächtnis Moltke´s: Stärkung der sinkenden Wehrkraft, Berlin, 1892.

Vieth, G. U. A., *Versuch einer Encyklopädie der Leibesübungen*, Berlin, 1795.

Vogelsang, T., 'Neue Dokumente zur Geschichte der Reichswehr 1930–1933', *Vierteljahrshefte für Zeitgeschichte* 2 (1954), pp. 397–436.

Vogl, A. v., *Die wehrpflichtige Jugend Bayerns*, Munich, 1905.

Vom Sinn des Soldatseins. Ein Ratgeber für den Soldaten, 34th edn, Berlin, 1984.

Die Vorrechte der Offiziere im Staate und in der Gesellschaft, Berlin, 1883.

Wagner, C. and Röder H. F., *Die Allgemeine Wehrpflicht*, Berlin, 1935.

Wallraf, M., *Aus einem rheinischen Leben*, Hamburg, 1926.

Warburg, M. M., *Aus meinen Aufzeichnungen*, Glückstadt, 1952.

Weber, Marianne, *Max Weber. Ein Lebensbild*, Heidelberg, 1950.

Weber, M., *Jugendbriefe*, Tübingen, 1936.

Weismann, H., *Das allgemeine deutsche Schützenfest zu Frankfurt am Main, Juli 1862. Ein Gedenkbuch*, Frankfurt, 1863.

Weißbuch 1970. Zur Sicherheit der Bundesrepublik Deutschland und zur Lage der Bundeswehr, ed. Bundesminister der Verteidigung, Bonn, 1970.

Weißbuch 1985. Zur Lage und Entwicklung der Bundeswehr, ed. Bundesminister der Verteidigung, Bonn, 1985.

Welcker, C., *Geschlechtsverhältnisse*, in *Staats-Lexikon*, vol. 6, Altona, 1838, pp. 629–65.

Welcker, C., *Anhang zum Artikel Heerwesen (Landwehrsystem)*, in *Staats-Lexikon*, vol. 7, Altona, 1839, pp. 589–607.

Welcker, C., *Bürgertugend und Bürgersinn*, in *Staats-Lexikon*, 2nd edn, vol. 2, Altona, 1846, S. 763–70.

Wermuth, A., *Ein Beamtenleben. Erinnerungen*, Berlin, 1922.

Westphal, A., *Das Deutsche Kriegervereinswesen, seine Ziele und seine Bedeutung für den Staat*, Berlin, 1903.

Westphal, A., *Handbuch für die Kriegervereine des Preußischen Landes-Kriegerverbandes*, Berlin, 1906.

Westphalen, L. Graf v. (ed.), *Die Tagebücher des Oberpräsidenten Ludwig Freiherrn Vincke 1813–1818*, Münster, 1980.

Wieber, F., *Aus meinem Leben*, Berlin, 1924.

Wigard, F. (ed.), *Stenographischer Bericht über die Verhandlungen der Deutschen Constituierenden Nationalversammlung zu Frankfurt am Main*, 9 vols, Frankfurt/Leipzig, 1848/49.

Wilke, A. v., *Altberliner Erinnerungen*, Berlin, 1930.

Wille, B., *Aus Traum und Kampf. Mein 60jähriges Leben*, Berlin, 1920.

Willich, A. v., *Im preußischen Heere!*, Mannheim, 1848.

Winter, G. (ed.), *Die Reorganisation des Preußischen Staats unter Stein und Hardenberg*, vol. 1, Part 1, Leipzig, 1931.

Wirth, J. G. A., *Das Nationalfest der Deutschen zu Hambach*, issue 2, Neustadt, 1832.

Wolf, G. (ed.), *Anna Louisa Karschin. Gedichte und Briefe*, Berlin, 1981.

Wolff, A., *Berliner Revolutions-Chronik*, 3 vols, Berlin, 1851/1854.

Wolff, M., *Leben und Briefe*, ed. F. Wolff, Hamburg, 1925.

Woltmann, K. v., *Über Natur, Bestimmung, Tugend und Bildung der Frauen*, Vienna, 1826.

Wuttke, A., *Der deutsche Volksaberglaube der Gegenwart*, Berlin, 1900.

Wyneken, G., 'Die Militarisierung der deutschen Jugend (1913)' in G. Wyneken, *Der Kampf für die Jugend*, Jena, 1919, pp. 204–214.

Zweig, S., *Die Welt von gestern. Erinnerungen eines Europäers*, Stockholm, 1944.

IV. Most Important Secondary Literature

Abenheim, D., *Bundeswehr und Tradition. Die Suche nach dem gültigen Erbe des deutschen Soldaten*, Munich, 1989.

Bibliography

Absolon, R., *Wehrgesetz und Wehrdienst 1933–1945*, Boppard, 1960.

Absolon, R., *Die Wehrmacht im Dritten Reich*, vol. 3, Boppard, 1975.

Albrecht-Heide, A. and Bujewski-Crawford, U., *Frauen – Krieg – Militär. Images und Phantasien*, Tübingen, 1991.

Anfänge westdeutscher Sicherheitspolitik 1945–1956, ed. Militärgeschichtliches Forschungsamt, vol. 1: *Von der Kapitulation bis zum Pleven-Plan*, Munich, 1982; vol. 2: *Die EVG-Phase*, Munich, 1990; vol. 3: *Die NATO-Option*, Munich, 1993.

Angress, W. T., 'Prussia´s Army and the Jewish Reserve Officer Controversy before World War I', in *Year Book XVII*, ed. Leo Baeck Institute, London, 1972, pp. 19–42.

Angress, W. T., '*Das deutsche Militär und die Juden im Ersten Weltkrieg*', *Militärgeschichtliche Mitteilungen* 1/1976, pp. 77–146.

Backerra, M. (ed.), *NVA. Ein Rückblick für die Zukunft*, Cologne, 1992.

Bald, D., 'Von der Wehrmacht zur Bundeswehr. Kontinuität und Neubeginn', in W. Conze and M. R. Lepsius (eds), *Sozialgeschichte der Bundesrepublik Deutschland*, Stuttgart, 1983, pp. 287–409.

Bald, D., *Militär und Gesellschaft 1945–1990. Die Bundeswehr der Bonner Republik*, Baden-Baden, 1994.

Bald, D., 'Alte Kameraden. Offizierskader der Bundeswehr', in U. Breymayer et al. (eds), *Willensmenschen. Über deutsche Offiziere*, Frankfurt, 1999, pp. 50–64.

Bald, D. (ed.), *Die Nationale Volksarmee*, Baden-Baden, 1992.

Bald, D. et. al. (eds), *Nationale Volksarmee – Armee für den Frieden*, Baden-Baden, 1995.

Bartjes, H., 'Der Zivildienst als die modernere "Schule der Nation"?', in Kühne, *Kriegskultur*, pp. 128–143.

Bartov, O., *The Eastern Front, 1941–45. German Troops and the Barbarisation of Warfare*, New York, 1986.

Bartov, O., *Hitler´s Army. Soldiers, Nazis, and War in the Third Reich*, New York, 1991.

Baumann, U., *Vom Recht auf den eigenen Tod. Die Geschichte des Suizids vom 18. bis zum 20. Jahrhundert*, Weimar, 2001.

Becker, F., *Bilder von Krieg und Nation. Die Einigungskriege in der bürgerlichen Öffentlichkeit Deutschlands 1864–1913*, Munich, 2001.

Behrenbeck, S., *Der Kult um die toten Helden. Nationalsozialistische Mythen, Rituale und Symbole 1923–1945*, Vierow, 1996.

Berger, L., *Der alte Harkort*, 3rd edn, Leipzig, 1895.

Berghahn, V. R., *Der Stahlhelm. Bund der Frontsoldaten 1918–1935*, Düsseldorf, 1966.

Berghahn, V. R. (ed.), *Militarismus*, Cologne, 1975.

Bibliography

Berghahn, V. R., *Militarism: The History of an International Debate*, Leamington Spa, 1981.

Bessel, R. J., 'Militarismus im innenpolitischen Leben der Weimarer Republik: Von den Freikorps zur SA', in Müller/Opitz, *Militär*, pp. 193–222.

Bessel, R. J., *Political Violence and the Rise of Nazism. The Storm Troopers in Eastern Germany 1925–1934*, New Haven, 1984.

Bessel, R., *Germany after the First World War*, Oxford, 1993.

Best, G., *War and Society in Revolutionary Europe, 1770–1870*, New York, 1986.

Best, G., 'The Militarization of European Society, 1870–1914', in Gillis, *Militarization*, pp. 13–29.

Beutel, G., *Dresdner Bürgersoldaten des 19. Jahrhunderts*, Dresden, 1926.

Biefang, A., *Politisches Bürgertum in Deutschland 1857–1868. Nationale Organisationen und Eliten*, Düsseldorf, 1994.

Birckenbach, H., 'Wehrdienst als Verlust – und Befreiung von der zivilen Lebensweise', in R. Steinweg (ed.), *Unsere Bundeswehr? Zum 25jährigen Bestehen einer umstrittenen Institution*, Frankfurt, 1981, pp. 197–233.

Birckenbach, H.-M., *Mit schlechtem Gewissen – Wehrdienstbereitschaft von Jugendlichen. Zur Empirie der psychosozialen Vermittlung von Militär und Gesellschaft*, Baden-Baden, 1985.

Blessing, W., *Staat und Kirche in der Gesellschaft. Institutionelle Autorität und mentaler Wandel in Bayern während des 19. Jahrhunderts*, Göttingen, 1982.

Blessing, W. K., 'Disziplinierung und Qualifizierung. Zur kulturellen Bedeutung des Militärs im Bayern des 19. Jahrhunderts', *Geschichte und Gesellschaft* 17 (1991), pp. 459–479.

Bond, B., 'The British Experience of National Service', 1947–1963, in *Foerster, Wehrpflicht*, pp. 207–215.

Bozon, M., *Les conscrits*, Paris, 1981.

Brändli, S., 'Von "schneidigen Offizieren" und "Militärcrinolinen": Aspekte symbolischer Männlichkeit am Beispiel preußischer und schweizerischer Uniformen des 19. Jahrhunderts', in U. Frevert, *Militär*, pp. 201–28.

Bramke, W., 'Die Funktion des Kyffhäuserbundes im System der militaristischen Organisationen in der Weimarer Republik', *Zeitschrift für Militärgeschichte* (1971), pp. 64–78.

Brauns, H., *Die Hannoverschen Bürgerwehren*, Hannover, 1911.

Brockmann, H., 'Das wiederbewaffnete Militär. Eine Analyse der Selbstdarstellung der Bundeswehr zwischen 1977 und 1994', *Soziale Welt* 45 (1994), pp. 279–303

Bröckling, U. and Sikora, M. (eds), *Armeen und ihre Deserteure*, Göttingen, 1998.

Broszat, M. et al. (eds), *Von Stalingrad zur Währungsreform*, Munich, 1988.

Bibliography

Bruder, T., *Nürnberg als bayerische Garnison von 1806 bis 1914*, Nuremberg, 1992.

Bucher, P., 'Zur Geschichte der Einwohnerwehren in Preußen 1918–1921', *Militärgeschichtliche Mitteilungen* 10 (1971), pp. 15–59.

Budde, G.-F., *Auf dem Weg ins Bürgerleben. Kindheit und Erziehung in deutschen und englischen Bürgerfamilien 1840–1914*, Göttingen, 1994.

Büsch, O., *Militärsystem und Sozialleben im alten Preußen 1713–1807*, 2nd edn, Frankfurt, 1981.

Calließ, J., *Militär in der Krise. Die bayerische Armee in der Revolution 1848/49*, Boppard, 1976.

Canetti, E., *Crowds and Power*, Harmondsworth, 1973.

Caplan, G., 'Militärische Männlichkeit in der deutsch-jüdischen Geschichte', *Die Philosophin* 22 (2000), pp. 85–100.

Carsten, F. L., *The Reichswehr and Politics: 1918–1933*, Oxford, 1966.

Chambers II, J. W, *To Raise an Army: The Draft Comes to Modern America*, New York, 1987.

Chambers II, J. W., *Draftees or Volunteers: A Documentary History of the Debate over Military Conscription in the United States, 1787–1973*, New York, 1975.

Chickering, R., 'Der "Deutsche Wehrverein" und die Reform der deutschen Armee 1912–1914', *Militärgeschichtliche Mitteilungen* 25 (1979), pp. 7–33.

Chickering, R., '"Casting Their Gaze More Broadly": Women´s Patriotic Activism in Imperial Germany', *Past and Present* 118 (1988), pp. 156–85.

Coetzee, M. S., *The German Army League. Popular Nationalism in Wilhelmine Germany*, New York, 1990.

Colley, L., *Britons. Forging the Nation 1707–1837*, New Haven, 1992.

Craig, G. A., *The Politics of the Prussian Army 1640–1945*, London, 1964.

Dammer, S., *Mütterlichkeit und Frauendienstpflicht. Versuche der Vergesellschaftung "weiblicher Fähigkeiten" durch eine Dienstverpflichtung (Deutschland 1890–1918)*, Weinheim, 1988.

Daniel, U., 'Die Vaterländischen Frauenvereine in Westfalen', *Westfälische Forschungen* 39 (1989), pp. 158–79.

Danyel, J., 'Die Erinnerung an die Wehrmacht in beiden deutschen Staaten. Vergangenheitspolitik und Gedenkrituale', in R.-D. Müller and H.-E. Volkmann (eds), *Die Wehrmacht. Mythos und Realität*, Munich, 1999, pp. 1139–1149.

Deák, I., *Beyond Nationalism. A Social and Political History of the Habsburg Officer Corps, 1848–1918*, New York, 1990.

Deist, W., 'Die Armee in Staat und Gesellschaft 1890–1914', in M. Stürmer (ed.), *Das kaiserliche Deutschland*, Kronberg, 1977, pp. 312–39.

Deist, W., 'Die Aufrüstung der Wehrmacht', in W. Deist et al. (eds), *Ursachen und Voraussetzungen des Zweiten Weltkrieges*, Frankfurt, 1989, pp. 439–637.

Deist, W., *Militär, Staat und Gesellschaft*, Munich, 1991.

Bibliography

Demeter, K., *Das deutsche Offizierkorps in Gesellschaft und Staat 1650–1945*, 2nd edn, Frankfurt, 1962.

Diedrich, T. et al. (eds), *Im Dienste der Partei. Handbuch der bewaffneten Organe der DDR*, Berlin, 1998.

Diehl, J. M., *Paramilitary Politics in Weimar Germany*, Bloomington, 1977.

Dieners, P., *Das Duell und die Sonderrolle des Militärs*, Berlin, 1992.

Doering-Manteuffel, A., *Katholizismus und Wiederbewaffnung. Die Haltung der deutschen Katholiken gegenüber der Wehrfrage 1948–1955*, Mainz, 1981.

Dörner, A., 'Die symbolische Politik der Ehre', in L. Vogt and A. Zingerle (eds), *Ehre*, Frankfurt, 1994, pp. 78–95.

Dülffer, J. (ed.), *Bereit zum Krieg. Kriegsmentalität im wilhelminischen Deutschland 1890–1914*, Göttingen, 1986.

Dunker, U., *Der Reichsbund jüdischer Frontsoldaten 1919–1938. Geschichte eines jüdischen Abwehrvereins*, Düsseldorf, 1977.

Eifert, C., *Paternalismus und Politik. Preußische Landräte im 19. Jahrhundert*, Münster, 2003.

Eifler, C. and Seifert, R. (eds), *Soziale Konstruktionen – Militär und Geschlechterverhältnis*, Münster, 1999.

Eley, G., *Reshaping the German Right: Radical Nationalism and Political Change after Bismarck*, New Haven, 1980.

Eley, G., 'Army, State and Civil Society: Revisiting the Problem of German Militarism', in G. Eley, *From Unification to Nazism*, Boston, 1986, pp. 85–109.

Elliott, C.J., 'The Kriegervereine and the Weimar Republic', *Journal of Contemporary History* 10 (1975), pp. 109–29.

Endres, F. C., 'Soziologische Struktur und ihr entsprechende Ideologien des deutschen Offizierkorps vor dem Weltkriege', *Archiv für Sozialwissenschaft und Sozialpolitik* 58 (1927), pp. 282–319.

Enloe, C., 'Beyond Steve Canyon and Rambo: Feminist Histories of Militarized Masculinity', in J. R. Gillis, (ed.), *The Militarization of the Western World*, New Brunswick, 1989, pp. 119–40.

Ewald, W., *Die rheinischen Schützengesellschaften*, Düsseldorf, 1933.

Finer, S. E., 'State- and Nation-Building in Europe: The Role of the Military', in C. Tilly (ed.), *The Formation of National States in Western Europe*, Princeton, 1975, pp. 84–163.

Fischer, H., *Judentum, Staat und Heer in Preußen im frühen 19. Jahrhundert*, Tübingen, 1968.

Foerster, R. G. (ed.), *Die Wehrpflicht*, Munich, 1994.

Förster, S., *Der doppelte Militarismus. Die deutsche Heeresrüstungspolitik zwischen Status-Quo-Sicherung und Aggression 1890–1913*, Stuttgart, 1985.

Forrest, A., '*La patrie en danger*: The French Revolution and the First *Levée en masse*', in D. Moran and A. Waldron (eds), *The People in Arms: Military Myth and National Mobilization since the French Revolution*, Cambridge, 2003, pp. 8–32.

Frank, M., *Dörfliche Gesellschaft und Kriminalität. Das Fallbeispiel Lippe 1650– 1800*, Paderborn, 1995

Frei, N., *Vergangenheitspolitik. Die Anfänge der Bundesrepublik und die NS- Vergangenheit*, München, 1996.

Frei, N., *Adenauer´s Germany and the Nazi Past: The Politics of Amnesty and Integration*, New York, 2002.

Frevert, U., *Women in German History: From Bourgeois Emancipation to Sexual Liberation*, Oxford, 1989.

Frevert, U., *"Mann und Weib, und Weib und Mann". Geschlechter-Differenzen in der Moderne*, Munich, 1995.

Frevert, U., *Men of Honour. A Social and Cultural History of the Duel*, Cambridge, 1995.

Frevert, U., 'Herren und Helden', in R. v. Dülmen (ed.), *Erfindung des Menschen*, Vienna, 1998, pp. 323–344.

Frevert, U. (ed.), *Militär und Gesellschaft im 19. und 20. Jahrhundert*, Stuttgart, 1997.

Fricke, D., 'Zur Rolle des Militarismus nach innen in Deutschland vor dem ersten Weltkrieg', *Zeitschrift für Geschichtswissenschaft* 6 (1958), pp. 1298–1310.

Fricke, D., 'Zum Bündnis des preußisch-deutschen Militarismus mit dem Klerus gegen die sozialistische Arbeiterbewegung am Ende des 19. Jahrhunderts', *Zeitschrift für Geschichtswissenschaft* 8 (1960), pp. 1378–1395.

Fricke, D., *Handbuch zur Geschichte der deutschen Arbeiterbewegung 1869 bis 1917*, 2 vols, Berlin, 1987.

Friedeburg, R. v., 'Klassen-, Geschlechter- oder Nationalidentität? Handwerker und Tagelöhner in den Kriegervereinen der neupreußischen Provinz Hessen- Nassau 1890–1914', in U. Frevert, *Militär*, pp. 229–244.

Gall, L., *Bürgertum in Deutschland*, Berlin, 1989.

Gebhardt, D., 'Militär und Krieg im Geschichtsunterricht nach 1945', *Geschichte in Wissenschaft und Unterricht* 41 (1990), pp. 81–100.

Gembruch, W., 'Bürgerliche Publizistik und Heeresreform in Preußen (1805– 1808)', in M. Messerschmidt et al. (eds), *Militärgeschichte*, Stuttgart, 1982, pp. 124–49.

Gersdorff, U. v., *Frauen im Kriegsdienst 1914–1945*, Stuttgart, 1969.

Gerteis, K., *Die deutschen Städte in der Frühen Neuzeit*, Darmstadt, 1986.

Gestrich, A., *Traditionelle Jugendkultur und Industrialisierung. Sozialgeschichte der Jugend in einer ländlichen Arbeitergemeinde Württembergs, 1800–1820*, Göttingen, 1986.

Geyer, M., 'Die Geschichte des deutschen Militärs von 1860 bis 1945', in H.-U. Wehler (ed.), *Die moderne deutsche Geschichte in der internationalen Forschung*, Göttingen, 1978, pp. 256–86.

Geyer, M., 'Der zur Organisation erhobene Burgfrieden', in K.-J. Müller and E. Opitz (eds), *Militär und Militarismus in der Weimarer Republik*, Düsseldorf, 1978, pp. 15–100.

Geyer, M., *Aufrüstung oder Sicherheit. Die Reichswehr in der Krise der Machtpolitik 1924–1936*, Wiesbaden, 1980.

Geyer, M., 'Eine Kriegsgeschichte, die vom Tod spricht', in T. Lindenberger and A. Lüdtke (eds), *Physische Gewalt*, Frankfurt, 1995, pp. 136–61.

Gillis, J. R. (ed.), *The Militarization of the Western World*, New Brunswick, 1989.

Gilman, S. L., *Rasse, Sexualität und Seuche*, Reinbek, 1992.

Girardet, R., *La société militaire de 1815 à nos jours*, Paris, 1998.

Goffman, E., *Asylums. Essays on the Social Situation of Mental Patients and Other Inmates*, New York, 1961.

Göttsch, S., '"Der Soldat, der Soldat ist der erste Mann im Staat…". Männerbilder in volkstümlichen Soldatenliedern 1855–1875', in W. Schmale (ed.), *MannBilder*, Berlin, 1998, pp. 131–54.

Groh, D. and Brandt P., *"Vaterlandslose Gesellen". Sozialdemokratie und Nation 1860–1990*, Munich, 1992.

Gruner, W. D., *Das Bayerische Heer 1825 bis 1864*, Boppard, 1972.

Hachtmann, R., *Berlin 1848. Eine Politik- und Gesellschaftsgeschichte der Revolution*, Bonn, 1997.

Hagemann, K., 'Of "Manly Valor" and "German Honor": Nation, War, and Masculinity in the Age of the Prussian Uprising against Napoleon', *Central European History* 31 (1998), pp. 187–220.

Hagemann, K., 'A Valorous *Volk* family: The Nation, the Military, and the Gender Order in Prussia in the Time of the Anti-Napoleonic Wars, 1806–15', in I. Blom et al. (eds), *Gendered Nations*, Oxford, 2000, pp. 179–205.

Hagemann, K., *"Mannlicher Muth und Teutsche Ehre". Nation, Militär und Geschlecht zur Zeit der Antinapoleonischen Kriege Preußens*, Paderborn, 2002.

Hagemann, K. and Pröve, R. (eds), *Landsknechte, Soldatenfrauen und Nationalkrieger. Militär, Krieg und Geschlechterordnung im historischen Wandel*, Frankfurt, 1998.

Hagen, M. v., 'The Levée en Masse from Russian Empire to Soviet Union, 1874–1938', in D. Moran and A. Waldron (eds), *The People in Arms: Military Myth and National Mobilization since the French Revolution*, Cambridge, 2003, pp. 159–88.

Hammer, M., *Volksbewegung und Obrigkeiten. Revolution in Sachsen 1830/31*, Weimar, 1997.

Handbuch der deutschen Bildungsgeschichte, vol. 4: *1870–1918*, ed. C. Berg, Munich 1991; vol. 5: *1918–1945*, ed. D. Langewiesche and H.-E. Tenorth, Munich 1989.

Bibliography

Handbuch zur deutschen Militärgeschichte 1648–1939, ed. Militärgeschichtliches Forschungsamt, Bd. 1–7, Frankfurt, 1964–1979.

Harnisch, H., 'Preußisches Kantonsystem und ländliche Gesellschaft: Das Beispiel der mittleren Kammerdepartements', in B. R. Kroener and R. Pröve (eds), *Krieg und Frieden*, pp. 137–65.

Harris, J. F., 'Arms and the people. The Bürgerwehr of Lower Franconia in 1848 and 1849', in K. H. Jarausch and L. E. Jones (eds), *In Search of a Liberal Germany*, New York, 1990, pp. 133–60.

Hass, G., 'Zum Bild der Wehrmacht in der Geschichtsschreibung der DDR', in R.-D. Müller and H.-E. Volkmann (eds), *Die Wehrmacht. Mythos und Realität*, Munich, 1999, pp. 1100–1112.

Hecker, G., *Walter Rathenau und sein Verhältnis zu Militär und Krieg*, Boppard, 1983.

Heer, H. and Naumann, Klaus (eds), *War of Extermination: The German Military in World War II*, New York, 2000.

Helmert, H., *Militärsystem und Streitkräfte im Deutschen Bund am Vorabend des preußisch-österreichischen Krieges von 1866*, Berlin, 1964.

Henning, H., 'Kriegervereine in den preußischen Westprovinzen', *Rheinische Vierteljahresblätter* 32 (1968), pp. 430–74.

Herbell, H., *Staatsbürger in Uniform 1789 bis 1961. Ein Beitrag zur Geschichte des Kampfes zwischen Demokratie und Militarismus in Deutschland*, Berlin, 1969.

Herrmann, U. (ed.), *Volk – Nation – Vaterland*, Hamburg, 1996.

Herwig, H. H., *The German Naval Officer Corps: A Social and Political History 1890–1918*, Oxford, 1973.

Hettling, M., *Bürger oder Soldaten? Kriegerdenkmäler 1848 bis 1854*, in R. Koselleck and M. Jeismann (eds), *Der politische Totenkult*, Munich, 1994, pp. 147–93.

Hödl, K., *Die Pathologisierung des jüdischen Körpers. Antisemitismus, Geschlecht und Medizin im Fin de Siècle*, Vienna, 1997.

Hofmann, H., 'Grundpflichten und Grundrechte', in J. Isensee and P. Kirchhof (eds) *Handbuch des Staatsrechts der Bundesrepublik Deutschland*, vol. 5, Heidelberg, 1992.

Höhn, R., *Verfassungskampf und Heereseid. Der Kampf des Bürgertums um das Heer (1815–1850)*, Leipzig, 1938.

Höhn, R., *Die Armee als Erziehungsschule der Nation. Das Ende einer Idee*, Bad Harzburg, 1963.

Höhn, R., *Sozialismus und Heer*, vol. 3, Bad Harzburg, 1969.

Holm, T., *Allgemeine Wehrpflicht*, Munich, 1953.

Homer, *The Odyssey*, trans. E. V. Rieu, Penguin Books, 1987.

Honegger, C., *Die Ordnung der Geschlechter*, Frankfurt, 1991.

Huber, E. R., *Deutsche Verfassungsgeschichte seit 1789*, vol. 1, Stuttgart, 1957.

Ibbeken, R., *Preußen 1807–1813*, Cologne, 1970.

Ingenlath, M., *Mentale Aufrüstung. Militarisierungstendenzen in Frankreich und Deutschland vor dem Ersten Weltkrieg*, Frankfurt, 1998.

Isaksson, E. (ed.), *Women and the Military System*, New York, 1988.

Jacobsen, H.-A., 'Zur Rolle der öffentlichen Meinung bei der Debatte um die Wiederbewaffnung 1950–1955', in Militärgeschichtlichen Forschungsamt (ed.) *Aspekte der deutschen Wiederbewaffnung bis 1945*, Boppard, 1975, pp. 61–98.

Jahr, C., 'British Prussianism – Überlegungen zu einem europäischen Militarismus im 19. und frühen 20. Jahrhundert', in W. Wette (ed.), *Militarismus in Deutschland 1871 bis 1945*, Münster, 1999, pp. 293–309.

Jany, C., *Geschichte der Königlich Preußischen Armee*, vol. 3, reprint Osnabrück, 1967; vol. 4, Berlin, 1933.

Jaun, R., 'Vom Bürger-Militär zum Soldaten-Militär: Die Schweiz im 19. Jahrhundert', in U. Frevert, *Militär*, pp. 48–77.

John, H., *Das Reserveoffizierkorps im Deutschen Kaiserreich 1890–1914*, Frankfurt, 1981.

Jones, K., 'Dividing the Ranks: Women and the Draft', in J. B. Elshtain and S. Tobias (eds), *Women, Militarism and War*, Savage, 1990, pp. 125–36.

Jung, R., 'Das Frankfurter Bürgermilitär im XVIII. Jahrhundert', *Alt-Frankfurt*, vol. 4, 1912, S. 40–50.

Kabel, R., *Die Militarisierung der Sowjetischen Besatzungszone Deutschlands*, Bonn, 1966.

Keane, J., *Civil Society: Old Images, New Visions*, Stanford, 1998.

Kehr, E., 'Zur Genesis des Königlich Preußischen Reserveoffiziers', in E. Kehr, *Der Primat der Innenpolitik*, Berlin, 1965, pp. 53–63.

Keim, W., *Erziehung unter der NS-Diktatur*, 2 vols, Darmstadt, 1995/97.

Kerber, L. K., *No Constitutional Right to Be Ladies. Women and the Obligations of Citizenship*, New York, 1998.

Kirkpatrick, C. E., 'Entscheidung für den Berufssoldaten. Die Armee der Vereinigten Staaten und die Aufhebung der Wehrpflicht gegen Ende des Vietnam-Krieges 1969' in R. G. Foerster (ed.), *Die Wehrpflicht*, Munich, 1994, pp. 241–258.

Klönne, A., *Jugend im Dritten Reich*, Munich, 1990.

Kloosterhuis, J., *Bauern, Bürger und Soldaten. Quellen zur Sozialisation des Militärsystems im preußischen Westfalen, 1713–1803*, 2 vols, Münster, 1992.

Kloosterhuis, J., 'Zwischen Aufruhr und Akzeptanz: Zur Ausformung und Einbettung des Kantonsystems in die Wirtschafts- und Sozialstrukturen des preußischen Westfalen', in B. R. Kroener and R. Pröve (eds), *Krieg und Frieden*, pp. 167–90.

Kleßmann, C., *Die doppelte Staatsgründung. Deutsche Geschichte 1945–1955*, Göttingen, 1989.

Kleßmann, C., *Zwei Staaten, eine Nation. Deutsche Geschichte 1955–1970*, Bonn, 1988.

Klotzbach, K., *Der Weg zur Staatspartei. Programmatik, praktische Politik und Organisation der deutschen Sozialdemokratie 1945 bis 1965*, Berlin, 1982.

Kocka, J., 'Zivilgesellschaft als historisches Problem und Versprechen', in M. Hildermeier et al. (eds), *Europäische Zivilgesellschaft in Ost und West*, Frankfurt, 2000, pp. 13–39.

Könenkamp, W.-D., 'Über Entlassungsbräuche der Soldaten', in *Beiträge zur deutschen Volks- und Altertumskunde*, vol. 16, 1972, pp. 43–72.

Koppmann, K., 'Die Exercitien der Bürgergarde', in *Beiträge zur Geschichte der Stadt Rostock*, vol. 2, Rostock, 1899, S. 93–96.

Koselleck, R. and Jeismann, M. (eds), *Der politische Totenkult*, Munich, 1994.

Kraake, S., *Frauen zur Bundeswehr – Analyse und Verlauf einer Diskussion*, Frankfurt, 1992.

Krabbe, W., *Die gescheiterte Zukunft der Ersten Republik. Jugendorganisationen bürgerlicher Parteien im Weimarer Staat (1918–1933)*, Opladen, 1995.

Krabbe, W. (ed.), *Politische Jugend in der Weimarer Republik*, Bochum, 1993.

Kraus, J., *Das Militärwesen der Reichsstadt Augsburg 1548–1806*, Augsburg, 1980.

Krölls, A., *Kriegsdienstverweigerung: Das unbequeme Grundrecht*, Frankfurt, 1980.

Kroener, B. R., 'Auf dem Weg zu einer "nationalsozialistischen Volksarmee". Die soziale Öffnung des Heeresoffizierkorps im Zweiten Weltkrieg', in M. Broszat, *Von Stalingrad zur Währungsreform*, Munich, 1988, pp. 651–82.

Kroener, B. R. and Pröve, R. (eds), *Krieg und Frieden*, Paderborn, 1996.

Krumeich, G., 'Zur Entwicklung der "nation armée" in Frankreich bis zum Ersten Weltkrieg', in R. G. Foerster (ed.), *Die Wehrpflicht*, Munich, 1994, pp. 133–145.

Kruse, W. (ed.), *Eine Welt von Feinden. Der Große Krieg 1914–1918*, Frankfurt, 1997.

Kühne, T., 'Gruppenkohäsion und Kameradschaftsmythos in der Wehrmacht', in R.-D. Müller and H.-E. Volkmann (eds), *Die Wehrmacht. Mythos und Realität*, Munich, 1999, pp. 534–49.

Kühne, T., 'Der Soldat', in U. Frevert and H.-G. Haupt (eds), *Der Mensch des 20. Jahrhunderts*, Frankfurt, 1999, pp. 344–72.

Kühne, T. (ed.), *Von der Kriegskultur zur Friedenskultur? Zum Mentalitätswandel in Deutschland seit 1945*, Münster, 2000.

Kühne, T. and Ziemann, B. (eds), *Was ist Militärgeschichte?*, Paderborn, 2000.

Kundrus, B., 'Nur die halbe Geschichte. Frauen im Umfeld der Wehrmacht zwischen 1939 und 1945', in R.-D. Müller and H.-E. Volkmann (eds), *Die Wehrmacht. Mythos und Realität*, Munich, 1999, pp. 719–35.

Kunisch, J., 'Das "Puppenwerk" der stehenden Heere', *Zeitschrift für Historische Forschung* 17 (1990), pp. 49–83.

Kutz, M., 'Militär und Gesellschaft im Deutschland der Nachkriegszeit (1946–1995)', in U. Frevert (ed.), *Militär und Gesellschaft im 19. und 20. Jahrhundert*, Stuttgart, 1997 , pp. 277–313.

Langewiesche, D., *Nation, Nationalismus, Nationalstaat in Deutschland und Europa*, Munich, 2000.

Large, D. C., *Germans to the Front. West German Rearmament in the Adenauer Era*, Chapel Hill, 1996.

Levi, M., *Consent, Dissent, and Patriotism*, Cambridge, 1997.

Leyh, M., 'Die bayerische Heeresreform unter König Ludwig II. 1866–1870', in *Darstellungen aus der Bayerischen Kriegs- und Heeresgeschichte*, issue 23, Munich, 1923.

Lindenberger, T. and Lüdtke, A. (eds), *Physische Gewalt*, Frankfurt, 1995.

Lindner, E., *Patriotismus deutscher Juden von der napoleonischen Ära bis zum Kaiserreich*, Frankfurt, 1997.

Lipp, C. (ed.), *Schimpfende Weiber und patriotische Jungfrauen. Frauen im Vormärz und in der Revolution 1848/49*, Moos, 1986.

Lippert, E., 'Lagefeststellung "Der Wehrpflichtige"', in P. Klein (ed.), *Wehrpflicht und Wehrpflichtige heute*, Baden-Baden, 1991, pp. 9–28.

Lissarrague, François, 'Figures of Women', in *A History of Women in the West, vol. I: From Ancient Godesses to Christian Saints*, ed. Pauline Schmitt Pantel (Cambridge and London: Belknap Press, 1992) pp. 139–229, especially pp. 172–81.

Lloyd, G., 'Selfhood, War, and Masculinity', in C. Pateman and E. Gross (eds), *Feminist Challenges. Social and Political Theory*, Sydney, 1986, pp. 63–76.

Lockenour, J., *Soldiers as Citizens: Former Wehrmacht Officers in the Federal Republic of Germany, 1945–1955*, Lincoln, 2001.

Lüdtke, A., '"Wehrhafte Nation" und "innere Wohlfahrt": Zur militärischen Mobilisierbarkeit der bürgerlichen Gesellschaft', *Militärgeschichtliche Mitteilungen* 30 (1981), pp. 7–56.

Lüdtke, A., *"Gemeinwohl", Polizei und "Festungspraxis". Staatliche Gewaltsamkeit und innere Verwaltung in Preußen, 1815–1850*, Göttingen, 1982.

Lutz, D. S., *Krieg und Frieden als Rechtsfrage im Parlamentarischen Rat 1948/49*, Baden-Baden, 1982.

Lutz, K.-H., *Das badische Offizierskorps 1840–1870/71*, Stuttgart, 1997.

Mallmann, K.-M., *Kommunisten in der Weimarer Republik*, Darmstadt, 1996.

Meier-Dörnberg, W., 'Die Auseinandersetzung um die Einführung der Wehrpflicht in der Bundesrepublik Deutschland', in R. G. Foerster (ed.), *Die Wehrpflicht*, Munich, 1994, pp. 107–18.

Meinecke, F., *Das Leben des Generalfeldmarschalls Hermann von Boyen*, 2 vols, Stuttgart, 1896/99.

Meinecke, F., *Die deutsche Katastrophe*, 6th edn, Wiesbaden, 1965.

Mertens, L., 'Das Privileg des Einjährig-Freiwilligen Militärdienstes im Kaiserreich und seine gesellschaftliche Bedeutung', *Militärgeschichtliche Mitteilungen* 35 (1986), pp. 59–66.

Messerschmidt, M., *Die Wehrmacht im NS-Staat. Zeit der Indoktrination*, Hamburg, 1969.

Messerschmidt, M., 'Die Armee in Staat und Gesellschaft – Die Bismarckzeit', in M. Stürmer (ed.), *Das kaiserliche Deutschland*, Kronberg, 1977, pp. 89–118.

Messerschmidt, M., 'Preußens Militär in seinem gesellschaftlichen Umfeld', in: H.-J. Puhle and H.-U. Wehler (eds), *Preußen im Rückblick*, Göttingen, 1980, pp. 43–88.

Messerschmidt, M. et al. (eds), *Militärgeschichte*, Stuttgart, 1982.

Meyer, G., *Soldaten ohne Armee*, in M. Broszat (ed.), *Von Stalingrad zur Währungsreform*, Munich, 1988, pp. 683–750.

Michaelis, H.-T., *Unter schwarz-rot-goldenem Banner und dem Signum des Doppeladlers. Gescheiterte Volksbewaffnungs- und Vereinigungsbestrebungen in der Deutschen Nationalbewegung und im Deutschen Schützenbund 1859–1869*, Frankfurt, 1993.

Mommsen, H., 'Militär und zivile Militarisierung in Deutschland 1918 bis 1938', in U. Frevert (ed.), *Militär und Gesellschaft im 19. und 20. Jahrhundert*, Stuttgart, 1997, pp. 265–276.

Mommsen, H. (ed.), *Der Erste Weltkrieg und die europäische Nachkriegsordnung*, Cologne, 2000.

Moran, D. and Waldron, A. (eds), *The People in Arms: Military Myth and National Mobilization since the French Revolution*, Cambridge, 2003.

Mosse, G. L., *Fallen Soldiers: Reshaping the Memory of the World Wars*, Oxford, 1990.

Müller, K.-J., *Armee und Drittes Reich 1933–1939*, Paderborn, 1987.

Müller, K.-J. and Opitz, E. (eds), *Militär und Militarismus in der Weimarer Republik*, Düsseldorf, 1978.

Müller, R.-D. and Volkmann, H.-E. (eds), *Die Wehrmacht. Mythos und Realität*, Munich, 1999.

Müller, S., 'Soldaten, Bürger, Barrikaden. Konflikte und Allianzen während der Revolution von 1848/49', in C. Jansen and T. Mergel (eds), *Die Revolutionen von 1848/49*, Göttingen, 1998, pp. 37–53.

Bibliography

Müller, S., *Soldaten in der deutschen Revolution von 1848/49*, Paderborn, 1999.

Münchow-Pohl, B. v., *Zwischen Reform und Krieg. Untersuchungen zur Bewußtseinslage in Preußen 1809–1812*, Göttingen, 1987.

Mürmann, A., *Die öffentliche Meinung in Deutschland über das preußische Wehrgesetz von 1814 während der Jahre 1814–1819*, Berlin, 1910.

Nolte, P., *Gemeindebürgertum und Liberalismus in Baden 1800–1850*, Göttingen, 1994.

Olenhusen, I. G. v., 'Vom Jungstahlhelm zur SA: Die junge Nachkriegsgeneration in den paramilitärischen Verbänden der Weimarer Republik', in W. R. Krabbe, *Politische Jugend*, pp. 146–82.

Opitz, C., 'Der Bürger wird Soldat – und die Bürgerin...? Die Revolution, der Krieg und die Stellung der Frau nach 1789', in V. Schmidt-Linsenhoff (ed.), *Sklavin oder Bürgerin? Französische Revolution und Neue Weiblichkeit 1760–1830*, Frankfurt, 1989, pp. 38–54.

Opitz, E., 'Sozialdemokratie und Militarismus in der Weimarer Republik', in K.-J. Müller and E. Opitz (eds), *Militär und Militarismus in der Weimarer Republik*, Düsseldorf, 1978, pp. 269–86.

Ostertag, H., *Bildung, Ausbildung und Erziehung des Offizierkorps im deutschen Kaiserreich 1871 bis 1918*, Frankfurt, 1990.

Paret, P., 'Conscription and the End of the Old Regime in France and Prussia', in P. Paret, *Understanding War*, Princeton, 1992, pp. 53–74.

Pinkow, H.-W., *Der literarische und parlamentarische Kampf gegen die Institution des Stehenden Heeres in Deutschland in der ersten Hälfte des XIX. Jahrhunderts (1815–1848)*, Berlin, 1912.

Planert, U. (ed.), *Nation, Politik und Geschlecht*, Frankfurt, 2000.

Pröve, R., *Stehendes Heer und städtische Gesellschaft im 18. Jahrhundert. Göttingen und seine Militärbevölkerung 1713–1756*, Munich, 1995.

Pröve, R., 'Bürgerwehren in den europäischen Revolutionen 1848', in D. Dowe et al. (eds), *Europa 1848*, Bonn, 1998, pp. 901–14.

Pröve, R., 'Politische Partizipation und soziale Ordnung. Das Konzept der "Volksbewaffnung" und die Funktion der Bürgerwehren 1848/49', in W. Hardtwig (ed.), *Revolution in Deutschland und Europa 1848/49*, Göttingen, 1998, pp. 109–32.

Pröve, R., '"Der Mann des Mannes". "Civile" Ordnungsformationen, Staatsbürgerschaft und Männlichkeit im Vormärz', in K. Hagemann and R. Pröve (eds), *Landsknechte, Soldatenfrauen und Nationalkrieger. Militär, Krieg und Geschlechterordnung im historischen Wandel*, Frankfurt, 1998, pp. 103–20.

Pröve, R., *Stadtgemeindlicher Republikanismus und die "Macht des Volkes". Civile Ordnungsformationen und kommunale Leitbilder politischer Partizipation in den deutschen Staaten vom Ende des 18. bis zur Mitte des 19. Jahrhunderts*, Göttingen, 2000.

Quataert, H. J., 'German Patriotic Women's Work in War and Peace Time, 1864–1890', in S. Förster and J. Nagler (eds), *On the Road to Total War*, New York, 1997, pp. 448–77.

Quataert, H., *Staging Philanthropy: Patriotic Women and the National Imagination in Dynastic Germany, 1813–1916*, Ann Arbor, 2001.

Rattelmüller, P. E., *Das Bayerische Bürgermilitär*, Munich, 1969.

Rautenberg, H.-J., 'Die Bundeswehr von der Gründung bis zu ihrer Konsolidierung (1955/56–1962)', in A. Fischer (ed.), *Wiederbewaffnung in Deutschland nach 1945*, Berlin, 1986, pp. 125–42.

Rautenberg, H.-J. and Wiggershaus, N., 'Die "Himmeroder Denkschrift" vom Oktober 1950', *Militärgeschichtliche Mitteilungen* 21 (1977), pp. 135–206.

Reder, D. A., *Frauenbewegung und Nation. Patriotische Frauenvereine in Deutschland im frühen 19. Jahrhundert (1813–1830)*, Cologne, 1998.

Reder, D. A., '"Aus reiner Liebe für Gott, für den König und das Vaterland". Die "patriotischen Frauenvereine" in den Freiheitskriegen von 1813–1815', in K. Hagemann and R. Pröve (eds), *Landsknechte, Soldatenfrauen und Nationalkrieger. Militär, Krieg und Geschlechterordnung im historischen Wandel*, Frankfurt, 1998, pp. 199–222.

Ritter, G., 'Das Problem des Militarismus in Deutschland', *Historische Zeitschrift* 177 (1954), pp. 21–48.

Ritter, G., *Staatskunst und Kriegshandwerk. Das Problem des "Militarismus" in Deutschland*, 4 vols, Munich, 1954–1968.

Ritter, G. A. and Tenfelde, K. *Arbeiter im Deutschen Kaiserreich 1871 bis 1914*, Bonn, 1992.

Rohe, K., *Das Reichsbanner Schwarz Rot Gold. Ein Beitrag zur Geschichte und Struktur der politischen Kampfverbände zur Zeit der Weimarer Republik*, Düsseldorf, 1966.

Rohkrämer, T., *Der Militarismus der "kleinen Leute". Die Kriegervereine im Deutschen Kaiserreich 1871–1914*, Munich, 1990.

Rosenhaft, E., 'Gewalt in der Politik: Zum Problem des "Sozialen Militarismus"', in K.-J. Müller and E. Opitz (eds), *Militär und Militarismus in der Weimarer Republik*, Düsseldorf, 1978, pp. 237–59.

Rosenhaft, E., *Beating the Fascists? The German Communists and Political Violence 1929–1933*, Cambridge, 1983.

Rosenhaft, E., 'Links gleich rechts? Militante Straßengewalt um 1930', in T. Lindenberger and A. Lüdtke (eds), *Physische Gewalt*, Frankfurt, 1995, pp. 238–75.

Ruhland, V., *Untersuchungen zu Rolle und Formen der Bürgermilizen im Prozeß der bürgerlichen Umwälzung in Deutschland, unter besonderer Berücksichtigung der Kommunalgarden im Königreich Sachsen*, 2 vols, Dresden, 1987.

Ruhland, V. and Zeise, R., 'Entstehung und Charakter der Kommunalgarden im Königreich Sachsen 1830/31', *Jahrbuch für Regionalgeschichte* 14 (1987), pp. 228–42.

Rumschöttel, H., *Das bayerische Offizierkorps 1866–1914*, Berlin, 1973.

Rychner, M. and Däniker, K., 'Unter "Männern". Geschlechtliche Zuschreibungen in der Schweizer Armee zwischen 1870 und 1914', in R. Jaun and B. Studer (eds), *Weiblich-männlich. Geschlechterverhältnisse in der Schweiz*, Zürich, 1995, pp. 159–70.

Salewski, M., *Entwaffnung und Militärkontrolle in Deutschland 1919–1927*, Munich, 1966.

Sander, E., 'Die Wehrhoheit in den deutschen Städten', *Archiv für Kulturgeschichte* 36 (1954), pp. 333–56.

Sauer, P., *Das württembergische Heer in der Zeit des Deutschen und des Norddeutschen Bundes*, Stuttgart, 1958.

Sauer, P., *Revolution und Volksbewaffnung*, Ulm, 1976.

Saul, K., 'Der "Deutsche Kriegerbund". Zur innenpolitischen Funktion eines "nationalen" Verbandes im kaiserlichen Deutschland', *Militärgeschichtliche Mitteilungen* 6 (1969), pp. 95–159.

Saul, K., 'Der Kampf um die Jugend zwischen Volksschule und Kaserne. Ein Beitrag zur "Jugendpflege" im Wilhelminischen Reich 1890–1914', *Militärgeschichtliche Mitteilungen* 9 (1971), pp. 97–143.

Schaser, A., 'Women in a Nation of Men: The Politics of the League of German Women´s Associations (BDF) in Imperial Germany, 1894–1914', in I. Blom et al. (eds), *Gendered Nations*, Oxford, 2000, pp. 249–68.

Schmidt, D., *Die preußische Landwehr*, Berlin, 1981.

Schmidt, M., 'Die Apotheose des Krieges im 18. und frühen 19. Jahrhundert im deutschen Dichten und Denken', in W. Huber and J. Schwerdtfeger (eds), *Kirche zwischen Krieg und Frieden. Studien zur Geschichte des deutschen Protestantismus*, Stuttgart, 1976, pp. 130–66.

Schmidt, W., *Eine Stadt und ihr Militär. Regensburg als bayerische Garnisonsstadt im 19. und frühen 20. Jahrhundert*, Regensburg, 1993.

Schnabel-Schüle, H., *Überwachen und Strafen im Territorialstaat*, Cologne, 1997.

Schneider, H., *Revolutionäre Lieder und vaterländische Gesänge*, in U. Herrmann (ed.), *Volk – Nation – Vaterland*, Hamburg, 1996, pp. 291–324.

Schodrok, K.-H., *Militärische Jugend-Erziehung in Preußen 1806–1820*, Olsberg, 1989.

Schoenbaum, D., *Hitler´s Social Revolution. Class and Status in Nazi Germany 1933–1939*, New York, 1966.

Schubert, K. v., *Wiederbewaffnung und Westintegration. Die innere Auseinandersetzung um die militärische und außenpolitische Orientierung der Bundesrepublik 1950–1952*, Stuttgart, 1970.

Schumann, D., 'Einheitssehnsucht und Gewaltakzeptanz. Politische Grund-positionen des deutschen Bürgertums nach 1918', in H. Mommsen (ed.), *Der Erste Weltkrieg und die europäische Nachkriegsordnung*, Cologne, 2000, pp. 83–105.

Schuster, K., *Der Rote Frontkämpferbund 1924–1929*, Düsseldorf, 1975.

Schütte, L., 'Das Warendorfer Landwehrbataillon und der Feldzug in Baden nach dem Tagebuch des Majors Kayser', *Warendorfer Schriften* 18 (1988), pp. 181–228.

Schwieger, K., 'Militär und Bürgertum. Zur gesellschaftlichen Prägkraft des preußischen Militärsystems im 18. Jahrhundert', in D. Blasius (ed.), *Preußen in der deutschen Geschichte*, Königstein, 1980, pp. 179–99.

Seifert, R., 'Gender, Nation und Militär – Aspekte von Männlichkeitskonstruktion und Gewaltsozialisation durch Militär und Wehrpflicht', in E. Opitz and F. S. Rödiger (eds), *Allgemeine Wehrpflicht. Geschichte, Probleme, Perspektiven*, Bremen, 1994, pp. 179–94.

Seyppel, M., 'Die Kölner Bürgerwehr 1848', *Geschichte in Köln* 17 (1985), pp. 75–115.

Shklar, J. N., *American Citizenship: The Quest for Inclusion*, Cambridge, 1991.

Sicken, B. (ed.), *Stadt und Militär 1815–1914. Wirtschaftliche Impulse, infra-strukturelle Beziehungen, sicherheitspolitische Aspekte*, Paderborn, 1998.

Siedenhans, M., 'Nationales Vereinswesen und soziale Militarisierung. Die Kriegervereine im wilhelminischen Bielefeld', in J. Meynert et al. (eds), *Unter Pickelhaube und Zylinder. Das östliche Westfalen im Zeitalter des Wilhelminismus 1888–1914*, Bielefeld, 1991, pp. 369–99.

Sikora, M., *Disziplin und Desertion. Strukturprobleme militärischer Organisation im 18. Jahrhundert*, Berlin, 1996.

Sikora, M., 'Scharnhorst und die militärische Revolution', in J. Kunisch and H. Münkler (eds), *Die Wiedergeburt des Krieges aus dem Geist der Revolution*, Berlin, 1999, pp. 153–83.

Smets, J., 'Von der "Dorfidylle" zur preußischen Nation. Sozialdisziplinierung der linksrheinischen Bevölkerung durch die Franzosen am Beispiel der allgemeinen Wehrpflicht (1802–1814)', *Historische Zeitschrift* 262 (1996), pp. 695–738.

Soeding, E., *Die Harkorts*, 2 vols, Münster, 1957.

Spiers, E. M., *The Army and Society*, London, 1980.

Stargardt, N., *The German Idea of Militarism. Radical and Socialist Critics, 1866–1914*, Cambridge, 1994.

Stein, H.-P., *Symbole und Zeremoniell in deutschen Streitkräften vom 18. bis zum 20. Jahrhundert*, Herford, 1984.

Steinhilber, W., *Die Heilbronner Bürgerwehren 1848 und 1849 und ihre Beteiligung an der badischen Mai-Revolution des Jahres 1849*, Heilbronn, 1959.

Stern, F., *Gold and Iron*, New York, 1977.

Stern, K., *Das Staatsrecht der Bundesrepublik Deutschland*, vol. 3.2, Munich, 1994.

Stoehr, I., 'Phalanx der Frauen? Wiederaufrüstung und Weiblichkeit in Westdeutschland 1950–1957', in C. Eifler and R. Seifert (eds), *Soziale Konstruktionen – Militär und Geschlechterverhältnis*, Münster, 1999, pp. 187–204.

Strachan, H., *The Politics of the British Army*, Oxford, 1997.

Strachan, H. 'Militär, Empire und *Civil Society* Großbritannien im 19. Jahrhundert', in U. Frevert (ed.), *Militär und Gesellschaft im 19. und 20. Jahrhundert*, Stuttgart, 1997, pp. 78–93.

Strachan, H. (ed.), *The British Army, Manpower and Society into the 21st century*, London, 2000.

Stübig, H., *Armee und Nation. Die pädagogisch-politischen Motive der preußischen Heeresreform, 1807–1814*, Frankfurt, 1971.

Studiengruppe Militärpolitik, *Die Nationale Volksarmee. Ein Anti-Weißbuch zum Militär in der DDR*, Reinbek, 1976.

Stumpf, R., 'Die Wiederverwendung von Generalen und die Neubildung militärischer Eliten in Deutschland und Österreich nach 1945', in M. Messerschmidt et al. (eds), *Militärgeschichte*, Stuttgart, 1982, pp. 478–97.

Süchting-Hänger, A., '"Gleichgroße mut´ge Helferinnen" in der weiblichen Gegenwelt: Der Vaterländische Frauenverein und die Politisierung konservativer Frauen 1890–1914', in U. Planert (ed.), *Nation, Politik und Geschlecht*, Frankfurt, 2000, pp. 131–46.

Taylor, P. K., *Indentured to Liberty. Peasant Life and the Hessian Military State, 1688–1815*, Ithaca, 1994.

Thompson, D. F., *The Democratic Citizen. Social Science and Democratic Theory in the Twentieth Century*, Cambridge, 1970.

Thoß, B. (ed.), *Volksarmee schaffen – ohne Geschrei! Studien zu den Anfängen einer ´verdeckten Aufrüstung´ in der SBZ/DDR 1947–1952*, Munich, 1994.

Thoß, B. (ed.), *Vom Kalten Krieg zur deutschen Einheit*, Munich, 1995.

Trox, E., *Militärischer Konservativismus. Kriegervereine und ´Militärpartei´ in Preußen zwischen 1815 und 1848/49*, Stuttgart, 1990.

Trox, E., 'Kriegerfeste, militärische Männerbünde und politisierte Offiziere', *Militärgeschichtliche Mitteilungen* 51 (1992), pp. 23–46.

Vaisse, M. (ed.), *Aux armes, citoyens! Conscription et armée de métier des Grecs à nos jours*, Paris, 1998.

Verhey, J., *The Spirit of 1914: Militarism, Myth, and Mobilization in Germany*, Cambridge, 2000.

Verteidigung im Bündnis. Planung, Aufbau und Bewährung der Bundeswehr 1950–1972, ed. Militärgeschichtliches Forschungsamt, Munich, 1975.

Vogel, J., *Nationen im Gleichschritt. Der Kult der ´Nation in Waffen´ in Deutschland und Frankreich, 1871–1914*, Göttingen, 1997.

Vogel, J., 'Stramme Gardisten, temperamentvolle Tirailleurs und anmutige Damen. Geschlechterbilder im deutschen und französischen Kult der "Nation in Waffen"', in U. Frevert (ed.), *Militär und Gesellschaft im 19. und 20. Jahrhundert*, Stuttgart, 1997, pp. 245–62.

Vogel, J., '"En revenant de la revue". Militärfolklore und Folkloremilitarismus in Deutschland und Frankreich 1871–1914', *Österreichische Zeitschrift für Geschichtswissenschaften* 9 (1998), pp. 9–30.

Vogelsang, T., *Reichswehr, Staat und NSDAP. Beiträge zur deutschen Geschichte 1930–1932*, Stuttgart, 1962.

Vogt, W. R., *Militär und Demokratie. Funktionen und Konflikte der Institution des Wehrbeauftragten*, Hamburg, 1972.

Walzer, M., *Obligations: Essays on Disobedience, War, and Citizenship*, Cambridge, 1970.

Walzer, M., 'The Concept of Civil Society', in M. Walzer (ed.), *Toward a Global Civil Society*, Providence, 1995, pp. 7–27.

Wandruszka, A. and Urbanitsch, P. (eds), *Die Habsburgermonarchie 1848–1918*, vol. 5: *Die bewaffnete Macht*, Vienna, 1987.

Weber, E., *Lyrik der Befreiungskriege (1812–1815)*, Stuttgart, 1991.

Weber, E., 'Zwischen Emanzipation und Disziplinierung. Zur meinungs- und willensbildenden Funktion politischer Lyrik in Zeitungen zur Zeit der Befreiungskriege', in U. Herrmann (ed.), *Volk – Nation – Vaterland*, Hamburg, 1996, pp. 325–52.

Weber, E., *Peasants into Frenchmen. The Modernization of Rural France 1870–1914*, Stanford, 1976.

Wegner, B., *Hitlers Politische Soldaten: Die Waffen-SS 1933–1945*, 5th edn, Paderborn, 1996.

Wegner, B., 'Anmerkungen zur Geschichte der Waffen-SS aus organisations- und funktionsgeschichtlicher Sicht', in R.-D. Müller and H.-E. Volkmann (eds), *Die Wehrmacht. Mythos und Realität*, Munich, 1999, pp. 405–19.

Wehler, H.-U., *Deutsche Gesellschaftsgeschichte*, vol. 3, Munich, 1995.

Wehrpflicht, Wehrrecht und Kriegsdienstverweigerung in beiden deutschen Staaten, ed. Friedrich-Ebert-Stiftung, Bonn, 1980.

Weisbrod, B., 'Gewalt in der Politik. Zur politischen Kultur in Deutschland zwischen den beiden Weltkriegen', *Geschichte in Wissenschaft und Unterricht* 43 (1992), pp. 391–404.

Wenzke, R., 'Auf dem Wege zur Kaderarmee. Aspekte der Rekrutierung, Sozial-struktur und personellen Entwicklung des entstehenden Militärs in der SBZ/DDR bis 1952/53', in B. Thoß (ed.), *Volksarmee schaffen – ohne Geschrei! Studien zu den Anfängen einer ´verdeckten Aufrüstung´ in der SBZ/DDR 1947–1952*, Munich, 1994, pp. 205–72.

Wenzke, R., 'Die Wehrpflicht im Spiegel der marxistisch-leninistischen Theorie und der "realsozialistischen" Praxis in der DDR', in R. G. Foerster (ed.), *Die Wehrpflicht*, Munich, 1994, pp. 118–30.

Wenzke, R., 'Das unliebsame Erbe der Wehrmacht und der Aufbau der DDR-Volksarmee', in R.-D. Müller and H.-E. Volkmann (eds), *Die Wehrmacht. Mythos und Realität*, Munich, 1999, pp. 1113–1138.

Wette, W., 'Ideologien, Propaganda und Innenpolitik als Voraussetzung der Kriegspolitik des Dritten Reiches', in W. Deist et al., *Ursachen und Voraussetzungen des Zweiten Weltkrieges*, Frankfurt, 1989, pp. 25–208.

Wette, W., 'Deutsche Erfahrungen mit der Wehrpflicht 1918–1945', in R. G. Foerster (ed.), *Die Wehrpflicht*, Munich, 1994, pp. 91–106.

Wette, W., 'Das Bild der Wehrmacht-Elite nach 1945', in G. R. Ueberschär (ed.), *Hitlers militärische Elite*, vol. 2, Darmstadt, 1998, pp. 293–308.

Wette, W. (ed.), *Militarismus in Deutschland 1871 bis 1945*, Münster, 1999.

Wettig, G., *Entmilitarisierung und Wiederbewaffnung in Deutschland 1943–1955*, Munich, 1967.

Wiedner, H., 'Soldatenmißhandlungen im Wilhelminischen Kaiserreich (1890–1914)', *Archiv für Sozialgeschichte* 22 (1982), pp. 159–99.

Wildenthal, L., *German Women for Empire, 1884–1945*, Durham, 2001.

Wilke, J., 'Der nationale Aufbruch der Befreiungskriege als Kommunikationsereignis', in U. Herrmann (ed.), *Volk – Nation – Vaterland*, Hamburg, 1996, pp. 353–68.

Wirtz, R., *'Widersetzlichkeiten, Excesse, Crawalle, Tumulte und Skandale'. Soziale Bewegung und gewalthafter sozialer Protest in Baden 1815–1848*, Berlin, 1981.

Witt, P.-C., 'Monarchen und Bürger. Über Untertanen und Untertänigkeit im wilhelminischen Deutschland (1890–1914)', in H. Lademacher and L. Geeraedts (eds), *Freiheitsstreben – Demokratie – Emanzipation*, Münster, 1993, pp. 139–87.

Ziemann, B., *Front und Heimat. Ländliche Kriegserfahrungen im südlichen Bayern 1914–1923*, Essen, 1997.

Ziemann, B., 'Republikanische Kriegserinnerung in einer polarisierten Öffentlichkeit. Das Reichsbanner Schwarz-Rot-Gold als Veteranenverband der sozialistischen Arbeiterschaft', *Historische Zeitschrift* 267 (1998), pp. 357–98.

Ziemann, B., 'Der "Hauptmann von Köpenick" – Symbol für den Sozialmilitarismus im wilhelminischen Deutschland?' In V. Precan (ed.), *Grenzüberschreitungen*, Prag, 1999, pp. 252–64.

Ziemann, B., 'Das "Fronterlebnis" des Ersten Weltkrieges – eine sozialhistorische Zäsur?', in H. Mommsen (ed.), *Der Erste Weltkrieg und die europäische Nachkriegsordnung*, Cologne, 2000, pp. 43–82.

Bibliography

Ziemann, B., 'Sozialmilitarismus und militärische Sozialisation im deutschen Kaiserreich 1870–1914', *Geschichte in Wissenschaft und Unterricht* 53 (2002), pp. 148–64.

Zimmermann, H.-P., *"Der feste Wall gegen die rote Flut". Kriegervereine in Schleswig-Holstein 1864–1914*, Neumünster, 1989.

Zimmermann, W., *Die Wehrpolitik der Zentrumspartei in der Weimarer Republik*, Frankfurt, 1994.

Zunkel, F., *Der Rheinisch-Westfälische Unternehmer 1834–1879*, Cologne, 1962.

Index

Index

Schiller, Friedrich, 12, 41n14
Schmid, Carlo, 260, 272
schools, 5, 25, 40, 53, 105, 109, 155, 170, 174, 185, 215, 217–18, 248
Schulze-Delitzsch, Hermann, 134–5
Seeckt, Hans v., 242, 264
sexuality, 28, 39, 78, 167, 169, 173–8
sexually transmitted diseases, 78, 173–4
shooting clubs, 16, 18, 122, 135–6, 181, 203
Siemens, Werner, 154, 158
Social Democrats, 150, 194–206 passim, 214, 231n149, 240–1, 245, 247–8, 250–1, 260, 263, 266–1, 274, 276
Stein, Freiherr vom, 15–16, 19, 21, 28, 65, 105, 153, 157
students, 24, 50, 54, 71, 73, 79, 89, 101, 123, 127, 151, 164–70 passim, 214, 244, 248
substitution, 16, 18–19, 23–4, 30, 49, 90, 101, 103–5, 107–9, 114–15, 120, 132, 140
suicide, 111, 185, 197, 200, 231n155
Switzerland, 12, 76, 101, 133, 136

theologians, 54, 80, 174, 186
tin soldiers, 161, 214, 218
'total institution', 3, 75, 171, 182, 186, 201
Treitschke, Heinrich v., 150, 200, 210, 281
Twesten, Carl, 156

uniform, 2, 12, 18, 24, 29, 31, 56, 59–60, 64–5, 72, 74, 77, 79–80, 86, 88–9, 122–3, 129, 135, 140, 159–60, 168, 173, 179–82, 190, 198, 203, 206–7, 212, 217, 220, 237, 239, 243, 250–1, 269, 271, 275
urban/rural, 78, 117, 126, 171, 178, 191–2
USA, 1, 136, 237–8, 269, 277–8, 281

veterans' associations, 202–9, 213, 220–1, 232, 240, 243–4, 250, 261
Vincke, Ludwig v., 13, 16, 23, 29, 31, 37, 63, 68–9
violence, 2–6 passim, 9–13, 34, 40, 64, 82–3, 112, 124–5, 131, 157, 172, 175, 180–1, 185,

197–8, 200, 212, 221–2, 238–9, 241, 245–7, 249, 268, 272, 277–8, 280
Virchow, Rudolf, 153

Warburg, Max, 160
Warsaw Pact, see NATO
Wars of Unification, 9, 140, 149, 152, 157, 199, 209
weapons, 2, 12, 17, 28, 31, 33–4, 39–40, 49, 59–60, 71, 74, 77, 83–4, 110, 112, 114–15, 117, 119, 122–31, 134, 136–7, 139, 146n95, 151, 154, 162, 171, 178, 180–3, 191, 194, 202, 209–15, 217, 220–1, 223, 231n155, 235, 237, 239–40, 242–3, 256–7, 259, 262, 279
Weber, Max, 150, 164–170 passim, 189
Wehrmacht, 249, 251–65 passim, 269
Wehrvereine, see defence associations
Welcker, Carl, 64, 75–6, 108, 115–20 passim, 125, 132, 210
Wilhelm I, 158, 195, 205
Wilhelm II, 158, 183, 195
women, 2, 5–6, 13, 25–6, 28, 30–9, 74–78, 97n102, 98n106, 98n107, 118–19, 127–31, 149–50, 163, 167, 173, 175–80 passim, 203, 208–12, 221, 227n80, 228n108, 237, 244–5, 255–6, 259, 262, 272, 274–5, 279–80
housewives, 27, 37, 39, 212
wives, 26, 31–2, 35, 58, 75, 86, 98, 130, 158, 173, 179, 187, 207, 223
women's associations, 35–9, 209–11
workers, day labourers, 50, 52, 55, 70, 104, 125, 137, 140, 151, 169–70, 180, 183, 186, 192–3, 194–5, 203, 208, 234n201, 244
workers' associations, workers' groupings, 136–8
working-class movement, labour movement, 138, 240
World War I, 101, 209, 214, 218, 221–3, 237–8, 240, 246, 256–8
World War II, 237–8, 254–5, 258, 264, 277–8, 281